Get the eBook FREE!
(PDF, ePub, Kindle, and liveBook all included)

We believe that once you buy a book from us, you should be able to read it in any format we have available. To get electronic versions of this book at no additional cost to you, purchase and then register this book at the Manning website..

Go to https://www.manning.com/freebook and follow the instructions to complete your pBook registration.

That's it!
Thanks from Manning!

Julia for Data Analysis

Julia for Data
Analysis

BOGUMIŁ KAMIŃSKI

FOREWORD BY VIRAL SHAH

MANNING
SHELTER ISLAND

For online information and ordering of this and other Manning books, please visit
www.manning.com. The publisher offers discounts on this book when ordered in quantity.
For more information, please contact

> Special Sales Department
> Manning Publications Co.
> 20 Baldwin Road
> PO Box 761
> Shelter Island, NY 11964
> Email: orders@manning.com

Manning Publications Co.
20 Baldwin Road
PO Box 761
Shelter Island, NY 11964

Development editor:	Marina Michaels
Technical development editors:	German Gonzalez-Morris
Review editor:	Adriana Sabo
Production editor:	Deirdre S. Hiam
Copy editor:	Sharon Wilkey
Proofreader:	Melody Dolab
Technical proofreader:	Mike Haller
Typesetter and cover designer:	Marija Tudor

ISBN 9781633439368
Printed in the United States of America

brief contents

1 ▪ Introduction   1

PART 1   ESSENTIAL JULIA SKILLS **17**

  2 ▪ Getting started with Julia   19

  3 ▪ Julia's support for scaling projects   49

  4 ▪ Working with collections in Julia   70

  5 ▪ Advanced topics on handling collections   100

  6 ▪ Working with strings   123

  7 ▪ Handling time-series data and missing values   154

PART 2   TOOLBOX FOR DATA ANALYSIS **183**

  8 ▪ First steps with data frames   185

  9 ▪ Getting data from a data frame   209

  10 ▪ Creating data frame objects   233

  11 ▪ Converting and grouping data frames   265

  12 ▪ Mutating and transforming data frames   291

  13 ▪ Advanced transformations of data frames   327

  14 ▪ Creating web services for sharing data analysis results   365

contents

foreword xiii
preface xv
acknowledgments xvii
about this book xix
about the author xxiv
about the cover illustration xxv

1 Introduction 1

1.1 What is Julia and why is it useful? 2

1.2 Key features of Julia from a data scientist's perspective 6

Julia is fast because it is a compiled language 6 ▪ Julia provides full support for interactive workflows 8 ▪ Julia programs are highly reusable and easy to compose together 8 ▪ Julia has a built-in state-of-the-art package manager 9 ▪ It is easy to integrate existing code with Julia 10

1.3 Usage scenarios of tools presented in the book 10

1.4 Julia's drawbacks 11

1.5 What data analysis skills will you learn? 13

1.6 How can Julia be used for data analysis? 13

PART 1 ESSENTIAL JULIA SKILLS 17

2 Getting started with Julia 19

2.1 Representing values 20

2.2   Defining variables   23

2.3   Using the most important control-flow constructs   26

   Computations depending on a Boolean condition   26 ▪ *Loops   32*
   Compound expressions   33 ▪ *A first approach to calculating the*
   winsorized mean   35

2.4   Defining functions   36

   Defining functions using the function keyword   37 ▪ *Positional*
   and keyword arguments of functions   37 ▪ *Rules for passing*
   arguments to functions   39 ▪ *Short syntax for defining simple*
   functions   39 ▪ *Anonymous functions   40* ▪ *Do blocks   41*
   Function-naming convention in Julia   42 ▪ *A simplified*
   definition of a function computing the winsorized mean   43

2.5   Understanding variable scoping rules   44

3   Julia's support for scaling projects   49

3.1   Understanding Julia's type system   50

   A single function in Julia may have multiple methods   50
   Types in Julia are arranged in a hierarchy   51 ▪ *Finding all*
   supertypes of a type   52 ▪ *Finding all subtypes of a type   52*
   Union of types   53 ▪ *Deciding what type restrictions to put in*
   method signature   54

3.2   Using multiple dispatch in Julia   55

   Rules for defining methods of a function   55 ▪ *Method*
   ambiguity problem   56 ▪ *Improved implementation of*
   winsorized mean   57

3.3   Working with packages and modules   59

   What is a module in Julia?   59 ▪ *How can packages be used*
   in Julia?   61 ▪ *Using StatsBase.jl to compute the winsorized*
   mean   63

3.4   Using macros   65

4   Working with collections in Julia   70

4.1   Working with arrays   70

   Getting the data into a matrix   72 ▪ *Computing basic*
   statistics of the data stored in a matrix   76 ▪ *Indexing into*
   arrays   78 ▪ *Performance considerations of copying vs.*
   making a view   81 ▪ *Calculating correlations between*
   variables   82 ▪ *Fitting a linear regression   83* ▪ *Plotting*
   the Anscombe's quartet data   86

4.2   Mapping key-value pairs with dictionaries   88

4.3 Structuring your data by using named tuples 93

*Defining named tuples and accessing their contents   94
Analyzing Anscombe's quartet data stored in a named
tuple   95 ▪ Understanding composite types and mutability
of values in Julia   96*

5 Advanced topics on handling collections   100

5.1 Vectorizing your code using broadcasting 101

*Understanding syntax and meaning of broadcasting in
Julia   101 ▪ Expanding length-1 dimensions in
broadcasting   103 ▪ Protecting collections from being
broadcasted over   106 ▪ Analyzing Anscombe's quartet
data using broadcasting   109*

5.2 Defining methods with parametric types 112

*Most collection types in Julia are parametric   112 ▪ Rules for
subtyping of parametric types   114 ▪ Using subtyping rules to
define the covariance function   116*

5.3 Integrating with Python 117

*Preparing data for dimensionality reduction using t-SNE   117
Calling Python from Julia   118 ▪ Visualizing the results of
the t-SNE algorithm   120*

6 Working with strings   123

6.1 Getting and inspecting the data 124

*Downloading files from the web   125 ▪ Using common
techniques of string construction   125 ▪ Reading the
contents of a file   127*

6.2 Splitting strings 128

6.3 Using regular expressions to work with strings 130

*Working with regular expressions   130 ▪ Writing a parser of a
single line of movies.dat file   131*

6.4 Extracting a subset from a string with indexing 132

*UTF-8 encoding of strings in Julia   132 ▪ Character vs. byte
indexing of strings   133 ▪ ASCII strings   134 ▪ The Char
type   135*

6.5 Analyzing genre frequency in movies.dat 135

*Finding common movie genres   135 ▪ Understanding genre
popularity evolution over the years   137*

6.6 Introducing symbols 140

Creating symbols   140 ▪ Using symbols   141

6.7 Using fixed-width string types to improve performance 143

Available fixed-width strings 143 • Performance of fixed-width strings 144

6.8 Compressing vectors of strings with PooledArrays.jl 146

Creating a file containing flower names 146 • Reading in the data to a vector and compressing it 147 • Understanding the internal design of PooledArray 148

6.9 Choosing appropriate storage for collections of strings 151

7 **Handling time-series data and missing values 154**

7.1 Understanding the NBP Web API 155

Getting the data via a web browser 155 • Getting the data by using Julia 157 • Handling cases when an NBP Web API query fails 159

7.2 Working with missing data in Julia 163

Definition of the missing value 163 • Working with missing values 164

7.3 Getting time-series data from the NBP Web API 169

Working with dates 170 • Fetching data from the NBP Web API for a range of dates 172

7.4 Analyzing data fetched from the NBP Web API 173

Computing summary statistics 174 • Finding which days of the week have the most missing values 174 • Plotting the PLN/USD exchange rate 175

PART 2 TOOLBOX FOR DATA ANALYSIS 183

8 **First steps with data frames 185**

8.1 Fetching, unpacking, and inspecting the data 187

Downloading the file from the web 187 • Working with bzip2 archives 188 • Inspecting the CSV file 190

8.2 Loading the data to a data frame 190

Reading a CSV file into a data frame 190 • Inspecting the contents of a data frame 192 • Saving a data frame to a CSV file 195

8.3 Getting a column out of a data frame 196

Understanding the data frame's storage model 196 • Treating a data frame column as a property 197 • Getting a column by

*using data frame indexing   200 ▪ Visualizing data stored in
columns of a data frame   202*

8.4   Reading and writing data frames using different
       formats   203

Apache Arrow   204 ▪ SQLite   205

9   *Getting data from a data frame   209*

9.1   Advanced data frame indexing   210

*Getting a reduced puzzles data frame   212 ▪ Overview
of allowed column selectors   215 ▪ Overview of allowed
row-subsetting values   220 ▪ Making views of data frame
objects   223*

9.2   Analyzing the relationship between puzzle difficulty and
       popularity   225

*Calculating mean puzzle popularity by its rating   225
Fitting LOESS regression   229*

10   *Creating data frame objects   233*

10.1   Reviewing the most important ways to create
        a data frame   234

*Creating a data frame from a matrix   235 ▪ Creating a data
frame from vectors   237 ▪ Creating a data frame using a
Tables.jl interface   244 ▪ Plotting a correlation matrix of data
stored in a data frame   246*

10.2   Creating data frames incrementally   248

*Vertically concatenating data frames   248 ▪ Appending a
table to a data frame   253 ▪ Adding a new row to an
existing data frame   256 ▪ Storing simulation results in
a data frame   257*

11   *Converting and grouping data frames   265*

11.1   Converting a data frame to other value types   266

*Conversion to a matrix   268 ▪ Conversion to a named tuple of
vectors   269 ▪ Other common conversions   276*

11.2   Grouping data frame objects   280

*Preparing the source data frame   280 ▪ Grouping a data
frame   281 ▪ Getting group keys of a grouped data frame   282
Indexing a grouped data frame with a single value   283
Comparing performance of indexing methods   285 ▪ Indexing a
grouped data frame with multiple values   286 ▪ Iterating a
grouped data frame   288*

12 **Mutating and transforming data frames   291**

12.1   Getting and loading the GitHub developers
       data set   292

Understanding graphs   293 ▪ *Fetching GitHub developer data
from the web   294* ▪ *Implementing a function that extracts
data from a ZIP file   296* ▪ *Reading the GitHub developer
data into a data frame   298*

12.2   Computing additional node features   303

Creating a SimpleGraph object   303 ▪ *Computing features of
nodes by using the Graphs.jl package   305* ▪ *Counting a node's
web and machine learning neighbors   307*

12.3   Using the split-apply-combine approach to predict
       the developer's type   311

*Computing summary statistics of web and machine learning
developer features   311* ▪ *Visualizing the relationship between
the number of web and machine learning neighbors of a
node   315* ▪ *Fitting a logistic regression model predicting
developer type   319*

12.4   Reviewing data frame mutation operations   321

Performing low-level API operations   321 ▪ *Using the
insertcols! function to mutate a data frame   323*

13 **Advanced transformations of data frames   327**

13.1   Getting and preprocessing the police stop data set   328

Loading all required packages   328 ▪ *Introducing the
@chain macro   329* ▪ *Getting the police stop data
set   331* ▪ *Comparing functions that perform operations
on columns   333* ▪ *Using short forms of operation
specification syntax   336*

13.2   Investigating the violation column   337

Finding the most frequent violations   337 ▪ *Vectorizing
functions by using the ByRow wrapper   340* ▪ *Flattening data
frames   341* ▪ *Using convenience syntax to get the number of
rows of a data frame   341* ▪ *Sorting data frames   342*
Using advanced functionalities of DataFramesMeta.jl   343

13.3   Preparing data for making predictions   345

Performing initial transformation of the data   345 ▪ *Working
with categorical data   347* ▪ *Joining data frames   349*
Reshaping data frames   350 ▪ *Dropping rows of a data
frame that hold missing values   353*

13.4   Building a predictive model of arrest probability   354

*Splitting the data into train and test data sets   354 ▪ Fitting a
logistic regression model   356 ▪ Evaluating the quality of a
model's predictions   357*

13.5   Reviewing functionalities provided by DataFrames.jl   361

14 **Creating web services for sharing data analysis results   365**

14.1   Pricing financial options by using a Monte Carlo
simulation   366

*Calculating the payoff of an Asian option definition   366
Computing the value of an Asian option   368 ▪ Understanding
GBM   369 ▪ Using a numerical approach to computing the
Asian option value   370*

14.2   Implementing the option pricing simulator   372

*Starting Julia with multiple-thread support   372 ▪ Computing
the option payoff for a single sample of stock prices   373
Computing the option value   375*

14.3   Creating a web service serving the Asian option
valuation   379

*A general approach to building a web service   379 ▪ Creating
a web service using Genie.jl   381 ▪ Running the web
service   383*

14.4   Using the Asian option pricing web service   383

*Sending a single request to the web service   384 ▪ Collecting
responses to multiple requests from a web service in a data
frame   386 ▪ Unnesting a column of a data frame   387
Plotting the results of Asian option pricing   389*

appendix A   First steps with Julia   393

appendix B   Solutions to exercises   405

appendix C   Julia packages for data science   427

index   431

foreword

Today, the world is awash with lots of software tools for data analysis. The reader may wonder, why *Julia for Data Analysis*? This book answers both the "why" and the "how."

Since the reader may not be familiar with me, I would like to introduce myself. I am one of the creators of the Julia language and co-founder and CEO of Julia Computing. We started the Julia language with a simple idea—build a language that is as fast as C, but as easy as R and Python. This simple idea has had an immense impact in a lot of different areas as the Julia community has built a wonderful set of abstractions and infrastructure surrounding it. Bogumił, along with many co-contributors, has built a high performance and easy-to-use package ecosystem for data analysis.

Now, you may wonder, why one more library? Julia's data analysis ecosystem is built from the ground up leveraging some of the fundamental ideas in Julia itself. These libraries are "Julia all the way down," meaning they have been implemented fully in Julia—the DataFrames.jl library for working with data, the CSV.jl library for reading data, the JuliaStats ecosystem for statistical analysis, and so on. These libraries have built on ideas specifically developed in R and taken forward. For example, the infrastructure for working with missing data in Julia is a core part of the Julia ecosystem. It took many years to get it right and to make the Julia compiler efficient in order to reduce the overhead of working with missing data. A completely Julia native DataFrames.jl library means that you no longer have to be restricted to vectorized coding style for high performance data analysis. You can simply write `for` loops over multi-gigabyte datasets, use multi-threading for parallel data processing, integrate with computational libraries in the Julia ecosystem, and even deploy these as web APIs to be consumed by other systems. All these features are presented in the book. One of the things I really enjoyed in this book is that the examples that Bogumił introduces to the reader are not just neat, small, tabular datasets, but real-world data—for instance, a set of chess puzzles with 2 million rows!

The book is divided into two parts. The first part introduces the basic concepts of the Julia language, introducing the type system, multiple dispatch, data structures, etc. The second part then builds on these concepts and presents data analysis—reading data, selecting, creating a DataFrame, split-apply-combine, sorting, joining, and reshaping—and finally finishes with a complete application. There is also a discussion of the Arrow data exchange format that allows Julia programs to co-exist with data analysis tools in R, Python, and Spark, to mention a few. The code patterns in all the chapters teach the reader good practices that result in high-performance data analysis.

Bogumił is not only a major contributor to Julia's data analysis and statistical ecosystem, but also has built several courses (like the one on JuliaAcademy) and has blogged extensively about the internals of these packages. Thus, he is one of the best authors to present how Julia can effectively be used for data analysis.

— VIRAL SHAH, CO-FOUNDER AND CEO OF JULIA COMPUTING

preface

I have been using the Julia language since 2014. Before that, I mainly used R for data analysis (Python was not then mature enough in the field). However, in addition to exploring data and building machine learning models, I often needed to implement custom compute-intensive code, which required days to finish the computations. I mostly worked with C or Java for such applications. Constantly switching between programming languages was a pain.

After I learned about Julia, I immediately felt that it was an exciting technology matching my needs. Even in its early days (before its 1.0 release), I was able to successfully use it in my projects. However, as with every new tool, it still needed to be polished.

Then I decided to start contributing to the Julia language and to packages related to data management functionalities. Over the years, my focus evolved, and I ended up as one of the main maintainers of the DataFrames.jl package. I am convinced that Julia is now ready for serious applications, and DataFrames.jl has reached a state of stability and is feature rich. Therefore, I decided to write this book sharing my experiences with using Julia for data analysis.

I have always believed that it's important for software to not only provide great functionality, but to also offer adequate documentation. For this reason, for several years I have maintained these online resources: The Julia Express (https://github .com/bkamins/The-Julia-Express), a tutorial giving a quick introduction to the Julia language; An Introduction to DataFrames.jl (https://github.com/bkamins/Julia-Data Frames-Tutorial), a collection of Jupyter notebooks; and a weekly blog about Julia (https://bkamins.github.io/). Additionally, last year Manning invited me to prepare the *Hands-On Data Science with Julia* liveProject (https://www.manning.com/ liveprojectseries/data-science-with-julia-ser), a set of exercises covering common data science tasks.

Having written all these teaching materials, I felt strongly that a piece of the puzzle was still missing. People who wanted to start doing data science with Julia had a hard time finding a book that would gradually introduce them to the fundamentals required in order to perform data analysis using Julia. This book fills this gap.

The Julia ecosystem has hundreds of packages that can be used in your data science projects, and new ones are being registered daily. My objective for this book is to teach Julia's most important features and selected popular packages that any user will find useful when doing data analysis. After reading the book, you should be ready to do the following on your own:

- Perform data analysis with Julia.
- Learn the functionalities provided by specialized packages that go beyond data analysis and are useful when doing data science projects. Appendix C provides an overview of tools I recommend that are available in the Julia ecosystem, categorized by application area.
- Comfortably study more advanced aspects of Julia that are relevant for package developers.
- Benefit from discussions about Julia on social media such as Discourse (https://discourse.julialang.org/), Slack (https://julialang.org/slack/), and Zulip (https://julialang.zulipchat.com/register/), confident that you understand the key concepts and terminology that other users reference in their comments.

acknowledgments

This book is an important part of my journey with the Julia language. Therefore, I would like to thank many people for helping me.

Let me start by thanking the Julia community members from whom I've both learned a lot and taken inspiration for my contributions. There are too many of them to name, so I had the hard choice of picking a few. In my early days, Stefan Karpinski helped me a lot in getting started as a Julia contributor when I supported his efforts toward shaping the string-processing functionalities in Julia. In the data science ecosystem, Milan Bouchet-Valat has been my most important partner for many years now. His custodianship efforts on the Julia data and statistics ecosystem are invaluable. The most important thing I learned from him is attention to detail and consideration of the long-term consequences of design decisions that package maintainers make. The next key person is Jacob Quinn, who designed and implemented a large part of the functionalities I discuss in this book. Finally, I would like to mention Peter Deffebach and Frames Catherine White, who are both significant contributors to the Julia data analysis ecosystem and are always ready to provide invaluable comments and advice from the package users' perspective.

I would also like to acknowledge my editor at Manning, Marina Michaels, technical editor Chad Scherrer, and technical proofreader German Gonzalez-Morris, as well as the reviewers who took the time to read my manuscript at various stages during its development and who provided invaluable feedback: Ben McNamara, Carlos Aya-Moreno, Clemens Baader, David Cronkite, Dr. Mike Williams, Floris Bouchot, Guillaume Alleon, Joel Holmes, Jose Luis Manners, Kai Gellien, Kay Engelhardt, Kevin Cheung, Laud Bentil, Marco Carnini, Marvin Schwarze, Mattia Di Gangi, Maureen Metzger, Maxim Volgin, Milan Mulji, Neumann Chew, Nikos Tzortzis Kanakaris, Nitin Gode, Orlando Méndez Morales, Patrice Maldague, Patrick Goetz, Peter Henstock,

Rafael Guerra, Samuel Bosch, Satej Kumar Sahu, Shiroshica Kulatilake, Sonja Krause-Harder, Stefan Pinnow, Steve Rogers, Tom Heiman, Tony Dubitsky, Wei Luo, Wolf Thomsen, and Yongming Han. Finally, the entire Manning team that worked with me on the production and promotion of the book: Deirdre Hiam, my project manager; Sharon Wilkey, my copyeditor; and Melody Dolab, my page proofer.

Finally, I would like to express my gratitude to my scientific collaborators, especially Tomasz Olczak, Paweł Prałat, Przemysław Szufel, and François Théberge, with whom I've published multiple papers using the Julia language.

about this book

This book was written in two parts to help you get started using Julia for data analysis. It begins by explaining Julia's most important features that are useful in such applications. Next, it discusses the functionalities of selected core packages used in data science projects.

The material is built around complete data analysis projects, starting from data collection, though data transformation, and finishing with visualization and building basic predictive models. My objective is to teach you the fundamental concepts and skills that are useful in any data science project.

This book does not require prior knowledge of advanced machine learning algorithms. This knowledge is not necessary for understanding the fundamentals of data analysis in Julia, and I do not discuss such models in this book. I do assume that you have knowledge of basic data science tools and techniques such as generalized linear regression or LOESS regression. Similarly, from a data engineering perspective, I cover the most common operations, including fetching data from the web, writing a web service, working with compressed files, and using basic data storage formats. I left out functionalities that require either additional complex configuration that is not Julia related or specialist software engineering knowledge.

Appendix C reviews the Julia packages that provide advanced functionalities in the data engineering and data science domains. Using the knowledge you glean from this book, you should be able to confidently learn to use these packages on your own.

Who should read this book

This book is for data scientists or data engineers who would like to learn how Julia can be used for data analysis. I assume that you have some experience in doing data analysis using a programming language such as R, Python, or MATLAB.

How this book is organized: A roadmap

The book, which is divided into two parts, has 14 chapters and three appendices.

Chapter 1 provides an overview of Julia and explains why it is an excellent language for data science projects.

The chapters in part 1 follow, teaching you essential Julia skills that are most useful in data analysis projects. These chapters are essential for readers who do not know the Julia language well. However, I expect that even people who use Julia will find useful information here, as I have selected the topics for discussion based on issues commonly reported as difficult. This part is not meant to be a complete introduction to the Julia language, but rather is written from the perspective of usefulness in data science projects. The part 1 chapters are as follows:

- Chapter 2 discusses the basics of Julia's syntax and common language constructs and the most important aspects of variable scoping rules.
- Chapter 3 introduces Julia's type system and methods. It also introduces working with packages and modules. Finally, it discusses using macros.
- Chapter 4 covers working with arrays, dictionaries, tuples, and named tuples.
- Chapter 5 discusses advanced topics related to working with collections in Julia, including broadcasting and subtyping rules for parametric types. It also covers integrating Julia with Python.
- Chapter 6 teaches you how to work with strings in Julia. Additionally, it covers the topics of using symbols, working with fixed-width strings, and compressing vectors by using the PooledArrays.jl package.
- Chapter 7 concentrates on working with time-series data and missing values. It also covers fetching data by using HTTP queries and parsing JSON data.

In part 2, you'll learn how to build data analysis pipelines with the help of the Data-Frames.jl package. While, in general, you could perform data analysis using only the data structures you will learn in part 1, building your data analysis workflows by using data frames will be easier and at the same time will ensure that your code is efficient. Here's what you'll learn in part 2:

- Chapter 8 teaches you how to create a data frame from a CSV file and perform basic operations on data frames. It also shows how to process data in the Apache Arrow and SQLite databases, work with compressed files, and do basic data visualization.
- Chapter 9 shows you how to select rows and columns from a data frame. You will also learn how to build and visualize locally estimated scatterplot smoothing (LOESS) regression models.
- Chapter 10 covers various ways of creating new data frames and populating existing data frames with new data. It discusses the Tables.jl interface, an implementation-independent abstraction of a table concept. You will also learn to integrate Julia with R and to serialize Julia objects.

- Chapter 11 teaches you how to convert data frames into objects of other types. One of the fundamental types is the grouped data frame. You will also learn about the important general concepts of type-stable code and type piracy.
- Chapter 12 focuses on transformation and mutation of data frame objects—in particular, using the split-apply-combine strategy. Additionally, this chapter covers the basics of using the Graphs.jl package to work with graph data.
- Chapter 13 discusses advanced data frame transformation options provided by the DataFrames.jl package, as well as data frame sorting, joining, and reshaping. It also teaches you how to chain multiple operations in data processing pipelines. From a data science perspective, this chapter shows you how to work with categorical data and evaluate classification models in Julia.
- Chapter 14 shows you how to build a web service in Julia that serves data produced by an analytical algorithm. Additionally, it shows you how to implement Monte Carlo simulations and make them run faster by taking advantage of Julia's multithreading capabilities.

The book ends with three appendices. Appendix A provides essential information about Julia's installation and configuration, as well as common tasks related to working with Julia—in particular, package management. Appendix B contains solutions to the exercises presented in the chapters. Appendix C gives a review of the Julia package ecosystem that you will find useful in your data science and data engineering projects.

About the code

This book contains many examples of source code, both in numbered listings and in line with normal text. In both cases, source code is formatted in a `fixed-width font like this` to separate it from ordinary text. Sometimes code is also **in bold** to highlight code that has changed from previous steps in the chapter, such as when a new feature adds to an existing line of code.

Additionally, comments in the source code have often been removed from the listings when the code is described in the text. Code annotations accompany many of the listings, highlighting important concepts.

All the code used in this book is available on GitHub at https://github.com/bkamins/JuliaForDataAnalysis. The code examples are intended to be executed in an interactive session in the terminal. Therefore, in the book, in most cases, the code blocks show both Julia input prefixed with the `julia>` prompt and the produced output below the command. This style matches the display in your terminal. Here is an example:

```
julia> 1 + 2
3
```

3 is the output printed by Julia in the terminal.

1 + 2 is the Julia code executed by the user.

All the material presented in this book can be run on Windows, macOS, or Linux. You should be able to run all examples on a machine with 8 GB of RAM. However, some code listings require more RAM; in those cases, I give a warning in the book.

How to run the code presented in the book

To ensure that all code presented in the book runs correctly on your machine, it is essential that you first follow the configuration steps described in appendix A.

This book was written and tested with Julia 1.7.

An especially important point is that before running example code, you should always activate the project environment provided in the book's GitHub repository at https://github.com/bkamins/JuliaForDataAnalysis.

In particular, in the book, we use the DataFrames.jl package a lot. All the code is written and tested in version 1.3 of this package. You can find versions of all other packages used in the book in the Manifest.toml file available in the book's GitHub repository.

The code presented in the book is not meant to be executed by copying and pasting it to your Julia session. Always use the code that you can find in the book's GitHub repository. For each chapter, the repository has a separate file containing all code from that chapter.

---

liveBook discussion forum

Purchase of *Julia for Data Analysis* includes free access to liveBook, Manning's online reading platform. Using liveBook's exclusive discussion features, you can attach comments to the book globally or to specific sections or paragraphs. It's a snap to make notes for yourself, ask and answer technical questions, and receive help from the author and other users. To access the forum, go to https://livebook.manning.com/book//julia-for-data-analysis/discussion. You can also learn more about Manning's forums and the rules of conduct at https://livebook.manning.com/discussion.

Manning's commitment to our readers is to provide a venue where a meaningful dialogue between individual readers and between readers and the author can take place. It is not a commitment to any specific amount of participation on the part of the author, whose contribution to the forum remains voluntary (and unpaid). We suggest you try asking the author some challenging questions lest his interest stray! The forum and the archives of previous discussions will be accessible from the publisher's website as long as the book is in print.

Other online resources

Here is a list of selected online resources that you might find useful when reading this book:

- DataFrames.jl documentation (https://dataframes.juliadata.org/stable/) with links to tutorials

- *Hands-on Data Science with Julia* liveProject (https://www.manning.com/live projectseries/data-science-with-julia-ser), designed as a follow-up resource you can use after reading this book to test your skills and learn how to use advanced machine learning models with Julia
- My weekly blog (https://bkamins.github.io/), where I write about the Julia language

In addition, there are numerous valuable sources of general information on Julia. Here is a selection of some of the most popular ones:

- The Julia language website (https://julialang.org)
- JuliaCon conference (https://juliacon.org)
- Discourse (https://discourse.julialang.org)
- Slack (https://julialang.org/slack/)
- Zulip (https://julialang.zulipchat.com/register/)
- Forem (https://forem.julialang.org)
- Stack Overflow (https://stackoverflow.com/questions/tagged/julia)
- Julia YouTube channel (www.youtube.com/user/julialanguage)
- Talk Julia podcasts (www.talkjulia.com)
- JuliaBloggers blog aggregator (https://www.juliabloggers.com)

about the author

 **BOGUMIŁ KAMIŃSKI** is a lead developer of DataFrames.jl, the core package for data manipulation in the Julia ecosystem. He has over 20 years of experience delivering data science projects for corporate customers. Bogumił also has over 20 years of experience teaching data science at the undergraduate and graduate levels.

about the cover illustration

The figure on the cover of *Julia for Data Analysis* is "Prussienne de Silésie," or "Prussian of Silesia" taken from a collection by Jacques Grasset de Saint-Sauveur, published in 1797. Each illustration is finely drawn and colored by hand.

In those days, it was easy to identify where people lived and what their trade or station in life was just by their dress. Manning celebrates the inventiveness and initiative of the computer business with book covers based on the rich diversity of regional culture centuries ago, brought back to life by pictures from collections such as this one.

Introduction 1

This chapter covers

- Julia's key features
- Why do data science with Julia?
- Patterns for data analysis in Julia

Data analysis has become one of the core processes in virtually any professional activity. The collection of data has become easier and less expensive, so we have easy access to it. The crucial aspect is that data analysis allows us to make better decisions cheaper and faster.

The need for data analysis has given rise to several new professions, among which a data scientist often comes to mind first. A *data scientist* is a person skilled at collecting data, analyzing it, and producing actionable insights. As with all craftsmen, data scientists need tools that will help them deliver their products efficiently and reliably.

Various software tools can help data scientists do their jobs. Some of those tools use a graphical interface and thus are easy to work with, but also usually have limitations on how they can be used. The vast array of tasks that data scientists need to do typically leads them to quickly conclude that they need to use a programming language to achieve the required flexibility and expressiveness.

1

Developers have come up with many programming languages that data scientists commonly use. One is *Julia*, which was designed to address challenges that data scientists face when using other tools. Quoting the Julia creators, it "runs like C, but reads like Python." Julia, like Python, supports an efficient and convenient development process. At the same time, programs developed in Julia have performance comparable to C.

In section 1.1, we will discuss the results of exemplary benchmarks supporting these claims. Notably, in 2017, a program written in Julia achieved a peak performance of 1.54 petaflops (quadrillions of floating-point operations per second) using 1.3 million threads when processing astronomical image data. Before, only software implemented in C, C++, and Fortran achieved processing speeds of over 1 petaflop (https://julia computing.com/case-studies/celeste/).

In this book, you'll learn how to use the Julia language to perform tasks that data scientists need to do routinely: reading and writing data in different formats, as well as transforming, visualizing, and analyzing it.

1.1 *What is Julia and why is it useful?*

Julia is a programming language that is both high level and has a high execution speed. It's fast to both create and run Julia programs. In this section, I discuss the reasons why Julia is becoming increasingly popular among data scientists.

Various programming languages are commonly used for data analysis, such as (in alphabetical order) C++, Java, MATLAB, Python, R, and SAS. Some of these languages—for instance, R—were designed to be very expressive and easy to use in data science tasks; however, this typically comes at a cost of slower execution times of their programs. Other languages, like C++, are more low level, which allows them to process data quickly; unfortunately, the user usually must pay the price of writing more verbose code with a lower level of abstraction.

Figure 1.1 compares the execution speed and code size (one of the possible measures of programming language expressiveness) of C, Java, Python, and Julia for 10 selected problems. Since these comparisons are always hard to do objectively, I have chosen the Computer Language Benchmarks Game (http://mng.bz/19Ay), which has a long history of development and maintainers who have tried, in my opinion, to make it as objective as possible.

On both subplots in figure 1.1, C has a reference value of 1 for each problem; values smaller than 1 show that the code runs faster (left plot) or is smaller (right plot) than C. On the left plot, the y-axis representing execution time has a logarithmic scale. Code size on the right plot is the size of the gzip archive of the program written in each language.

In terms of execution speed (left plot), C is fastest, and Julia (represented with circles) comes in second. Notably, Python (represented with diamonds) is, in many tasks, orders of magnitude slower than all other displayed languages (I had to plot the y-axis on a log scale to make the left plot legible).

When considering the code size (right plot), Julia leads in 8 of 10 tasks, while for C and Java, we see the largest measurements. In addition to code size, a language's ease of use is also relevant. I prepared the plots in figure 1.1 in Julia in an interactive session that allowed me to easily tune it; you can check the source code in the GitHub repository accompanying the book (https://github.com/bkamins/JuliaForDataAnalysis). This would also be convenient in Python, but more challenging with Java or C.

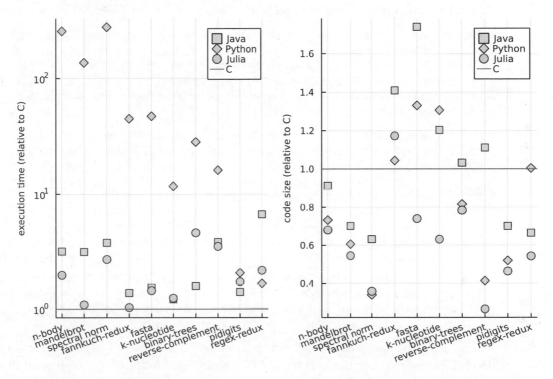

Figure 1.1 **Comparing code size and execution speed of C, Python, Java, and Julia for 10 selected computational problems**

In the past, developers faced a tradeoff between language expressiveness and speed. However, in practice, they wanted both. The ideal programming language should be easy to learn and use, like Python, but at the same time allow high-speed data processing like C.

This often required data scientists to use two languages in their projects. They prototyped their algorithms in an easy-to-code language (for example, Python) and then identified performance bottlenecks and ported selected parts of the code to a fast language (for example, C). This translation takes time and can introduce bugs. Maintaining a codebase that has significant parts written in two programming languages can be challenging and introduces the complications of integrating several technologies. Finally, when working on challenging and novel problems, having code written in two programming languages makes quick experimentation difficult, which increases the time from the product's concept to its market availability.

Timeline case study

Let me give you an example from my experience of working with Julia. *Timeline* is a web app that helps financial advisers with retirement financial planning. Such an application, to supply reliable recommendations, requires a lot of on-demand calculations. Initially, Timeline's creators began prototyping in MATLAB, switching to Elixir for online deployment. I was involved in migrating the solution to Julia.

After the code rewrite, the system's online query time was reduced from 40 seconds to 0.6 seconds. To assess the business value of such a speedup, imagine you are a Timeline user having to wait for 40 seconds for your web browser's response. Now assume the wait is 0.6 seconds. Apart from increased customer satisfaction, faster processing time also decreases the cost and complexity of the technical infrastructure required to operate this system.

However, execution speed is only one aspect of the change. The other is that Timeline reports that switching to Julia saved tens of thousands of dollars in programming time and debugging. Software developers have less code to write, while data scientists who communicate with them now use the same tool. You can find out more about this use case at https://juliacomputing.com/case-studies/timeline/.

In my opinion, the Timeline example is especially relevant for managers of data science teams that deploy the results of their work to production. Even a single developer will appreciate the productivity boost of using a single language for prototyping and writing high-performance production code. However, the real gains in time to production and development cost are visible when you have a mixed team of data scientists, data engineers, and software developers that can use a single tool when collaborating.

The Timeline case study shows how Julia was used to replace the combination of MATLAB and Elixir languages in a real-life business application. To complement this example, it's instructive to check which languages are used to develop popular open source software projects that data scientists routinely use (statistics collected on October 11, 2021). Table 1.1 shows the top two programming languages used (in percentages of lines of source code) to implement three R and Python packages.

Table 1.1 Languages used to implement selected popular open source packages

Package	Functionality	URL	Languages
data.table	Data frame package for R	https://github.com/Rdatatable/data.table	C 36.3%, R 62.4%
randomForest	Random forest algorithm for R	https://github.com/cran/randomForest	C 50.3%, R 39.9%
PyTorch	Machine learning library for Python	https://github.com/pytorch/pytorch	C++ 52.6%, Python 36.6%

All these examples share a common feature: data scientists want to use a high-level language, like Python or R, but because parts of the code are too slow, the package writer must switch to a lower-level language, like C or C++.

To solve this challenge, a group of developers created the Julia language. In their manifesto, "Why We Created Julia," Julia's developers call this issue the *two-language problem* (http://mng.bz/Poag).

The beauty of Julia is that we do not have to make such a choice. It offers data scientists a language that is high level, easy to use, and fast. This fact is reflected by the source code structure of Julia and its packages. Table 1.2 lists packages approximately matching the functionality of those in table 1.1.

Table 1.2 Julia packages matching functionality of packages listed in table 1.1

Package	Functionality	URL	Languages
DataFrames.jl	Data frame package	https://github.com/JuliaData/DataFrames.jl	Julia 100%
DecisionTree.jl	Random forest library	https://github.com/bensadeghi/Decision Tree.jl	Julia 100%
Flux.jl	Machine learning package	https://github.com/FluxML/Flux.jl	Julia 100%

All of these packages are written purely in Julia. But is this important for users?

As I also did several years ago, you might think that this feature is more relevant for package developers than for end-user data scientists. Python and R have mature package ecosystems, and you can expect that most compute-intensive algorithms are already implemented in a library that you can use. This is indeed true, but we quickly hit three significant limitations when moving from implementing toy examples to complex production solutions:

- "Most algorithms" is different from "all algorithms." While in most of your code you can rely on the packages, once you start doing more advanced projects, you quickly realize that you'll write your own code that needs to be fast. Most likely, you do not want to switch the programming language you use for such tasks.
- Many libraries providing implementations of data science algorithms allow users to pass custom functions that are meant to perform computations as a part of the main algorithm. An example is passing an objective function (also called a *loss function*) to an algorithm that performs training of a neural network. Typically, during this training, the objective function is evaluated many times. If you want your computations to be fast, you need to make sure that evaluation of the objective function is fast.

  If you are using Julia, you have the flexibility of defining custom functions the way you want and can be sure that the whole program will run fast. The reason is that Julia compiles code (both library code and your custom code) together, thus allowing optimizations that are not possible when precompiled binaries are used or when a custom function is written in an interpreted language. Examples of such optimizations are function inlining (http://mng.bz/ya4y) and constant propagation (http://mng.bz/M02o). I do not discuss these topics in detail as you will not need to know exactly how the Julia compiler works in order to use it efficiently; you can refer to the preceding links for more information about compiler design.

- As a user, you will want to analyze the source code of packages you use, because you'll often need to understand in detail how something is implemented. This is much easier to do if the package is implemented in a high-level language. What is more, in some cases, you'll want to use the package's source code—for example, as a starting point for implementing a feature that its designers have not envisioned. That is simpler to do if the package is written in the same language as the language you use to call it.

To explain the claims presented here in more detail, the next section presents the key features of Julia that data scientists typically find essential.

1.2   Key features of Julia from a data scientist's perspective

Julia and its package ecosystem have five key characteristics that are relevant for a data scientist:

- Speed of code execution
- Designed for interactive use
- Composability, leading to highly reusable code that is easy to maintain
- Package management
- Ease of integration with other languages

Let's dive into each of these features in more detail.

1.2.1   Julia is fast because it is a compiled language

We start with *execution speed*, as this is the first promise Julia makes. The key design element that enables this feature is that Julia is a *compiled language*. In general, before Julia code is executed, it is compiled to native assembly instructions, using the LLVM technology (https://llvm.org/). The choice to use LLVM ensures that Julia programs are easily portable across various computing environments and that their execution speed is highly optimized. Other programming languages, like Rust and Swift, also use LLVM for the same reasons.

The fact that Julia is compiled has one major benefit from a performance perspective. The trick is that the compiler can perform many optimizations that do not change the result of running the code but improve its performance. Let's see this at work. The following example code should be easy to understand, even for those of you without prior experience with Julia:

```
julia> function sum_n(n)
           s = 0
           for i in 1:n
               s += i
           end
           return s
       end
sum_n (generic function with 1 method)

julia> @time sum_n(1_000_000_000)
  0.000001 seconds
500000000500000000
```

NOTE You can find an introduction to Julia syntax in chapter 2, and appendix A will guide you through the process of Julia's installation and configuration.

In this example, we define the function sum_n that takes one parameter, n, and calculates the sum of numbers from 1 to n. Next, we call this function, asking to produce a sum for n equal to one billion. The @time annotation in front of the function call asks Julia to print the execution time of our code (technically, it is a macro, which I explain in chapter 3). As you can see, the result is produced very fast.

You can probably imagine that executing one billion iterations of the loop defined in the body of the sum_n function in this time frame would be impossible; it surely would have taken much more time. Indeed, this is the case. What the Julia compiler did is realize that we are taking a sum of a sequence of numbers, so it applied a well-known formula for a sum of numbers from 1 to n, which is $n(n + 1)/2$. This allows Julia to drastically reduce the computation time.

This is only one example of an optimization that the Julia compiler can perform. Admittedly, implementations of languages like R or Python also try to perform optimizations to speed up code execution. However, in Julia, more information about the types of processed values and the structure of the executed code is available during compilation, and therefore many more optimizations are possible. "Julia: A Fresh Approach to Numerical Computing" by Jeff Bezanson et al. (the creators of the language; see http://mng.bz/JVvP) provides more detailed explanations about the design of Julia.

This is just one example of how the fact that Julia is compiled can speed up code execution. If you are interested in analyzing the source code of carefully designed benchmarks comparing different programming languages, I recommend you check out the Computer Language Benchmarks Game (http://mng.bz/19Ay) that I used to create figure 1.1.

Another related aspect of Julia is that it has built-in support for multithreading (using several processors of your machine in computations) and distributed computing (being able to use several machines in computations). Also, by using additional packages like CUDA.jl (https://github.com/JuliaGPU/CUDA.jl), you can run Julia code on GPUs (have I mentioned that this package is 100% written in Julia?). This essentially means that Julia allows you to fully use the computing resources you have available to reduce the time you need to wait for the results of your computations.

1.2.2   *Julia provides full support for interactive workflows*

A natural question you might now ask is this: Since Julia is compiled to native machine code, how it is possible that data scientists—who do most of their work in an exploratory and interactive manner—find it convenient to use? Typically, when we use compiled languages, we have an explicit separation of compilation and execution phases, which does not play well with the need for a responsive environment.

But here comes the second feature of the Julia language: it is *designed for interactive use*. In addition to running Julia scripts, you can use the following:

- An interactive shell, typically called a read-eval-print loop (REPL).
- Jupyter Notebook (you might have heard that Jupyter's name is a reference to the three core programming languages that are supported: Julia, Python and R).
- Pluto.jl notebooks (https://github.com/fonsp/Pluto.jl), which, using the speed of Julia, take the concept of a notebook to the next level. When you change something in your code, Pluto.jl automatically updates all affected computation results in the entire notebook.

In all these scenarios, the Julia code is compiled when the user tries to execute it. Therefore, the compilation and execution phases are blended and hidden away from the user, ensuring an experience that is like using an interpreted language.

The similarity does not end at this point; like R or Python, Julia is *dynamically typed*. Therefore, when writing your code, you do not have to (but can) specify the types of variables you use. The beauty of the Julia design is that because it is compiled, this dynamism still allows Julia programs to run fast.

It is important to highlight here that it is only the user who does not have to annotate the types of variables used. When running the code, Julia is aware of these types. This not only ensures the speed of code execution but also allows for writing highly composable software. Most Julia programs try to follow the well-known UNIX principle: do one thing and do it well. You'll see one example in the next section and will learn many more throughout this book.

1.2.3   *Julia programs are highly reusable and easy to compose together*

When writing a function in Python, you often must think about whether the user will pass a standard `list`, a NumPy `ndarray`, or a pandas `Series` to it. This often requires writing similar code several times. However, in Julia, you normally can write one function that will be passed a vector, and then this function will just work. The concrete vector implementation that the user passes does not matter to your code, as the code can be fully generic. During compilation, Julia will pick the most efficient way to execute the code (this is achieved using *multiple dispatch*, covered in chapter 3).

This is precisely the approach taken in the DataFrames.jl package that we use a lot in this book. The objects of `DataFrame` are used to work with tabular data and can store arbitrary columns. The DataFrames.jl package (https://github.com/JuliaData/DataFrames.jl) does not make any restrictions here.

For example, a `DataFrame` can store columns that have custom types defined in the Arrow.jl package (https://github.com/JuliaData/Arrow.jl). These columns do not have a standard Julia `Vector` type, but instead follow the Apache Arrow format (https://arrow.apache.org/). You will learn how to work with this data in chapter 8. The custom types implementing this format in Julia are designed so that reading even potentially very large Arrow data is extremely fast.

For reference, let me give you some brief information about Apache Arrow. This language-independent columnar memory format is organized for efficient analytic operations. It can be used for reading and writing Apache Parquet files (https://parquet.apache.org/) and is supported by popular frameworks including PySpark (https://spark.apache.org/docs/latest/api/python/) and Dask (https://docs.dask.org/en/stable/).

From the perspective of Julia language design principles, it is important to highlight that DataFrames.jl and Arrow.jl are completely independent packages. While they do not know about each other's existence, they seamlessly work together because they rely on common interfaces (in this case, this interface is provided via the `AbstractVector` type that we discuss in chapters 2 and 3). At the same time, when Julia executes your code, it generates efficient native assembly instructions that take advantage of the concrete vector types that you used. Therefore, if, in your project, you need to use a proprietary vector type for some reason, DataFrames.jl would not have a problem, and things not only would work but also would be efficient.

Let me highlight here that composability in Julia is naturally combined with optional type restrictions for function arguments that Julia allows for (you will learn how to write methods that have argument type restrictions in chapter 3). You will appreciate this feature when working with large projects, as it allows you to easily find bugs in the code or understand how the code works when you read it. If you use Python, you probably know that since version 3.5, it supports type hints because they are useful, particularly when many developers work on large projects. The difference between Python and Julia is that in Python, type hints are only annotations, and no type checking happens at run time (https://peps.python.org/pep-0484/). On the other hand, in Julia, if you supply type restrictions in your code, the compiler will enforce them so you can be sure that only what you expect gets executed without error.

1.2.4   *Julia has a built-in state-of-the-art package manager*

Let's now turn to the aspects of Julia that are important from a software engineering perspective. First, Julia is shipped with a state-of-the-art package manager, which allows you to easily manage the computational environment state that your code was designed to run under. I explain its details in appendix A, but a practical way of thinking about it is as follows.

To fully specify the state of your Julia environment, it is enough to share two files, Project.toml and Manifest.toml, that uniquely identify the package versions that your code uses, along with the sources of your program. If you do this, Julia will automatically re-create the entire configuration of the runtime environment that your code requires to run correctly. In this way, Julia ensures the reproducibility of your programs' results. Additionally, Julia resolves the common problem of managing dependencies of code written in other languages (often called *dependency hell*), in which a programmer has a tough time properly setting up packages required by other software.

1.2.5 *It is easy to integrate existing code with Julia*

The second engineering aspect is ease of integration with other languages. The creators of Julia were aware that when considering using this language, you might have tons of existing solutions written in other languages. Therefore, Julia is shipped with native support for calling C and Fortran code, while integration with C++, Java, MATLAB, Python, and R code is provided by packages.

This approach minimizes the cost of using Julia as a language of choice in corporate environments with significant legacy codebases. In chapter 5, you will see an example of integrating Julia with Python, and in chapter 10, with R. Packages also exist that make it easy to call Julia code from other languages, like C, Python, or R.

In this section, I have focused on the features of the Julia language. However, like every technology, Julia has its limitations. Next, I describe the types of computing tasks that the packages presented in this book are designed for.

1.3 *Usage scenarios of tools presented in the book*

This book focuses on showing you how to perform the analysis of tabular data. *Tabular data* is a two-dimensional structure consisting of *cells*. Each row has the same number of cells and provides information about one observation of the data. Each column has the same number of cells, stores information about the same feature across observations, and has a name that you can refer to.

While it might sound restrictive, the tabular data format is highly flexible and easy to work with. While, admittedly, you will sometimes want to work with unstructured data, even for those projects, you will end up processing tabular data. Therefore, learning how to do it is a good starting point when doing data science with Julia.

Here is a printout of a sample table that has the `DataFrame` type from the DataFrames.jl package:

```
julia> using DataFrames

julia> DataFrame(id=1:3,
                 name=["Alice", "Bob", "Clyde"],
                 age=[19, 24, 21], friends=[[2], [1, 3], [2]],
                 location=[(city="Atlanta", state="GA"),
                           (city="Boston", state="MA"),
                           (city="Austin", state="TX")])
```

```
3×5 DataFrame
 Row │ id     name    age    friends  location
     │ Int64  String  Int64  Array…   NamedTup…
─────┼────────────────────────────────────────────────────────────
   1 │     1  Alice      19  [2]      (city = "Atlanta", state = "GA")
   2 │     2  Bob        24  [1, 3]   (city = "Boston", state = "MA")
   3 │     3  Clyde      21  [2]      (city = "Austin", state = "TX")
```

This table has three rows, each of which holds information about one student. The
table also has five columns:

- `id`—Integer indicating a student's identifier.
- `name`—String indicating the student's name.
- `age`—Integer indicating the student's age.
- `friends`—Variable-length vectors of IDs of the given student's friends. This
  type of data is often called *nested*, as individual elements of the column are collections of data.
- `location`—Another nested column holding information about the city and
  state where the student lives (technically, elements of this column have the
  `NamedTuple` type; I will show you how to work with these objects in part 1).

In part 1, we will discuss the data types stored in the columns of this table in detail.
However, you may have already noted a great flexibility in the kind of information you
can store in `DataFrame` columns.

In this book, we will mostly talk about tools for working with data that can be
stored in random access memory (RAM) of a single computer and processed using
CPU. This is currently a common application scenario for data analysis. The packages
you are going to learn guarantee that this data processing can be done conveniently
and efficiently.

However, in general, we might want to work with data that is larger than the amount
of available RAM, perform its distributed processing across multiple machines, or perform computations using GPUs. If you are interested in these applications, I recommend as a starting reference point the "Parallel Computing" section of the Julia Manual
(http://mng.bz/E08q). Also, appendix C presents various options that Julia provides in
terms of database support and data storage formats.

1.4   Julia's drawbacks

When you were reading about the advantages of Julia, you likely thought that it's trying to "have its cake and eat it too" when combining the code compilation and dynamism required by interactive use cases. There surely must be a catch.

Indeed, there is. The problem is easy to identify: the compilation takes time. The
first time you run a function, it must be compiled before it is executed. For small functions, this cost is negligible, but for complex ones, execution can take up to several
seconds. This issue is called the *time to first plot problem* in the Julia community. I'll show
you a timing of producing a simple plot in a fresh Julia session in the next listing.

> **Listing 1.1   Measuring time to first plot**
>
> ```julia
> julia> @time using Plots
>   4.719333 seconds (9.27 M allocations: 630.887 MiB, 6.32% gc time,
>                     20.23% compilation time)
>
> julia> @time plot(1:10)
>   2.542534 seconds (3.75 M allocations: 208.403 MiB, 1.86% gc time,
>                     99.63% compilation time)
>
> julia> @time plot(1:10)
>   0.000567 seconds (1.42 k allocations: 78.898 KiB)
> ```

Time taken to load the Plots.jl package

Time taken to produce a first plot

Time taken to produce the same plot again

The call to the @time macro (as noted previously, you will learn about macros in chapter 3) asks Julia to produce statistics for the execution time of the expression following it. In this case, loading the Plots.jl package takes almost 5 seconds, and producing a first plot takes around 2.5 seconds (note that over 99% of this time is compilation). Producing a plot again, however, is fast because the plot function is already compiled.

The reason for the rather long compilation time in this specific example is that plotting requires very complex code underneath (imagine all possible options you get when styling the produced figures). In the early days of Julia, this issue was quite significant, but Julia's core developers have put a lot of effort into minimizing it. Currently, it is much less of a problem, and with every release of Julia, this will improve. Still, this issue will always be there to some extent, as this is an inherent characteristic of the design of the language.

A natural question is in which scenarios we should expect the compilation cost to matter. The cost is relevant if two conditions are met jointly: the first is working with a small amount of data, and the second is that the Julia process performs only a few operations before terminating. If you have a large amount of data (for example, taking an hour for processing), having to pay several seconds of compilation cost is not noticeable. Similarly, if you start a long interactive session or start a Julia server that responds to many requests without being terminated (as in the Timeline case study), the amortized cost of compilation is negligible because you pay it only the first time a function is run. However, if you want to quickly start Julia, do one plot of simple data, and exit Julia, the compilation time would be noticeable and most likely annoying (in listing 1.1, we can see performing such a task on my laptop requires around 7 seconds).

Users also often ask if it is possible to create an executable from Julia code that can be run on a machine that does not have Julia installed, without sacrificing execution speed. This is possible using the PackageCompiler.jl package (https://github.com/JuliaLang/PackageCompiler.jl). However, such applications will have a larger executable file size and larger RAM memory footprint when run in comparison to, for example, applications written in C (I have found that on a laptop, a fresh Julia 1.7.1 process under Windows 11 uses 134 MB of RAM). In some contexts where RAM is scarce (for example, embedded systems), users might find this problematic. You can expect that this situation will improve in future releases of Julia.

Finally, you have likely heard that Julia is a relatively new player in the field of programming languages. This naturally raises a question about its maturity and stability. In this book, we will focus on packages that have reached a production-ready stability level. As you will learn, these packages provide all standard functionalities that a data scientist typically needs.

However, the breadth of the package ecosystem in Python or R is much more extensive. Therefore, in some specific situations, you might not find a suitable package in the Julia ecosystem or might consider a package not mature enough to warrant its use for production purposes. You'll then need to decide whether you should opt out of using Julia or use the packages like RCall.jl or PyCall.jl that allow you to easily use R or Python libraries in your Julia programs (which is what I typically do). In the book, you will see examples of such an integration so that you can verify that it is indeed convenient.

1.5 What data analysis skills will you learn?

This book gives you a hands-on introduction to data analysis using the Julia language. The target audience of this book includes data scientists, data engineers, computer scientists, and business analysts who want to learn an exciting new technology that can help you get valuable insights into data in an efficient and convenient way.

Readers preferably have some experience with Julia programming to benefit most from reading it. However, I recognize that Julia is a new technology, with a limited number of data scientists that already know it. Therefore, part 1 includes several chapters introducing the Julia language. In part 2, you will learn the following skills in Julia:

- Reading and writing data in various common formats
- Performing common tasks when working with tabular data, including subsetting, grouping, summarizing, transforming, sorting, joining, and reshaping
- Visualizing your data by using various types of plots
- Performing data analysis and building predictive models using the collected data
- Creating complex data processing pipelines combining all the components described in the preceding list items

1.6 How can Julia be used for data analysis?

Most data analysis projects follow a similar workflow. In this section, I sketch a high-level map of the steps of this process (figure 1.2). For each step, I name typical tasks that a data scientist performs to accomplish it. Julia provides a full set of functionalities allowing you to perform these tasks in real-life projects, and in the following chapters, you will learn how to carry out all of them.

Figure 1.2 A typical data processing pipeline. Using the Julia language, the data scientist can perform all steps of data analysis.

The tools available in the Julia package ecosystem cover all the steps in a typical data analysis pipeline:

- *Source data ingestion*—Julia can natively read data from a variety of sources—for example, in formats including comma-separated values (CSV), Arrow, Microsoft Excel, or JavaScript Object Notation (JSON). It is worth highlighting that compared to R or Python, Julia is an excellent tool for writing efficient custom-made parsers for data coming from nonstandard sources, which is a common scenario in Internet of Things (IoT) applications.
- *Data preparation*—Typical data operations performed in this step include joining, reshaping, sorting, subsetting, transforming, and fixing quality issues. In this book, we will mostly work with the DataFrames.jl package to accomplish these tasks; the package was designed to be convenient to use and efficient, especially when performing nonstandard data transformations that require writing custom functions. As I have already discussed in this chapter, doing proper performance benchmarking is challenging, but if you are a pandas user in Python, you can expect that your complex split-apply-combine operations or large joins (these two classes of operations are often the most time-consuming steps in data preparation) will typically take an order of magnitude less time after switching to DataFrames.jl.
- *Data analysis*—After the data is prepared, the data scientist wants to gain insights from it; data can be analyzed in multiple ways, including by aggregating and summarizing it, visualizing, performing statistical analysis, or building machine learning models. In a similar way to the data preparation step, you will benefit most from using Julia if you create complex solutions. In my experience, Julia is especially convenient to use and efficient in comparison to R or Python if you need to combine machine learning, optimization, and simulation components in a single model. In part 2, we will create an example project showing how simulation can be integrated into a data analysis pipeline.
- *Sharing the results*—The last step of any analysis is to make its results available to an external audience. This can be as simple as saving the data to persistent storage, but also covers serving the results, for example, via an interactive dashboard or web service (covered in chapter 14) or deploying a created machine learning model to a production environment. Here, the key benefit of Julia is that if you deploy your models to production, you do not have to port them to another

language to achieve high performance of execution; I presented the Timeline case study as an example in section 1.1. In part 2, I'll show you how to create a web service in Julia that provides users with your data analysis results.

It is important to highlight that the preceding steps are typically done in two modes:

- *Interactive*—The data scientist works with the data in an exploratory and iterative way, with the aim of understanding it, and draws valuable business conclusions. This mode is usually used when working in a development environment.
- *Fully automated*—All analyses are performed without any intervention of a data scientist. The Julia programs automatically execute all the steps of the data processing pipeline and serve the results to outside processes. This mode is typically used when the code is deployed to a production environment.

Julia and its data-science–related ecosystem were designed so that they can conveniently be used in both interactive and fully automated modes. This book presents examples of code prepared for both scenarios.

Methodologies for data analysis

This section has presented a simplified view of the data analysis process. If you would like to learn more about standards developed in this area, here are a few references that will provide you with more in-depth information:

- Team Data Science Process (TDSP), http://mng.bz/wyOW
- Cross-industry standard process for data mining (CRISP-DM), http://www .statoo.com/CRISP-DM.pdf
- Knowledge discovery in databases (KDD), https://link.springer.com/chapter/ 10.1007/0-387-25465-X_1
- Sample, explore, modify, model, and assess (SEMMA), http://mng.bz/7Zjg

---

Summary

- Julia is a modern programming language created to meet the requirements of data scientists: it is fast and at the same time expressive and easy to use both interactively and in production.
- Julia programs are highly composable, which means that the various packages and functionalities provided by the language can be easily used together while ensuring high execution speed.
- Julia's design is engineering friendly: it has an advanced package management functionality built in and offers an easy way to integrate with other programming languages. Additionally, when you define functions in Julia, you can restrict the types of arguments they accept. This is especially useful when working with large projects, as it allows you to quickly catch bugs in the code and makes it simple to understand how the code works.

- In this book, you will learn how to work with tabular data by using the Julia packages that are mature and ready for serious production use.
- Packages from the Julia ecosystem allow you to easily read and write data in various formats, process the data, visualize it, and create both statistical and machine learning models.

Part 1

Essential Julia skills

In this first part of the book, you will learn key Julia skills that are useful in data science projects. I have organized the content to gradually become more advanced. We start with the basic syntax of Julia and finish with advanced topics like parsing JSON data and working with missing values.

This part consists of six chapters organized as follows:

- Chapter 2 discusses the basics of Julia's syntax and common language constructs, as well as the most important aspects of variable scoping rules.
- Chapter 3 introduces Julia's type system and defining methods. It also introduces working with packages and modules. Finally, it discusses using macros.
- Chapter 4 covers working with arrays, dictionaries, tuples, and named tuples.
- Chapter 5 discusses advanced topics related to working with collections in Julia: broadcasting and subtyping rules for parametric types. It also covers integrating Julia with Python, using an example of a t-SNE dimensionality reduction algorithm.
- Chapter 6 teaches you various aspects of working with strings in Julia. Additionally, it covers the topics of using symbols, fixed-width strings, and compressing vectors by using the PooledArrays.jl package.
- Chapter 7 concentrates on working with time-series data and missing values. It also covers fetching data by using HTTP queries and parsing JSON data.

Getting started with Julia

This chapter covers

- Understanding values and variables
- Defining loops, conditional expressions, and functions
- Variable scoping rules in Julia

If you are new to the Julia language, in this chapter, you will learn its basic syntax and most important concepts. We'll focus on the aspects that are different from those in Python and R. Even if you already know Julia, I recommend that you quickly go through this chapter to make sure you have a complete understanding of the basic concepts.

If you are not sure how to install, set up, and use your working environment, how to get help, or how to install and manage packages, refer to appendix A.

Note that the chapters in part 1 are not meant to be a full course on Julia. They contain only essential information required for you to start doing data science in Julia. I recommend you refer to the books listed on the Julia project "Books" page

19

(https://julialang.org/learning/books/) or to the Julia Manual (https://docs.julialang .org/en/v1/) for a complete introduction to Julia programming.

In this chapter, our goal is to write a function that calculates a winsorized mean of a vector. Informally speaking, a *winsorized mean* replaces the smallest and largest values with the less extreme observations closest to them. This is done to limit the effect of outliers on the result (http://mng.bz/m2yM). Let me start with explaining how you can compute this mean.

Assume you have a sequence of numbers stored as a vector and want to compute its mean. However, you are aware that your data might include extreme values (outliers) that could significantly affect the result. In this situation, you can use the winsorized mean, which is a modification of a standard mean. The idea is to replace the most extreme observed values with less extreme ones. Let's start with a definition that we will want to implement.

The *k-times winsorized mean* of a vector x is the mean of the elements of this vector, where each of its k smallest elements is replaced by the (k + 1)st smallest element, and similarly, each of the k largest elements is replaced by the (k + 1)st largest element (http://mng.bz/5mWD).

If we assume that the vector x is sorted in ascending order and has length n, as is done, for example, at the Xycoon Statistics-Econometrics-Forecasting site (www .xycoon.com/winsorized_mean.htm), then when calculating the k-times winsorized mean, we replace the elements x[1], x[2], ..., x[k] with element x[k + 1] and elements x[n], x[n - 1], ..., x[n - k + 1] with element x[n - k].

Here is an example. Assuming we want to calculate the two-times winsorized mean of the vector [1, 2, 3, 4, 5, 6, 7, 8], we replace 1 and 2 with 3; similarly, 7 and 8 are replaced by 6. This operation gives us a vector [3, 3, 3, 4, 5, 6, 6, 6], whose mean is equal to 4.5. Now you know what we need to implement. The question is how to do it in Julia.

To develop a function calculating the winsorized mean, we need to introduce various important parts of the Julia language, starting from values and variables, and continuing with control flow and functions.

2.1   *Representing values*

To create a function calculating the winsorized mean, we first need to learn how Julia represents numbers and vectors. More generally, it is important to understand how Julia handles values.

A *value* is a representation of an entity that is stored in a computer's memory and can be manipulated by a Julia program. In this book, I also use the term *object* to refer to values, especially when referring to values that have a complex internal structure (for example, data frames, which are discussed in part 2). However, Julia is not an object-oriented programming language, and objects do not have methods attached to them. Instead, Julia supports multiple dispatch, as we will briefly discuss later in this chapter.

Before discussing how to manipulate values, let's see how to create them in the next listing. Every value is a result of evaluating a Julia expression. Here are a few basic example values created by the evaluation of *literals* (which represent values in the source code).

Listing 2.1 Creating values by evaluating literals

```
julia> 1
1

julia> true
true

julia> "Hello world!"
"Hello world!"

julia> 0.1
0.1

julia> [1, 2, 3]
3-element Vector{Int64}:
 1
 2
 3
```

These values are, consecutively, an integer 1, Boolean true, string "Hello world!", floating-point number 0.1, and a three-element vector [1, 2, 3].

In Julia, an extremely important property of each value is its type, which you can check by using the typeof function. In Julia, when you define a function, you can optionally declare the types of arguments that the function accepts. For example, in our k-times winsorized mean function of a vector x, we will want to make sure that k is an integer and x is a vector. Let's try using the typeof function on the values from listing 2.1 in the next listing.

Listing 2.2 Checking types of values

```
julia> typeof(1)
Int64

julia> typeof(true)
Bool

julia> typeof("Hello world!")
String

julia> typeof(0.1)
Float64

julia> typeof([1, 2, 3])
Vector{Int64} (alias for Array{Int64, 1})
```

You might notice two things here. First, for integer and floating-point values, you have a number 64 that is a part of the type name—namely, Int64 and Float64. This value is important. It signals to the user that both these values take up 64 bits of memory. In general, you have flexibility here if needed. You could, for example, use Int8 values that use only 8 bits of memory at the cost of being able to represent a narrower range of values: from –128 to 127. You can create an Int8 value by writing Int8(1).

In Julia, you can check, if needed, the exact memory layout of numbers by using the bitstring function, producing a string holding a sequence of bits that make the passed value. I show this in the following code to convince you that, indeed, 1 and 1.0 take 64 bits on my machine, and Int8(1) takes 8 bits. Note that although these three values represent the number 1, they all have different storage in computer memory because they have different types (if you would like to learn more about how floating-point numbers, like 1.0, are stored in computer memory, check out http://mng.bz/ aPDo):

```
julia> bitstring(1)
"0000000000000000000000000000000000000000000000000000000000000001"

julia> bitstring(1.0)
"0011111111110000000000000000000000000000000000000000000000000000"

julia> bitstring(Int8(1))
"00000001"
```

In this book, we will typically use the default 64-bit numbers. It is useful to know that on 64-bit machines (the kind of computer you are most likely using), you can refer to the Int64 type more briefly by just typing Int:

```
julia> Int
Int64
```

The second thing to notice is the type of the [1, 2, 3] vector, which is Vector{Int64} (alias for Array{Int64, 1}). It seems quite verbose. Let's dissect this.

Start with Array{Int64, 1}. We see that our vector is of the Array type. In the curly brackets, we get the *parameters* of this type: {Int64, 1}. The subtypes of AbstractArray normally take two parameters, and Array takes exactly two parameters. The first parameter is the type of elements that the array can store (in our case, Int64). The second parameter is the dimension of the array, which is 1 in this example.

Because one-dimensional arrays are typically called *vectors* in mathematics, Julia allows you to just write Vector{Int64}, which means the same as Array{Int64, 1}. Since the type name is Vector, which means it is a one-dimensional array, we can omit passing the dimension parameter. However, we still need to pass the element type that the vector is allowed to store so it gets one parameter, in this case, {Int64}. Figure 2.1 illustrates these concepts.

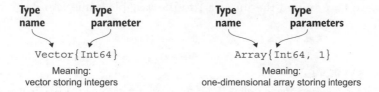

Meaning:
vector storing integers

Meaning:
one-dimensional array storing integers

Figure 2.1 Rules of reading the names of types having parameters. Both definitions are equivalent, as vectors are one-dimensional arrays; the second parameter of `Array{Int64, 1}` is an array dimension (in this case, 1), so this is a vector. Type parameters are wrapped in curly brackets.

In addition to getting the type of a value with the `typeof` function, you can conveniently test whether a value is of a particular type by using the `isa` operator. Let's check this `[1, 2, 3]` vector:

```
julia> [1, 2, 3] isa Vector{Int}
true

julia> [1, 2, 3] isa Array{Int64, 1}
true
```

Note that in this example, in `Vector{Int}`, both `Vector` and `Int` are aliases, and `Array{Int64, 1}` is the same type.

When writing your own code, you will most likely not use the `typeof` function and the `isa` operator often since Julia automatically uses type information when running your code. However, it is important to learn how to manually inspect the type of a value to build your understanding of how Julia works. For example, knowing types of variables is important when debugging your code. In chapter 3, you will learn how the information about the type of a variable is used when defining functions in Julia.

2.2 Defining variables

Now that you know what a value is, you are ready to learn about variables. In our winsorized mean function, we need variables to refer to the values passed by the user to the function.

A *variable* is a name that is bound to a value. The simplest way to bind a value to a variable name is to use the assignment operator = (equals sign):

```
julia> x = 1
1

julia> y = [1, 2, 3]
3-element Vector{Int64}:
 1
 2
 3
```

In this example, we have bound the integer 1 to the variable name x and the vector [1, 2, 3] to the variable name y.

> ### Binding vs. copying values
>
> It is important to highlight that in Julia, the assignment operator (=) performs only binding of values to variables. The process of binding does not involve copying values. Python also follows this approach. However, in R, this is not the case.
>
> This distinction is most important when working with collections of data, like vectors, if you mutate them (for example, adding or changing stored elements). In Julia, if a vector is bound to two different variables and you mutate it, the change will be visible in both variables. For example, in Julia, if you write x = [1, 2] and then y = x, then the x and y variables are bound to the same value. If you next write x[1] = 10, both the x and y variables have the value [10, 2]. If you would like to bind to a variable y a copy of a value bound to variable x, write y = copy(x). In this case, changing the value bound to x will not affect y.
>
> Understanding when value binding versus copying happens is especially important when working with columns of a data frame. In my experience as a maintainer of the DataFrames.jl package, this issue is one of the major sources of bugs in users' code. In part 2, you will learn how, when working with DataFrames.jl, to decide whether the operation you perform should copy data.

It is important to highlight here that Julia is a dynamically typed language, so it does not need to know the types bound to variables during compile time. The practical consequence of this fact is that you can bind values of different types to the same variable name in your code. Here is an example:

```
julia> x = 1
1

julia> x
1

julia> typeof(x)
Int64

julia> x = 0.1
0.1

julia> x
0.1

julia> typeof(x)
Float64
```

In this example, we first bind an integer 1 of type Int64 to the variable x. Next, we assign 0.1 of type Float64 to the same variable name. This behavior is something that users of R or Python naturally expect, as they also belong to the class of dynamically typed programming languages.

Avoid binding values of different types to the same variable name

For convenience, Julia allows you to bind values of different types to the same variable name. However, that is not recommended for performance reasons.

As we discussed in chapter 1, Julia is a compiled language. During compilation, Julia tries to automatically find all possible types of values that can be bound to a given variable name. If the Julia compiler can prove that this is a single type (or, in some cases, a closed list of a few types), then Julia is able to generate more-efficient code.

In the Julia Manual, code that avoids changing the type of values bound to a variable is called *type stable*. Writing type-stable code is one of the most important performance recommendations in Julia (http://mng.bz/69N6). We will get back to the topic of writing type-stable code in the context of working with DataFrames.jl in part 2.

Julia offers a lot of flexibility in naming your variables. You can use Unicode characters in variable names, and they are case-sensitive. Here are three examples:

```julia
julia> Kamiński = 1
1

julia> x₁ = 0.5
0.5

julia> ε = 0.0001
0.0001
```

The first example uses ń (a letter in the Polish alphabet) in the variable name. The second example has a subscript 1 in the name of the variable x_1. The last example uses the Greek letter ε. This flexibility is most useful when you have source material (for example, documentation or a research paper) and want to use the same symbols in the code as are used in the text to make it easier to understand the code.

You might ask how we can type characters such as $_1$ or ε. It is easy to check. In the Julia REPL, switch to help mode by pressing the question mark key (?) on your keyboard (appendix A explains how to use help in Julia), and then paste the character you want to investigate. Here is the truncated output you will get:

```julia
help?> ₁
"₁" can be typed by \_1<tab>

help?> ε
"ε" can be typed by \varepsilon<tab>
```

As you can see, typing in these characters is convenient, especially if you are a LaTeX user. This method of input is supported in all standard environments under which you can expect to write Julia code—for example, Julia REPL, Visual Studio Code, and

Jupyter Notebook. In the Julia Manual, you can find a complete list of Unicode characters that can be entered via tab completion in the Julia REPL (http://mng.bz/o5Gv).

2.3   *Using the most important control-flow constructs*

As explained in this chapter's introduction, to write a function calculating a winsorized mean, we need to iterate over values stored in a vector and conditionally change them. In this section, you will learn how to perform these operations.

The three kinds of control-flow constructs that we will often use in this book are as follows:

- Conditional evaluation
- Loops
- Compound expressions

For a complete list, see the "Control Flow" section of the Julia Manual (http://mng.bz/ne24). I will now explain how you can use each of them.

2.3.1   *Computations depending on a Boolean condition*

Conditional evaluation is used when we want to take different actions depending on the value of a particular condition. In this section, I'll show you how to use conditional expressions in Julia and the common patterns you should know when working with Boolean conditions.

THE CONDITIONAL EXPRESSION

In Julia, *conditional expressions* are written using the if-elseif-else-end syntax. Figure 2.2 illustrates an example of a conditional expression.

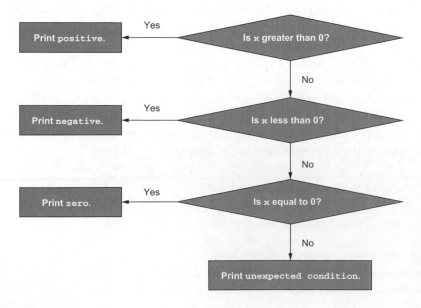

**Figure 2.2
Explanation of how
the code in listing
2.3 works**

The following listing shows how to implement the conditional expression presented in figure 2.2 in Julia. Note that we test two values for equality in Julia by using the == operator.

Listing 2.3 Defining a conditional expression

```
julia> x = -7
-7

julia> if x > 0
           println("positive")
       elseif x < 0
           println("negative")
       elseif x == 0
           println("zero")
       else
           println("unexpected condition")
       end
negative
```

Because x is negative, x > 0 produces false, and x < 0 produces true, so negative is printed.

In this syntax, the elseif and else parts can be omitted. It is important to stress that the expression passed after if must have a logical value. The type of the value of the expression must be Bool; otherwise, an error is thrown:

```
julia> x = -7
-7

julia> if x
           println("condition was true")
       end
ERROR: TypeError: non-boolean (Int64) used in boolean context
```

CODE INDENTATION IN JULIA

In listing 2.3, I indented the code four spaces. This is a standard practice in Julia and is also used in other cases that we discuss later in this chapter (loops, functions, etc.).

In Julia, as opposed to Python, using indentation is optional and serves the purpose of improving code readability. In general, Julia identifies the end of a code block when it encounters the end keyword or other keywords that are specific to a given statement (for example, in a conditional expression, these additional keywords are else and elseif).

RULES FOR COMPARING FLOATING-POINT NUMBERS

In listing 2.3, when we checked whether x was positive, negative, or zero, you might have been surprised that I included the else part printing unexpected condition. It would seem natural to expect that if x is a number, it must meet one of these conditions.

Unfortunately, things are more complex than that. The Institute of Electrical and Electronics Engineers (IEEE) 754 standard for floating-point arithmetic defines a special NaN (*not a number*) value that, when compared to other values using <, <=, >, >=, and ==, always produces `false`, as you can see here:

```
julia> NaN > 0
false

julia> NaN >= 0
false

julia> NaN < 0
false

julia> NaN <= 0
false

julia> NaN == 0
false
```

According to the IEEE 754 standard, comparing NaN to a value produces `true` only when the not-equal operator (!=) is used:

```
julia> NaN != 0
true

julia> NaN != NaN
true
```

This shows us that we must be careful when using common knowledge from mathematics in the context of programming language—not all things work the same way in theory and when implemented on a computer. Also, in general, different programming languages might implement different rules for working with numbers. When working with floating-point numbers, Julia follows the IEEE 754 standard.

CONSEQUENCES OF INEXACT REPRESENTATION OF NUMBERS BY FLOATING-POINT VALUES

Another similar problem arises because floating-point numbers only approximately represent real numbers. Therefore, for instance, we have this:

```
julia> 0.1 + 0.2 == 0.3
false
```

This is surprising. The reason for this is that none of the `Float64` values created by the evaluation of literals `0.1`, `0.2`, and `0.3` exactly represent the written real numbers. What Julia does is store the `Float64` values that are the closest representation of the requested numbers. Therefore, we have a small, but often nonzero, error. By writing this

```
julia> 0.1 + 0.2
0.30000000000000004
```

we can see that the sum of 0.1 and 0.2 is a bit more than 0.3. What should a data scientist do in such a case? In Julia, you can use the isapprox function to perform an approximate comparison:

```
julia> isapprox(0.1 + 0.2, 0.3)
true
```

You can control how isapprox treats the *approximately equals* statement by passing appropriate arguments; see the Julia Manual (http://mng.bz/gR4x) for details. You can also conveniently use the isapprox function with a default tolerance level, which defaults to around 1.5e-8 relative tolerance for Float64 values via an infix operator:

```
julia> 0.1 + 0.2 ≈ 0.3          ◁──┐  Do not confuse the ≈ character
true                               │  with the = character.
```

You can get the approx (≈) character in the Julia REPL by typing \approx and pressing Tab.

COMBINING SEVERAL LOGICAL CONDITIONS

You should now be comfortable with writing a single condition. However, we often want to test several conditions at once. For example, we might want to check whether a number is both positive and less than 10. In Julia, you can combine conditions by using the && (and) and || (or) operators. Here are two examples:

```
julia> x = -7
-7

julia> x > 0 && x < 10
false

julia> x < 0 || log(x) > 10
true
```

As a convenience, when comparisons against the same value are joined using the && operator, they can be written more concisely. Therefore, instead of writing x > 0 && x < 10, you could write 0 < x < 10, just as you would do when writing a condition in a mathematical text.

SHORT-CIRCUIT EVALUATION OF CONDITIONS IN JULIA

Another important feature of && and || operators in Julia is that they perform *short-circuit* evaluation: they evaluate only as many conditions (starting from the leftmost) as are needed to determine the logical value of the whole expression. You have already seen this feature at work when we evaluated the expression x < 0 || log(x) > 10. The reason is that log(x) throws an error if x has a negative real value, as you can see here:

```
julia> x = -7
-7

julia> log(x)
ERROR: DomainError with -7.0:
log will only return a complex result if called with a complex argument.
Try log(Complex(x)).
```

The reason we have not seen this error when evaluating $x < 0$ || $\log(x) > 10$ is that since x is equal to -7, the first condition $x < 0$ is `true`, so Julia never checks the second condition. Therefore, if you write

```
x > 0 && println(x)
```

Julia interprets it in the same way as

```
if x > 0
    println(x)
end
```

Similarly,

```
x > 0 || println(x)
```

is the same as

```
if !(x > 0)
    println(x)
end
```

As a consequence, the `&&` and `||` operators can be used to conveniently write one-liners performing conditional evaluation:

```
julia> x = -7
-7

julia> x < 0 && println(x^2)
49

julia> iseven(x) || println("x is odd")
x is odd
```

This pattern is used in Julia to improve code readability when simple conditions are used.

Let me highlight that in these scenarios, the second part of the expression does not have to produce a `Bool` value. The reason for this is that the short-circuiting behavior of `&&` and `||` in our examples is equivalent to writing the following `if` expressions:

```
julia> x = -7
-7

julia> if x < 0
           println(x^2)
       end
49

julia> if !iseven(x)
           println("x is odd")
       end
x is odd
```

Remember, however, that as I have explained, using an expression that does not produce a `Bool` value in a normal `if` condition is not allowed and throws an error:

```
julia> x = -7
-7

julia> if x < 0 && x^2
           println("inside if")
       end
ERROR: TypeError: non-boolean (Int64) used in boolean context
```

TERNARY OPERATOR

Before we wrap up the discussion on checking conditions, let's introduce the *ternary operator*, borrowed from the C programming language. Writing

```
x > 0 ? sqrt(x) : sqrt(-x)
```

is equivalent to writing

```
if x > 0
    sqrt(x)
else
    sqrt(-x)
end
```

As you can see, before the ? symbol, we pass the expression that is the condition. Then, after ?, we pass two expressions separated by :, of which only one is evaluated, depending on whether the passed condition is true or false.

The ternary operator is used in short one-line conditions. Here is one more example:

```
julia> x = -7
-7

julia> x > 0 ? println("x is positive") : println("x is not positive")
x is not positive
```

CONDITIONAL EXPRESSIONS RETURN A VALUE

The if-elseif-else-end expressions and the ternary operator return a value that is the return value of the last executed expression in the branch that was chosen. This is often useful if you want to bind this return value to a variable.

As an example, assume that we want to compute the square root of an absolute value of a given number x and store the result in variable y. You could write this operation as y = sqrt(abs(x)), but let me show you how to do it by using a conditional expression:

```
julia> x = -4.0
-4.0

julia> y = if x > 0
               sqrt(x)
           else
               sqrt(-x)
           end
2.0

julia> y
2.0
```

The same rule applies to the ternary operator:

```
julia> x = 9.0
9.0

julia> y = x > 0 ? sqrt(x) : sqrt(-x)
3.0

julia> y
3.0
```

2.3.2   *Loops*

In Julia, you can use two kinds of loops: `for`-end and `while`-end. The `for` loop is arguably the more common one in practice. It iterates over values of a collection. The next listing shows a working example.

> **Listing 2.4   Defining a `for` loop**

```
julia> for i in [1, 2, 3]
           println(i, " is ", isodd(i) ? "odd" : "even")
       end
1 is odd
2 is even
3 is odd
```

Here we have a vector `[1, 2, 3]` containing three values. The `i` variable in each iteration of the loop takes the consecutive values from this vector, and the body of the loop is executed. The `isodd(i) ? "odd" : "even"` expression is a ternary operator (introduced in section 2.3.1).

On the other hand, the `while` loop produces values as long as a certain condition is met, as the following listing shows.

> **Listing 2.5   Defining a `while` loop**

```
julia> i = 1
1

julia> while i < 4
           println(i, " is ", isodd(i) ? "odd" : "even")
           global i += 1
       end
1 is odd
2 is even
3 is odd
```

Here we have a variable `i`. If the condition following the `while` keyword is `true`, the body of the loop is executed. In this case, we test whether `i` is less than 4. Note that in the body of the loop, we increment `i` by 1 so eventually the loop terminates.

In this example, you can see the `global` keyword, which I will explain when we discuss variable scoping rules in section 2.5. For now, it is enough to understand that this keyword signals Julia that it should use the `i` variable that we defined outside the `while` loop.

Another style that I have not explained yet is `i += 1`. This statement means the same as writing `i = i + 1` but is a bit shorter to type. In this case, it increments the variable `i` by 1. You can use shorthand for other operators as well—for example, `-=`, `*=`, or `/=`.

In both `for` and `while` loops, you can use two special keywords:

- `continue` immediately stops an iteration and moves to the next one.
- `break` immediately terminates the loop.

It is easiest to understand how these keywords work by example:

```julia
julia> i = 0
0

julia> while true
           global i += 1
           i > 6 && break
           isodd(i) && continue
           println(i, " is even")
       end
2 is even
4 is even
6 is even
```

Observe that we write `while true` to set up the loop. Since this condition is always true, unless we have another means to interrupt the loop, it would run infinitely many times. This is exactly what the `break` keyword achieves. To understand this, let's review the body of the loop line by line.

In this loop, in each iteration, the variable `i` gets incremented by 1. Next, we check whether we have reached a value greater than 6, and if so, terminate the loop. If `i` is less than or equal to 6, we check whether it is odd. If this is the case, we skip the rest of the body of the loop; otherwise, (if `i` is even), we execute `println(i, " is even")`.

2.3.3 *Compound expressions*

When processing data, it is often useful to perform several operations but bundle them together so that from the outside, they look like one expression returning the value of the last expression inside it. In Julia, you have two options for packing several expressions into one.

The first is using `begin-end` blocks. The second is more lightweight and allows chaining expressions by using the semicolon (`;`). Often, we need to wrap a chain of expressions separated by `;` in parentheses to delimit the range of the compound expression. The next listing shows some examples.

Listing 2.6   Defining compound expressions using `begin-end` blocks or a semicolon (`;`)

```
julia> x = -7
-7

julia> x < 0 && begin
           println(x)        ⟵——  Prints –7
           x += 1
           println(x)        ⟵——  Prints –6
           2 * x             ⟵——┐ The value of the whole code block
       end                        is –12, which Julia displays.
-7
-6
-12
                                              First prints –5, and
                                              since the whole
                                              compound expression is
julia> x > 0 ? (println(x); x) : (x += 1; println(x); x)  ⟵——  also –5, Julia displays it
-5
-5
```

In the first case, we use the short-circuiting `&&` operator. However, it requires a single expression on both its left and right side. In this example, we use a `begin-end` block to conveniently create a single expression from a sequence of expressions spanning multiple lines. Observe that apart from printing two values, the whole expression returns `-12`, which is the value of `2 * x`, the last expression in the chain. The expression on the right-hand side of `&&` does not have to produce a Boolean value, as opposed to the expression on the left-hand side of `&&`.

In the second example, we use a ternary operator. It similarly requires passing single expressions to all of its parts to work correctly. Since our code is relatively short, we use the semicolon to create a single expression from several expressions. We use parentheses to clearly delimit the range of the chain of expressions. Using the enclosing parentheses is not always strictly required by the Julia parser, but it is a good practice, so I recommend you always use them when chaining several expressions together.

In summary, compound expressions are useful when you are required to pass a single expression in part of the code, but you need to perform several operations. Typically, the `begin-end` block is used for longer expressions that span multiple lines, while chaining with the semicolon is preferred for shorter cases fitting onto a single line.

In practice, you should not overuse compound expressions as they might lead to less readable code. Often it is better, for example, to use the standard conditional expression or define a helper function to improve code clarity. However, you are likely to encounter compound expressions in the source code of various packages, so it is important that you know how to interpret them.

Let me again highlight the stylistic convention that we used in the preceding code. In Julia, code blocks use four spaces for indentation. However, this is only a convention. Proper code formatting is not enforced by Julia and does not affect how code is executed, but it is highly recommended to follow this convention as it greatly improves code readability.

> ## Comments in code
>
> A special part of the source code that we often need is comments. They are not a control-flow construct but affect how Julia interprets code, so I include this note here.
>
> If you put a hash character (#) in your code, everything from the point where this character is placed until the end of the line is ignored by the Julia parser.

2.3.4 A first approach to calculating the winsorized mean

We are now ready to calculate the k-times winsorized mean of a vector. For now, we'll do that without using functions, but only in the Julia REPL. Let's try to compute it for the vector [8, 3, 1, 5, 7] by using what you have already learned. In our calculation, we want to perform the following steps:

1 Initialize the input data. Vector x holds the data for which we want to compute the mean, and integer k indicates the number of smallest and largest values to replace.

2 Sort the vector x and store the result in a variable y. This way, k smallest values are at the beginning of the vector y, and k largest are at its end.

3 Replace k smallest values by the (k + 1)st smallest value in vector y by using a loop. Similarly, replace k largest values by the (k + 1)st largest value.

4 Calculate the mean of vector y by first summing its elements and then dividing the result by the length of the vector. The obtained result is the k-times winsorized mean of the original vector x.

First, bind variable x to the input vector, and let k be equal to 1:

```
julia> x = [8, 3, 1, 5, 7]
5-element Vector{Int64}:
 8
 3
 1
 5
 7

julia> k = 1
1
```

In the simplest approach (we will discuss more advanced methods in chapter 3), as the next step, we sort this vector and bind the result to a variable:

```
julia> y = sort(x)
5-element Vector{Int64}:
 1
 3
 5
 7
 8
```

Next, we replace k smallest values with the (k + 1)st smallest one. We do the same with largest values and inspect the y vector after the change:

```julia
julia> for i in 1:k
           y[i] = y[k + 1]
           y[end - i + 1] = y[end - k]
       end

julia> y
5-element Vector{Int64}:
 3
 3
 5
 7
 7
```

Here we additionally see two new constructs. First, when we write 1:k, we create a range of values starting from 1 and then containing all integer values up to k inclusive (as opposed to Python, in which the last element of the range is not included).

The second feature is vector indexing. We discuss this in more detail in chapter 4, but for now, it is important to note the following:

- Vectors in Julia use 1-based indexing.
- You get the i-th element of a vector x by using the syntax x[i].
- As a convenience, when doing indexing, if you write end inside square brackets, it gets replaced by the length of the vector; so, x[end] refers to the last element of the vector x.

We now can calculate the mean of the vector y:

```julia
julia> s = 0
0

julia> for v in y
           global s += v
       end

julia> s
25

julia> s / length(y)
5.0
```

At this point, you are most likely eager to wrap our code in a function to make it reusable. This is the topic of the next section.

2.4 Defining functions

You already know how to work with variables and use control-flow constructs, so the next step is to understand how functions are defined in Julia. This is a broad topic, and if you are interested in all the details about defining and calling functions, I recommend checking the Julia Manual (http://mng.bz/vX4r).

This section covers the most common patterns used in practice so you can learn how to define your own function calculating a winsorized mean.

2.4.1 Defining functions using the function keyword

Let's start with a basic definition of a function taking a single positional argument in the next listing.

Listing 2.7 Defining functions by using the `function` keyword

```
julia> function times_two(x)
           return 2 * x
       end
times_two (generic function with 1 method)

julia> times_two(10)
20
```

This function takes a single argument x and returns a twice-as-big value. As you can see, the definition starts with the function keyword. Next, we pass a function name, followed by a list of its arguments wrapped in parentheses. The function body follows.

The function definition is finished when the end keyword is reached. You can use the return keyword to return the value of the expression following it. Defining a function without the return keyword is allowed, in which case the value of the last expression in the body of the function is returned (just as in R). In this book, I use the return keyword in functions to explicitly signal which value I want to be returned from the function.

2.4.2 Positional and keyword arguments of functions

In general, Julia allows you to define functions with positional arguments and keyword arguments that optionally can get a default value. Also, a function can return more than one value. The following listing shows an example of a definition using these features and several ways the function can be called.

Listing 2.8 Using positional and keyword arguments and providing their default values

```
julia> function compose(x, y=10; a, b=10)
           return x, y, a, b
       end
compose (generic function with 2 methods)

julia> compose(1, 2; a=3, b=4)
(1, 2, 3, 4)

julia> compose(1, 2; a=3)
(1, 2, 3, 10)

julia> compose(1; a=3)
(1, 10, 3, 10)
```

```
julia> compose(1)
ERROR: UndefKeywordError: keyword argument a not assigned

julia> compose(; a=3)
ERROR: MethodError: no method matching g(; a=3)
```

Figure 2.3 explains the meaning of each argument in the compose function definition.

The rules of function definitions are as follows:

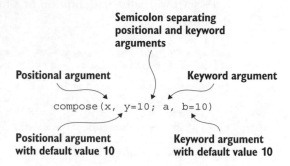

Figure 2.3   Definition of the compose function

- Multiple positional arguments (in this example, x and y) are separated by a comma. When you call a function, you pass only the values of positional arguments (without their names) in the sequence in which they were defined. The argument position matters; you are allowed to set a default value of a positional argument by using the assignment syntax (like y=10 in this example). If you give a positional argument a default value, all positional arguments that follow it also must be given a default value; in other words, all positional arguments without a default value must be placed before any positional argument that has a default value.

- To create keyword arguments (in this example, a and b), you use a semicolon (;) to separate them from the positional arguments. When you call a function, you need to pass the name of the keyword argument and then its value linked by the = character. Here, default values are also allowed. When calling a function, you can pass keyword arguments in any order.

- If an argument (positional or keyword) has a default value, you can omit passing it when you call a function.

- When calling a function that takes both positional and keyword arguments, it is good practice to separate them by using a semicolon (;), just as when you define a function. This is the convention that I use in this book; however, using a comma is also allowed.

- You can omit passing a value of arguments (positional or keyword) that have a default value defined. However, you must always pass values for all arguments that do not have a default value specified.

- If you want to return multiple values from a function, separate them by a comma (,). In chapter 4, you will learn that technically, Julia creates a Tuple from these values and returns it.

You can find additional information about optional arguments and keyword arguments in the Julia Manual at http://mng.bz/49Kv and http://mng.bz/QnqQ.

2.4.3   Rules for passing arguments to functions

The way default values of the arguments are defined via the = assignment also high-lights one important feature of Julia. If you pass a value to a function, Julia binds the function argument name to this value, just as it would if you performed an assignment (see section 2.2 for a discussion of how binding of a variable to a value works).

This feature, called *pass-by-sharing*, means that Julia never copies data when arguments are passed to a function. Here is an example:

```
julia> function f!(x)
           x[1] = 10
           return x
       end
f! (generic function with 1 method)

julia> x = [1, 2, 3]
3-element Vector{Int64}:
 1
 2
 3

julia> f!(x)
3-element Vector{Int64}:
 10
  2
  3

julia> x
3-element Vector{Int64}:
 10
  2
  3
```

We name this function f!. Adding ! as a suffix to a function name is a stylistic convention that signals its users that it may mutate its arguments (we will discuss this convention in more detail later in this chapter).

This is a behavior that you might know from Python, but is different from, for example, R, in which copying function arguments is performed. One of the benefits of pass-by-sharing behavior is that function calls in Julia are very fast. In general, you can safely split your code into multiple functions without fearing that it will significantly degrade its performance. The downside of pass-by-sharing is that if you pass mutable objects to a function (we discuss mutability in more detail in chapter 4) and modify it inside this function, this modification will be, in effect, after the function finishes its execution.

2.4.4   Short syntax for defining simple functions

To define short functions, Julia allows you to use a shorter syntax that uses the assignment = operator. You can then omit the function and end keyword arguments in the definition, subject to a limitation that the body of the function must be a single expression.

The next listing shows an example of defining the functions `times_two` and `compose`, again using this syntax.

Listing 2.9 Defining short functions by using the assignment syntax

```
julia> times_two(x) = 2 * x
times_two (generic function with 1 method)

julia> compose(x, y=10; a, b=10) = x, y, a, b
compose (generic function with 2 methods)
```

Let me give you a warning about a common typing mistake that significantly changes the meaning of the code. If you type `times_two(x) = 2 * x`, you define a new function; however, if you type `times_two(x) == 2 * x`, you perform a logical comparison of equality of `f(x)` and `2 * x`. As you can see, the code examples differ only in `=` versus `==`. The potential pitfall is that both are valid, so you might not get what you want, while Julia would still accept and execute the code.

FUNCTIONS CAN BE PASSED AS ARGUMENTS TO OTHER FUNCTIONS IN JULIA

A useful feature of Julia is that functions are first-class objects, as in functional programming. Therefore, they can be passed around and assigned to variables, and each function has its distinct type. Here is an example:

```
julia> map(times_two, [1, 2, 3])
3-element Vector{Int64}:
 2
 4
 6
```

In this code, we use the `map` function that takes two arguments: a function (`times_two`, in this case, defined previously) and a collection (a vector `[1, 2, 3]`, in this example). The returned value is the passed collection transformed by applying the `times_two` function to each element.

2.4.5 Anonymous functions

When you pass a function as an argument to another function, you'll often want to define a function that does not need a name. You just want to temporarily define this function and pass it to another function. In Julia, you can define nameless functions, which are called *anonymous functions*.

The syntax is similar to the short syntax introduced previously, except that you skip the function name and replace `=` with `->`, as the next listing shows.

Listing 2.10 Defining anonymous functions by using the `->` syntax

```
julia> map(x -> 2 * x, [1, 2, 3])
3-element Vector{Int64}:
 2
 4
 6
```

In this example, the anonymous function is x -> 2 * x. In Python, an equivalent would be to use a lambda function with the following syntax: lambda x: 2 * x.

Note that in the x -> 2 * x definition, we skip the parentheses around the argument. But in general, if we use more than one argument, parentheses are needed, as in this definition: (x, y) -> x + y.

Julia has many functions that take functions as their arguments. Here's one more example:

```
julia> sum(x -> x ^ 2, [1, 2, 3])
14
```

We calculate the sum of squares of the values stored in the vector. In this case, the key benefit of being able to use a function as a first argument of the sum function is the following. A natural way to compute the sum of squares of a vector is to first square its elements, store the result in a temporary vector, and then calculate its sum. However, this approach is expensive because it needs to allocate this temporary vector. When sum(x -> x ^ 2, [1, 2, 3]) is executed, no allocations are performed.

Multiple dispatch when calling the sum function

In the preceding sum(x -> x ^ 2, [1, 2, 3]) example, you saw Julia use multiple dispatch. We discuss this topic in chapter 3, but I describe it briefly here because it is one of the fundamental design concepts in Julia.

Normally, you pass to the sum function a single collection and get its sum in return. For example, executing sum([1, 2, 3]) produces 6. However, for a single function, like sum in the preceding example, Julia allows you to define multiple *methods*.

Each method of a function takes a different set of arguments. When we write sum([1, 2, 3]), Julia invokes the method taking a single argument. However, when we write sum(x -> x ^ 2, [1, 2, 3]), another method of the sum function is called. In this case, the method expects that the first argument is a function, and the second argument is a collection and returns a sum of elements of this collection after they are transformed by the function passed as a first argument.

2.4.6 *Do blocks*

One last convenience syntax that you should learn is the do-end block. These blocks are used if (1) you use a function that accepts another function as its first positional argument and (2) you want to pass an anonymous function composed of several expressions (so a standard anonymous function definition style is not convenient).

Here is an example of a do-end block:

```
julia> sum([1, 2, 3]) do x
           println("processing ", x)
           return x ^ 2
       end
processing 1
```

A do-end block defines an anonymous function taking a single argument x. This anonymous function is passed as a first argument to the sum function.

```
processing 2
processing 3
14
```

As you can see, in this case, we use the sum function. As I have explained, one of its methods expects two arguments: the first should be a function, and the second a collection. When using the do-end syntax, you skip the function that you want to pass in the arguments of the called function and instead add the do keyword argument followed by an argument name of the anonymous function you want to define. Then the function body is normally defined as for any other function and is terminated by the end keyword argument.

2.4.7 *Function-naming convention in Julia*

Before we wrap up this section, let's discuss one convention that is related to the way functions are named in Julia. Often you will see an exclamation mark (!) at the end of the function name—for example, sort!. Users sometimes think this means that Julia treats these functions in a nonstandard way; for example, in Rust, the ! suffix indicates a macro. This is not the case; such a name gets no special treatment.

However, a Julia convention recommends that developers add ! at the end of functions they create if those functions modify their arguments. Here is an example comparison of how the sort and sort! functions work. Both return a sorted collection. However, sort does not change its argument, while sort! modifies it in place:

```
julia> x = [5, 1, 3, 2]
4-element Vector{Int64}:
 5
 1
 3
 2

julia> sort(x)
4-element Vector{Int64}:
 1
 2
 3
 5

julia> x
4-element Vector{Int64}:
 5
 1
 3
 2

julia> sort!(x)
4-element Vector{Int64}:
 1
 2
 3
 5
```

```
julia> x
4-element Vector{Int64}:
 1
 2
 3
 5
```

You might wonder why this convention is useful. Although most functions do not modify their arguments, Julia uses pass-by-sharing when passing arguments to functions, so all functions potentially could modify their arguments. Therefore, it is useful to visually warn the user that a given function indeed takes advantage of pass-by-sharing and modifies its arguments (usually the benefit of modifying the arguments in place is improved performance).

2.4.8   *A simplified definition of a function computing the winsorized mean*

Now we are ready to create and test our first version of the function calculating the winsorized mean. We follow the same steps as in section 2.3.4, but this time, we wrap the code in a function:

```
julia> function winsorized_mean(x, k)
           y = sort(x)
           for i in 1:k
               y[i] = y[k + 1]
               y[end - i + 1] = y[end - k]
           end
           s = 0
           for v in y
               s += v
           end
           return s / length(y)
       end
winsorized_mean (generic function with 1 method)

julia> winsorized_mean([8, 3, 1, 5, 7], 1)
5.0
```

In defining the winsorized_mean function, an important difference from the code in section 2.3.4 is that the line s += v has no global prefix (in section 2.3.4, this line is global s += v). The reason is that this time, the s variable is local since it is defined in the body of the function.

We now have a working function allowing us to calculate the k-times winsorized mean. It could be used in practice. I reused the steps from section 2.3.4 on purpose to show you how to wrap code in a function. However, this implementation can be improved both in terms of correctness (think of how it would behave if we passed inappropriate values for x or k) and in terms of performance. In chapter 3, after you learn more about how Julia programs are written, you will see how this code can be improved.

2.5   *Understanding variable scoping rules*

You have learned the basic constructs of the Julia language. A natural question is how these constructs interact with variables. In other words, what are the rules that allow Julia to determine which variables are visible in which regions of code? This topic is fundamentally important for any programmer, and since the way scoping works in Julia is different from, for example, Python, it should be discussed here.

We won't develop any new features of our winsorized mean function in this section (we will get back to that in chapter 3). However, we already implicitly relied on Julia's variable scoping rules in our code in the preceding section, so it is important to explicitly explain how scoping works.

In general, the rules of variable scoping are complex, as they need to cover many possible scenarios. This section concentrates on the major concepts that are sufficient to deal with most situations. If you want to learn more details, check out the Julia Manual (http://mng.bz/Xarp).

If you define a variable in a top-level scope of your code (outside any construct introducing local scope, such as functions), that variable is created in a *global scope*. Julia allows users to define global variables, as this is often convenient, especially when working interactively with the Julia REPL. However, using global variables is discouraged, as it can have a negative impact on code execution speed.

> ### Using global variables can have a negative impact on code execution speed
>
> A call to avoid global variables is one of the first rules listed in the "Performance Tips" section of the Julia Manual (http://mng.bz/epPP). Through Julia 1.7, this is a general rule. In Julia 1.8, a possibility of fixing the type of a global variable is introduced, so starting from Julia 1.8, the limitations I describe here apply only to untyped global variables.
>
> Let me explain why global variables have a negative impact on code execution speed. As you have already learned, Julia compiles functions before executing them. We also discussed in section 2.2 that to ensure that compilation results in fast native code, the variables used inside a function must be type stable. Finally, you also know that Julia is dynamically typed, which means that you can bind values of any type to a variable.
>
> Now assume that you reference a global variable inside a function. To produce fast code, Julia would have to be sure of the variable's type. However, since the variable is global, no such guarantee is possible. Therefore, the Julia compiler must assume that the global variable is not type stable, and consequently, the code will be slow.
>
> A crucial question is why the Julia compiler can't determine the type of the global variable when it compiles the function. The answer is that it could, but this type can change after Julia compiles the function.
>
> Let me give you an example. As mentioned in chapter 1, Julia comes with built-in support for multithreading. This powerful feature allows you to use all cores of your CPU when doing computations. However, this power comes at a price. Assume you have

two threads running in parallel. In the first thread, you run a function using a global variable. In the second thread, another function is executed in parallel that changes the same global variable. Therefore, the function running in the second thread could alter the type of the global variable used in thread one after the function running in this thread was compiled.

You probably want to know how to avoid the problems caused by using global variables inside function definitions. The simplest solution is to pass these variables as function arguments.

The following types of constructs that you have learned already create a new scope (called *local scope*). In the list, I omit several more advanced constructs that we do not use in this book):

- Functions, anonymous functions, `do-end` blocks
- `for` and `while` loops
- `try-catch-end` blocks (discussed in section chapter 7)
- Comprehensions (discussed in chapter 4)

Notably, the `if` blocks and `begin-end` blocks *do not* introduce a new scope. Variables defined in these blocks leak out to the enclosing scope.

For completeness of the discussion, let me add that modules, which are discussed in chapter 3, introduce a new global scope.

Let's look at several examples of these rules in action. Start a fresh Julia REPL, and follow these code examples. In each, we define a function with a slightly different scoping behavior. We begin with a basic scenario:

```
julia> function fun1()
           x = 1
           return x + 1
       end
fun1 (generic function with 1 method)

julia> fun1()
2

julia> x
ERROR: UndefVarError: x not defined
```

This example shows that a variable defined within a function (local scope) does not get to the enclosing scope if it is not defined there. Next, I will illustrate the consequences of `if` blocks not introducing a new scope:

```
julia> function fun2()
           if true
               x = 10
           end
           return x
       end
```

```
fun2 (generic function with 1 method)

julia> fun2()
10
```

By executing `fun2()`, you can see that the x variable is defined in an `if` block, but since the `if` block does not introduce a scope, the x variable is also visible outside of the block.

Unlike `if` blocks, loops introduce a new local scope. The most important scenarios of a loop introducing a new local scope are shown in the following four examples:

```
julia> function fun3()
           x = 0
           for i in [1, 2, 3]
               if i == 2
                 · x = 2
               end
           end
           return x
       end
fun3 (generic function with 1 method)

julia> fun3()
2
```

From the result of the `fun3()` call, you can see that if we nest local scopes and variable x is defined in the outer local scope, it is reused by the inner local scope (introduced by the `for` loop, in this case). If we omit x = 0 in the definition, the function will not work:

```
julia> function fun4()
           for i in [1, 2, 3]
               if i == 2
                   x = 2
               end
           end
           return x
       end
fun4 (generic function with 1 method)

julia> fun4()
ERROR: UndefVarError: x not defined
```

The reason for the error in the `fun4()` call is that the `for` loop introduces a new local scope, and since x is not defined in the outer scope of the `fun4` function, it does not leak out of the `for` loop.

Moreover, a loop-local variable, like x in the preceding example, is freshly defined for each iteration of the loop, so the following code also fails:

```
julia> function fun5()
           for i in [1, 2, 3]
               if i == 1
                   x = 1
```

```
                    else
                        x += 1
                    end
                    println(x)
                end
            end
fun5 (generic function with 1 method)

julia> fun5()
1
ERROR: UndefVarError: x not defined
```

Let's try to understand what happens in the code when we call `fun5()`. In the first iteration of the loop, we perform the `x = 1` assignment and print `1`. In the second iteration, `x` from the first iteration is discarded (it is freshly allocated in each iteration), so its value is not available when the `x += 1` operation is attempted. The workaround for this problem is to reintroduce the variable `x` in the scope enclosing the `for` loop, as shown in the following listing.

> **Listing 2.11   Updating a local variable defined in the enclosing scope of the `for` loop**

```
julia> function fun6()
           x = 0
           for i in [1, 2, 3]
               if i == 1
                   x = 1
               else
                   x += 1
               end
               println(x)
           end
       end
fun6 (generic function with 1 method)

julia> fun6()
1
2
3
```

Now all works as expected when we call `fun6()`, as the `x` variable is stored in the scope of the `fun6` function and thus is not freshly allocated in each iteration.

> **The nothing value**
>
> In listing 2.11, we define the function `fun6` that does not return any value by using the `return` keyword. Also, the last part of the function body is a `for` loop that does not produce a value that would be returned by the function in the absence of the `return` keyword. In such cases, the return value of the function is `nothing`, which is used by convention when there is no value to return.

Before I finish this section, let me stress again that what we have discussed here are simplified scoping rules used by Julia. All the details about how scoping works in Julia are given in the Julia Manual (http://mng.bz/Xarp), along with an explanation of the rationale behind the design.

Summary

- Every value in Julia has a type. Examples of numeric types are `Int64` and `Float64`. Values that are collections, like vectors, have types that have parameters; `Vector{Float64}` is an example of a type indicating a vector that can store `Float64` numbers.
- Julia is dynamically typed, which means that only values have types. Variable names are dynamically bound to values, which implies that, in general, variables can change the type of value that is bound to them.
- Julia provides great flexibility in naming your variables. Additionally, the Julia REPL and common editors make it easy to use nonstandard characters using LaTeX completions.
- Julia provides all the standard control-flow constructs. For user convenience, it also introduces several syntaxes to make it easier to write code: ternary operator, short-circuit evaluation, single-expression function definitions, anonymous functions, and the `do-end` block syntax.
- In Julia, you can define functions in three ways: using the `function` keyword, using the assignment operator =, and defining an anonymous function with the `->` operator.
- In Julia, functions and `for` and `while` loops introduce a new scope, but `if` and `begin-end` blocks do not.

Julia's support for scaling projects

This chapter covers

- Using Julia's type system
- Defining multiple methods for a function
- Working with modules and packages
- Using macros

In this chapter, you will learn elements of the Julia language that are important when creating larger projects. We start with exploring Julia's type system. Understanding how type hierarchy works is essential to learning how to define multiple methods for a single function, a topic we started discussing in section 2.4. Similarly, when you use an existing function, you must know how to find out which types of arguments it accepts. Getting an exception because you tried to pass an argument of incorrect type when calling a function is one of the most common errors when working in Julia. To avoid such problems, you must have a good understanding of how Julia's type system is designed.

When you define methods for a function, you can restrict the types of arguments they accept. This feature makes your Julia programs faster, allows you to catch bugs more easily, and makes it easier to understand how the code works.

If your projects grow larger, you will need to use third-party functionalities provided as packages or organize your source code into modules. In this chapter, you will learn how to do that with Julia.

Finally, in some cases, it is convenient to automatically generate Julia code. This is achieved in Julia with macros. The topic of writing your own macros is advanced, so in this chapter, you will learn how to use macros that are available in Julia.

To show you the practical usefulness of the material I introduce in this chapter, we will improve the `winsorized_mean` function initially implemented in chapter 2 in terms of its performance, code safety, and readability.

3.1 Understanding Julia's type system

As discussed in chapter 2, the `winsorized_mean` function implemented in section 2.4 will not work with all possible values of arguments that you could pass to it. How can we make sure that it will correctly handle various types of passed arguments? To understand this, we first need to discuss the Julia type system.

3.1.1 A single function in Julia may have multiple methods

When learning about Julia, you might have heard that it uses *multiple dispatch* (mentioned in section 2.4). You can define multiple methods for the same function with different implementations, depending on the types of the passed arguments. You can use the `methods` function to get the list of methods defined for a given function. Here is an example list of methods for the `cd` function that sets the Julia working directory:

```
julia> methods(cd)
# 4 methods for generic function "cd":
[1] cd() in Base.Filesystem at file.jl:88
[2] cd(dir::AbstractString) in Base.Filesystem at file.jl:83
[3] cd(f::Function) in Base.Filesystem at file.jl:141
[4] cd(f::Function, dir::AbstractString) in Base.Filesystem at file.jl:91
```

You can see that some of the arguments of the functions have type annotations; in this case, they are `::Function` and `::AbstractString`, which restrict the types of values allowed by the given methods and change their behavior, depending on types of passed values.

Let's focus here on the `Function` type. Intuitively, all functions should have this type, and this is typically the case:

```
julia> sum isa Function
true
```

However, if we check the type of the `sum` function, we see that it is not `Function`:

```
julia> typeof(sum)
typeof(sum)
```

```
julia> typeof(sum) == Function
false
```

To understand what is going on here, we need to know that in Julia, types are organized in a hierarchy. This allows the bundling together of several types when defining methods for functions. For instance, in the preceding example, the cd function can take any function as an argument.

3.1.2   Types in Julia are arranged in a hierarchy

In Julia, all types are arranged in a tree, and each type has a parent. This parent, called a *supertype*, can be checked using the supertype function:

```
julia> supertype(typeof(sum))
Function
```

So, indeed, we see that the type of the sum function is a *subtype* of the Function type. The following rules govern how the type tree works (here I show the main mental model and omit discussion of some corner cases):

- The root type of the tree is called Any. All other types are subtypes of the Any type. If you define a function without specifying its argument(s) type, as we did in section 2.4, Julia assumes by default that the Any type is allowed; that is, you can pass a value of any type to such a function.
- Only the types that are leaves can have instances (that is, have objects that are of that specific type). The types that can be instantiated are called *concrete*. In other words, if you have a value, you can be sure that its type is concrete and that it is a leaf type. For this reason, there is no function whose type is Function. Every function has its own unique concrete type that is a subtype of the Function type.
- The types that are not leaves of the type tree (for example, Any or Function) cannot be instantiated. They serve only as intermediate types allowing for logical grouping of other types and are called *abstract*. You can find the list of subtypes of an abstract type by calling the subtypes function.

Concrete vs. abstract types

Only concrete types can be instantiated and cannot have concrete subtypes. You can check whether a given type is concrete by using the isconcretetype function. Abstract types cannot have instances but can have subtypes. You can check whether a given type is abstract by using the isabstracttype function. Therefore, it is not possible for a type to be both abstract and concrete.

However, some types are neither abstract nor concrete. You will encounter these types in chapter 4 when you learn more about parametric types. An example of such a type is Vector. (Note that this type has its parameter left out, and this is why it is not concrete; in section 2.1, you saw an example of a value having Vector{Int}, which is a concrete type as it has a fully specified parameter, Int in that case.)

3.1.3   Finding all supertypes of a type

Let's see the `supertype` and `subtypes` functions in action. First, we start with the `Int64` type that you already know and check which supertypes it has. For this, we define the following recursive function:

```julia
julia> function print_supertypes(T)
           println(T)
           T == Any || print_supertypes(supertype(T))
           return nothing
       end
print_supertypes (generic function with 1 method)

julia> print_supertypes(Int64)
Int64
Signed
Integer
Real
Number
Any
```

> The print_supertypes function accepts a type as its argument.

As you can see, the type hierarchy is quite deep. This allows your functions to have fine-grained control of the types of arguments they accept.

In our function, we traverse the type tree recursively. In this example, we start with the `Int64` type. We first print it. Next, we check whether it is equal to the `Any` type. `Int64` is not equal to `Any`; therefore, since we used the `||` operator, we execute the `print_supertypes(supertype(T))` expression. It calls the `print_supertypes` function again with a supertype of `Int64`, which is `Signed`. The process is repeated recursively until `print_supertypes` is passed the `Any` type as an argument, the root of the type tree. At that point, we do not perform a recursive call of the `print_supertypes` function, and the process terminates. Figure 3.1 illustrates the result; the arrow indicates the subtype relationship.

Also, you might have noticed the `return nothing` line in our code. It serves the purpose discussed in section 2.4—namely, the recommendation that all functions should explicitly specify the value they want to return. In this case, because we do not want any specific value to be returned, we return the `nothing` value to signal that there's nothing to return from the function. If a function returns `nothing`, the Julia REPL does not print any return value to the terminal. Therefore, in this example, the only things that get printed are the types outputted by the `println(T)` operation.

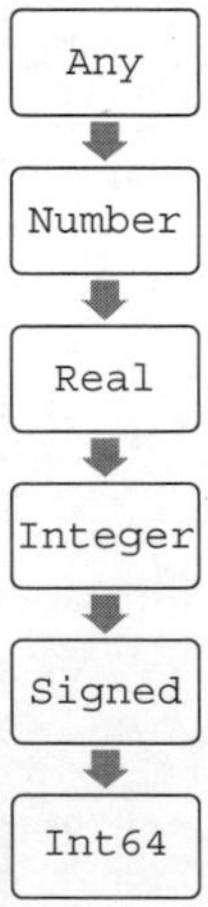

Figure 3.1   The print_supertypes function accepts a type as its argument.

3.1.4   Finding all subtypes of a type

Now we will do the reverse operation and try to print all subtypes of the `Integer` abstract type. Here is the code that performs this operation. In this example, we use recursion again. This time, the recursion stops when a type does not have any subtypes:

```
julia> function print_subtypes(T, indent_level=0)
           println(" " ^ indent_level, T)
           for S in subtypes(T)
               print_subtypes(S, indent_level + 2)
           end
           return nothing
       end
print_subtypes (generic function with 2 methods)

julia> print_subtypes(Integer)
Integer
  Bool
  Signed
    BigInt
    Int128
    Int16
    Int32
    Int64
    Int8
  Unsigned
    UInt128
    UInt16
    UInt32
    UInt64
    UInt8
```

You have learned that the Integer type has three subtypes: Bool, Signed, and Unsigned. The Bool type does not have a subtype, while Signed and Unsigned are abstract and have a wide range of subtypes with differing memory footprints in bits (indicated by the number in the type name; see section 2.1 for a discussion about bitwise representation of different numeric types). Figure 3.2 presents this type hierarchy.

You might ask what the " " ^ indent_level expression does in the preceding code. It simply repeats the " " string indent_level times. Chapter 6 covers more details about working with strings in Julia.

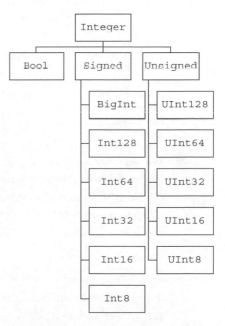

Figure 3.2   Hierarchy of subtypes of the Integer type

3.1.5   *Union of types*

Referring to collections of types by using abstract types is useful. However, sometimes you might want to specify a list of types that do not have the respective node (abstract type) in the type tree. For instance, what if you want to allow only signed or unsigned integers in your code but not Bool values? You could use the Union keyword. In our scenario, if you write Union{Signed, Unsigned}, you tell Julia that you allow any of the types specified inside the curly brackets after the Union keyword.

In data science workflows, the `Union` keyword is often used when we specify a union between a certain type and the `Missing` type. For instance, if you write `Union{String, Missing}`, you indicate that a value must be a `String` but can optionally be missing. Chapter 7 covers handling missing values in more detail.

3.1.6 *Deciding what type restrictions to put in method signature*

Let's now go back to our `winsorized_mean` function from section 2.4. It takes two arguments: an integer `k` and a vector `x`. What are appropriate type restrictions for these arguments? For `k`, this is easy. From what you have learned, it is natural to require that `k` is an `Integer`. What about `x`? Let's check the type and the supertype of the vector `[1.0, 2.0, 3.0]` and range `1:3` by using the `print_supertypes` function we defined previously:

```
julia> print_supertypes(typeof([1.0, 2.0, 3.0]))
Vector{Float64}
DenseVector{Float64}
AbstractVector{Float64}
Any

julia> print_supertypes(typeof(1:3))
UnitRange{Int64}
AbstractUnitRange{Int64}
OrdinalRange{Int64, Int64}
AbstractRange{Int64}
AbstractVector{Int64}
Any
```

We see that the type hierarchy is a bit deep, but the types seem to meet at `Abstract-Vector` level; the only problem is that in the first case, we have a `Float64` parameter of the type, and in the second case, `Int64`. An intuitive and correct solution is to just drop the parameter and require `x` to be `AbstractVector`. This is what we will do in section 3.2. Let's see what `AbstractVector` is:

```
julia> AbstractVector
AbstractVector (alias for AbstractArray{T, 1} where T)
```

The `where T` addition in the alias explanation means that `T` can be any type. An alternative way to learn the correct common type of `[1.0, 2.0, 3.0]` and `1:3` would be to use the `typejoin` function:

```
julia> typejoin(typeof([1.0, 2.0, 3.0]), typeof(1:3))
AbstractVector{T} where T (alias for AbstractArray{T, 1} where T)
```

The `typejoin` function finds the narrowest type that is a supertype of types passed as its arguments. You will not need this function often, but it is useful to confirm our intuition in this case.

The topic of working with types is much more complex than what we have covered here. We will come back to it in chapter 5, which covers parametric types and the `where` keyword. However, I still skip many concepts related to types in this book.

When doing data science, you will usually not need to define your own types, so I have left out the process of creating your own types, defining constructors, and defining type promotion and conversion rules. A definitive guide to these topics is the "Types" section of the Julia Manual (https://docs.julialang.org/en/v1/manual/types/).

3.2   *Using multiple dispatch in Julia*

Now that you know how to define functions and how type hierarchy works, you are ready to learn to define functions that have different methods. You can then apply this knowledge to our `winsorized_mean` function.

3.2.1   *Rules for defining methods of a function*

Fortunately, defining methods is relatively easy if you understand the principles of how Julia's type system works. You just add the type restriction to the arguments of the function after `::`. As discussed in section 3.1, if the type specification part is omitted, Julia assumes that a value of `Any` type is allowed.

Assume we want to create the function `fun` by taking a single positional argument with the following behavior:

- If `fun` is passed a number, it should print `a number was passed`, unless it is a value having `Float64` type, in which case we want a `Float64 value` printed.
- In all other cases, we want to print `unsupported type`.

Here is an example of implementing this behavior by defining three methods for a function `fun`:

```
julia> fun(x) = println("unsupported type")
fun (generic function with 1 method)

julia> fun(x::Number) = println("a number was passed")
fun (generic function with 2 methods)

julia> fun(x::Float64) = println("a Float64 value")
fun (generic function with 3 methods)

julia> methods(fun)
# 3 methods for generic function "fun":
[1] fun(x::Float64) in Main at REPL[3]:1
[2] fun(x::Number) in Main at REPL[2]:1
[3] fun(x) in Main at REPL[1]:1

julia> fun("hello!")
unsupported type

julia> fun(1)
a number was passed

julia> fun(1.0)
a Float64 value
```

In this example, `1` is a `Number` (as it is `Int`) but is not `Float64`, for instance, so the most specific matching method is `fun(x::Number)`.

3.2.2   *Method ambiguity problem*

When defining multiple methods for a function, you must avoid method ambiguities. They happen when the Julia compiler is not able to decide which method for a given set of arguments should be selected.

It is easier to understand the problem with an example. Assume you want to define a bar function taking two positional arguments. The bar function should inform you if any of these arguments are numbers. Here is a first attempt to implement this function:

```
julia> bar(x, y) = "no numbers passed"
bar (generic function with 1 method)

julia> bar(x::Number, y) = "first argument is a number"
bar (generic function with 2 methods)

julia> bar(x, y::Number) = "second argument is a number"
bar (generic function with 3 methods)

julia> bar("hello", "world")
"no numbers passed"

julia> bar(1, "world")
"first argument is a number"

julia> bar("hello", 2)
"second argument is a number"

julia> bar(1, 2)
ERROR: MethodError: bar(::Int64, ::Int64) is ambiguous. Candidates:
  bar(x::Number, y) in Main at REPL[2]:1
  bar(x, y::Number) in Main at REPL[3]:1
Possible fix, define
  bar(::Number, ::Number)
```

As you can see, everything works nicely until we want to call bar by passing a number as both its first and second argument. In this case, Julia complains that it does not know which method should be called, as two of them potentially could be selected. Fortunately, we get a hint as to how to resolve the situation. We need to define an additional method that fixes the ambiguity:

```
julia> bar(x::Number, y::Number) = "both arguments are numbers"
bar (generic function with 4 methods)

julia> bar(1, 2)
"both arguments are numbers"

julia> methods(bar)
# 4 methods for generic function "bar":
[1] bar(x::Number, y::Number) in Main at REPL[8]:1
[2] bar(x::Number, y) in Main at REPL[2]:1
[3] bar(x, y::Number) in Main at REPL[3]:1
[4] bar(x, y) in Main at REPL[1]:1
```

Why is multiple dispatch useful?

Understanding how methods work in Julia is essential. As you could see in the preceding examples, this knowledge allows users to differentiate behavior of functions, based on the type of any positional argument of the function. Combined with the flexible type hierarchy system discussed in section 3.1, multiple dispatch allows Julia programmers to write highly flexible and reusable code.

Observe that by specifying types at a suitable level of abstraction, the user does not have to think of every possible concrete type that could be passed to the function while still retaining control of the kind of values that are accepted. For instance, if you define your own `Number` subtype—as is done, for example, by the Decimals.jl package (https://github.com/JuliaMath/Decimals.jl) that features types supporting decimal floating-point calculations of arbitrary precision—you do not have to rewrite your code. Everything will just work with the new type, even if the original code was not developed specifically to target this use case.

3.2.3   *Improved implementation of winsorized mean*

We are ready to improve our `winsorized_mean` function definition. Here is how you could implement it more carefully than we did in section 2.4:

```julia
julia> function winsorized_mean(x::AbstractVector, k::Integer)
           k >= 0 || throw(ArgumentError("k must be non-negative"))
           length(x) > 2 * k || throw(ArgumentError("k is too large"))
           y = sort!(collect(x))
           for i in 1:k
               y[i] = y[k + 1]
               y[end - i + 1] = y[end - k]
           end
           return sum(y) / length(y)
       end
winsorized_mean (generic function with 1 method)
```

First note that we have restricted the allowed types for x and k; therefore, if you try to invoke the function, its arguments must match the required types:

```julia
julia> winsorized_mean([8, 3, 1, 5, 7], 1)
5.0

julia> winsorized_mean(1:10, 2)
5.5

julia> winsorized_mean(1:10, "a")
ERROR: MethodError: no method matching
winsorized_mean(::UnitRange{Int64}, ::String)
Closest candidates are:
  winsorized_mean(::AbstractVector{T} where T, ::Integer) at REPL[6]:1

julia> winsorized_mean(10, 1)
ERROR: MethodError: no method matching winsorized_mean(::Int64, ::Int64)
Closest candidates are:
  winsorized_mean(::AbstractVector{T} where T, ::Integer) at REPL[6]:1
```

Additionally, we can see several changes in the code that make it more robust. First, we check if passed arguments are consistent; that is, if k is negative or too large, it is invalid, in which case we throw an error by calling the throw function with ArgumentError as its argument. See what happens if we pass the wrong k:

```
julia> winsorized_mean(1:10, -1)
ERROR: ArgumentError: k must be non-negative

julia> winsorized_mean(1:10, 5)
ERROR: ArgumentError: k is too large
```

Next, make a copy of the data stored in the x vector before sorting it. To achieve this, we use the collect function, which takes any iterable collection and returns an object storing the same values that has a Vector type. We pass this vector to the sort! function to sort it in place.

You might ask why using the collect function to allocate a new Vector is needed. The reason is that, for example, ranges like 1:10 are read-only; therefore, later, we would not be able to update y with y[i] = y[k + 1] and y[end – the + 1] = y[end -- k]. Additionally, in general, Julia can support non-1-based indexing in arrays (see https://github.com/JuliaArrays/OffsetArrays.jl). However, Vector uses 1-based indexing. In summary, using the collect function turns any collection or general AbstractVector into a standard Vector type defined in Julia that is mutable and uses 1-based indexing.

Finally, note that instead of performing the for loop manually, we have just used the sum function, which is both simpler and more robust.

Does adding argument type annotations in methods improve their execution speed?

You have seen in section 3.2 that adding type annotations to function arguments makes the Julia code easier to read and safer. A natural question that users often ask is whether this improves code execution speed.

If you have a single method for a function, adding type annotations does not improve code execution speed. The reason is that when a function is called, the Julia compiler knows the types of arguments that you have passed to it and generates the native machine code using this information. In other words, type restriction information does not affect code generation.

However, the situation is different if you have multiple methods defined for a function. This is because type restrictions influence method dispatch. Then, each method can have a different implementation using an algorithm optimized for a value of a given type. Using multiple dispatch allows the Julia compiler to pick the implementation that is best for your data.

Let's look at an example. Consider the sort function introduced in chapter 2. By calling methods(sort), you can learn that it has five methods defined in Base Julia (and possibly more if you loaded Julia packages). There is a general method for sorting vectors with the signature `sort(v::AbstractVector; kwthe.)` and a specialized method for sorting ranges like `1:3` that has the signature `sort(r::Abstract-UnitRange)`.

What is the benefit of having this specialized method? The second method is defined as `sort(r::AbstractUnitRange) = r`. Since we know that objects of type `AbstractUnitRange` are already sorted (they are ranges of values with an increment equal to 1), we can just return the passed value. In this case, taking advantage of type restriction in the method signature can significantly improve the `sort` operation performance. In section 3.4, you will learn how to check that this is indeed the case by using benchmarking.

3.3 Working with packages and modules

Larger programs in Julia require structure that helps organize their code. Therefore, it is likely that someone already implemented a function like our `winsorized_mean` because it is a commonly used statistical method. In Julia, such functions are shared using packages. So, if someone did create a function like ours, then instead of writing our own function, we could use the one defined in a package. That's why you need to know how to use packages in Julia.

3.3.1 What is a module In Julia?

A starting point in this discussion is understanding the concept of a *module* and how it is related to *packages* and *files*. Let's start by working with multiple files, as this is the easiest to understand.

Assume your code is split into three files—file1.jl, file2.jl, and file3.jl—and you want to create a main file—call it, for example, main.jl—that uses these three files. You can achieve this by using the `include` function. Assume that the source code of your main.jl file is the following:

```
include("file1.jl")
include("file2.jl")
include("file3.jl")
```

Then, if you execute it, simplifying a bit, it would work as if you had copied and pasted the contents of file1.jl into it, then copied and pasted the contents of file2.jl into it, and finally copied and pasted file3.jl. As you can see, the logic of the `include` function is easy. It just allows you to split the code into multiple files to make them smaller.

In Julia, the pattern I have just shown you is common. You create one main file that does have a minimal amount of logic and mostly serves as a place to include other files where the actual code is stored.

So, what are modules? *Modules* are a way to define separate variable namespaces. Back in section 2.4, I told you there that there is one global scope in your program. Now you will learn that there can be many, as each module defines its own separate global scope. The default global scope when you work with Julia is also a module that is called `Main` (therefore, in many of the listings in this chapter, you have seen that functions are defined in `Main`).

You can define the module `ExampleModule` that defines a single function called `example` by using the `module` keyword argument like this:

```
module ExampleModule

function example()
    println("Hello")
end

end # ExampleModule
```

You might have noticed two stylistic things in this example:

- Code inside the module is not indented as a convention (unlike all other blocks in Julia). Modules can get very large (spanning even thousands of lines), so using four-space indentation for the entire content of the module would not be practical.
- There is a convention to put a comment with the module name after the `end` keyword argument. Again, modules typically contain hundreds or even thousands of lines of code. Therefore, it is often hard to visually identify that the `end` keyword is finishing the definition of the module. For this reason, it is useful to explicitly indicate the end by using a comment.

When doing data science projects with Julia, you most often will not need to define your own modules, so let me highlight some key practical concepts:

- Unlike Python, modules have no relationship with how the code is organized into files. You can have many modules in a single file, or a single module can be defined in multiple files (combined using the `include` function). Modules are used only to give a logical structure to your code by defining separate variable namespaces and module-specific global scopes.
- A module designer can decide which variables and functions are exposed to the module users by using the `export` keyword.

If someone creates a module that is intended to be shared with other Julia users, it can be registered with the Julia general registry (https://github.com/JuliaRegistries/General). These modules must have a special structure, and after being registered, they become available as *packages*. You can find instructions for managing packages in appendix A.

Simplifying a bit, you can think of modules and packages as follows. Modules give you the capability to organize code into coherent units. When a developer decides to share the functionality provided by a module with other Julia users, this module can be annotated with proper metadata (like its version) and registered as a package. You can find detailed information about package creation, development, and management in the Pkg.jl package documentation at https://pkgdocs.julialang.org/v1/.

> **Julia's standard library**
>
> Normally, when you want to use a package, you need to install it (installation is explained in appendix A). However, Julia gets shipped with a set of standard library modules. These behave like regular Julia packages, but you don't need to install them explicitly. An example of such a module that we use in this chapter is `Statistics`. You can find documentation of all standard library modules in the "Standard Library" section of the Julia Manual (https://docs.julialang.org/en/v1/).

3.3.2 How can packages be used in Julia?

Knowing how to use modules that are bundled into packages is important for a data scientist. You have two basic ways to make the functionality of an installed package usable in your code: using the `import` or `using` keyword arguments. When you use `import`, only the module name is brought into the scope of your code. To access variables and functions defined by the module, you need to prefix their names with the module name, followed by a dot. Here is an example:

```
julia> import Statistics

julia> x = [1, 2, 3]
3-element Vector{Int64}:
 1
 2
 3

julia> mean(x)
ERROR: UndefVarError: mean not defined

julia> Statistics.mean(x)
2.0
```

The `Statistics` module is shipped with the Julia standard library. It defines basic statistical functions like `mean`, `std`, `var`, and `quantile`. As you can see, when we used `import`, we had to prefix the function name with `Statistics` to make things work.

  Instead, with the `using` keyword, we bring all exported functionalities of the module into the scope so they can be used directly. Therefore, following the preceding example, we have this:

```
julia> using Statistics

julia> mean(x)
2.0
```

This code works because the `mean` function is exported by the `Statistics` module.

  Now you might wonder if you should be using the `import` or the `using` statements in your code. This is a question often asked by Python users who learn that it is safe to import only the functions or variables that they plan to use in code. This is not the case in Julia.

In most Julia code, you can safely employ the using statement, and this is what people normally do. You already know the reason: the Julia language can automatically detect if a name you are trying to use conflicts with an identical name already introduced with, for example, the using keyword. In such cases, you will be informed that there is a problem.

Let me go through the most common situations where you might see name conflict problems. In the first example, you define a variable name that is later introduced from the module with the using statement. Start a fresh Julia session for this:

```
julia> mean = 1
1

julia> using Statistics
WARNING: using Statistics.mean in module Main conflicts with
an existing identifier.

julia> mean
1
```

As you can see, since you already defined the mean variable, loading the Statistics module, which exports the mean function, produces a warning but does not overshadow your definition. You would have to call the mean function from this module by using the form with the prefix—that is, Statistics.mean.

In the second scenario, you try to make an assignment to a variable that has a name that conflicts with a function from a loaded module that was already used (start a fresh Julia session again):

```
julia> using Statistics

julia> mean([1, 2, 3])
2.0

julia> mean = 1
ERROR: cannot assign a value to variable Statistics.mean from module Main
```

This time, you get an error; from the point where you have used the mean function from the Statistics module, you are not allowed to assign a value to it in your code.

In the last scenario, you first load a module and then define a conflicting variable name before using the same name defined in the module (start a fresh Julia session):

```
julia> using Statistics

julia> mean = 1
1

julia> mean([1, 2, 3])
ERROR: MethodError: objects of type Int64 are not callable
```

Now you are allowed to freely define the mean variable without a warning. Later, if you want to use the mean function from the Statistics module, you again would need to write Statistics.mean. For convenience, you're allowed to define the variable in your global scope in this case without an error or a warning. If you are never planning to use a certain name from a loaded module, it is not brought into scope. This is useful when you already have some working code and need to start using an additional module that exports the name that you already use in your code.

In such a scenario, this behavior ensures that you do not have to change your original code; it will keep working as it did before. The mental model that you can build to understand this behavior is that Julia is lazy; it introduces a variable into scope and resolves its name the first time it is used.

3.3.3   Using StatsBase.jl to compute the winsorized mean

We are now ready to go back to our `winsorized_mean` example. Assuming you have the StatsBase.jl package installed, you can find that it provides the `winsor` function. After loading `Statistics` and `StatsBase`, you can check its help (start a fresh Julia session):

```
julia> using Statistics

julia> using StatsBase

help?> winsor
search: winsor winsor! winsorized_mean

  winsor(x::AbstractVector; prop=0.0, count=0)

  Return an iterator of all elements of x that replaces either count or
  proportion prop of the highest elements with the previous-highest
  element and an equal number of the lowest elements with the next-lowest
  element.

  The number of replaced elements could be smaller than specified if
  several elements equal the lower or upper bound.

  To compute the Winsorized mean of x, use mean(winsor(x)).
```

Let's check to see if it indeed produces the same result as `winsorized_mean` for our data:

```
julia> mean(winsor([8, 3, 1, 5, 7], count=1))
5.0
```

> **Why do you need to restart your Julia session?**
>
> In several examples in this section, I have prompted you to start a fresh Julia session. This is because it is currently impossible to fully reset the workspace after you have defined variables or functions in it. For instance, as you saw in our examples, after we used the `mean` function from the `Statistics` module, we were not allowed to create a variable that would have the `mean` name.
>
> Since users often need this functionality when working interactively, the Julia development team plans to add the capability to clear the workspace without restarting Julia sessions in the future.

As usual, if you would like to learn more details about modules, refer to the Julia Manual (https://docs.julialang.org/en/v1/manual/modules/). Detailed information about how to create packages and how the Julia package manager works is provided in the Pkg.jl package documentation (https://pkgdocs.julialang.org/v1/). Appendix A explains how to install packages in Julia and get help regarding their functionality.

Wrapping up the discussion about modules and packages, it is important to discuss the Julia community's conventions for managing their functionality. The design of Julia, in terms of provided functionalities and functions, follows a similar principle to Python's "batteries included" approach:

- By default, you are given access to a very limited set of functions, defined in the Base module that is always loaded when you start Julia.
- Julia comes with many preinstalled packages that form a Julia standard library that you can load if needed. These modules provide functionality such as string handling, working with dates and time, multithreading and distributed computing, I/O, sorting, basic statistics, random number generation, linear algebra, serialization of Julia objects, and testing.

If you require functionality that is unavailable in the standard library, the easiest thing to do is to look for it in packages. JuliaHub (https://juliahub.com/ui/Packages) provides a flexible web interface allowing you to browse available packages.

The meaning of the Base Julia term

Often, in this book, as well as in other resources on Julia, you'll see the term *Base Julia*. This refers to the Base module that Julia defines. This module provides a set of definitions that are always loaded by Julia when you run it.

Doing statistics with Julia

Julia comes with the Statistics module as part of its standard library. This module contains basic statistics functionalities that allow you to compute the mean, variance, standard deviation, Pearson correlation, covariance, median, and quantiles of your data.

More advanced statistical functionalities are provided by the packages from the JuliaStats collection (https://juliastats.org/). The StatsBase.jl package discussed in this chapter is part of JuliaStats. This package defines functions that allow you to compute weighted statistics of your data, and provides functionalities such as rankings and rank correlations, along with various data-sampling algorithms.

Other popular packages from JuliaStats are Distributions.jl (providing support for various probability distributions), HypothesisTests.jl (defining many commonly used statistical tests), MultivariateStats.jl (for multivariate statistical analysis like principal component analysis), Distances.jl (for efficient computing of distances between vectors), KernelDensity.jl (for kernel density estimation), Clustering.jl (providing algorithms for data clustering), and GLM.jl (allowing you to estimate generalized linear models).

3.4 *Using macros*

The last important feature of Julia that you are going to encounter in this book is the macro. As a data scientist, you likely will not need to define your own macros, but expect to use them quite often, especially in part 2, when we will discuss the domain-specific language (DSL) defined in the DataFramesMeta.jl package that allows working conveniently with data frames.

For our current purposes, we will need to use the @time macro to compare the performance of our winzorized_mean function against the implementation provided by the StatsBase.jl package.

So, what does a macro do? *Macros* are used to generate your program's code. You can think of macros as functions that take a parsed representation of Julia code and return its transformation (technically, macros operate at a level of *abstract syntax trees* [http://mng.bz/5mKZ]).

It is important to understand that macros are executed after Julia code is parsed, but before it is compiled. If you know the Lisp programming language, you will notice similarities in the way Julia and Lisp support macros. Note that in Julia, macros are different from C macros that perform textual manipulation of the source code.

You can easily recognize macro calls in the code, as a macro is always prefixed with the @ character. Here is an example of a macro call:

```
julia> @time 1 + 2
  0.000000 seconds
3
```

In this example, we use the @time macro and pass the 1 + 2 expression to it. This macro executes the passed expression and prints the time it took to execute. As you can see, unlike functions, you can call macros without using parentheses. However, you could also enclose the expression passed to the macro in parentheses:

```
julia> @time(1 + 2)
  0.000000 seconds
3
```

Here is an example of calling a macro taking two arguments:

```
julia> @assert 1 == 2 "1 is not equal 2"
ERROR: AssertionError: 1 is not equal 2

julia> @assert(1 == 2, "1 is not equal 2")
ERROR: AssertionError: 1 is not equal 2
```

Note that if you do not use parentheses, the expressions passed to the macro should be separated with a space (a comma must not be used in this case).

You now know how macros are called, but what do they do? As I have said, they rewrite your code to generate new, transformed code. You can easily see this rewritten code by using the @macroexpand macro. Let's start with a simple example of the @assert macro:

```
julia> @macroexpand @assert(1 == 2, "1 is not equal 2")
:(if 1 == 2
      nothing
  else
      Base.throw(Base.AssertionError("1 is not equal 2"))
  end)
```

As you can see, in this case, the generated code is relatively simple. The `@assert` macro has created the `if` block, which does nothing if the assertion is true and throws an error if the assertion is false.

Of course, normally macros can generate much more complex code. For example, the `@time` macro performs multiple operations to ensure proper measurement of the execution time of the passed expression:

```
julia> @macroexpand @time 1 + 2
quote
    #= timing.jl:206 =#
    while false
        #= timing.jl:206 =#
    end
    #= timing.jl:207 =#
    local var"#11#stats" = Base.gc_num()
    #= timing.jl:208 =#
    local var"#14#compile_elapsedtime" =
    Base.cumulative_compile_time_ns_before()
    #= timing.jl:209 =#
    local var"#13#elapsedtime" = Base.time_ns()
    #= timing.jl:210 =#
    local var"#12#val" = 1 + 2
    #= timing.jl:211 =#
    var"#13#elapsedtime" = Base.time_ns() - var"#13#elapsedtime"
    #= timing.jl:212 =#
    var"#14#compile_elapsedtime" =
    Base.cumulative_compile_time_ns_after() - var"#14#compile_elapsedtime"
    #= timing.jl:213 =#
    local var"#15#diff" = Base.GC_Diff(Base.gc_num(), var"#11#stats")
    #= timing.jl:214 =#
    Base.time_print(var"#13#elapsedtime", (var"#15#diff").allocd,
    (var"#15#diff").total_time, Base.gc_alloc_count(var"#15#diff"),
    var"#14#compile_elapsedtime", true)
    #= timing.jl:215 =#
    var"#12#val"
end
```

As you can see, a seemingly simple operation of measuring execution time is, in fact, quite complex.

Now you might ask why `@time` is a macro and not just a function. If you were to define the `time` function instead and write `time(1 + 2)`, the `1 + 2` expression would be evaluated before it was passed to the function, so it would be impossible to measure the time it took to execute it. To measure the execution time of an expression, we must augment it with proper code before the expression is run. This is possible only during parsing of the Julia code.

It is worth remembering the @macroexpand macro, as you will find it useful when learning the DataFramesMeta.jl package in part 2.

As usual in this chapter, let's use the winsorized_mean example to test macros. We'll compare the performance of our solution with the performance of the implementation from StatsBase.jl. For benchmarking, we will use the @benchmark macro from the BenchmarkTools.jl package. It differs from the @time macro in that it runs the expression many times and then calculates the statistics of the observed run times (before running this code, define the winsorized_mean function by using the code from section 3.2). In the example code, I added a semicolon (;) after the rand(10^6) expression to suppress printing of its value to the terminal.

We start with the benchmark of our winsorized_mean function:

```
julia> using BenchmarkTools

julia> x = rand(10^6);          ⊲⎯┐ Uses ; at the end of the expression passed in the
                                    REPL to suppress printing its value to the terminal

julia> @benchmark winsorized_mean($x, 10^5)  ⊲⎯┐ Since x is a global variable, uses
                                                 $x to ensure proper benchmarking
                                                 of the tested code
```

You should get a timing similar to the one presented in figure 3.3 (exact timings might differ slightly on your machine).

```
BenchmarkTools.Trial: 89 samples with 1 evaluation.
 Range (min … max):  54.292 ms … 62.020 ms │ GC (min … max): 0.00% … 0.00%
 Time  (median):     56.013 ms             │ GC (median):    0.00%
 Time  (mean ± σ):   56.421 ms ±  1.454 ms │ GC (mean ± σ):  0.61% ± 1.40%

  ▁  ▁ ▁█ ▁▁█ ▁ ▁ ▁▁ ▁ ▁  ▁ ▁  ▁▁  ▁ ▁ ▁ ▁       ▁
  █▁▁█▁██▁███▁█▁█▁██▁█▁█▁▁█▁█▁▁██▁▁█▁█▁█▁█▁▁▁▁▁▁▁▁█ ▁
  54.3 ms         Histogram: frequency by time        60.7 ms <

 Memory estimate: 7.63 MiB, allocs estimate: 2.
```

Figure 3.3   Benchmark of execution time of the winsorized_mean function

Now we benchmark computation of the winsorized mean by using the functions provided by the packages from the Julia statistics ecosystem:

```
julia> using Statistics

julia> using StatsBase

julia> @benchmark mean(winsor($x; count=10^5))
```

The code produces the timing presented in figure 3.4. Using library functions is noticeably faster.

```
BenchmarkTools.Trial: 369 samples with 1 evaluation.
 Range (min … max):  12.321 ms … 16.754 ms │ GC (min … max): 0.00% … 14.17%
 Time  (median):     13.292 ms             │ GC (median):    0.00%
 Time  (mean ± σ):   13.543 ms ± 848.854 µs │ GC (mean ± σ):  2.64% ±  5.27%
```

```
 12.3 ms          Histogram: frequency by time         15.8 ms <
```

```
Memory estimate: 7.63 MiB, allocs estimate: 2.
```

Figure 3.4   Benchmark of execution time when using the `winsor` function

In the example, we first generate one million random floats from the range `[0, 1]` by using the `rand` function. The results of the benchmarks show that the library function is around four times faster than our code. The reason for this is relatively easy to guess. In our function, we sort the whole vector, while most of the time it is not needed, as `k` is typically relatively small in comparison to the size of the vector. The library solution uses the `partialsort!` function to improve its efficiency.

An important aspect of using the `@benchmark` macro is that we use `$x` instead of just `x`. This is needed to get a correct assessment of execution time of the expressions we check. As a rule, remember to prefix with `$` all global variables you use in the expressions you want to benchmark (this applies only to benchmarking and is not a general rule when using macros). For details about this requirement, refer to the documentation of the BenchmarkTools.jl package (https://github.com/JuliaCI/BenchmarkTools.jl). The short explanation is as follows. Recall that since `x` is a global variable, code using it is not type stable. When the `@benchmark` macro sees the `$x`, it is instructed to turn the `x` variable into one that is local (and thus type stable) before running the benchmarks.

The BenchmarkTools.jl package also provides the `@btime` macro that accepts the same arguments as `@benchmark`. The difference is that it produces less-verbose output, similar to `@time`, and the printed time is the minimum elapsed time measured during benchmarking. Here is an example:

```
julia> @btime mean(winsor($x; count=10^5))
  12.542 ms (2 allocations: 7.63 MiB)
0.5003188657625405
```

Note that the reported time is similar to the minimum time produced by `@benchmark mean(winsor($x; count=10^5))`.

As a final example of applying macros, try writing the following in your Julia REPL:

```
julia> @edit winsor(x, count=10^5)
```

`@edit` is one of my favorite macros. In your source code editor, it takes you directly to the source code of the function you are using (you can specify which editor should be used by setting the JULIA_EDITOR environment variable; see http://mng.bz/yaJy). A huge benefit of using Julia is that this function is most likely written in Julia, so you can easily inspect its implementation. I recommend you check how the winsor function is implemented to find out the tricks its creators used to make it fast.

EXERCISE 3.1 Create an x variable that is a range of values from 1 to 10^6. Now, using the collect function, create a y vector holding the same values as the x range. Using the @btime macro, check the time of sorting x and y by using the sort function. Finally, using the @edit macro, check the implementation of the sort function that would be invoked when you sort the x range.

That is all you need to know about macros to use them. You will hardly ever need to write your own macros, as most of the time, writing functions is enough to get what you want. However, sometimes you want certain actions to be performed on your code before the code is executed. In these cases, macros are the way to achieve the desired result.

Summary

- Types of variables have a hierarchical relationship and form a tree. The root of the tree is the Any type that matches any value. Types that have subtypes are called *abstract* and cannot have instances. Types that can have instances cannot have subtypes and are called *concrete*.
- A single function can have multiple methods. Each method has a unique set of argument types that it allows.
- In Julia, modules are used to create separate namespaces (global scopes). The most common use of modules is for creation of packages. Packages can be registered with the Julia general registry and made available for all developers.
- Macros in Julia allow you to transform code into other code before it gets executed. They are sometimes useful when functions do not allow you to achieve the desired result.
- When you install Julia, it comes with "batteries included." Many modules are shipped as part of the standard library and provide essential functionalities that are commonly needed in practice. You can explore the additional packages in the Julia ecosystem in JuliaHub.

Working with collections in Julia

This chapter covers

- Working with arrays
- Using dictionaries to handle key-value mappings
- Handling immutable collection types: tuples and named tuples

In chapters 2 and 3, you learned basic elements of the Julia language. We have mostly used scalar types (like numbers) in all the examples. However, in data science, you will typically work with data *collections*, groupings of a variable number of data items. One collection type already introduced in chapter 2 is a vector.

In this chapter, you will learn how to use several fundamental collections that are most used in practical scenarios: arrays, dictionaries, tuples, and named tuples.

4.1 Working with arrays

In this section, you will learn the basics of working with arrays in Julia: their creation, indexing into arrays, and the most common operations you can expect to perform with them. Arrays are commonly used collections in data science. Most machine learning algorithms expect data stored in arrays as their inputs. In Julia (as opposed to, for example, Python), arrays are part of the language specification, so they are equipped with a convenient syntax. Working with them requires learning only one set of rules, and they are fast.

To learn how to work with arrays in Julia, we will analyze Anscombe's quartet data (http://mng.bz/69ZZ). As you will learn in this section, it consists of four data sets that have identical simple descriptive statistics but very different distributions. Each of the four data sets consists of 11 observations and has two variables: one feature denoted as x and one target denoted as y. Table 4.1 shows the data.

Table 4.1   Anscombe's quartet data

Data set 1		Data set 2		Data set 3		Data set 4	
x	y	x	y	x	y	x	y
10.0	8.04	10.0	9.14	10.0	7.46	8.0	6.58
8.0	6.95	8.0	8.14	8.0	6.77	8.0	5.76
13.0	7.58	13.0	8.74	13.0	12.74	8.0	7.71
9.0	8.81	9.0	8.77	9.0	7.11	8.0	8.84
11.0	8.33	11.0	9.26	11.0	7.81	8.0	8.47
14.0	9.96	14.0	8.10	14.0	8.84	8.0	7.04
6.0	7.24	6.0	6.13	6.0	6.08	8.0	5.25
4.0	4.26	4.0	3.10	4.0	5.39	19.0	12.50
12.0	10.84	12.0	9.13	12.0	8.15	8.0	5.56
7.0	4.82	7.0	7.26	7.0	6.42	8.0	7.91
5.0	5.68	5.0	4.74	5.0	5.73	8.0	6.89

Our goal is to perform the following operations on each of these data sets:

- Calculate the mean and standard deviation of x and y variables
- Calculate Pearson's correlation coefficient of x and y variables
- Fit a linear regression explaining y by x and compute its coefficient of determination R^2
- Investigate the data visually by using plots

Terminology used in the book for tabular data

When describing tabular data in this book, I use the following terminology. Rows of data are called *observations*, and columns are called *variables*.

> *(continued)*
>
> In the context of a predictive model, a variable that is explained by the model is called a *target* (other names that are alternatively used are *output* or *dependent variable*). The variables used to make a prediction are called *features* (other names include *input* or *independent variable*).
>
> The same terminology is used in the MLJ.jl ecosystem (https://github.com/alan-turing-institute/MLJ.jl), which is a popular toolbox for machine learning in Julia.

4.1.1　Getting the data into a matrix

We want to analyze data stored in table 4.1. The table has eight columns and 11 rows. Each column represents one variable. Note that columns 1, 3, 5, and 7 (odd columns) are the x feature variables in data sets 1, 2, 3, and 4, respectively. Likewise, columns 2, 4, 6, and 8 (even columns) are the y target variables in the respective data sets.

CREATING A MATRIX

Before analyzing the data, we need to store it in the computer's memory. Since the data is of a homogeneous type (these are all numbers), it is natural to use a matrix as a container. In this section, you will see how to create this matrix and check its basic properties.

We start with creating a variable bound to a matrix storing our data, as shown in the following listing.

Listing 4.1　Defining a matrix storing Anscombe's quartet data

```
julia> aq = [10.0    8.04   10.0   9.14   10.0    7.46    8.0    6.58
              8.0    6.95    8.0   8.14    8.0    6.77    8.0    5.76
             13.0    7.58   13.0   8.74   13.0   12.74    8.0    7.71
              9.0    8.81    9.0   8.77    9.0    7.11    8.0    8.84
             11.0    8.33   11.0   9.26   11.0    7.81    8.0    8.47
             14.0    9.96   14.0   8.1    14.0    8.84    8.0    7.04
              6.0    7.24    6.0   6.13    6.0    6.08    8.0    5.25
              4.0    4.26    4.0   3.1     4.0    5.39   19.0   12.50
             12.0   10.84   12.0   9.13   12.0    8.15    8.0    5.56
              7.0    4.82    7.0   7.26    7.0    6.42    8.0    7.91
              5.0    5.68    5.0   4.74    5.0    5.73    8.0    6.89]
11×8 Matrix{Float64}:
 10.0    8.04   10.0   9.14   10.0    7.46    8.0    6.58
  8.0    6.95    8.0   8.14    8.0    6.77    8.0    5.76
 13.0    7.58   13.0   8.74   13.0   12.74    8.0    7.71
  9.0    8.81    9.0   8.77    9.0    7.11    8.0    8.84
 11.0    8.33   11.0   9.26   11.0    7.81    8.0    8.47
 14.0    9.96   14.0   8.1    14.0    8.84    8.0    7.04
  6.0    7.24    6.0   6.13    6.0    6.08    8.0    5.25
  4.0    4.26    4.0   3.1     4.0    5.39   19.0   12.5
 12.0   10.84   12.0   9.13   12.0    8.15    8.0    5.56
  7.0    4.82    7.0   7.26    7.0    6.42    8.0    7.91
  5.0    5.68    5.0   4.74    5.0    5.73    8.0    6.89
```

The `aq` variable is a `Matrix` holding `Float64` values. Note that in Julia, it is easy to create a matrix storing predefined data. You just need to write each row of data as a single line of the input, using whitespace as a separator of columns, and wrap everything in square brackets. If you would like to learn about additional options for constructing arrays, consult the "Array Literals" section of the Julia Manual (http://mng.bz/M0vo).

In the head of the output of our operation in listing 4.1, we can see that the matrix has 11 rows and eight columns. We can check this by using the `size` function:

```
julia> size(aq)
(11, 8)

julia> size(aq, 1)
11

julia> size(aq, 2)
8
```

The `size` function can take either one argument, in which case it returns a tuple of dimensions, or two arguments, where the second argument is the dimension that we want to investigate (where 1 stands for rows and 2 stands for columns).

WORKING WITH TUPLES

Before moving forward, let's briefly discuss what a *tuple* is. You can think of it as a vector but with a fixed length and immutable. It is created using parentheses, while vectors are created with square brackets. You can get elements of the tuple, as with vectors, but you cannot set them, unlike with vectors, because tuples are immutable; see figure 4.1. Tuples in Julia are similar to tuples in Python, and their type is `Tuple`.

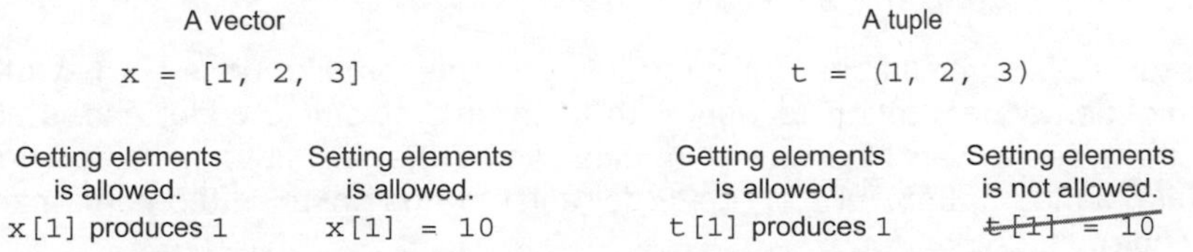

A vector		A tuple	
x = [1, 2, 3]		t = (1, 2, 3)	
Getting elements is allowed.	Setting elements is allowed.	Getting elements is allowed.	Setting elements is not allowed.
x[1] produces 1	x[1] = 10	t[1] produces 1	~~t[1] = 10~~

Figure 4.1 A comparison of a vector and a tuple. You can get elements of vectors and tuples, but Julia allows setting elements of only a vector.

The results of the operations shown in figure 4.1, executed in the Julia REPL, are as follows:

```
julia> v = [1, 2, 3]
3-element Vector{Int64}:
 1
 2
 3
```

```
julia> t = (1, 2, 3)
(1, 2, 3)

julia> v[1]
1

julia> t[1]
1

julia> v[1] = 10
10

julia> v
3-element Vector{Int64}:
 10
  2
  3

julia> t[1] = 10
ERROR: MethodError: no method matching
setindex!(::Tuple{Int64, Int64, Int64}, ::Int64, ::Int64)
```

In this example, note that both vectors and tuples use *1-based indexing*. This means, as discussed in chapter 2, that the first element of a vector and a tuple has an index of 1. The same convention is used in R, Fortran, and MATLAB. This is especially important to remember if you work a lot with Python, Java, or C++, since these programming languages use 0-based indexing.

Tuples vs. vectors

You might ask what the benefit is of using tuples instead of vectors. The considerations are as follows.

Tuples are immutable, so if in your code you want to ensure that the user will not be able to change them, they are safer to use.

Since tuples are immutable, they are faster, as the compiler does not have to use dynamic memory allocation to work with them (in type-stable code) and is able to know the types of variables stored in them even if they are heterogeneous (refer to the Julia Manual, http://mng.bz/epPP, for a list of tips ensuring the performance of Julia code).

As a downside, I do not recommend creating tuples that store a large number of elements (they are best suited to holding small collections). Large tuples may lead to significant compilation time of your programs.

Representation of vectors in Julia

In this section, we are discussing a basic kind of a vector used in Julia that has the Vector type. In general, Julia supports other vector types, and you will learn about several in the following chapters. In particular, it is useful to know that, unlike the Vector type, some vector types are not mutable or do not use 1-based indexing.

For more technically oriented readers, let me mention that in Julia, tuples are allocated on the stack, and standard arrays are heap allocated. If you do not know these memory allocation models, see http://mng.bz/o5a2. For working efficiently with Julia, you do not need to know the details of how memory management is handled. It's enough to understand that heap allocation is slower than stack allocation. Additionally, heap allocation requires an additional process called *garbage collection* (*GC*) to be run. GC is responsible for releasing the memory that has been heap allocated and is not referenced anymore.

Figure 4.2 shows a benchmark for creating a tuple versus a vector. You can see in the `Memory estimate` section (marked with a rectangle) that creating a vector requires one memory allocation, while creating a tuple does not lead to any allocations. Therefore, in the `GC` section (marked with a rounded rectangle), you can see that when benchmarking the creation of a tuple, GC is never triggered, while when benchmarking a vector, GC is occasionally run.

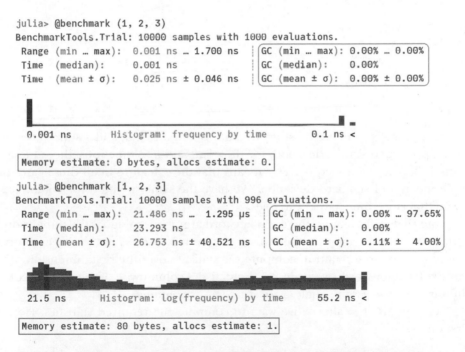

```
julia> @benchmark (1, 2, 3)
BenchmarkTools.Trial: 10000 samples with 1000 evaluations.
 Range (min … max):  0.001 ns … 1.700 ns  ┊ GC (min … max): 0.00% … 0.00%
 Time  (median):     0.001 ns              ┊ GC (median):    0.00%
 Time  (mean ± σ):   0.025 ns ± 0.046 ns   ┊ GC (mean ± σ):  0.00% ± 0.00%


 0.001 ns       Histogram: frequency by time       0.1 ns <

 Memory estimate: 0 bytes, allocs estimate: 0.

julia> @benchmark [1, 2, 3]
BenchmarkTools.Trial: 10000 samples with 996 evaluations.
 Range (min … max):  21.486 ns …  1.295 µs  ┊ GC (min … max): 0.00% … 97.65%
 Time  (median):     23.293 ns              ┊ GC (median):    0.00%
 Time  (mean ± σ):   26.753 ns ± 40.521 ns  ┊ GC (mean ± σ):  6.11% ±  4.00%


 21.5 ns        Histogram: log(frequency) by time      55.2 ns <

 Memory estimate: 80 bytes, allocs estimate: 1.
```

Figure 4.2   A benchmark comparing the creation time of a tuple and a vector. Creating tuples is faster and does not lead to memory allocation on the heap. Run using `BenchmarkTools` before executing the computations presented in this figure.

To wrap up the comparison of vectors and tuples, let's discuss their construction when you pass data of mixed types. When you construct a vector using square brackets, Julia will try to promote all passed elements to a common type, while constructing a tuple does not result in such a conversion. Here is an example:

```
julia> [1, 2.0]
2-element Vector{Float64}:
 1.0
 2.0

julia> (1, 2.0)
(1, 2.0)
```

In the code, when constructing a vector, we pass 1 (an integer) and 2.0 (a floating-point value). In the produced vector, the integer 1 is converted to floating-point 1.0. When constructing a tuple, the passed values are stored in it without any conversion.

4.1.2 *Computing basic statistics of the data stored in a matrix*

Now we are ready to compute means and standard deviations of variables stored in the aq matrix. For this, we will use the mean and std functions defined in the Statistics module:

```
julia> using Statistics

julia> mean(aq; dims=1)
1×8 Matrix{Float64}:
 9.0  7.50091  9.0  7.50091  9.0  7.5  9.0  7.50091

julia> std(aq; dims=1)
1×8 Matrix{Float64}:
 3.31662  2.03157  3.31662  2.03166  3.31662  2.03042  3.31662  2.03058
```

In the aq matrix defined in listing 4.1, the columns 1, 3, 5, and 7 store the x feature. In the presented summaries, both for the mean and std functions, the values in positions 1, 3, 5, and 7 are equal. This means that the x feature in all these cases has the same mean and standard deviation. We have the same situation for columns 2, 4, 6, and 8 that store the y target variables.

Note that we have used the dims keyword argument to signal the dimension along which we want to compute the statistics. Here it is dims=1, as we have observations stored in rows, so we want to compute the statistics over the first dimension of the aq matrix. In other words, we compute the statistics columnwise of the aq matrix because the variables we want to analyze are stored as its columns.

Let's discuss two alternative ways to compute the required statistics. Here is the first one:

```
julia> map(mean, eachcol(aq))
8-element Vector{Float64}:
 9.0
 7.500909090909093
 9.0
 7.500909090909091
 9.0
 7.500000000000001
 9.0
 7.50090909090909
```

```
julia> map(std, eachcol(aq))
8-element Vector{Float64}:
 3.3166247903554
 2.031568135925815
 3.3166247903554
 2.0316567355016177
 3.3166247903554
 2.030423601123667
 3.3166247903554
 2.0305785113876023
```

Let's dissect this example. The `eachcol(aq)` call returns a collection iterating columns of our matrix (for reference, `eachrow(aq)` would iterate its rows). Next, we apply the `map` function (discussed in chapter 2), which applies the appropriate function (`mean` and `std`, respectively) to each of the columns. As a reminder from chapter 2, note that we could have used the do-end notation with the `map` function like this:

```
map(eachcol(aq)) do col
    mean(col)
end
```

However, in this case, this would be more verbose than just passing the `mean` function as a first positional argument to `map`.

Instead of using the `map` function, we could have used a comprehension to create a vector by iterating columns of the `aq` matrix:

```
julia> [mean(col) for col in eachcol(aq)]
8-element Vector{Float64}:
 9.0
 7.500909090909093
 9.0
 7.500909090909091
 9.0
 7.500000000000001
 9.0
 7.50090909090909
```

```
julia> [std(col) for col in eachcol(aq)]
8-element Vector{Float64}:
 3.3166247903554
 2.031568135925815
 3.3166247903554
 2.0316567355016177
 3.3166247903554
 2.030423601123667
 3.3166247903554
 2.0305785113876023
```

As you can see, the comprehension uses the `for` keyword argument, after which we specify which variable (`col`, in this case) should store values produced by an iterator (`eachcol(aq)`, in this case). Then, before the `for` keyword, we write the expression that should be evaluated, which can depend on the `col` variable. As a result, we get an array collecting the produced results. Figure 4.3 compares the syntax when using the map function and the comprehension.

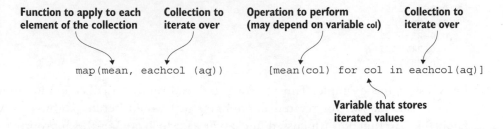

Figure 4.3   Syntax used when working with the map function and the comprehension. When using a comprehension, you explicitly give a name to the variable that is used to store the values you iterate (col in our case).

In most scenarios, the choice between using a comprehension and using the map function follows programmer's convenience and code readability (in particular, you can expect similar performance). Their differences are most visible if you want to operate on several collections at the same time. Refer to the Julia Manual at http://mng.bz/aPZo and http://mng.bz/gR1x for examples. Another difference is that comprehensions always produce arrays, while the map function can produce values of a different type. Here is an example of taking the absolute value of several numbers stored in a tuple. A comprehension produces a vector, while map returns a tuple:

```julia
julia> x = (-2, -1, 0, 1, 2)
(-2, -1, 0, 1, 2)

julia> [abs(v) for v in x]
5-element Vector{Int64}:
 2
 1
 0
 1
 2

julia> map(abs, x)
(2, 1, 0, 1, 2)
```

4.1.3   *Indexing into arrays*

Often you want to select part of a matrix to be able to work with it later. This is easily done using indexing.

We illustrate indexing by presenting yet another way to specify the computation of column statistics in our aq matrix:

```julia
julia> [mean(aq[:, j]) for j in axes(aq, 2)]
8-element Vector{Float64}:
```

```
9.0
7.500909090909093
9.0
7.500909090909091
9.0
7.500000000000001
9.0
7.50090909090909

julia> [std(aq[:, j]) for j in axes(aq, 2)]
8-element Vector{Float64}:
 3.3166247903554
 2.031568135925815
 3.3166247903554
 2.0316567355016177
 3.3166247903554
 2.030423601123667
 3.3166247903554
 2.0305785113876023
```

This time, we are using indexing in the aq matrix. The axes function is similar to the size function discussed previously. The difference is that instead of returning the length of the given dimension, it produces a valid range of indices in a given dimension. In this example, it is as follows:

```
julia> axes(aq, 2)
Base.OneTo(8)

help?> Base.OneTo
  Base.OneTo(n)

  Define an AbstractUnitRange that behaves like 1:n, with the added
  Distinction that the lower limit is guaranteed (by the type system)
  to be 1.
```

As you can see, the indices start from 1 and span through 8. I have included the documentation of the OneTo object that is returned so that you know exactly what it represents. In practice, you will not need to construct it yourself, but occasionally you might encounter it produced by standard Julia functions, so it's worthwhile to be aware of what it does.

Why is OneTo prefixed with Base?

We can see that Julia prints the information about the OneTo type by prefixing it with Base—for example, Base.OneTo(8). This output gives us two pieces of information:

- The OneTo type is defined in the Base module (the default module that is always loaded when you start Julia).
- This type is not exported to the Main module. Therefore, you can access it only by prefixing its name with the name of the module that defines it.

Section 3.3 explains the Base and Main modules and how name exporting works.

In our comprehension, since we now iterate indices of the second dimension of our matrix, we need to extract its single column. This is done using the `aq[:, j]` expression. The colon (`:`) means that we pick all rows of the j-th column of `aq`.

Matrix indexing: practical guidance

If you use matrices, use two indices (for rows and for columns) to access its elements, just as in the preceding example. Similarly, when indexing vectors, use a single index. In general, Julia allows for other indexing styles, which come in handy when writing advanced generic code, but I recommend you stick to the basic rule of *as many indices as dimensions of an array*, as this will make your code readable and easier to debug.

A final note related to the `aq[:, j]` expression is that it makes a copy of the j-th column of our matrix. Sometimes, for performance reasons, you might prefer not to copy data, but use a view into the `aq` matrix instead. This can be done using the `view` function or the `@view` macro as follows:

```
julia> [mean(view(aq, :, j)) for j in axes(aq, 2)]
8-element Vector{Float64}:
 9.0
 7.500909090909093
 9.0
 7.500909090909091
 9.0
 7.500000000000001
 9.0
 7.50090909090909

julia> [std(@view aq[:, j]) for j in axes(aq, 2)]
8-element Vector{Float64}:
 3.3166247903554
 2.031568135925815
 3.3166247903554
 2.0316567355016177
 3.3166247903554
 2.030423601123667
 3.3166247903554
 2.0305785113876023
```

In the first example, when calculating the mean, we use the `view` function. In this case, we pass the indices as consecutive arguments to it. When using the `@view` macro, we can use the standard indexing syntax. I have shown this approach when calculating the standard deviation. Apart from syntax differences, writing `view(aq, :, j)` and `@view aq[:, j]` are equivalent.

> ### What is a view?
>
> In Julia, if you have an array and create its view, no data from the parent array is copied. Instead, a lightweight object is created that lazily references the parent array. Therefore, the parent and its view share the same memory to store data. If you modify data stored in a view, this change is also visible in the parent.

In the context of the `@view` macro, let me remind you of one important aspect of the way macros work in Julia (we discussed this in chapter 3). If you invoke a macro without parentheses, it eagerly considers all that follows as an expression; as much code as possible is taken to be an expression.

Here is an example where that leads to a problem. Assume you want to create a tuple consisting of two views of a vector, and try the following code:

```
julia> x = [1, 2, 3, 4]
4-element Vector{Int64}:
 1
 2
 3
 4

julia> (@view x[1:2], @view x[3:4])
ERROR: LoadError: ArgumentError: Invalid use of @view macro:
argument must be a reference expression A[...].
```

What is the reason for the error? The problem is that the `x[1:2], @view[3:4]` part of the code is a single expression passed to the first `@view` call. To solve this problem, you need to use the second style of macro invocation that uses parentheses (just as when you call functions):

```
julia> (@view(x[1:2]), @view(x[3:4]))
([1, 2], [3, 4])
```

4.1.4 *Performance considerations of copying vs. making a view*

You might ask how much making a copy affects the performance of operations. This section presents how to compare the performance of copying to that of making a view. To do this, we will need a data set much bigger than our `aq` matrix, as it is too small for a practically relevant benchmark.

Here's an example benchmark on a matrix of 10,000,000 rows and 10 columns:

```
julia> using BenchmarkTools

julia> x = ones(10^7, 10)
10000000×10 Matrix{Float64}:
 1.0  1.0  1.0  1.0  1.0  1.0  1.0  1.0  1.0  1.0
 1.0  1.0  1.0  1.0  1.0  1.0  1.0  1.0  1.0  1.0
 1.0  1.0  1.0  1.0  1.0  1.0  1.0  1.0  1.0  1.0
 1.0  1.0  1.0  1.0  1.0  1.0  1.0  1.0  1.0  1.0
 ⋮                        ⋮
```

```
1.0   1.0   1.0   1.0   1.0   1.0   1.0   1.0   1.0   1.0
1.0   1.0   1.0   1.0   1.0   1.0   1.0   1.0   1.0   1.0
1.0   1.0   1.0   1.0   1.0   1.0   1.0   1.0   1.0   1.0
1.0   1.0   1.0   1.0   1.0   1.0   1.0   1.0   1.0   1.0
```

```
julia> @btime [mean(@view $x[:, j]) for j in axes($x, 2)];
  39.193 ms (1 allocation: 144 bytes)
```

```
julia> @btime [mean($x[:, j]) for j in axes($x, 2)];
  201.935 ms (21 allocations: 762.94 MiB)
```

```
julia> @btime mean($x, dims=1);
  38.959 ms (7 allocations: 688 bytes)
```

> Recall from chapter 3 that we write $x in the code to get a proper benchmark result because x is a global variable.

We first create a large matrix filled with 1s, using the ones function. As you can see from the benchmarks, using the views uses up much less memory and is faster. In the benchmark, we additionally include the mean(x, dims=1) call that also produces the expected result. This function is built into standard Julia distribution and tuned for performance. The benchmark shows that our code is roughly as efficient.

4.1.5   *Calculating correlations between variables*

Let's apply what you've learned to calculate correlations between the studied variables, as this is also a statistic that we want to compute. The difference from our examples of calculating the mean and the standard deviation is that when computing correlation, we need to pass two columns to a function simultaneously. In this section, you will learn how to do that.

We want to calculate the correlation of columns 1 and 2, 3 and 4, 5 and 6, and 7 and 8. Here is a simple approach using the cor function from the Statistics module:

```
julia> [cor(aq[:, i], aq[:, i+1]) for i in 1:2:7]
4-element Vector{Float64}:
 0.8164205163448398
 0.8162365060002429
 0.8162867394895983
 0.8165214368885028
```

This time, the cor function is passed two vectors (related to the x and y variables, respectively). As you can see, the correlations are similar. Let me comment on the 1:2:7 expression. You've already learned about ranges of the form start:stop that span all values starting from start and finishing at stop, inclusive, with step equal to 1. The style start:step:stop is a generalization of this syntax, allowing you to specify the step of the range via the parameter step; see figure 4.4.

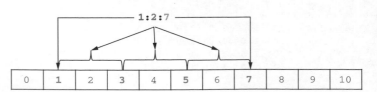

Figure 4.4   Interpretation of range syntax with a custom step size. In this example, step has the value 2, so we are iterating odd numbers: 1, 3, 5, 7.

Let's check that the step parameter works as I explained by using the `collect` function that you learned about in chapter 3:

```
julia> collect(1:2:7)
4-element Vector{Int64}:
 1
 3
 5
 7
```

In the `[cor(aq[:, i], aq[:, i+1]) for i in 1:2:7]` expression, I have used copying operations on purpose. I encourage you to rewrite this code by using views as an exercise.

> **EXERCISE 4.1**   Rewrite the expression `[cor(aq[:, i], aq[:, i+1]) for i in 1:2:7]` by using views (either the `view` function or the `@view` macro). Compare the performance of both approaches by using the `@benchmark` macro from the BenchmarkTools.jl package.

4.1.6   *Fitting a linear regression*

We can now turn to fitting a linear regression by using ordinary least squares (OLS). Later you will learn a more general and convenient API for estimating parameters of such models using the GLM.jl package, but for now, we restrict ourselves to a basic approach to learn how to work with matrices in Julia. The linear regression that we want to fit has the form $y = a + b * x + error$, where a and b are unknown coefficients that must be estimated. We will choose them so that the sum of squares of *error* terms across all observations is minimized.

As you might know from an introductory statistics course, to estimate the parameters of the linear regression, we need a vector `y` holding the target variable and a matrix of model features. It is crucially important that, since we want to learn two parameters, a and b, we have two features in our model. The feature related to the a parameter is called a *constant term* and must be represented as a column consisting only of 1s. The second feature should be our *x* variable. Let's build the target vector `y` and the feature matrix `X` from our aq data set by extracting the first set of *x* and *y* variables at indices 1 and 2:

```
julia> y = aq[:, 2]
11-element Vector{Float64}:
  8.04
  6.95
  7.58
  8.81
  8.33
  9.96
  7.24
  4.26
 10.84
  4.82
  5.68
```

```
julia> X = [ones(11) aq[:, 1]]
11×2 Matrix{Float64}:
 1.0  10.0
 1.0   8.0
 1.0  13.0
 1.0   9.0
 1.0  11.0
 1.0  14.0
 1.0   6.0
 1.0   4.0
 1.0  12.0
 1.0   7.0
 1.0   5.0
```

◁── **We use 11 because we know our data has 11 observations.**

What might surprise you is the `[ones(11) aq[:, 1]]` syntax. However, you've already learned all the building blocks we use here. The `ones` function generates a vector of eleven 1s. Then we use the method of constructing matrices in which you merge columns by separating them with a whitespace and wrapping them in square brackets. This is the same approach we used at the beginning of this section. The only difference is that now we are horizontally concatenating whole vectors, not just single cells of a matrix.

This operation works as expected, because in Julia vectors are always considered to be columnar. When you write `[1, 2, 3]`, which is a literal defining a vector, with a syntax that is visually horizontal (to save vertical space in your code), the produced object is a columnar vector. This is highlighted by the fact that Julia prints the vectors vertically in the REPL, as opposed to R, which prints them horizontally.

We are ready to estimate the parameters of our model. You can use the backslash (\) operator:

```
julia> X \ y
2-element Vector{Float64}:
 3.000090909090909
 0.500090909090909
```

In this case, the constant term is approximately estimated to be `3.0`, and the coefficient with the *x* variable to be `0.5`.

The \ operator

The result of the A \ B operation, when A is a matrix, depends on its shape.

If A is square, the result X is such that A * X = B.

If A is not square, the result X is a minimizer of the expression `norm(A * X - B)`, where `norm` is a function computing the Euclidean norm; it is defined in the `LinearAlgebra` module.

In the context of linear regression, when A is a feature matrix and B is a target variable vector, then A \ B produces the least squares estimate or regression parameters.

We are now ready to estimate all four models:

```
julia> [[ones(11) aq[:, i]] \ aq[:, i+1] for i in 1:2:7]
4-element Vector{Vector{Float64}}:
 [3.000090909090909, 0.500090909090909]
 [3.0009090909090905, 0.5]
 [3.0024545454545457, 0.4997272727272727]
 [3.001727272727273, 0.4999090909090908]
```

Again, all models are almost identical. Notice that this time, we have created a vector that contains vectors. In Julia, arrays can store objects of any type, which includes other arrays (typically called *nested arrays*). If you expect to work a lot with these data structures, you might consider learning the features provided by the ArraysOfArrays.jl package.

> **Precision of floating-point calculations**
>
> Floating-point operations are done with finite precision. One consequence is that running the same Julia code on different hardware or using different implementations of libraries performing linear algebra operations might produce a slightly different result. (Julia allows switching linear algebra libraries; see https://github.com/JuliaLinearAlgebra/MKL.jl.)
>
> You might see this effect when working with examples in this book. For example, the X \ y expression we used in this section can produce an output different from what I showed previously. The differences could be seen in the least significant digits of the output.

We are now ready to compute the R^2 coefficient of determination:

```
julia> function R²(x, y)
           X = [ones(11) x]
           model = X \ y
           prediction = X * model
           error = y - prediction
           SS_res = sum(v -> v ^ 2, error)
           mean_y = mean(y)
           SS_tot = sum(v -> (v - mean_y) ^ 2, y)
           return 1 - SS_res / SS_tot
       end
R² (generic function with 1 method)

julia> [R²(aq[:, i], aq[:, i+1]) for i in 1:2:7]
4-element Vector{Float64}:
 0.6665424595087751
 0.6662420337274844
 0.6663240410665592
 0.6667072568984652
```

First, we define the R² function that takes the x feature and y target. Remember that if you do not remember how to type ², you can easily get help by pressing ? and pasting ²:

```
help?> ²
"²" can be typed by \^2<tab>
```

In the R^2 function, we first reproduce the steps to estimate the model parameters we just discussed. Then we make a prediction by using this model with the `X * model` expression. Here we take advantage of the fact that the multiplication operator in Julia performs matrix multiplication out of the box. Next, we store the prediction errors in the `error` variable. The coefficient of determination is defined as 1 minus the ratio of the sum of squared errors of the model and the sum of deviations of the target variable from its mean. We compute these quantities in the last part of our function. In the body of the R^2 function, we use the `mean` function, which requires that you first load the `Statistics` module to ensure that the computations are executed without error.

As you can see, applying the R^2 function to our data produces almost the same result for all four data sets. This is the last analysis we wanted to perform.

4.1.7   *Plotting the Anscombe's quartet data*

Now you are ready to learn why the Anscombe's quartet data is so famous. Let's plot the data to discover that the distribution of all four data sets is radically different. We will use the Plots.jl package to do the plotting. First, we plot the first data set on a scatterplot to warm up:

```
julia> using Plots

julia> scatter(aq[:, 1], aq[:, 2]; legend=false)
```

Figure 4.5 presents the output you should see.

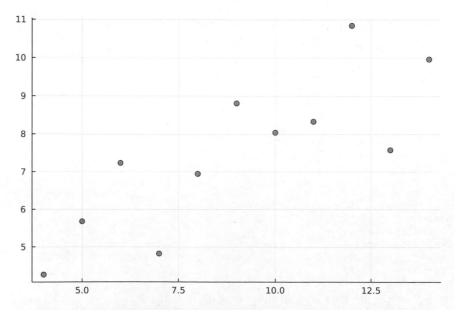

Figure 4.5   The plot of the first data set from Anscombe's quartet. The points are scattered but seem to roughly follow a linear trend.

If you run the example code, you will see that the time to produce the plot for the first time is noticeable. As explained in section 1.4, this is expected, as Julia needs to compile the function we call. Fortunately, this is a one-time cost, and consecutive plots are produced quickly.

Now let's visualize the four plots. With Plots.jl, this is quite easy. You just need to wrap four `scatter` calls with a `plot` function:

```julia
julia> plot(scatter(aq[:, 1], aq[:, 2]; legend=false),
            scatter(aq[:, 3], aq[:, 4]; legend=false),
            scatter(aq[:, 5], aq[:, 6]; legend=false),
            scatter(aq[:, 7], aq[:, 8]; legend=false))
```

This produces the plot shown in figure 4.6. As you can see, the four data sets look completely different.

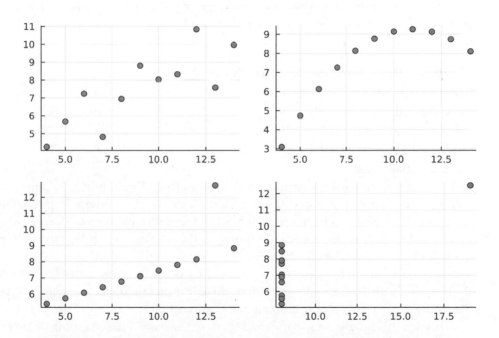

Figure 4.6 The plot of the four data sets from Anscombe's quartet. Although, as we have checked, all four data sets have identical basic summary statistics, the relationships between the x and y variables are completely different in each of them.

Before we finish this section, let me show you another way to make the last plot. You might have thought that there was a lot of unnecessary typing. Indeed, there was. Here is the code that uses a comprehension to achieve the same result:

```julia
julia> plot([scatter(aq[:, i], aq[:, i+1]; legend=false)
            for i in 1:2:7]...)
```

Observe, however, that we had to add one small detail. Since the `plot` function accepts subplots as its consecutive positional arguments, we cannot just pass a vector produced by our comprehension to it, as that would produce an error. We need to expand the vector into multiple positional arguments in the function call. This operation, called *splatting*, is performed using the triple dots (`...`). In our code, they directly follow the comprehension expression inside the function call.

If you are interested in more details about working with arrays, check out the Julia Manual section on multidimensional arrays (https://docs.julialang.org/en/v1/manual/arrays/). You also can check http://mng.bz/neYe to find out how the problem we have described can be solved using DataFrames.jl (we will work with this package in part 2).

At this point, you should have a working knowledge of how to create vectors and arrays, manipulate them, and pass them to statistical and plotting functions. Arrays are a special type of collection in which every dimension can be indexed into with a continuous range of integers. However, sometimes you need a data structure that allows you to use any values for indexing. This is possible with dictionaries, which we discuss next.

4.2   *Mapping key-value pairs with dictionaries*

Another type of standard collection often used when doing data science is the dictionary. We will introduce dictionaries by solving the famous Sicherman dice puzzle. In this section, you will learn how to create a dictionary, add keys to a dictionary, retrieve values from it, and compare dictionaries.

THE SICHERMAN PUZZLE

A standard die has six sides, with faces numbered from 1 to 6. In many games, players roll two standard dice and sum the obtained results. In the Sicherman puzzle, we are asked to check if it is possible to number the faces of a pair of cubes in a way completely different from that of standard dice so that the cubes can be used in any dice game and all the odds will be the same as they are when standard dice are used. More formally, we want to check if there exist other pairs of two six-sided dice, not necessarily identical, with faces numbered with positive integers that have the same probability distribution for the sum of rolled values as standard dice.

To solve this puzzle, we will use dictionaries. A *dictionary* is a mapping of keys to values. In our example, since we consider two six-sided dice, we can have 36 distinct toss results (we have six sides of each die, and $6 \times 6 = 36$ possible combinations of outcomes). Therefore, our mapping will tell us, for every value of the sum of rolled values, how many times (out of the total 36) it occurs.

CREATING A DICTIONARY

Let's first create a dictionary of this distribution for a pair of standard dice:

```
julia> two_standard = Dict{Int, Int}()
Dict{Int64, Int64}()
```

```
julia> for i in [1, 2, 3, 4, 5, 6]
           for j in [1, 2, 3, 4, 5, 6]
               s = i + j
               if haskey(two_standard, s)
                   two_standard[s] += 1
               else
                   two_standard[s] = 1
               end
           end
       end

julia> two_standard
Dict{Int64, Int64} with 11 entries:
  5  => 4
  12 => 1
  8  => 5
  6  => 5
  11 => 2
  9  => 4
  3  => 2
  7  => 6
  4  => 3
  2  => 1
  10 => 3
```

In our code, we first create an empty `two_standard` dictionary. Note that by writing `Dict{Int, Int}`, we specify two parameters for our type. The first parameter is the type of allowed keys, and the second is the type of allowed values.

Next, using a double-nested loop, we traverse 36 combinations of possible outcomes of tosses and sum them, storing the sum in the `s` variable. Inside the loop, using the `haskey` function, we check whether the dictionary already contains a mapping for the `s` key. If it does, we increase the count for the entry of the dictionary by one. Otherwise, this is the first time we encounter the given key, and we assign it the count equal to 1. Note that indexing into a dictionary uses square brackets, just like indexing into arrays or tuples.

We can easily extract a list of the keys and values of the dictionary:

```
julia> keys(two_standard)
KeySet for a Dict{Int64, Int64} with 11 entries. Keys:
  5
  12
  8
  6
  11
  9
  3
  7
  4
  2
  10
```

```
julia> values(two_standard)
ValueIterator for a Dict{Int64, Int64} with 11 entries. Values:
  4
  1
  5
  5
  2
  4
  2
  6
  3
  1
  3
```

You can see that the types of both values do not seem to be vectors. They are both just views of the dictionary contents. Therefore, if we wanted to plot the distribution of the sum of rolls, we would need to collect them, which materializes the views as vectors. Here's how this should be done:

```
julia> using Plots

julia> scatter(collect(keys(two_standard)),
               collect(values(two_standard));
               legend=false, xaxis=2:12)
```

Note that by using the xaxis keyword argument, we explicitly set the x-axis label in the plot. Figure 4.7 shows the plot you should obtain.

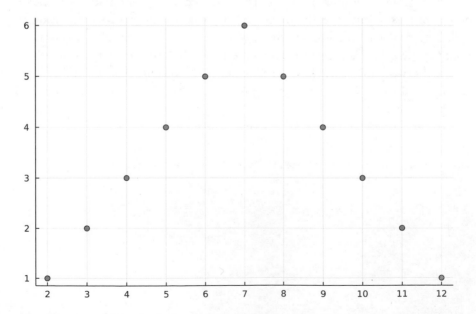

Figure 4.7   **Distribution of the sum of rolling two standard dice. The possible outcomes range from 2 to 12. The distribution is symmetric.**

In the preceding example, I wanted to show you the use of the `keys` and `values` functions. However, Plots.jl allows you to visualize the contents of the dictionaries more easily. You could write `scatter(two_standard; legend=false, xaxis=2:12)` to get the same plot.

SOLVING THE SICHERMAN PUZZLE

Now we are ready to start solving the puzzle. To reduce the search space, note that since the minimal sum equaling 2 occurs only once, we must have exactly one 1 on both dice. Similarly, note that the largest sum equals 12, so the maximum number on any die is 11. We thus concentrate on five sides of a die (one and only one side must contain 1, as discussed) with values ranging from 2 to 11. Let's generate a vector of all such dice. Notice that we can concentrate only on nondecreasing sequences of numbers posted on dice:

```julia
julia> all_dice = [[1, x2, x3, x4, x5, x6]
                   for x2 in 2:11
                   for x3 in x2:11
                   for x4 in x3:11
                   for x5 in x4:11
                   for x6 in x5:11]
2002-element Vector{Vector{Int64}}:
 [1, 2, 2, 2, 2, 2]
 [1, 2, 2, 2, 2, 3]
 [1, 2, 2, 2, 2, 4]
 [1, 2, 2, 2, 2, 5]
 ⋮
 [1, 10, 10, 10, 11, 11]
 [1, 10, 10, 11, 11, 11]
 [1, 10, 11, 11, 11, 11]
 [1, 11, 11, 11, 11, 11]
```

Notice that in this code, we have used a nice feature of comprehension syntax in Julia that we have not discussed yet. The `for` loops can be nested, and the loops that follow previous loops can use the variables defined in outer loops. Such a nested comprehension works as if we have written multiple `for` loops, one inside the other.

We now see that we have 2,002 such dice. We are ready to test all pairs of dice to check which have the same distribution as our `two_standard` distribution. Here is how to do this:

```julia
julia> for d1 in all_dice, d2 in all_dice
           test = Dict{Int, Int}()
           for i in d1, j in d2
               s = i + j
               if haskey(test, s)
                   test[s] += 1
               else
                   test[s] = 1
               end
           end
           if test == two_standard
               println(d1, " ", d2)
```

```
        end
      end
[1, 2, 2, 3, 3, 4] [1, 3, 4, 5, 6, 8]
[1, 2, 3, 4, 5, 6] [1, 2, 3, 4, 5, 6]
[1, 3, 4, 5, 6, 8] [1, 2, 2, 3, 3, 4]
```

In this code, we create the `test` dictionary in the same way as we created the `two_standard` dictionary earlier. The only difference is that we use a different, shorter style of writing the `for` loop. For instance, in `for i in d1, j in d2`, we immediately create a nested loop iterating over a Cartesian product of `d1` and `d2` values.

Also notice that we can use the `==` comparison to check whether two dictionaries have identical mappings of keys to values.

Our code outputs three pairs of dice. One is a pair of standard dice, as expected. The other two pairs are the same, just in reverse order. Thus, we have learned that there is a unique solution to the Sicherman dice puzzle. Somewhat surprisingly, we now know that if we take one die with numbers 1, 2, 2, 3, 3, 4 and the other with numbers 1, 3, 4, 5, 6, 8, then the distribution of the sum of their tossed values is indistinguishable from the distribution for the two standard dice.

The example code has one shortcoming. It violates the *don't repeat yourself* (*DRY*) principle. We have repeated the same code for filling the `Dict{Int, Int}` dictionary twice: the first time it was used to fill the `two_standard` dictionary, and the next time it was used to repeatedly fill the `test` dictionary. In such situations, I usually wrap the repeated code in a function. This operation is a task left for you as an exercise to reinforce your learning of function definition syntax in Julia.

EXERCISE 4.2   Rewrite the code solving the Sicherman puzzle, wrapping the logic of the processing in functions. Create one function, `dice_distribution`, that produces a dictionary with a distribution of the sum of possible combinations of values on two dice passed as its arguments. Next, write another function, `test_dice`, in which you create the `all_dice` variable, then the `two_standard` variable, and finally run the main loop comparing the distribution of all dice from the `all_dice` vector against the `two_standard` distribution.

Standard data collections in Julia

In this section, we have given one short example of using dictionaries. If you would like to learn more about other collection types that are supported by Base Julia, refer to the Julia Manual (https://docs.julialang.org/en/v1/base/collections/). Additionally, the DataStructures.ji package provides even more collection types that you might need in your code. Following are several collection types that are most needed in practice.

A data structure related to dictionaries, and sometimes used in data science workflows, is the *set*. The `Set` type is available in Base Julia. Instead of keeping key-value pairs, as dictionaries do, sets just keep a set of unique values. The basic operations

> that sets allow you to do are adding values, removing values, and quickly checking if a certain value is present in a set.
>
> Both the `Dict` and `Set` types in Base Julia store their elements in an undefined order. The types that preserve insertion order are provided in the DataStructures.jl package and are, respectively, `OrderedDict` dictionary and `OrderedSet` set.

If you are interested in an alternative solution to the Sicherman dice puzzle using DataFrames.jl, check out my blog post "Solving Sicherman Dice Puzzle Using Data-Frames.jl" (http://mng.bz/p692).

You now know how to work with dictionaries, which, unlike arrays, allow you to use any values for indexing. A natural question is whether we can have a data structure that would allow both integer indexing and selection of values by their name. Indeed, Julia provides such a collection. It is called `NamedTuple`, and we will discuss it next.

4.3 Structuring your data by using named tuples

When we were analyzing the Anscombe's quartet data in section 4.1, you might have had the feeling that we were missing some structure in our data. The `NamedTuple` type is a basic method to add structure to your code. You can think of a `NamedTuple` as a way to add names to the consecutive elements of a tuple.

In this section, you will learn how to create a `NamedTuple` and access its elements. You will also see how to fit linear models using the GLM.jl package.

We will rewrite the Anscombe's quartet data example using the `NamedTuple` type. Start with the `aq` matrix we already defined in listing 4.1 (repeated here for your convenience):

```
julia> aq = [10.0    8.04   10.0   9.14   10.0    7.46    8.0    6.58
              8.0    6.95    8.0   8.14    8.0    6.77    8.0    5.76
             13.0    7.58   13.0   8.74   13.0   12.74    8.0    7.71
              9.0    8.81    9.0   8.77    9.0    7.11    8.0    8.84
             11.0    8.33   11.0   9.26   11.0    7.81    8.0    8.47
             14.0    9.96   14.0   8.1    14.0    8.84    8.0    7.04
              6.0    7.24    6.0   6.13    6.0    6.08    8.0    5.25
              4.0    4.26    4.0   3.1     4.0    5.39   19.0   12.50
             12.0   10.84   12.0   9.13   12.0    8.15    8.0    5.56
              7.0    4.82    7.0   7.26    7.0    6.42    8.0    7.91
              5.0    5.68    5.0   4.74    5.0    5.73    8.0    6.89]
11×8 Matrix{Float64}:
 10.0    8.04   10.0   9.14   10.0    7.46    8.0    6.58
  8.0    6.95    8.0   8.14    8.0    6.77    8.0    5.76
 13.0    7.58   13.0   8.74   13.0   12.74    8.0    7.71
  9.0    8.81    9.0   8.77    9.0    7.11    8.0    8.84
 11.0    8.33   11.0   9.26   11.0    7.81    8.0    8.47
 14.0    9.96   14.0   8.1    14.0    8.84    8.0    7.04
  6.0    7.24    6.0   6.13    6.0    6.08    8.0    5.25
  4.0    4.26    4.0   3.1     4.0    5.39   19.0   12.5
 12.0   10.84   12.0   9.13   12.0    8.15    8.0    5.56
  7.0    4.82    7.0   7.26    7.0    6.42    8.0    7.91
  5.0    5.68    5.0   4.74    5.0    5.73    8.0    6.89
```

4.3.1   *Defining named tuples and accessing their contents*

First, create a named tuple for the first data set as an exercise:

```
julia> dataset1 = (x=aq[:, 1], y=aq[:, 2])
(x = [10.0, 8.0, 13.0, 9.0, 11.0, 14.0, 6.0, 4.0, 12.0, 7.0, 5.0],
 y = [8.04, 6.95, 7.58, 8.81, 8.33, 9.96, 7.24, 4.26, 10.84, 4.82, 5.68])
```

As you can see, creating a NamedTuple is easy. It is similar to a Tuple, except we are giving names to the elements. NamedTuple, just like a Tuple, is immutable. You can index into it by using a number, but you can also access its fields by using a dot (.) and field name:

```
julia> dataset1[1]
11-element Vector{Float64}:
 10.0
  8.0
 13.0
  9.0
 11.0
 14.0
  6.0
  4.0
 12.0
  7.0
  5.0

julia> dataset1.x
11-element Vector{Float64}:
 10.0
  8.0
 13.0
  9.0
 11.0
 14.0
  6.0
  4.0
 12.0
  7.0
  5.0
```

Let's now create a nested named tuple holding our four data sets in the next listing.

Listing 4.2   **Defining a named tuple storing Anscombe's quartet data**

```
julia> data = (set1=(x=aq[:, 1], y=aq[:, 2]),
               set2=(x=aq[:, 3], y=aq[:, 4]),
               set3=(x=aq[:, 5], y=aq[:, 6]),
               set4=(x=aq[:, 7], y=aq[:, 8]))
(set1 = (x = [10.0, 8.0, 13.0, 9.0, 11.0, 14.0, 6.0, 4.0, 12.0, 7.0, 5.0],
 y = [8.04, 6.95, 7.58, 8.81, 8.33, 9.96, 7.24, 4.26, 10.84, 4.82, 5.68]),
 set2 = (x = [10.0, 8.0, 13.0, 9.0, 11.0, 14.0, 6.0, 4.0, 12.0, 7.0, 5.0],
 y = [9.14, 8.14, 8.74, 8.77, 9.26, 8.1, 6.13, 3.1, 9.13, 7.26, 4.74]),
 set3 = (x = [10.0, 8.0, 13.0, 9.0, 11.0, 14.0, 6.0, 4.0, 12.0, 7.0, 5.0],
```

```
  y = [7.46, 6.77, 12.74, 7.11, 7.81, 8.84, 6.08, 5.39, 8.15, 6.42, 5.73]),
  set4 = (x = [8.0, 8.0, 8.0, 8.0, 8.0, 8.0, 8.0, 19.0, 8.0, 8.0, 8.0],
  y = [6.58, 5.76, 7.71, 8.84, 8.47, 7.04, 5.25, 12.5, 5.56, 7.91, 6.89]))
```

Now you can fetch a single data set from our collection like this:

```
julia> data.set1
(x = [10.0, 8.0, 13.0, 9.0, 11.0, 14.0, 6.0, 4.0, 12.0, 7.0, 5.0],
 y = [8.04, 6.95, 7.58, 8.81, 8.33, 9.96, 7.24, 4.26, 10.84, 4.82, 5.68])

julia> data.set1.x
11-element Vector{Float64}:
 10.0
  8.0
 13.0
  9.0
 11.0
 14.0
  6.0
  4.0
 12.0
  7.0
  5.0
```

4.3.2 Analyzing Anscombe's quartet data stored in a named tuple

We are now ready to reproduce selected steps of the analysis we did in section 4.1 by using the data variable. First, calculate the means of x variables in each set:

```
julia> using Statistics

julia> map(s -> mean(s.x), data)
(set1 = 9.0, set2 = 9.0, set3 = 9.0, set4 = 9.0)
```

In the code, we create an anonymous function `s -> mean(s.x)` that extracts the x field from a passed NamedTuple and computes its mean. An interesting feature to note is that the map function is smart enough to return a NamedTuple that keeps the names of processed fields from the source NamedTuple. Calculation of Pearson's correlation works similarly:

```
julia> map(s -> cor(s.x, s.y), data)
(set1 = 0.8164205163448398, set2 = 0.8162365060002429,
 set3 = 0.8162867394895983, set4 = 0.8165214368885028)
```

Finally, let's fit a linear model for the first data set by using the GLM.jl package. In the model, the target variable is y, and we have one feature x:

```
julia> using GLM

julia> model = lm(@formula(y ~ x), data.set1)
StatsModels.TableRegressionModel{LinearModel{GLM.LmResp{Vector{Float64}},
 GLM.DensePredChol{Float64, LinearAlgebra.CholeskyPivoted{Float64,
 Matrix{Float64}}}}, Matrix{Float64}}
```

y ~ 1 + x ◁——┐ **This indicates the formula**
              used to fit the model.

◁————————————┐
This part of the output indicates
the type of the model variable.
You can safely ignore it.

Coefficients:

	Coef.	Std. Error	t	Pr(>|t|)	Lower 95%	Upper 95%
(Intercept)	3.00009	1.12475	2.67	0.0257	0.455737	5.54444
x	0.500091	0.117906	4.24	0.0022	0.23337	0.766812

Observe several features in this code:

- We use the `@formula(y ~ x)` syntax to say that the x field of our `NamedTuple` is a feature and y is a target variable. Inside the `@formula` macro, we are passing the target variable name, followed by a tilde (~) and the feature variable name. In part 2, we will discuss how such formulas are constructed in more detail. If you would like to learn all the details of the `@formula` domain-specific language, you can find them in the StatsModels.jl package documentation (http://mng.bz/O6Qo).

- The first positional argument to the `lm` function is the model formula, and the second positional argument is a table represented by our `data.set1` named tuple. The `lm` function takes the data from the passed table and fits the linear regression model specified by the passed formula. The object returned by the `lm` function stores information about the estimated parameters of our model. When this object is printed in the REPL, it gives us a table with summary statistics of the model, in which the x variable and the intercept in our model automatically get proper names.

As you can see, the obtained estimates of our linear model are the same as obtained in section 4.1.

As the last example, let's use the `r2` function from GLM.jl to calculate the coefficient of determination of our model:

```
julia> r2(model)
0.666542459508775
```

Again, the results are in line with what we had earlier. Building models using the GLM.jl package is much more powerful than doing it manually, as we did in section 4.1. Now you are ready to reproduce figure 4.6 (showing scatterplots of all four data sets in one plot) using data stored in `NamedTuple`.

EXERCISE 4.3 Reproduce figure 4.6 using the `data` named tuple defined in listing 4.2.

4.3.3 *Understanding composite types and mutability of values in Julia*

Before we wrap up this section, it is worth discussing two important concepts in more depth: *composite structures* and *mutability* of values. I discuss these topics here to help you better understand the differences between arrays, dictionaries, named tuples, and other types discussed in this chapter.

COMPOSITE TYPES

The model variable that we worked with in section 4.3.2 has a TableRegression-Model type that is a composite type—namely, a struct. When doing basic operations, you will most likely not need to create them on your own, but you will often encounter them returned by functions from packages.

The TableRegressionModel type is defined in the StatsModels.jl package as follows:

```
struct TableRegressionModel{M,T} <: RegressionModel
    model::M
    mf::ModelFrame
    mm::ModelMatrix{T}
end
```

At a basic level, you do not need to understand all the details of this definition. What is important for us now is that the struct defines three fields: model, mf, and mm. When you get a value having such a type, you can easily access its fields by using a dot (.), just as for a NamedTuple (in part 2, you will learn that the way the dot operator works is a bit more complex, but by default it behaves in the way I describe here):

```
julia> model.mm
ModelMatrix{Matrix{Float64}}([1.0 10.0; 1.0 8.0; … ; 1.0 7.0; 1.0 5.0],
                             [1, 2])
```

Therefore, you can think of these objects as being similar to NamedTuple, with the difference being that their type has a specific name (TableRegressionModel, in our case), and it cannot be indexed with numbers like a NamedTuple. You can learn more about defining composite types in the Julia Manual (http://mng.bz/YKwK).

MUTABILITY OF VALUES

Julia distinguishes between mutable and immutable types. Here is a classification of selected types encountered so far in this book:

- *Immutable*—Int, Float64, String, Tuple, NamedTuple, struct
- *Mutable*—Array (so also Vector and Matrix), Dict, and struct created with mutable keyword added

You might ask how immutable and mutable types differ. The point is that mutable values can be changed. This might sound obvious, but the crucial thing is that they can also be changed by functions to which they are passed. Such side effects can be quite surprising. Therefore, as discussed in chapter 2, it is crucially important to annotate the functions that mutate their arguments with the exclamation point suffix (!). Also, as discussed in chapter 2, remember that adding ! at the end of a function is only a convention (functions whose names end with ! get no special treatment by the Julia compiler; the convention is only meant to make it visually explicit for the user that the function might mutate its arguments). Here are two examples of data mutation at work.

In the first example, we see the difference between calling the `unique` and `unique!` functions on a vector. They both remove duplicates from a collection. The difference between them is that `unique` returns a new vector, while `unique!` works in place:

```
julia> x = [3, 1, 3, 2]
4-element Vector{Int64}:
 3
 1
 3
 2
```

> **The unique function returns a new vector. It does not mutate the passed vector.**

```
julia> unique(x)
3-element Vector{Int64}:
 3
 1
 2
```

> **The x vector is unchanged.**

```
julia> x
4-element Vector{Int64}:
 3
 1
 3
 2
```

> **The unique! function changes the x vector in place.**

```
julia> unique!(x)
3-element Vector{Int64}:
 3
 1
 2
```

> **The x vector is changed.**

```
julia> x
3-element Vector{Int64}:
 3
 1
 2
```

The `unique` function does not change the passed argument, but instead allocates a new vector and de-duplicates it. On the other hand, the `unique!` function updates the passed vector in place.

The second example is meant to show you that even if your data structure is immutable, it might contain mutable elements that can be changed by a function. In this example, we use the `empty!` function that takes a mutable collection as its argument and removes all elements stored in it in place:

```
julia> empty_field!(nt, i) = empty!(nt[i])
empty_field! (generic function with 1 method)
```

> **The empty_field! function calls the empty! function on the i-th element of the nt object.**

```
julia> nt = (dict = Dict("a" => 1, "b" => 2), int=10)
(dict = Dict("b" => 2, "a" => 1), int = 10)
```

> **The nt named tuple has a dictionary as its first element; dictionaries are mutable.**

```
julia> empty_field!(nt, 1)
Dict{String, Int64}()
```

```
julia> nt
(dict = Dict{String, Int64}(), int = 10)
```

After executing the empty_field! function, the dictionary stored in the nt named tuple is empty.

In this example, we create the `empty_field!` function that takes an object and tries to index into it in position `i` and empty the stored value in place by using the `empty!` function. Next, we create a `NamedTuple` that has two fields: a dictionary and an integer. The `Dict("a" => 1, "b" => 2)` syntax is a convenient approach to initially populating a dictionary, where each element `"a" => 1` is a `Pair` object mapping a single key to a single value.

The crucial thing to observe is that when we call `empty_field!(nt, 1)`, the dictionary stored in the `nt` variable gets emptied, although `nt` is a `NamedTuple` that is immutable. However, it contains a mutable object as its field.

In summary, stressing what we have already discussed, Julia does not copy data when passing arguments to a function. If an object is passed to a function and contains a structure (even a nested one) that is mutable, that object can potentially be mutated by the function. If you want to create a fully independent object when passing a value to a function, to be sure that the original value is guaranteed not to be mutated, use the `deepcopy` function to create it.

Summary

- Arrays are the most common containers in Julia, as most machine learning algorithms take arrays as their input. In Julia, arrays are part of the core of the language, so they are efficient and easy to use.
- You can use the `Statistics` module and the GLM.jl package to easily perform analysis of your data, including determining the mean, standard deviation, correlation, and estimation of linear models. All functions providing these functionalities accept arrays as their input.
- Julia, like R, Fortran, and MATLAB, by default uses 1-based indexing for arrays.
- In Julia, vectors are always considered to be columnar.
- You can use dictionaries in Julia to store key-value mappings. It is important to remember that in Julia, keys in a dictionary can be values of any type.
- Arrays and dictionaries are mutable containers, which means that you can change their contents.
- Tuples and named tuples are similar to one-dimensional arrays, but they are immutable containers. After they are created, you are not allowed to change their contents.
- Named tuples differ from tuples in that all their elements, apart from having an index, also have names, which you can use to access them.

5

Advanced topics on handling collections

This chapter covers

- Vectorizing your code, aka broadcasting
- Understanding subtyping rules for parametric types
- Integrating Julia with Python
- Performing t-SNE dimensionality reduction

You already know from chapter 2 how to process vectors by using loops, the `map` function, and comprehensions. This chapter introduces another way that is commonly used in practice: broadcasting.

Section 5.2 explains a more advanced topic related to rules of subtyping for parametric types that often raises questions from people learning Julia. This issue is closely linked with collections because, as you will learn in this chapter, types of the most common collections like arrays or dictionaries are parametric. For this reason, you need to learn this topic if you want to know how to correctly write method signatures that allow for collections as their arguments.

Section 5.3 is devoted to integrating Julia with Python. You will learn that converting collections between the Julia format and the Python format is done automatically by the PyCall.jl package. Therefore, you can easily use existing Python code that performs operations on collections of data in your Julia projects. As an example of such integration, I will show you how to do t-SNE dimensionality reduction of data (https://lvdmaaten.github.io/tsne/) using the scikit-learn library from Python. Running the PyCall.jl examples requires having a properly configured Python installation on your computer. Therefore, please make sure to follow the environment setup instructions in appendix A.

5.1   Vectorizing your code using broadcasting

In the examples we worked through in chapters 2, 3, and 4, we used three ways to perform a repeated operation:

- `for` loops iterating a collection
- The `map` function applying a function to a collection
- Comprehension

These three syntaxes are powerful and flexible; however, many languages designed for data science provide ways to perform *vectorized operations*, also called *broadcasting*. In Julia, broadcasting is also supported. In this section, you will learn how to use it.

We will discuss how broadcasting works by going back to Anscombe's quartet data. However, let's start with an explanation of broadcasting on some toy examples.

5.1.1   Understanding syntax and meaning of broadcasting in Julia

An important design rule of the Julia language is that definitions of functions follow the rules of mathematics. You already saw this rule at work in chapter 4, which showed that the multiplication operator `*` uses matrix multiplication rules. Therefore, the following code follows matrix multiplication rules:

```julia
julia> x = [1 2 3]
1×3 Matrix{Int64}:
 1  2  3

julia> y = [1, 2, 3]
3-element Vector{Int64}:
 1
 2
 3

julia> x * y
1-element Vector{Int64}:
 14
```

The operation works as we multiply x, which is bound to a 1×3 matrix, and a three-element vector y, and in Julia vectors are always interpreted as columnar.

You might ask, then, how we should multiply two vectors elementwise, an operation known as a *Hadamard product* in mathematics. Clearly, this is not possible with just the `*` operator, as it does standard matrix multiplication:

```
julia> a = [1, 2, 3]
3-element Vector{Int64}:
 1
 2
 3

julia> b = [4, 5, 6]
3-element Vector{Int64}:
 4
 5
 6

julia> a * b
ERROR: MethodError: no method matching *(::Vector{Int64}, ::Vector{Int64})
```

You get an error, as multiplication of a vector by a vector is not a valid mathematical operation. Instead, we need to broadcast the multiplication. In Julia, adding broadcasting to an operator is easy. You just prefix it with a dot (.), like this:

```
julia> a .* b
3-element Vector{Int64}:
  4
 10
 18
```

When a broadcasted operator like .* is used, Julia iterates elements of passed collections (in our case, vectors a and b), and applies the operator after the dot (in our case, *) elementwise. Therefore, in this case, the broadcasting result is the same as that produced by the following operations:

```
julia> map(*, a, b)
3-element Vector{Int64}:
  4
 10
 18

julia> [a[i] * b[i] for i in eachindex(a, b)]
3-element Vector{Int64}:
  4
 10
 18
```

In this map example, we are passing two collections (instead of only one, as we did before when I explained how map works). The passed function (*, in this case) is applied iteratively elementwise to those collections until one of them gets exhausted.

In the comprehension example, it is worth commenting on the eachindex (a, b) expression, which produces the following:

```
julia> eachindex(a, b)
Base.OneTo(3)
```

The eachindex function produces indices that could be used to index into both a and b arguments passed to it. In this case, these are just integers from 1 to 3. Therefore,

you can index both a and b vectors with these values; for example, the following indexing expressions are valid: a[1], b[2], a[3], but a[0] or b[4] would not be valid as
they are not in the range specified by Base.OneTo(3).

   If the sizes of a and b do not match, we get an error:

```
julia> eachindex([1, 2, 3], [4, 5])
ERROR: DimensionMismatch("all inputs to eachindex must have the same
indices, got Base.OneTo(3) and Base.OneTo(2)")
```

This is an important difference from the map function, which does not use the
eachindex function internally, but instead iterates collections until either of them is
exhausted, as I have explained:

```
julia> map(*, [1, 2, 3], [4, 5])
2-element Vector{Int64}:
  4
 10
```

> **Practical considerations of using map**
>
> If you pass multiple collections to the map function, you should always check before-
> hand to make sure that they have the same length. Most of the time, using collec-
> tions of unequal lengths with the map function is a bug.

Broadcasting, like the eachindex function, checks to see if the dimensions of the
passed objects match:

```
julia> [1, 2, 3] .* [4, 5]
ERROR: DimensionMismatch("arrays could not be broadcast to a common size;
got a dimension with lengths 3 and 2")
```

5.1.2 Expanding length-1 dimensions in broadcasting

There is one exception to the rule that dimensions of all collections taking part in
broadcasting must match. This exception states that single-element dimensions get
expanded to match the size of the other collection by repeating the value stored in
this single element:

```
julia> [1, 2, 3] .^ [2]
3-element Vector{Int64}:
 1
 4
 9
```

You might ask why a single-element dimension gets expanded. The reason is practical:
in most cases, when your collection has a single element in a dimension, you want it to
get expanded. Here is an example:

```
julia> [1, 2, 3] .^ 2
3-element Vector{Int64}:
```

```
1
4
9
```

Here we are calculating a square of elements of a vector. Since 2 is a scalar, it is interpreted as having size 1 in each dimension. Most people agree that in such a case, dimension expansion should happen. You will see the same behavior in both Python and R.

Now let's consider a second example:

```
julia> [1, 2, 3, 4, 5, 6, 7, 8, 9, 10] .* [1 2 3 4 5 6 7 8 9 10]
10×10 Matrix{Int64}:
  1   2   3   4   5   6   7   8   9   10
  2   4   6   8  10  12  14  16  18   20
  3   6   9  12  15  18  21  24  27   30
  4   8  12  16  20  24  28  32  36   40
  5  10  15  20  25  30  35  40  45   50
  6  12  18  24  30  36  42  48  54   60
  7  14  21  28  35  42  49  56  63   70
  8  16  24  32  40  48  56  64  72   80
  9  18  27  36  45  54  63  72  81   90
 10  20  30  40  50  60  70  80  90  100
```

Here we have created a multiplication table. The specified operation works because we have a 10-element vector with one column and 10 rows, and a 10-element matrix with one row and 10 columns. In this case, dimension expansion happens for both the left- and right-hand sides of the operation.

This technique is often used in practice to get a *Cartesian product* of all inputs. For instance, in part 2, you will learn that when you write "x" => sum in DataFrames.jl, you ask the package to apply the sum function to the column x of the data frame. A common scenario is that we want to apply several functions to several columns of a data frame. Using broadcasting, this can be written concisely as follows:

```
julia> ["x", "y"] .=> [sum minimum maximum]
3×3 Matrix{Pair{String, _A} where _A}:
 "x"=>sum  "x"=>minimum  "x"=>maximum
 "y"=>sum  "y"=>minimum  "y"=>maximum
```

This expression asks for computation of sum, minimum, and maximum for columns x and y. The reason it works as expected is that we use the same pattern as in the multiplication table example. The ["x", "y"] expression creates a two-element vector (recall that vectors in Julia are columnar; in this case, the vector has one column and two rows), and the [sum minimum maximum] expression creates a matrix with one row and three columns.

When we apply broadcasting to the => operator, we get a Cartesian product of arguments passed to it. A single column of the ["x", "y"] vector is repeated three times to match the number of columns in the [sum minimum maximum] matrix. Similarly, a single row of the [sum minimum maximum] matrix is repeated two times to match the number of rows in the ["x", "y"] vector. Therefore, the `["x", "y"] .=> [sum minimum maximum]` operation produces the same result as the following more-verbose code:

```
julia> left_matrix = ["x" "x" "x"
                      "y" "y" "y"]
2×3 Matrix{String}:
 "x"  "x"  "x"
 "y"  "y"  "y"

julia> right_matrix = [sum minimum maximum
                       sum minimum maximum]
2×3 Matrix{Function}:
 sum  minimum  maximum
 sum  minimum  maximum

julia> left_matrix .=> right_matrix
2×3 Matrix{Pair{String}}:
 "x"=>sum  "x"=>minimum  "x"=>maximum
 "y"=>sum  "y"=>minimum  "y"=>maximum
```

Figure 5.1 illustrates the `["x", "y"] .=> [sum minimum maximum]` operation.

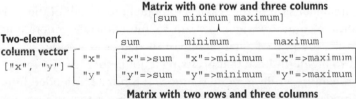

Figure 5.1 The `["x", "y"] .=> [sum minimum maximum]` operation results in a 2 × 3 matrix because we pass a two-element vector and a one-row matrix with three columns as arguments.

You now know that you can add a dot (.) before any operator to broadcast it. What about functions that are not operators? Here you also use a dot (.), but this time, you suffix it after the function name. Here is an example:

```
julia> abs.([1, -2, 3, -4])
4-element Vector{Int64}:
 1
 2
 3
 4
```

Let me stress that just applying the abs function to a vector results in an error:

```
julia> abs([1, 2, 3])
ERROR: MethodError: no method matching abs(::Vector{Int64})
```

The reason is the same as before: absolute value is mathematically defined for numbers but not defined for vectors. Of course, you can conveniently also apply broadcasting to a function taking multiple arguments. For example, the `string` function concatenates its arguments into a single string:

```
julia> string(1, 2, 3)
"123"
```

If we use broadcasting on this function, we get the following result:

```
julia> string.("x", 1:10)
10-element Vector{String}:
 "x1"
 "x2"
 "x3"
 "x4"
 "x5"
 "x6"
 "x7"
 "x8"
 "x9"
 "x10"
```

Here we expand the dimension of the scalar x to match the length of the `1:10` range. This operation is quite common when we want to automatically generate names for objects—for example, columns of a data frame or filenames in a folder.

It is important to highlight here that prefixing a dot before the operator or suffixing it to a function name is a fully general solution. It is not a hardcoded functionality of specific predefined operations. You can use broadcasting with any custom function. For instance:

```
julia> f(i::Int) = string("got integer ", i)
f (generic function with 2 methods)

julia> f(s::String) = string("got string ", s)
f (generic function with 2 methods)

julia> f.([1, "1"])
2-element Vector{String}:
 "got integer 1"
 "got string 1"
```

Here we define two methods for the f function. As you can see, by writing f., we have automatically broadcasted it without having to define anything extra.

5.1.3   *Protecting collections from being broadcasted over*

Before we go back to our Anscombe's quartet data, let me comment on one common case. What should we do if we do not want to broadcast a collection but want to force its reuse along all dimensions as if it were a scalar? To explain this issue, let me first introduce the `in` function.

The in function

The `in` function is used to check whether a certain value is contained in a collection. For example:

```
julia> in(1, [1, 2, 3])
true

julia> in(4, [1, 2, 3])
false
```

As a convenience, `in` also supports infix notation:

```
julia> 1 in [1, 2, 3]
true

julia> 4 in [1, 2, 3]
false
```

You already know this infix notation, as it is used when defining iterations in `for` loops; see section 2.2 for an explanation of how these loops work.

Now imagine you have a long vector of values and want to check whether they are contained in a vector. When you try the test without broadcasting, it does not work as you probably expect:

```
julia> in([1, 3, 5, 7, 9], [1, 2, 3, 4])
false
```

The problem is that the vector `[1, 3, 5, 7, 9]` is not an element of vector `[1, 2, 3, 4]`, so you get `false`. For reference, let's test the scenario where we put the `[1, 3, 5, 7, 9]` vector into the collection in which we look for it:

```
julia> in([1, 3, 5, 7, 9], [1, 2, 3, 4, [1, 3, 5, 7, 9]])
true
```

As expected, this time the `in` test returns `true`. Going back to the original test, note that broadcasting does not seem to work either:

```
julia> in.([1, 3, 5, 7, 9], [1, 2, 3, 4])
ERROR: DimensionMismatch("arrays could not be broadcast to a common size;
got a dimension with lengths 5 and 4")
```

How should we resolve this issue? The solution is to wrap the vector that we want to be reused as a whole with `Ref`. In this way, we will protect this object from being iterated over. Instead, it will be unwrapped from `Ref` and treated by broadcasting as if it were a scalar, and thus this value will be repeated to match the dimension of the other container:

```
julia> in.([1, 3, 5, 7, 9], Ref([1, 2, 3, 4]))
5-element BitVector:
 1
 1
```

```
0
0
0
```

This time we get the expected result.

What is Ref in Julia?

In Julia, when you write `r = Ref(x)`, you create a zero-dimensional container storing the `x` value as its only element. You can retrieve the `x` object from the `Ref` value `r` by writing `r[]` (notice that we do not pass any indices in the indexing syntax, as the `r` object is zero-dimensional). The type is named `Ref`; you can think of it as if `r` is a reference to `x`.

Since `Ref` objects are zero-dimensional and store exactly one element, they have length 1 in every dimension. Therefore, if you use the `r` object in broadcasting, the `x` value stored in it is used in all required dimensions, following the expansion rules discussed in section 5.1.2.

In the output, note that Boolean `true` is printed as 1, and Boolean `false` is printed as 0. This choice of display allows for more convenient visual inspection of large matrices containing Boolean values. To see why this is useful, consider that we wanted to use the `isodd` function to check which entries of the multiplication table created in section 5.1.2 are odd:

```
julia> isodd.([1, 2, 3, 4, 5, 6, 7, 8, 9, 10] .* [1 2 3 4 5 6 7 8 9 10])
10×10 BitMatrix:
 1  0  1  0  1  0  1  0  1  0
 0  0  0  0  0  0  0  0  0  0
 1  0  1  0  1  0  1  0  1  0
 0  0  0  0  0  0  0  0  0  0
 1  0  1  0  1  0  1  0  1  0
 0  0  0  0  0  0  0  0  0  0
 1  0  1  0  1  0  1  0  1  0
 0  0  0  0  0  0  0  0  0  0
 1  0  1  0  1  0  1  0  1  0
 0  0  0  0  0  0  0  0  0  0
```

In this example, you can see that broadcasting operations can be chained together in a single expression. In this case, we broadcast both the multiplication `*` and the `isodd` function.

For reference, let me show you how this matrix would be displayed if we changed its element type to `Any` (section 5.2 provides more details about type parameters):

```
julia> Matrix{Any}(isodd.([1, 2, 3, 4, 5, 6, 7, 8, 9, 10] .*
                          [1 2 3 4 5 6 7 8 9 10]))
10×10 Matrix{Any}:
  true  false   true  false   true  false   true  false   true  false
 false  false  false  false  false  false  false  false  false  false
  true  false   true  false   true  false   true  false   true  false
```

```
false   false   false   false   false   false   false   false   false   false
true    false   true    false   true    false   true    false   true    false
false   false   false   false   false   false   false   false   false   false
true    false   true    false   true    false   true    false   true    false
false   false   false   false   false   false   false   false   false   false
true    false   true    false   true    false   true    false   true    false
false   false   false   false   false   false   false   false   false   false
```

This time, `true` and `false` are printed to avoid potential confusion with integers 1 and 0 that could be potentially stored in this matrix, since its element type is `Any`. In my opinion, however, analyzing such a printout is less convenient than before.

To practice what you have learned, try the following exercise, which is a common task when processing data.

EXERCISE 5.1 The `parse` function can be used to convert a string into a number. For instance, if you want to parse a string as an integer, write `parse(Int, "10")` to get the integer 10. Assume you are given a vector of strings `["1", "2", "3"]`. Your task is to create a vector of integers by parsing the strings contained in the given vector.

5.1.4 Analyzing Anscombe's quartet data using broadcasting

Now we are ready to go back to our Anscombe's quartet data. Let's initialize the `aq` variable first, as we did in listing 4.1:

```
julia> aq - [10.0    8.04   10.0    9.14   10.0    7.46    8.0    6.58
              8.0    6.95    8.0    8.14    8.0    6.77    8.0    5.76
             13.0    7.58   13.0    8.74   13.0   12.74    8.0    7.71
              9.0    8.81    9.0    8.77    9.0    7.11    8.0    8.84
             11.0    8.33   11.0    9.26   11.0    7.81    8.0    8.47
             14.0    9.96   14.0    8.1    14.0    8.84    8.0    7.04
              6.0    7.24    6.0    6.13    6.0    6.08    8.0    5.25
              4.0    4.26    4.0    3.1     4.0    5.39   19.0   12.50
             12.0   10.84   12.0    9.13   12.0    8.15    8.0    5.56
              7.0    4.82    7.0    7.26    7.0    6.42    8.0    7.91
              5.0    5.68    5.0    4.74    5.0    5.73    8.0    6.89]
11×8 Matrix{Float64}:
 10.0    8.04   10.0   9.14   10.0    7.46    8.0    6.58
  8.0    6.95    8.0   8.14    8.0    6.77    8.0    5.76
 13.0    7.58   13.0   8.74   13.0   12.74    8.0    7.71
  9.0    8.81    9.0   8.77    9.0    7.11    8.0    8.84
 11.0    8.33   11.0   9.26   11.0    7.81    8.0    8.47
 14.0    9.96   14.0   8.1    14.0    8.84    8.0    7.04
  6.0    7.24    6.0   6.13    6.0    6.08    8.0    5.25
  4.0    4.26    4.0   3.1     4.0    5.39   19.0   12.5
 12.0   10.84   12.0   9.13   12.0    8.15    8.0    5.56
  7.0    4.82    7.0   7.26    7.0    6.42    8.0    7.91
  5.0    5.68    5.0   4.74    5.0    5.73    8.0    6.89

julia> using Statistics
```

We will reproduce two tasks we performed in section 4.1 using broadcasting: calculation of the mean of every variable and calculation of the coefficient of determination.

We first start with calculating the mean of the columns of the aq matrix. We want to apply the mean function to every column of the matrix. When thinking about how to do it, we notice that we need to broadcast the mean function over a collection of columns of aq. Fortunately, we know that the eachcol function gives us such a collection; therefore, we can write this:

```
julia> mean.(eachcol(aq))
8-element Vector{Float64}:
 9.0
 7.500909090909093
 9.0
 7.500909090909091
 9.0
 7.500000000000001
 9.0
 7.50090909090909
```

Note the dot (.) after mean, which means that we want to broadcast this function over the collection produced by eachcol(aq). If we were to forget to write the dot, we would get the following result:

```
julia> mean(eachcol(aq))
11-element Vector{Float64}:
  8.6525
  7.4525
 10.47125
  8.56625
  9.35875
 10.492500000000001
  6.3375
  7.03125
  9.71
  6.92625
  5.755000000000001
```

Since eachcol(aq) is a collection of eight vectors constituting columns of the aq matrix, the mean function computes their mean; that is, the function takes a sum of these eight vectors and divides it by 8. As a result, we get a vector of the means of the aq matrix's rows (note that the result has 11 elements, which is the number of rows of the aq matrix), and we want to compute the means of its columns.

As a second application, let's use broadcasting to rewrite the function calculating the coefficient of determination. Let me remind you of the original implementation:

```
function R²(x, y)
    X = [ones(11) x]
    model = X \ y
    prediction = X * model
    error = y - prediction
    SS_res = sum(v -> v ^ 2, error)
    mean_y = mean(y)
    SS_tot = sum(v -> (v - mean_y) ^ 2, y)
    return 1 - SS_res / SS_tot
end
```

If we wanted to use broadcasting, we could write this:

```
function R²(x, y)
    X = [ones(11) x]
    model = X \ y
    prediction = X * model
    SS_res = sum((y .- prediction) .^ 2)
    SS_tot = sum((y .- mean(y)) .^ 2)
    return 1 - SS_res / SS_tot
end
```

As you can see, we change formulas for `SS_res` and `SS_tot`. In both cases, we use the dot (`.`) twice. For example, in `(y .- prediction) .^ 2`, we are broadcasting both subtraction and exponentiation.

Efficiency of broadcasting in Julia

An important feature of Julia that differentiates it from R and Python is that if it encounters several broadcasting operations chained together in a single expression, it performs the operation in one pass without allocating any intermediate objects. This feature, called *broadcast fusion*, greatly improves the performance of complex broadcasted operations.

Broadcast fusion can be efficient because, as explained in chapter 1, Julia compiles your program as a whole, so when a broadcasting operation is encountered, the compiler can fully optimize the native code that gets executed. This is different from R and Python, where support for broadcasted operations is usually implemented in languages like C and stored in precompiled binaries for a limited predefined set of functions.

If you would like to learn more about how this feature of the Julia language works, I recommend you start with "Extensible Broadcast Fusion" by Matt Bauman (http://mng.bz/G1OR).

By now you know four ways of iteratively applying operations to elements of collections:

- Using `for` loops
- Using comprehensions
- Using the `map` function (and other similar higher-order functions that take functions as their arguments)
- Using broadcasting

You're probably asking yourself in which cases you should use which option. Fortunately, this is mostly a matter of convenience and code readability. In your projects, use the option that is easiest for you to use and that results in the most readable code. One of the great features of Julia is that all these options are fast. Most of the time, you won't sacrifice performance by choosing one over the other.

I say "most of the time" because exceptions to this rule exist. Apart from the differences already discussed in this section, one of the most important exceptions is that if you use a `for` loop or `map` function, you can optionally make the operation take advantage of all cores of your processor by using the `Threads` module or ThreadsX.jl package. The ability to easily support multithreaded execution of your code is a feature that distinguishes Julia from R and Python. Part 2 presents examples of how to take advantage of multithreading in your projects.

5.2 Defining methods with parametric types

In this section, we will write our own function that will calculate the covariance of two vectors. As you might guess, the `cov` function in the `Statistics` module does this calculation, but it is instructive to write this function as an exercise. Our objective is to write a function that takes two vectors holding real values and returns the covariance. The crucial part of my requirement is that the function should take as parameters two vectors that hold real values. In this section, you will learn how to specify such a restriction.

Defining functions that have complex type restrictions is challenging. Fortunately, in most of your code, you will not need to write your own methods and so won't require an advanced understanding of this topic. However, since packages written in Julia use these features heavily, you must know these concepts to be able to understand which arguments the functions provided by these packages accept and how to read error messages produced by Julia if you make a mistake when using them.

5.2.1 Most collection types in Julia are parametric

In chapter 3, you learned about Julia's type system and how to define methods. In this chapter, we discuss working with collections. You probably have noticed that most types representing collections are *parametric*: they specify the type of data that can be stored in them. Here are some examples:

```julia
julia> []
Any[]

julia> Dict()
Dict{Any, Any}()
```

Here, we create an empty vector and an empty dictionary. They can store any value, which is signaled by the `Any` parameter, so they work just like lists and dictionaries in Python.

With vectors, you can specify their element type by prefixing the opening square bracket with the type:

```julia
julia> Float64[1, 2, 3]
3-element Vector{Float64}:
 1.0
 2.0
 3.0
```

Note that although we enter 1, 2, and 3 as integers, they get converted to `Float64` because we request that the resulting vector should contain such values. Similarly, for the dictionary, we can write this:

```
julia> Dict{UInt8, Float64}(0 => 0, 1 => 1)
Dict{UInt8, Float64} with 2 entries:
  0x00 => 0.0
  0x01 => 1.0
```

As you can see, we force the conversion of both keys and values to UInt8 and Float64 types, respectively. As a side note, observe that Julia prints unsigned integers with the 0x prefix, and these values are using hexadecimal representation. For example, let's specify an explicit conversion from Int to UInt32:

```
julia> UInt32(200)
0x000000c8
```

As a last example, we create a vector that can store any Real value:

```
julia> Real[1, 1.0, 0x3]
3-element Vector{Real}:
    1
    1.0
 0x03
```

Notice that this time, no conversion of stored values happens, as Int, Float64 and UInt8 types are subtypes of Real (as you know from chapter 3). To check this, run typeof.(Real[1, 1.0, 0x3]), and you will get an [Int64, Float64, UInt8] vector as a result.

Before we move forward, let me introduce the eltype function. This function allows us to extract the type of elements that a collection can store. Here are a few examples:

```
julia> v1 = Any[1, 2, 3]
3-element Vector{Any}:
 1
 2
 3

julia> eltype(v1)
Any

julia> v2 = Float64[1, 2, 3]
3-element Vector{Float64}:
 1.0
 2.0
 3.0

julia> eltype(v2)
Float64

julia> v3 = [1, 2, 3]
3-element Vector{Int64}:
 1
 2
 3
```

```
julia> eltype(v3)
Int64

julia> d1 = Dict()
Dict{Any, Any}()

julia> eltype(d1)
Pair{Any, Any}

julia> d2 = Dict(1 => 2, 3 => 4)
Dict{Int64, Int64} with 2 entries:
  3 => 4
  1 => 2

julia> eltype(d2)
Pair{Int64, Int64}
```

For vectors, we just get the type. For dictionaries, we get a `Pair` type since, as already discussed, in Julia the key–value combination has a `Pair` type:

```
julia> p = 1 => 2
1 => 2

julia> typeof(p)
Pair{Int64, Int64}
```

5.2.2 *Rules for subtyping of parametric types*

Having seen these examples, we are now ready to go back to our task of defining a function that takes two vectors holding real values and returns their covariance. We want the function to accept any vector.

You already know from chapter 3 that we should use the `AbstractVector` type. We also want the function to accept only real values in these vectors. Similarly, we know that the element type of these vectors should be `Real`.

So, our first assumption is that `AbstractVector{Real}` should be the right type to use. Let's check this assumption by using the `isa` test discussed in chapter 3:

```
julia> [1, 2, 3] isa AbstractVector{Int}
true

julia> [1, 2, 3] isa AbstractVector{Real}
false
```

We see that, as expected, the type of `[1, 2, 3]` is a subtype of `Abstract-Vector{Int}`, but surprisingly, it is not a subtype of `AbstractVector{Real}`. This behavior of parameters in Julia is called *invariant* in computer science: although `Int` is a subtype of `Real`, `AbstractVector{Int}` is not a subtype of `Abstract-Vector{Real}`. You can find an in-depth discussion of this design decision in the "Parametric Composite Types" section of the Julia Manual (http://mng.bz/z5EX).

A vector whose type is a subtype of `AbstractVector{Real}` must allow any `Real` value to be stored in it. You saw the vector `Real[1, 1.0, 0x3]` in section 5.2.1, and we checked there that, indeed, its elements had different types. Hence, for example, Vector{Real} cannot be stored in memory as efficiently as Vector{Int}.

I will now focus on explaining how to specify a vector type whose element type is a subtype of Real. The syntax for this case is AbstractVector{<:Real}. The <: sequence means the element type of the vector can be any subtype of Real, not just Real. Equivalently, we could have used the where keyword that we already discussed in chapter 3:

```
julia> AbstractVector{<:Real} == AbstractVector{T} where T<:Real
true
```

The AbstractVector{T} where T<:Real form is encountered less often, but it can be useful if we want to refer to the variable T, which stores the element type of our vector, later in the code.

To summarize our discussion, let me give several specific examples of types and their meanings. The example is built around a Vector type:

- Int is a subtype of Real. This is because Real is an abstract concept referring to multiple numeric types; similarly, Real is a subtype of Any.
- Vector{Int} is not a subtype of Vector{Real}. This is because both Vector{Int} and Vector{Real}, as you have seen in this section, can have instances. One is a container that can store only integers. The other is a container that can store any Real values. These are two concrete and different containers. Neither is a subtype of the other.
- Vector{<:Real}, or, equivalently, Vector{T} where T<:Real, is a way to describe a union of all containers that can store Real values. Vector{<:Real} is an abstract concept referring to multiple containers. Both Vector{Int} and Vector{Real} are subtypes of Vector{<:Real}.
- Vector, Vector{<:Any}, and Vector{T} where T are each a way to describe a union of all containers having a Vector type without restricting their element type. This is different from Vector{Any}, which is a concrete type that can have an instance: it is a vector in which you can store any value. Note, though, that Vector{Any} is a subtype of Vector{<:Any}, which is in turn a subtype of Any (as every type in Julia is a subtype of Any).

Figure 5.2 illustrates these relationships.

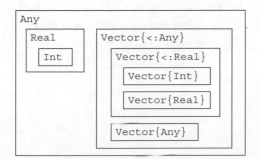

Figure 5.2 In this example of subtype relationships, a box represents a type. If a type is a subtype of a given type, it is put inside the box. Note that Vector{Int} **is not a subtype of** Vector{Real}**, although** Int **is a subtype of** Real**. Similarly,** Vector{Real} **is not a subtype of** Vector{Any}**, although** Real **is a subtype of** Any**.**

5.2.3   *Using subtyping rules to define the covariance function*

So, how should we define our covariance function? Here is a full method:

```julia
julia> using Statistics

julia> function ourcov(x::AbstractVector{<:Real},
                       y::AbstractVector{<:Real})
           len = length(x)
           @assert len == length(y) > 0
           return sum((x .- mean(x)) .* (y .- mean(y))) / (len - 1)
       end
ourcov (generic function with 1 method)
```

Section 3.4 explains how the @assert macro works. Section 2.3.1 explains how combining several logical conditions works.

In the preceding code, we use broadcasting to compute the covariance. Let's first check that the `ourcov` function works correctly:

```julia
julia> ourcov(1:4, [1.0, 3.0, 2.0, 4.0])
1.3333333333333333

julia> cov(1:4, [1.0, 3.0, 2.0, 4.0])
1.3333333333333333
```

It looks like it does work as required. Note that in the code, we mix a range of integers with a vector of floating-point values, and they get accepted and are handled correctly. However, if we pass a collection whose element type is not a subtype of `Real`, the function will fail, even if we do not change the specific values stored by the collection:

```julia
julia> ourcov(1:4, Any[1.0, 3.0, 2.0, 4.0])
ERROR: MethodError: no method matching ourcov(::UnitRange{Int64},
::Vector{Any})
Closest candidates are:
  ourcov(::AbstractVector{var"#s3"} where var"#s3"<:Real,
::AbstractVector{var"#s2"} where var"#s2"<:Real) at REPL[48]:1
```

This time, the function fails, as our second argument is a vector whose element type is `Any`, and `Any` is not a subtype of `Real`.

Before I wrap up this section, let me answer one common question. What if you have a container with a wide element type (for example, `Any`) and want to narrow it down to the element type of data stored in a collection? Fortunately, this is easy. You just need to broadcast the `identity` function (which returns its argument) over a collection. Then the broadcasting mechanisms that Julia has implemented will perform narrowing of the element type for you. Here you can see it in action:

```julia
julia> x = Any[1, 2, 3]
3-element Vector{Any}:
 1
 2
 3

julia> identity.(x)
3-element Vector{Int64}:
```

```
1
2
3

julia> y = Any[1, 2.0]
2-element Vector{Any}:
 1
 2.0

julia> identity.(y)
2-element Vector{Real}:
 1
 2.0
```

5.3 Integrating with Python

In this section, you will learn how to integrate Julia with Python when working with collections. You will see that conversion between collection types in Julia and in Python is done automatically. Knowing how to use Python code from Julia is useful, as in larger projects, you might need to build software from components that were developed using both technologies. I have chosen the example that we will use to additionally reinforce your understanding of how you can work with arrays in Julia and use broadcasting.

I have chosen to present integration with Python, as it is currently a very popular language. In chapter 10, you will learn how Julia and R can be integrated. If you would like to call C or Fortran code from Julia, refer to the Julia manual at http://mng.bz/0911. Bindings to other languages are provided by packages—for example, to C++ with Cxx.jl (https://github.com/JuliaInterop/Cxx.jl) or to Java with JavaCall.jl (https://github.com/JuliaInterop/JavaCall.jl).

5.3.1 Preparing data for dimensionality reduction using t-SNE

As an example application of integrating Julia with Python, I will show you how to perform dimensionality reduction using the t-SNE algorithm. *t-Distributed Stochastic Neighbor Embedding* (*t-SNE*) is a statistical method for giving each data point belonging to a high-dimensional space a location in a low-dimensional space (https://lvdmaaten.github.io/tsne/). In this case, we will use two-dimensional space as a target since it can then be easily visualized in a plot. The t-SNE performs a mapping in such a way that similar objects in the high-dimensional source space are nearby points in the low-dimensional target space, and dissimilar objects are distant points.

We start with generating random data in a five-dimensional space that we will later want to embed in two dimensions:

```
julia> using Random

julia> Random.seed!(1234);

julia> cluster1 = randn(100, 5) .- 1
100×5 Matrix{Float64}:
```

```
 -0.0293437   -0.737544    -0.613869   -1.31815    -2.95335
 -1.97922     -1.02224     -1.74252    -2.33397    -2.00848
    ⋮
 -1.55273     -1.09341     -0.823972   -3.41422    -2.21394
 -4.40253     -1.62642     -1.01099    -0.926064    0.0914986

julia> cluster2 = randn(100, 5) .+ 1
100×5 Matrix{Float64}:
   1.57447     1.40369      1.44851     1.27623     0.942008
   2.16312     1.88732      2.51227     0.533175   -0.520495
    ⋮
   1.47109     2.61912      1.80582     1.18953     1.41611
   2.77582     1.53736     -0.805129   -0.315228    1.35773
```

First, we use the `Random.seed!(1234)` command to set the seed of the random number generator in Julia. The name of the function is suffixed with `!` because it modifies the state of the global random number generator. This will ensure that the data I show you is the same as the data you obtain if you run this code under the same version of Julia. If you want to get different random numbers generated each time you run this code, skip setting the seed of the random number generator.

Next, using the `randn` function, we generate two matrices of 100 rows and five columns. The values stored in them are randomly sampled from standard normal distribution. Using broadcasting, we subtract 1 from all entries of the `cluster1` matrix and add 1 to all entries of the `cluster2` matrix. In this way, we separate points stored in both matrices. Data from cluster 1 is mostly negative, while in cluster 2, we have mostly positive entries.

Now, we vertically concatenate these matrices by using the `vcat` function to create a single matrix of 200 rows and five columns. We call the matrix `data5`, as it has five columns:

```
julia> data5 = vcat(cluster1, cluster2)
200×5 Matrix{Float64}:
 -0.0293437   -0.737544    -0.613869   -1.31815     -2.95335
 -1.97922     -1.02224     -1.74252    -2.33397     -2.00848
 -0.0981391   -1.39129     -1.87533    -1.76821     -1.23108
 -1.0328      -0.972379     0.600607   -0.0713489   -1.16386
    ⋮
  1.2327       2.37472      1.31467    -0.290594     3.00592
 -0.198159    -0.211778    -0.726857    0.194847     2.65386
  1.47109      2.61912      1.80582     1.18953      1.41611
  2.77582      1.53736     -0.805129   -0.315228     1.35773
```

We will want to see if, after using the t-SNE algorithm to perform dimensionality reduction to two dimensions, we will be able to visually confirm that these two clusters are indeed separated.

5.3.2 *Calling Python from Julia*

First, we need to load the required Python package by using the `pyimport` function from the PyCall.jl package:

```
julia> using PyCall

julia> manifold = pyimport("sklearn.manifold")
PyObject <module 'sklearn.manifold' from
'~\\.julia\\conda\\3\\lib\\site-packages\\sklearn\\manifold\\__init__.py'>
```

This operation could fail on your machine. If it does, the reason might be that either Python is not properly configured or `sklearn` from Python is not installed. You should receive information telling which operations you need to perform to fix this issue. If `sklearn` from Python is not installed, the following code is a standard way to add it:

```
using Conda
Conda.add("scikit-learn")
```

However, under some operating system configurations, this operation might fail. See the following sidebar for more options.

Using the PyCall.jl package to configure integration with Python

The PyCall.jl package allows you to interoperate with Python from the Julia language. It allows you to import Python modules from Julia, call Python functions (with automatic conversion of types), and even evaluate entire code blocks of Python code from Julia.

When you install PyCall.jl, then by default, on Mac and Windows systems, it will install a minimal Python distribution that is private to Julia. On GNU/Linux systems, the package will use the Python installation available in your PATH. Alternatively, you can use a different version of Python than the default, as explained on the PyCall.jl GitHub page (http://mng.bz/vXo1).

If you are on Mac or Windows and use the default configuration of Python, you can use the Conda.jl package to add packages to the Python distribution private to Julia. If you are on GNU/Linux, then, by default, you should be able to add packages by using the standard tools you use in your Python installation.

Unfortunately, unlike with Julia, which has a built-in standard package manager, properly configuring a Python environment and installing packages on your machine can sometimes be challenging. The PyCall.jl package maintainers have tried to make this process work automatically in most cases. However, if it fails, I recommend you refer to the PyCall.jl (https://github.com/JuliaPy/PyCall.jl) and Conda.jl (https://github.com/JuliaPy/Conda.jl) pages for more detailed instructions on resolving them.

After importing `sklearn.manifold` from Python and binding it to the `manifold` variable, we are ready to use the t-SNE algorithm. We store the result in the `data2` variable, as the resulting matrix has two columns after dimensionality reduction:

```
julia> tsne = manifold.TSNE(n_components=2, init="random",
                            learning_rate="auto", random_state=1234)
PyObject TSNE(init='random', learning_rate='auto', random_state=1234)
```

```
julia> data2 = tsne.fit_transform(data5)
200×2 Matrix{Float32}:
  1.25395   -14.9826
  0.448442  -12.2407
 -2.0488    -10.6652
  2.19538    -3.94876
  ⋮
  6.23544    10.1046
  5.49633     6.37504
 -1.82243    13.8231
  5.05417    13.2529
```

If you refer to the examples of using the t-SNE algorithm in the scikit-learn documentation (http://mng.bz/K0oZ), you can see that using Python in Julia is essentially transparent:

- You can call Python functions in exactly the same way as you would call them in Python. In particular, you can use dot (.) to refer to objects in the same way as in Python.
- An automatic conversion occurs between Julia and Python objects, so you do not have to think about it.

This level of integration means that using Python from Julia requires little mental effort for a developer. From my experience, most of the time, fixing the syntax differences is enough if you want to port some Python code to Julia, and things just work. For example, in Julia, string literals require double quotes ("), while typically in Python, a single quote (') is used.

This section presented only a minimal example of integrating Julia with Python. If you would like to learn more details, such as possible integration options, check the PyCall.jl package website at https://github.com/JuliaPy/PyCall.jl.

5.3.3   *Visualizing the results of the t-SNE algorithm*

To conclude our analysis, let's plot the `data2` matrix by using a scatterplot. We will color the first 100 points, representing cluster 1, with a different fill color than the last 100 points that are from cluster 2:

```
julia> using Plots

julia> scatter(data2[:, 1], data2[:, 2];
               color=[fill("black", 100); fill("gold", 100)],
               legend=false)
```

In this code, note the `[fill("black", 100); fill("gold", 100)]` expression. First, using the `fill` function, we create two vectors storing 100 constant values representing colors we want to use. Next, inside square brackets, using the semicolon (;), we vertically concatenate these two vectors to create a 200-element vector that is passed as a color keyword argument to the `scatter` function.

Figure 5.3 shows the resulting plot. Observe that, as expected, we have a separation of points from cluster 1 and cluster 2 (except for one outlier from cluster 1).

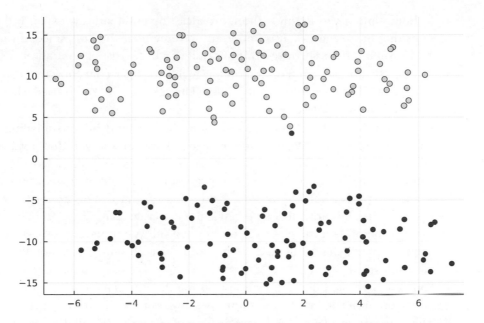

Figure 5.3 **Visualization of the result of t-SNE embedding. Data for clusters 1 and 2 (represented with different fill colors) are separated. The algorithm helps us identify one outlier in cluster 1; this is the black point that in embedded space is located closer to points from cluster 2.**

EXERCISE 5.2 Repeat the analysis presented in section 5.3, but instead of adding and subtracting 1 when creating data for clusters 1 and 2, add and subtract 0.4, respectively. This will reduce the separation between two clusters in five-dimensional space. Check to see if this will reduce their separation in the two-dimensional space generated by t-SNE.

Summary

- Julia provides four important ways to iterate over collections and transform them: loops, the map function (and other similar higher-order functions), comprehensions, and broadcasting. Each has slightly different rules of processing data. Therefore, you should choose one depending on your needs in a given situation.
- Most functions in Julia are defined to work on scalars. If you want to apply a function to a collection elementwise, you have to use one of the methods provided by Julia that allow you to iterate over collections.
- Broadcasting in Julia is a way to apply a function to a collection of values (an operation often called *vectorization* in other languages). You can broadcast any function (like sin or log) by suffixing it with a dot (.). Similarly, to vectorize an operator (like * or /), prefix it with a dot (.).
- Broadcasting in Julia is efficient, as it uses broadcast fusion. Julia does not need to allocate objects for storing intermediate results of processing data when executing complex broadcasted operations.

- In Julia, similarly to R and Python, broadcasting automatically expands dimensions that have length 1. It is important to remember this rule since, if you forget it, you might be surprised by the result of a broadcasting operation.
- If you have a broadcasted operation to which you pass a collection that you want to be treated as a scalar, wrap it in `Ref`. This approach is often used when performing a lookup into a reference table using the `in` function.
- When working with collections, you should understand Julia's subtyping rules for parametric types. Writing `Vector{Real}` specifies a type that a value can take. This value is a `Vector` that can store any `Real` number. On the other hand, `Vector{<:Real}` is used to represent a supertype of any `Vector` whose element type is a subtype of `Real`. No value can have the `Vector{<:Real}` type, because it is not a leaf type and is not concrete. Therefore, `Vector{Int}` is a subtype of `Vector{<:Real}` but is not a subtype of `Vector{Real}` (recall from chapter 3 that in Julia, if a type can have an instance, it is not allowed to have subtypes).
- You can integrate Julia with Python by using the PyCall.jl package. This integration is often needed when you want to use Python code in your Julia projects.
- The integration of Julia with Python provided by the PyCall.jl package allows you to call Python functions in exactly the same way as you would call them in Python, and an automatic conversion of collections between Julia and Python formats is performed. This means that using Python functionalities in Julia is easy, and only minimal changes in Python code are required to use them in Julia projects.

Working with strings

6

This chapter covers

- UTF-8 encoding of Julia strings; byte versus character indexing
- Manipulating strings: interpolation, splitting, using regular expressions, parsing
- Working with symbols
- Using the InlineStrings.jl package to work with fixed-width strings
- Using the PooledArrays.jl package to compress vectors of strings

In this chapter, you will learn how to handle text data in the Julia language. Text data is stored in strings. *Strings* are one of the most common data types that you will encounter when doing data science projects, especially involving natural language processing tasks.

As an application of string processing, we will analyze movie genres that were given ratings by Twitter users. We want to understand which movie genre is most common and how the relative frequency of this genre changes with the movie year.

For this analysis, we will use the movies.dat file. The file URL is http://mng.bz/ 9Vao, and the file is shared on the GitHub repository https://github.com/sidooms/ MovieTweetings under an MIT license.

We will analyze the movie genre data according to the following steps, which are described in the subsequent sections of this chapter and depicted in figure 6.1:

1 Get the data from the web.
2 Read in the data in Julia.
3 Parse the original data to extract the year and genre list for each analyzed movie.
4 Create frequency tables to find which movie genre is most common.
5 Create a plot of popularity of the most common genre by year.

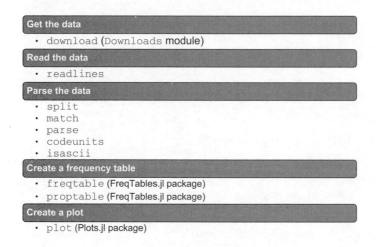

Figure 6.1   Steps of our analysis: each step lists the most important Julia functions used and the packages that provide them

Through the analysis, you will learn what it means that strings in Julia are UTF-8 encoded and how you should take this fact into account when working with strings.

At the end of this chapter, we will discuss performance issues when working with strings. You'll learn about the following:

- Using symbols instead of strings when analyzing text data
- Using fixed-width strings provided by the InlineStrings.jl package
- Compressing vectors of strings by using the PooledArrays.jl package

6.1 Getting and inspecting the data

In most data science workflows, the first task you will face is getting the data and reading it in before you can start analyzing it. Therefore, in this section, we start with learning how to download the source file from the web and inspect its contents (for your convenience, the file is also stored in the GitHub repository with the source code for this book).

6.1.1 Downloading files from the web

First, download the data, as shown in the next listing.

Listing 6.1 Fetching the movies.dat file from GitHub

```
julia> import Downloads
julia> Downloads.download("https://raw.githubusercontent.com/" *
                          "sidooms/MovieTweetings/" *
                          "44c525d0c766944910686c60697203cda39305d6/" *
                          "snapshots/10K/movies.dat",
                          "movies.dat")
"movies.dat"
```

We use the `download` function from the `Downloads` module that takes two arguments: the URL location of the file to fetch and the location path where it should be saved. In this case, we save the file as movies.dat in the working directory of Julia.

> **Downloading files on Julia versions earlier than 1.6**
>
> In Julia versions earlier than 1.6, the `download` function was available without having to use the `Downloads` module. Although this function is still available in Julia 1.7 (the version used in this book), it is deprecated, so I recommend you use the `Downloads` module.

Observe that in the preceding example, both arguments of the `download` function are string literals. Notice two important points:

- String literals are enclosed in double quotes (`"`).
- You can concatenate string literals by using the multiplication operator (`*`). In the preceding example, we split a long string into multiple lines of code and concatenated it by using `*` (in Python, you would use the addition operator (`+`) to concatenate strings).

Let me briefly comment next on several standard features that Julia strings support.

6.1.2 Using common techniques of string construction

The first convenient feature is that you can interpolate variables into strings by using $ inside a string literal. Here is an example:

```
julia> x = 10
10

julia> "I have $x apples"
"I have 10 apples"
```

In this code, the value bound to variable x is interpolated into the string, as we write $x inside the string literal. You can also interpolate more complex expressions this way, but then you need to wrap them in parentheses:

```
julia> "I have $(2 * x) apples"
"I have 20 apples"
```

The second feature is that you can use C's traditional escaped input forms (https://en.cppreference.com/w/cpp/language/escape) in string literals; for example, to create a string containing a newline, use the \n sequence. For instance, the string literal "a\nb" consists of three characters: a, followed by a newline, and finally b.

In addition to standard escape sequences, Julia introduces two extra ones. To write $, you need to escape it with \$. Unescaped $ is used for interpolation, as I have explained. Here is an example of the \$ escape sequence at work, showing you that using just $ leads to an error:

```
julia> "I have \$100."
"I have \$100.                ⟵⎯⎤  Julia displays strings in an interactive
                                  │  session by using an escaped form.
julia> "I have $100."
ERROR: syntax: invalid interpolation syntax: "$1"
```

The second extension is \ immediately followed by a newline. This sequence allows you to split long strings into multiple lines. Therefore, instead of using * in listing 6.1, we could have written this to get the same result:

```
Downloads.download("https://raw.githubusercontent.com/\
            sidooms/MovieTweetings/\
            44c525d0c766944910686c60697203cda39305d6/\
            snapshots/10K/movies.dat",
            "movies.dat")
```

In this case, the newline following the \ and any leading whitespace (typically used for code indentation) in the following line are ignored, as you can see here:

```
julia> "a\
       b\
       c"
"abc"
```

Sometimes you might want to avoid both special handling of C's escaped input forms and interpolation. You can easily avoid them by using the raw prefix in front of the string literal (these literals are then called *raw string literals*). I use this feature most often when I work on Windows and need to write paths. Here is an example. If you try writing a standard Windows path in a standard string literal, most likely you will get an error:

```
julia> "C:\my_folder\my_file.txt"
ERROR: syntax: invalid escape sequence
```

This error occurs because Julia treats \m as an invalid escape sequence. We can easily fix this problem with the raw prefix:

```
julia> raw"C:\my_folder\my_file.txt"
"C:\\my_folder\\my_file.txt"
```

Everything works this time. Note that the string is still displayed as a standard string. Each \ character is displayed as \\ because this is the escape sequence interpreted as \ in standard strings. If you would like to print the undecorated text representation of the string, use the print function:

```
julia> print(raw"C:\my_folder\my_file.txt")
C:\my_folder\my_file.txt
```

The second special string literal that you might encounter in Julia code is the triple quoted string. These literals begin and end with three quotes ("""). They are typically used to create longer blocks of text that span multiple lines. We do not use these literals in this book, but if you are interested in the details, you can find them in the Julia Manual at http://mng.bz/jAjp.

Now that you know the basics of creating string literals, let's see how to read strings from disk. First, we check that the movies.dat file was downloaded by using the isfile function to see if the file is present in the current working directory:

```
julia> isfile("movies.dat")
true
```

6.1.3 Reading the contents of a file

The function returns true, which means that the file is present. Let's read its contents line by line and bind the result to the movies variable in the next listing.

Listing 6.2 Reading the movies.dat file into a vector

```
julia> movies = readlines("movies.dat")
3096-element Vector{String}:
 "0002844::Fantômas - À l'ombre de la guillotine (1913)::Crime|Drama"
 "0007264::The Rink (1916)::Comedy|Short"
 "0008133::The Immigrant (1917)::Short|Comedy|Drama|Romance"
 "0012349::The Kid (1921)::Comedy|Drama|Family"
 ⋮
 "2748368::Neil (2013)::Short|Comedy"
 "2750600::A Different Tree (2013)::Short|Drama|Family"
 "2763252::Broken Night (2013)::Short|Drama"
 "2769592::Kiss Shot Truth or Dare (2013)::Short"
```

The readlines function reads all lines from the file as a vector of strings. Each string in the vector represents one line of our data.

Looking at the data, we can see that each entry about a movie (line in a file) has the following structure:

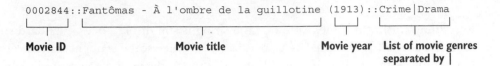

Movie ID   **Movie title**   **Movie year** **List of movie genres separated by |**

The first part is the movie's numeric identifier of a movie. It is followed, after the :: separator, by the movie title. Next follows the movie year in parentheses. Finally, after the next :: separator, we have genres that match the movie. If we have several genres, they are separated by a pipe (|).

6.2   *Splitting strings*

When working with data, you often face a challenge because it has to be preprocessed before it can be used for analysis. The most basic type of preprocessing is splitting strings containing multiple pieces of information. This is the skill that you will learn in this section.

For each movie, we'll extract the year of the movie from this string along with a list of its genres. However, before we do that for all strings, I'll show you how to do it on the first string in the list. We start by extracting it:

```
julia> movie1 = first(movies)
"0002844::Fantômas - À l'ombre de la guillotine (1913)::Crime|Drama"
```

Note that we have used the `first` function to fetch the first element of the vector `movies`. The first function we will use to work with this string is `split`. It takes two arguments: the string to split and a delimiter on which the string should be split. By default, the delimiter is whitespace, but in our case, we will first want to use ::. Let's try using the `split` function:

```
julia> movie1_parts = split(movie1, "::")
3-element Vector{SubString{String}}:
 "0002844"
 "Fantômas - À l'ombre de la guillotine (1913)"
 "Crime|Drama"
```

The `movie1_parts` variable now holds a vector of three strings, as expected.

You might have noticed that the `movies` vector has the type `Vector{String}`, while the `movie1_parts` vector has the type `Vector{SubString{String}}`. This is because Julia, for efficiency, when splitting a string with the `split` function, does not copy the string but instead creates a `SubString{String}` object that points to the slice of the original string. Having this behavior is safe, as strings in Julia are immutable (we already talked about mutable and immutable types in chapter 4).

Therefore, once the string is created, its contents cannot be changed. Creation of a substring of a string is guaranteed to be a safe operation. In your code, if you want to create a `SubString{String}`, you can use the `view` function or the `@view` macro on a `String`.

Since `String` and `SubString{String}` are both strings, there must be a more general, abstract concept of a string in Julia. Indeed, there is:

```
julia> supertype(String)
AbstractString

julia> supertype(SubString{String})
AbstractString
```

Both string types that we have encountered are subtypes of `AbstractString`. In Julia, `AbstractString` is the type representing all strings (in this chapter, we will soon discuss even more subtypes of this type).

When should AbstractString be used?

When annotating types of function arguments that should be strings, use `AbstractString` instead of `String` (unless you really require the `String` type, which is rare).

For instance, this is a good style of defining a function:

```
suffix_bang(s::AbstractString) = s * "!"
```

Using a `String` instead of `AbstractString` in this definition is not recommended, as then this function would not work with `SubString{String}` arguments.

The `split` function is one of many that are available in Base Julia for working with strings. You can find documentation for all of them in the "Strings" section of the Julia Manual (https://docs.julialang.org/en/v1/base/strings/). Here are several of the commonly used ones:

- `string`—Converts passed values to a string by using the `print` function
- `join`—Joins elements of an iterator into a string, inserting the given delimiter between joined items
- `occursin`—Checks if the first argument is a substring of the second argument
- `contains`—Checks if the second argument is a substring of the first argument
- `replace`—Finds in a given string passed patterns and replaces them with specified values
- `strip`—Strips leading and trailing characters (by default, whitespace) from a string (also related are `lstrip` and `rstrip` for stripping leading and trailing characters)
- `startswith`—Checks if a given string starts with a passed prefix

- endswith—Checks if a given string ends with a passed suffix
- uppercase—Uppercases a string
- lowercase—Lowercases a string
- randstring—Creates random strings (defined in the Random module)

6.3 *Using regular expressions to work with strings*

In the previous section, you learned to extract information from strings by using the split function when data is separated by a fixed character sequence. Now we move on to discussing how to use regular expressions to extract portions of a string following more general patterns.

Once we have created the movie1_parts variable, we can split its second element into movie name and year:

```
julia> movie1_parts[2]
"Fantômas - À l'ombre de la guillotine (1913)"
```

We will accomplish this by using regular expressions (www.regular-expressions.info).

6.3.1 *Working with regular expressions*

The topic of how to write regular expressions is wide; I recommend *Mastering Regular Expressions* by Jeffrey E. F. Friedl (O'Reilly, 2006) if you want to learn more about it. Julia supports Perl-compatible regular expressions, as provided by the Perl-Compatible Regular Expressions (PCRE) library (www.pcre.org). Here I show you the regular expression we will use and how to write regular expression literals in Julia:

```
julia> rx = r"(.+) \((\d{4})\)$"
r"(.+) \((\d{4})\)$"
```

To create a regular expression literal, prefix a string literal with the letter r. The meaning of this regular expression is explained in figure 6.2. Its most important part is that we create two capturing groups by using parentheses. A *capturing group* is a way to retrieve parts of the string that we match against a regular expression. In our example, we have designed two capturing groups: the first one will contain the movie name, and the second one will contain the movie year.

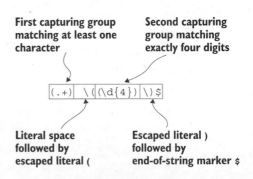

Figure 6.2 Interpretation of the r"(.+) \((\d{4})\)$" **regular expression**

You can easily match a regular expression against a string in Julia by using the match function:

```
julia> m = match(rx, movie1_parts[2])
RegexMatch("Fantômas - À l'ombre de la guillotine (1913)",
1="Fantômas - À l'ombre de la guillotine", 2="1913")
```

The m variable is bound to the object representing the result of matching the rx regular expression to the movie1_parts[2] string. When the object is displayed, we see that it has captured two groups, as expected. These groups can be easily retrieved from the m object by using indexing:

```
julia> m[1]
"Fantômas - À l'ombre de la guillotine"

julia> m[2]
"1913"
```

This approach is quite convenient. If we want to store the year as a number, we should parse it by using the parse function that we already discussed in chapter 5:

```
julia> parse(Int, m[2])
1913
```

This was a brief tutorial on regular expressions in Julia. I recommend you read the entire "Regular Expressions" section in the Julia Manual (http://mng.bz/WMBw) if you would like to learn more about how to use them.

6.3.2 *Writing a parser of a single line of movies.dat file*

We now have all the pieces to write a parser of a single line of the movies.dat file. I recommend defining this parser as a function. The next listing shows how you could define it.

> **Listing 6.3 Function parsing a single line of the movies.dat file**

```
function parseline(line::AbstractString)
    parts = split(line, "::")
    m = match(r"(.+) \((\d{4})\)", parts[2])
    return (id=parts[1],
            name=m[1],
            year=parse(Int, m[2]),
            genres=split(parts[3], "|"))
end
```

The parseline function takes a single line from our file and returns a NamedTuple containing the movie ID, name, year, and a list of genres. You can find all the parts of parsing of the line explained in sections 6.1.2 and 6.1.3. I will just comment that the expression split(parts[3], "|")) takes the third element of the parts vector, which contains a list of genres separated by a pipe (|), and then splits it again.

Let's see how the function works on the first line of our file:

```
julia> record1 = parseline(movie1)
(id = "0002844", name = "Fantômas - À l'ombre de la guillotine",
 year = 1913, genres = SubString{String}["Crime", "Drama"])
```

The obtained result is correct and follows what we expected. For example, to get a string with the name of the first movie, we can write record1.name.

6.4   *Extracting a subset from a string with indexing*

Before we move forward with our analysis of the movies.dat file, let's pause for a moment to discuss how strings are indexed in Julia. String indexing is often used to extract a subset of a string.

6.4.1   *UTF-8 encoding of strings in Julia*

To understand string indexing, you must know the fundamentals of UTF-8 encoding (http://mng.bz/49jD).

UTF-8 is a standard describing how individual characters in a string are represented by bytes. Its special feature is that different characters can use 1, 2, 3, or 4 bytes. This standard is the most frequently used today (http://mng.bz/QnWR), and, in particular, is followed in Julia. You can check the sequence of bytes in a given string by using the `codeunits` function. The following listing shows examples of strings consisting of one character, but having a different number of code units.

> **Listing 6.4   UTF-8 encodings of single-character strings with different byte lengths**

```
julia> codeunits("a")
1-element Base.CodeUnits{UInt8, String}:
 0x61

julia> codeunits("?")
2-element Base.CodeUnits{UInt8, String}:
 0xce
 0xb5

julia> codeunits("∀")
3-element Base.CodeUnits{UInt8, String}:
 0xe2
 0x88
 0x80
```

To understand the implications of a single character possibly using up a varying number of bytes, let's investigate the `record1.name` string that we created in section 6.3.2. To reduce the output in our analysis, we will restrict it to the first word in this string, which is *Fantômas*. We see that it consists of eight characters, so we will extract them from our string by using the `first` function:

```
julia> word = first(record1.name, 8)
"Fantômas"
```

The `first` function in this case takes two arguments: a string and the number of characters to take from its front—eight, in our case. You might wonder if we could have treated a string as a collection of characters and extracted them by using indexing. Let's try:

```
julia> record1.name[1:8]
"Fantôma"
```

6.4.2 Character vs. byte indexing of strings

The code works but produces an unexpected result. For some reason, Julia strips the last letter from the name. Why? The problem is that string indexing in Julia uses not character but byte offsets, and the letter ô in UTF-8 is encoded using 2 bytes. We can check this by using the `eachindex` function that you learned in chapter 5

```julia
julia> for i in eachindex(word)
           println(i, ": ", word[i])
       end
1: F
2: a
3: n
4: t
5: ô
7: m
8: a
9: s
```

or by using the `codeunits` function on the string consisting of a single letter ô:

```julia
julia> codeunits("ô")
2-element Base.CodeUnits{UInt8, String}:
 0xc3
 0xb4
```

Let's have a look at the code units that the `Fantômas` string consists of:

```julia
julia> codeunits("Fantômas")

9-element Base.CodeUnits{UInt8, String}:
 0x46
 0x61
 0x6e
 0x74
 0xc3
 0xb4
 0x6d
 0x61
 0x73
```

Indeed, we see that ô has a byte index equal to 5, but the next letter m has a byte index equal to 7, since ô is encoded using 2 bytes. In figure 6.3, you can see the mapping of characters, bytes (code units), byte index, and character index for the `Fantômas` string.

Character ⟶	F	a	n	t	ô		m	a	s
Byte (code unit) ⟶	0x46	0x61	0x6e	0x74	0xc3	0xb4	0x6d	0x61	0x73
Byte index ⟶	1	2	3	4	5	6	7	8	9
Character index ⟶	1	2	3	4	5		6	7	8

Figure 6.3 Mapping of characters, bytes (code units), byte index, and character index for the `Fantômas` string

This behavior of string indexing might at first be quite surprising. The reason for this behavior is that, depending on the context, you might want to perform either byte indexing or character indexing of your string, and Julia provides both options. Usually, when you need to parse nonstandard input data (for example, coming from an IoT sensor), you will need to work with bytes, and when you are processing standard text, you will need to work with characters.

Therefore, you must always check when using a function to see whether it works with byte indices or character indices. You have already seen that indexing using square brackets uses byte indexing and that the function `first` uses character counts. In my blog post "The String, or There and Back Again" (http://mng.bz/XaW1), I have created a glossary of the most commonly used functions when working with strings, including the kinds of indexing they use.

Using character counts when working with strings

In data science workflows, you will most commonly want to operate on strings using character counts, not byte indexing. Therefore, it is recommended that you do not index into strings using square brackets.

For matching complex patterns, use regular expressions. For simpler scenarios, here is a list of the most useful functions that use character counts for working with strings with an example usage:

- `length("abc")`—Returns the number of characters in a string; produces `3`.
- `chop("abcd", head=1, tail=2)`—Removes a given number of characters from the head or tail of the string. In this case, we strip one character from `head` and two from `tail`, producing `"b"`.
- `first("abc", 2)`—Returns a string consisting of the first two characters in the string; produces `"ab"`.
- `last("abc", 2)`—Returns a string consisting of the last two characters in the string; produces `"bc"`.

6.4.3   ASCII strings

In one case, byte and character indexing are guaranteed to produce the same result. This happens when your string consists only of ASCII characters. The most important examples of such characters are the digits 0 to 9, lowercase letters a to z, uppercase letters A to Z, and common symbols like !, +, -, *,), and (. Generally, any character that can be typed without using meta keys on a standard US keyboard is an ASCII character.

An important feature of ASCII characters is that they are always represented by a single byte in UTF-8 encoding. In Julia, you can easily check whether your string consists of only ASCII characters by using the `isascii` function:

```
julia> isascii("Hello world!")
true

julia> isascii("∀ x: x?0")
false
```

In the first case, the `Hello world!` string consists of only letters, a space, and an exclamation mark, which are all ASCII characters. In the second example, the ∀ and ? characters are not ASCII.

6.4.4   The Char type

Before I wrap up this discussion about indexing, let me briefly mention that when you pick a single character from a string by using indexing, you do not get a single-character string, as in R or Python, but rather a separate character type that is called `Char`. Here is an example:

```julia
julia> word[1]
'F': ASCII/Unicode U+0046 (category Lu: Letter, uppercase)

julia> word[5]
'ô': Unicode U+00F4 (category Ll: Letter, lowercase)
```

We do not need to work with single characters in this book, so I leave out all the details of how to use them. However, if you do a lot of natural language processing, I recommend reading the "Characters" section of the Julia Manual (http://mng.bz/820B).

6.5   Analyzing genre frequency in movies.dat

We are now ready to analyze movie genres in the movies.dat file. By doing this, you will learn how to create frequency tables, which are often used to summarize data.

Recall that we want to perform two tasks: find which movie genres are most common and understand how the relative frequency of a genre changes with the movie year.

6.5.1   Finding common movie genres

We start with the `movies` variable defined in listing 6.2 and process this vector by using the `parseline` function defined in listing 6.3:

```julia
julia> records = parseline.(movies)
3096-element Vector{NamedTuple{(:id, :name, :year, :genres),
Tuple{SubString{String}, SubString{String}, Int64,
Vector{SubString{String}}}}}:
 (id = "0002844", name = "Fantômas - À l'ombre de la guillotine",
  year = 1913, genres = ["Crime", "Drama"])
 (id = "0007264", name = "The Rink", year = 1916,
  genres = ["Comedy", "Short"])
 (id = "0008133", name = "The Immigrant", year = 1917,
  genres = ["Short", "Comedy", "Drama", "Romance"])
 (id = "0012349", name = "The Kid", year = 1921,
  genres = ["Comedy", "Drama", "Family"])
 ⋮
 (id = "2748368", name = "Neil", year = 2013, genres = ["Short", "Comedy"])
 (id = "2750600", name = "A Different Tree", year = 2013,
  genres = ["Short", "Drama", "Family"])
 (id = "2763252", name = "Broken Night", year = 2013,
  genres = ["Short", "Drama"])
 (id = "2769592", name = "Kiss Shot Truth or Dare", year = 2013,
  genres = ["Short"])
```

We add a dot (.) after the `parseline` function, which means that we are broadcasting it over all elements of the `movies` collection. As a result, we get a vector of named `tuples` describing the movies we want to analyze.

Let's first find out which genre is the most frequent in our data set. We will do this task in two steps:

1 Create a single vector containing genres from all movies we analyze.
2 Create a frequency table of this vector by using the `freqtable` function from the FreqTables.jl package.

The first step is to create a single vector of movie genres. We could perform this task in several ways. Here we will use the `append!` function, which appends one vector to another vector in place. Our code will start with an empty vector that can store strings and consecutively append to it vectors containing genres of all movies. Here is the code:

```
julia> genres = String[]
String[]

julia> for record in records
           append!(genres, record.genres)
       end

julia> genres
8121-element Vector{String}:
 "Crime"
 "Drama"
 "Comedy"
 "Short"
 ⋮
 "Family"
 "Short"
 "Drama"
 "Short"
```

The `append!` function takes two arguments. The first one is the vector to which we want to append data, and the second is the vector containing data to be appended.

Note one important detail in this code. The `genres` variable is a vector that stores `String` values. On the other hand, as we already discussed, `record.genres` is a collection of `SubString{String}` values. When you perform the `append!` operation, the `SubString{String}` values are automatically converted to `String`. This causes allocation of new strings in memory (recall that the point of using `Sub-String{String}` in the `split` function is to avoid such allocations). Since our data is small, I have decided that this is not a problem, as the extra execution time and memory consumption caused by this approach are negligible in this case.

Now we are ready to create a frequency table. We will perform this task in three steps:

1 Load the FreqTables.jl package.
2 Create a frequency table by using the `freqtable` function.

3 Sort the result in place by using the `sort!` function to find the least and most frequent genres.

Here is the code that performs this task:

```julia
julia> using FreqTables

julia> table = freqtable(genres)
25-element Named Vector{Int64}
Dim1          |
──────────────┼──────
              │   14
Action        │  635
Adventure     │  443
⋮             │    ⋮
Thriller      │  910
War           │  126
Western       │   35

julia> sort!(table)
25-element Named Vector{Int64}
Dim1          |
──────────────┼──────
News          │    4
Film-Noir     │   13
              │   14
⋮             │    ⋮
Thriller      │  910
Comedy        │ 1001
Drama         │ 1583
```

Note that the `freqtable` function returns a nonstandard array of type `Named-Vector`. This type allows you to use named indices. In our example, the names of the indices are genres. This type is defined in the NamedArrays.jl package, and you can find more information about how to work with it at https://github.com/davidavdav/NamedArrays.jl. Here, let me just mention that you can get access to the indices' names by using the `names` function and that sorting such arrays performs sorting on values (not on indices).

6.5.2 Understanding genre popularity evolution over the years

We have learned that `Drama` is the most frequent genre. We are now ready to find out how often this genre is present as a function of the movie year. We will do this analysis in the following steps:

1 Extract the year of each movie to a vector.
2 For each movie, check whether it has `Drama` as one of its genres.
3 Create a frequency table of proportions of the occurrence of `Drama` in movie genres by year.

Here is the code that accomplishes this task:

```julia
julia> years = [record.year for record in records]
3096-element Vector{Int64}:
 1913
 1916
 1917
 1921
    ⋮
 2013
 2013
 2013
 2013

julia> has_drama = ["Drama" in record.genres for record in records]
3096-element Vector{Bool}:
 1
 0
 1
 1
 ⋮
 0
 1
 1
 0

julia> drama_prop = proptable(years, has_drama; margins=1)
93×2 Named Matrix{Float64}
Dim1 ? Dim2 │    false      true
────────────┼──────────────────────
1913        │      0.0       1.0
1916        │      1.0       0.0
1917        │      0.0       1.0
⋮           │        ⋮         ⋮
2011        │ 0.484472  0.515528
2012        │ 0.577017  0.422983
2013        │ 0.623529  0.376471
```

In this code, to create both `years` and `has_drama` vectors, we use comprehensions. To check whether `Drama` is one of the genres, we use the `in` operator that we discussed in chapter 5. Finally, to calculate a frequency table of proportions, we use the `proptable` function from the FreqTables.jl package. We pass to it both `year` and `has_data` variables to create a cross-tabulation, and by passing `margins=1`, we are asking to compute the proportions over the first dimension (that is, rows). In this case, since the first variable passed to `proptable` is `year` and the second is `has_drama`, the proportions are calculated for each year. Observe that `proptable` automatically sorts its dimensions by the dimension values.

The `drama_prop` table is nice but is not easy to analyze. Let's create a plot of year against the proportion of the presence of `Drama` in the next listing.

> **Listing 6.5 Plotting the proportion of drama movies by year**

```julia
julia> using Plots

julia> plot(names(drama_prop, 1), drama_prop[:, 2]; legend=false,
            xlabel="year", ylabel="Drama probability")
```

We extract the years from the first axes of the drama_prop matrix by using the names function. To get the proportion of Drama by year, we extract the second column by using drama_prop[:, 2]. We additionally opt out from showing a plot legend and create labels for the *x* and *y* axes. Figure 6.4 shows the result.

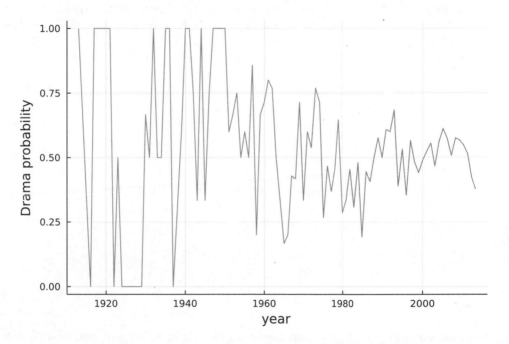

Figure 6.4 In plotting the proportion of the Drama genre as a function of year, no significant trend is visible.

As you can see in figure 6.4, no strong trend seems to be present. So, the Drama genre seems stable over the years. However, we can see that the variability of the Drama probability decreases with the year. This is most likely because in the initial years, there were few movies. Checking this is your exercise.

EXERCISE 6.1 Create a plot of the number of movies by year, using the years variable.

6.6   *Introducing symbols*

In some data science scenarios, you want to use strings as labels or tags of objects—for example, to denote a color of a product. You typically do not want to manipulate these labels; the only operation you perform on them is comparison for equality, and you want it to be very fast.

Julia has a special type called Symbol, which is similar to a string, that has exactly these features. This section first explains how to create values that have a Symbol type and then discusses their pros and cons in comparison to strings.

6.6.1   *Creating symbols*

Before I show you how to work with the Symbol type, you first need to learn how to construct these objects. You can create a value that has a Symbol type in two ways

The first is to call Symbol, passing it any value or sequence of values. Here are three examples:

```
julia> s1 = Symbol("x")
:x

julia> s2 = Symbol("hello world!")
Symbol("hello world!")

julia> s3 = Symbol("x", 1)
:x1
```

All three values bound to variables s1, s2, and s3 have the type Symbol:

```
julia> typeof(s1)
Symbol

julia> typeof(s2)
Symbol

julia> typeof(s3)
Symbol
```

Note two important points in this example. First, when you pass several values to Symbol, as in Symbol("x", 1), their string representations are concatenated.

Second, and more importantly, you can see that symbols are displayed using two styles. The first style is :x and :x1, and the second is more verbose: Symbol("hello world!").

You might wonder what rules govern this. The short style is used for printing a Symbol if it contains only characters that form a valid variable name. In this example, we use a space between the words hello and world, and since using a space in a variable name is not allowed, printing is done in the verbose form.

Here is one more example of the same rule at work:

```
julia> Symbol("1")
Symbol("1")
```

Since 1 is not a valid variable name (it is an integer literal), we get the symbol printed in a verbose form.

You might have guessed the second style that can be used to create symbols. If, and only if, the sequence of characters that we want to use to represent a Symbol is a valid variable name, we can prefix it with a colon (:) to create a Symbol value. Therefore, the following operations are valid:

```
julia> :x
:x

julia> :x1
:x1
```

However, remember that this syntax is not correct if the sequence of characters is not a valid variable name. Here is an example:

```
julia> :hello world
ERROR: syntax: extra token "world" after end of expression
```

We get an error. And here is a second example:

```
julia> :1
1
```

Here, we do not get an error, but instead of getting a Symbol, we get an integer 1.

6.6.2 Using symbols

You know how to create a value that has a Symbol type. Now we'll focus on working with them.

As I have mentioned, the Symbol type looks similar to a string, but it is not one. We can check this by testing its supertype:

```
julia> supertype(Symbol)
Any
```

Here, we see that the type is Any, not AbstractString. This means that no functions that operate on strings will work with values having a Symbol type. The only operation that in practice is useful on symbols in typical data science workflows is an equality comparison. So, we can write this:

```
julia> :x == :x
true

julia> :x == :y
false
```

The point is that an equality comparison for symbols is fast, much faster than testing strings for equality. The next listing shows a simple benchmark, in which we look for a value in a vector of one million elements.

Listing 6.6   Comparing the performance of working with `String` vs. `Symbol`

```
julia> using BenchmarkTools

julia> str = string.("x", 1:10^6)        ◁─┐  Creates a vector
1000000-element Vector{String}:             │  of String values
 "x1"
 "x2"
 "x3"
 ⋮
 "x999998"
 "x999999"
 "x1000000"

julia> symb = Symbol.(str)               ◁─┐  Creates a vector
1000000-element Vector{Symbol}:             │  of Symbol values
 :x1
 :x2
 :x3
 ⋮
 :x999998
 :x999999
 :x1000000
                                      Measures the performance of a value
                                      lookup in a vector of String values
julia> @btime "x" in $str;      ◁─┘
5.078 ms (0 allocations: 0 bytes)
                                      Measures the performance of a value
                                      lookup in a vector of Symbol values
julia> @btime :x in $symb;      ◁─┘
433.000 μs (0 allocations: 0 bytes)
```

Here we have two vectors: `str` consisting of `String`, and `symb` containing `Symbol` values. The benchmark results show that the lookup using symbols is, in this case, over 10 times faster than when we use strings.

You might ask how this is achieved. The trick is that Julia internally keeps a global pool of all symbols. If you introduce a new `Symbol`, Julia first checks whether it is already present in this pool, and if so, Julia reuses it. Therefore, when you compare two symbols, you can compare their address in memory without having to check their content.

This behavior has two additional consequences. On one hand, defining many identical symbols does not allocate new memory, as they will point to the same reference value. On the other hand, once `Symbol` is allocated in the global pool, it stays there until the end of the Julia session, which sometimes might look like a memory leak in the Julia program if you create a very large number of unique symbols.

Choosing between string and Symbol in your code

As a general recommendation, you should prefer strings over `Symbol` in your programs. Strings are more flexible and have multiple functions taking them as arguments. However, if you need to perform a lot of comparisons of string-like values in your program, but you do not expect to have to manipulate these values and you require maximum performance, you can consider using `Symbol`.

Before I wrap up the discussion of symbols, let me note that in this section, I have concentrated on symbols being used as data. Another application of symbols in Julia is for *metaprogramming*—programmatic manipulation of Julia code. We do not cover this advanced topic in this book, but if you would like to learn more about it, I recommend the "Metaprogramming" section in the Julia Manual (http://mng.bz/E0Dj) as a good place to start.

6.7   Using fixed-width string types to improve performance

In many data science workflows, we work with strings consisting of only a few characters. Think of codes of US states that consist of two letters, or the standard US ZIP code that consists of five digits. If you happen to work with such strings, Julia provides an even more efficient storage format than the standard `String` or `Symbol`.

6.7.1   Available fixed-width strings

These advanced string types are defined in the InlineStrings.jl package. Just like the standard `String` type, these string types are UTF-8 encoded, but they differ from the standard `String` type in two ways:

- As a benefit, they are as fast to work with as numbers (technically, they do not require being dynamically allocated in memory).
- As a limitation, they have a fixed maximum size in bytes.

The InlineStrings.jl package provides eight fixed-width string types:

- `String1`—Size up to 1 byte
- `String3`—Size up to 3 bytes
- `String7`—Size up to 7 bytes
- `String15`—Size up to 15 bytes
- `String31`—Size up to 31 bytes
- `String63`—Size up to 63 bytes
- `String127`—Size up to 127 bytes
- `String255`—Size up to 255 bytes

In practice, if you want to use these strings, you can pick the appropriate type manually, but typically, it is recommended to automatically perform type selection. If you call the `InlineString` function on a string, it will be converted to the narrowest fixed-width string that it matches. Similarly, if you call the `inlinestrings` function on a collection of strings, an appropriate common narrowest type for all passed strings will be automatically selected. Here are some examples of these functions at work:

```
julia> using InlineStrings

julia> s1 = InlineString("x")
"x"

julia> typeof(s1)
String1
```

```
julia> s2 = InlineString("∀")
"∀"

julia> typeof(s2)
String3

julia> sv = inlinestrings(["The", "quick", "brown", "fox", "jumps",
                           "over", "the", "lazy", "dog"])
9-element Vector{String7}:
 "The"
 "quick"
 "brown"
 "fox"
 "jumps"
 "over"
 "the"
 "lazy"
 "dog"
```

In this example, we can see that the "x" string can be encoded as String1 since the x character is represented by 1 byte in UTF-8 encoding. On the other hand, the ∀ character, as you have seen in listing 6.4, is represented using 3 bytes in UTF-8, so "∀" is converted to String3. In the last example of the sv variable, we have several strings, but none uses more than 7 bytes, while some are longer than 3 bytes. Therefore, as a result of the operation, we get a vector of String7 values.

6.7.2 *Performance of fixed-width strings*

To show you the potential benefits of using the string types defined in the Inline-Strings.jl package, let's perform a simple experiment. We want to generate a vector of strings in two variants: one using the String type, and the other using the fixed-width string.

Then we will perform two checks. In the first, we will see how much memory is required by the objects stored in both vectors. In the second, we will benchmark how fast Julia can sort these vectors. We start with setting up the data in the next listing.

Listing 6.7 **Setting up the data for performance comparison of different string types**

```
julia> using Random

julia> using BenchmarkTools

julia> Random.seed!(1234);          ◁──┐  Sets random number
                                         generator seed to ensure
                                         reproducibility of the example

julia> s1 = [randstring(3) for i in 1:10^6]    ◁──┐  Generates a vector of random
1000000-element Vector{String}:                     strings of type String
 "KYD"
 "tLO"
 "xnU"
 ⋮
 "Tt6"
```

```
 "19y"
 "GQ7"

julia> s2 = inlinestrings(s1)          ◁──┐  Converts the vector to a vector of
1000000-element Vector{String3}:          │  values having the String3 type
 "KYD"
 "tLO"
 "xnU"
?
 "Tt6"
 "19y"
 "GQ7"
```

We first load the required packages Random and BenchmarkTools. Next, we set the seed of the Julia random number generator with the Random.seed!(1234) command. I perform this step to ensure that, if you are on the same version of Julia used to write this book, you will get the same data as is shown in listing 6.7.

Then we generate a vector consisting of one million random strings of the String type, using a comprehension and the randstring function to generate random strings. We use the randstring(3) call to make sure our strings consist of three characters. Finally, using the inlinestrings function, we create a vector of String3 strings and bind it to the s2 variable. Since all our strings consist of three ASCII characters, the String3 type is automatically detected by the inlinestrings function.

Our test is to compare how much memory, in bytes, is used by all objects stored in vectors s1 and s2 by using the function Base.summarysize:

```
julia> Base.summarysize(s1)
19000040

julia> Base.summarysize(s2)
4000040
```

In this case, the s2 vector uses less than 25% of the memory used by the s1 vector, as our strings are short and have a uniform length.

The second test checks the performance of sorting both the s1 and s2 vectors:

```
julia> @btime sort($s1);
  227.507 ms (4 allocations: 11.44 MiB)

julia> @btime sort($s2);
  6.019 ms (6 allocations: 7.65 MiB)
```

In this case, we can see that sorting s2 is around 40 times faster than sorting s1.

In part 2 of this book, you will learn that when getting your data from a CSV file, the Julia CSV reader can automatically detect that it is useful to use fixed-width strings instead of the standard String type. Therefore, in practice, it is usually enough to be aware of the existence and meaning of fixed-width strings, so that when you see them in a data frame, you are not surprised to encounter a column consisting of String3 strings.

EXERCISE 6.2   Using the s1 vector from listing 6.7, create the s3 vector consisting of symbols representing the same strings contained in the s1 vector. Next, benchmark how fast you can sort the s3 vector. Finally, benchmark how fast you can de-duplicate the s1, s2, and s3 vectors by using the unique function.

6.8   *Compressing vectors of strings with PooledArrays.jl*

The last scenario related to the efficiency of the storage of strings that we will discuss in this chapter is the compression of vectors of strings. *Compression* is used to save memory if you have large vectors containing few unique values relative to the number of elements stored in the vector.

Consider the following scenario. In 1936, the British statistician and biologist Ronald Fisher studied three species of Iris flower: *Iris setosa*, *Iris virginica*, and *Iris versicolor*. You likely have heard of this experiment if you've studied machine learning models; if not, you can find the reference to this data set at https://archive.ics.uci .edu/ml/ datasets/iris.

We will not analyze this data set in this book, as it is covered in many other resources, including *Practical Data Science with R* by Nina Zumel and John Mount (Manning, 2019). However, I will use the names of the flowers to show you the potential benefits of string compression. As an additional skill, you will learn to write data to a file. After we create the file, we will read it back as a vector of strings. Next, we will compress this vector and compare the memory footprint of uncompressed versus compressed data.

6.8.1   *Creating a file containing flower names*

We will start by creating the file with the names of the flowers. Next, we will read this data back to a Vector of String values and to a PooledArray of such values to compare how much memory they occupy. As an additional skill, you will learn how to write data to a text file in Julia.

Here is the code that writes three million rows of data by repeating the names *Iris setosa*, *Iris virginica*, and *Iris versicolor* in it. The file in which we store the data is called iris.txt.

Listing 6.8   Writing names of Iris flowers to a file

```julia
julia> open("iris.txt", "w") do io
           for i in 1:10^6
               println(io, "Iris setosa")
               println(io, "Iris virginica")
               println(io, "Iris versicolor")
           end
       end
```

We first use the open function to open the file iris.txt for writing. We indicate that we want to write to the file by passing w as a second positional argument. Observe that we use the do-end block notation that you learned in chapter 2. In this notation, io is a name of the variable to which the opened file descriptor is bound. Then, inside the do-end block, you can write data to your file. The key value of using the do-end block is that the file descriptor is guaranteed to be closed after the operation is completed (even if an exception would be raised within the do-end block).

In this case, we use the println function to write data to the file; the first argument passed is the file descriptor to which we want to write, and the second argument is data we want to be written. The println function inserts a newline character after it writes data to the file. If we wanted to avoid the newline character, we would use the print function instead.

Let's check to see if the file was indeed created before we proceed:

```
julia> isfile("iris.txt")
true
```

6.8.2   *Reading in the data to a vector and compressing it*

We have created the iris.txt file; now let's read it back using the readlines function that you already learned in this chapter:

```
julia> uncompressed = readlines("iris.txt")
3000000-element Vector{String}:
 "Iris setosa"
 "Iris virginica"
 "Iris versicolor"
 ⋮
 "Iris setosa"
 "Iris virginica"
 "Iris versicolor"
```

Now compress this vector by using the PooledArray constructor from the Pooled-Arrays.jl package:

```
julia> using PooledArrays

julia> compressed = PooledArray(uncompressed)
3000000-element PooledVector{String, UInt32, Vector{UInt32}}:
 "Iris setosa"
 "Iris virginica"
 "Iris versicolor"
 ⋮
 "Iris setosa"
 "Iris virginica"
 "Iris versicolor"
```

We have created a vector that has the PooledVector type. First, let's use the Base.summarysize function to check that the compressed vector indeed uses less memory than the uncompressed vector:

```
julia> Base.summarysize(uncompressed)
88000040

julia> Base.summarysize(compressed)
12000600
```

Notice that the memory size of the compressed object is 85% smaller than the uncompressed one. Let me explain how this compression is achieved.

6.8.3   *Understanding the internal design of PooledArray*

To understand why compressed vectors can use less memory than uncompressed ones, figure 6.5 shows the most important elements of how `PooledVector{String, UInt32, Vector{UInt32}}` is internally implemented.

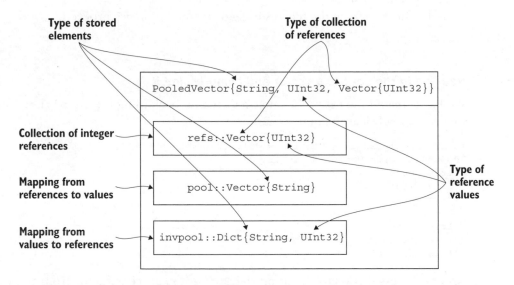

Figure 6.5   The `PooledVector` of strings contains a collection of integer references and two mappings: one from string values to integer references, and the other from integer references to string values. You can get a list of all fields of `PooledArray` by writing `fieldnames(PooledArray)`.

What is important is that the `compressed` pooled vector does not store the strings directly. Instead, it assigns an integer reference value to each unique string it stores. The `invpool` dictionary indicates the number assigned to each unique stored string:

```
julia> compressed.invpool
Dict{String, UInt32} with 3 entries:
  "Iris virginica"  => 0x00000002
  "Iris versicolor" => 0x00000003
  "Iris setosa"     => 0x00000001
```

In this case, `"Iris setosa"` has been assigned to number 1, `"Iris virginica"` to number 2, and `"Iris versicolor"` to number 3.

Observe that the assigned numbers start from 1. Therefore, it is easy to encode the inverse mapping from numbers to values by using a vector. This is achieved in the `pool` field:

```
julia> compressed.pool
3-element Vector{String}:
 "Iris setosa"
 "Iris virginica"
 "Iris versicolor"
```

Now, if we want to find which string has been assigned number 1 in our compressed pooled vector, we just take the first element of the `compressed.pool` vector, which is `"Iris setosa"` in our case.

It is crucial to observe that mappings in `invpool` and `pool` are consistent. As a result, if we take a reference number `i`, the following invariant is guaranteed to hold: `compressed.invpool[compressed.pool[i]]` is equal to `i`.

You are now ready to understand how compression is achieved. Note that the integer number assigned to the string uses less memory than the string itself. Therefore, instead of storing the strings, we store only the numbers assigned to them in the `refs` vector. Next, if the user wants to get an element of the `compressed` vector instead, the reference number of this element is retrieved from the `refs` vector, and then the actual value is looked up in the `pool` vector. Therefore, the following two lines of code are equivalent:

```
julia> compressed[10]
"Iris setosa"
```

```
julia> compressed.pool[compressed.refs[10]]
"Iris setosa"
```

In our example, the integer reference numbers assigned to strings have the `UInt32` type, so they use 4 bytes of memory, as explained in chapter 2. On the other hand, our strings use more memory, which we again can check using the `Base.summarysize` function, this time broadcasting it over elements of the `compressed.pool` vector:

```
julia> Base.summarysize.(compressed.pool)
3-element Vector{Int64}:
 19
 22
 23
```

We can see that these strings take up much more memory than 4 bytes. Additionally, we need to consider that apart from the raw size of the strings in the `uncompressed` vector, we additionally need to separately keep pointers to these vectors. Taking those two elements into consideration, you can now see the reason for the over seven-fold compression of the memory footprint of `compressed` versus `uncompressed` vectors.

I have spent so much time explaining how a pooled vector is implemented because it is important to help you understand when this data structure should be used. Using pooled vectors will be beneficial if you have a collection of strings with few unique values in comparison to the number of elements of the original collection. If this is not the case, you will not benefit from using the pooled vector, as instead of just storing the data, you'll also need to store three objects: `refs`, `pool`, and `invpool`. It is crucial to note that `pool` and `invpool` have sizes proportional to the number of unique elements in a collection. So, they are small if there are few such unique values, but are quite large if there are many unique values.

In conclusion, let's construct a large vector containing all unique values by using the `string` function that you learned in chapter 5 and then compare the size of a normal vector storing such strings to the size of the pooled vector:

```
julia> v1 = string.("x", 1:10^6)
1000000-element Vector{String}:
 "x1"
 "x2"
 "x3"
 ⋮
 "x999998"
 "x999999"
 "x1000000"

julia> v2 = PooledArray(v1)
1000000-element PooledVector{String, UInt32, Vector{UInt32}}:
 "x1"
 "x2"
 "x3"
 ⋮
 "x999998"
 "x999999"
 "x1000000"

julia> Base.summarysize(v1)
22888936

julia> Base.summarysize(v2)
54152176
```

As expected, since both the `v1` and `v2` vectors have all unique elements, the compressed vector `v2` uses more than two times more memory than the uncompressed `v1`.

In a similar vein to fixed-width strings discussed in section 6.7, in part 2, you will learn that when getting your data from a CSV file, the Julia CSV reader can automatically detect that it is useful to use compressed vectors instead of standard vectors by analyzing how many unique values are present in data in relation to the number of stored elements.

If you are using pandas in Python and know about the `Categorical` type, or you've used `factor` in R, you might ask how they are related to PooledArrays.jl. The PooledArrays.jl objective is to provide compression only. It does not provide additional logic allowing you to work with categorical values (in a data science sense). In chapter 13, you will learn about the CategoricalArrays.jl package, which provides a carefully designed implementation of categorical values for Julia. (If you would like to get a quick comparison of PooledArrays.jl and CategoricalArrays.jl, I recommend reading my "Categorical vs. Pooled Arrays" blog post at http://mng.bz/N547.)

6.9 *Choosing appropriate storage for collections of strings*

At this point, you might be overwhelmed by the number of options that Julia provides for storing collections of strings. Fortunately, as I have already hinted in sections 6.7 and 6.8, when reading in, for example, a CSV file, the reader automatically makes the right choice. However, it is useful to summarize the rules that can guide your choices if you want to make them yourself:

- If your collection of strings is a few elements or you do not expect memory or performance to be crucial for your program, you can safely just use a standard `String` and store it in a standard collection type (for example, a `Vector`).
- If you have a lot of strings to store, you have the following choices:
  - If the number of unique values relative to the number of elements of your collection is small, you can still just use `String`, but store it in a `Pooled-Array` provided by the PooledArrays.jl package.
  - Otherwise, if your strings are short and have similar lengths, you can use fixed-width strings (`String1`, `String3`, `String7`, etc.) provided by the InlineStrings.jl package and store them in a standard collection (for example, a `Vector`).
  - Finally, if you have many strings that have many unique values, of which at least some are quite long, you need to make a final decision. If you are interested in treating these strings as labels and intend to only compare them for equality, use `Symbol` (remember that, technically, symbols are not strings, but if you want to only compare them, this most likely should not be an issue). Otherwise, use the standard `String` type. In both cases, you can use a standard collection (for example, a `Vector`).

As a summary, I will quote computer scientist Donald Knuth: "Premature optimization is the root of all evil." How does this relate to our subject? Normally, when I start writing my Julia code, I most often use `Vector{String}` to store my strings (unless a package like CSV.jl automatically makes an optimal decision for me, as then I get optimization out of the box for free). Next, I check whether I run into any performance or memory bottlenecks (the simplest approach is to use the `@time` macro; more advanced profiling techniques are described in the Julia Manual at https://docs.julialang.org/en/v1/manual/profile/), and if so, appropriately adjust the data types that are used.

An extremely convenient feature of multiple dispatch in Julia, discussed in chapter 3, is that changing the data types will not require rewriting the rest of your code. Provided you have not hardcoded concrete data types, but instead have properly used abstract types, like `AbstractString`, Julia will automatically handle changing the concrete implementation of the string container you decided to perform.

Summary

- In Julia, you can use the `download` function from the `Downloads` module to download files from the web. This is an operation that you will frequently need to perform in practice.

- You can concatenate strings by using the `*` character, so `"a" * "b"` produces `"ab"`. This is often useful when you need to add a prefix or suffix to a string.

- Using the `$` character, you can interpolate values into a string. If you have a variable x bound to value `10`, and you type `"x = $x"`, you get `"x = 10"`. This functionality is often used in practice, for example, to display intermediate results of computations.

- You can use raw string literals to avoid special treatment of `\` and `$` in string literals. This is useful when specifying paths in Windows. The `raw"C:\DIR"` literal is an example; if we omitted the `raw` prefix, we would get an error.

- The `readlines` function can be used to read the contents of a file into a vector of strings, where each element of a resulting vector is a string representing a single line of the source file. This way of reading in files is convenient, as most text data is later parsed line by line.

- The `split` function can be used to split a string into multiple strings on a specified delimiter. For example, `split("a,b", ",")` produces an `["a", "b"]` vector. This kind of parsing of source data is often needed in practice.

- A standard string type in Julia is `String`. However, since strings in Julia are immutable, some standard functions, when applied to a string of the `String` type, return a view into it that has the `SubString{String}` type. The benefit of such views is that they do not require allocating additional memory to store them.

- When you write your own functions that accept strings, specify `AbstractString` as a type parameter in the function definition to ensure that it will work with any string type that the user might want to pass. Because Julia has many string types, your functions should be implemented in a generic way.

- Julia has full support for working with regular expressions, which are useful in extracting information from string data. You can create regular expression literals by prefixing a string with `r`—for example, the `r"a.a"` pattern matches a three-character sequence that starts and ends with a and contains any character in the middle. Regular expressions are commonly used to extract data from text sources.

- You can use the `parse` function to convert strings to numbers; for example, `parse(Int, "10")` returns the integer 10. This functionality is often needed when processing numeric data stored in text files.

- Strings in Julia use UTF-8 encoding, so each character can take up 1, 2, 3, or 4 bytes in a string. ASCII characters always use 1 byte in this encoding. Therefore, in general, the number of characters in a string can be less than the number of bytes in this string.

- When manipulating strings, you can use byte or character counts to refer to a concrete section of the string. For ASCII strings, these approaches are equivalent, but in general, they are not. You must always check whether the function you use operates on byte or character counts.

- String indexing with square brackets—for example, `"abc"[2:3]`—uses byte indexing. Because strings in Julia are UTF-8 encoded, not all indices are valid for this kind of indexing.

- Commonly used functions that use character indexing are `length`, `chop`, `first`, and `last`.

- The FreqTables.jl package provides `freqtable` and `proptable` functions that allow you to easily create frequency tables from your data. These summaries of source data are commonly used in data science workflows.

- `Symbol` is a special type that is not a string but is sometimes used when your strings are considered labels and you only need to compare them, while requiring that the comparison is performed fast.

- Symbols that are valid variable name identifiers can be conveniently created with a colon (`:`) prefix—for example, `:some_symbol`.

- The InlineStrings.jl package defines several fixed-width string types: `String1`, `String3`, `String7`, etc. If your strings are short and have a uniform length, such nonstandard string types will use less memory and will be faster to process in many operations such as sorting.

- You can open files for writing by using the `open` function. You can then write to them by using, for example, the `println` function if you pass the file descriptor (indicating where the data should be written) as a first argument.

- Values of the `PooledArray` type from the PooledArrays.jl package let you compress the memory size of collections of strings if you only have a few unique values in them. In such cases, using this functionality can save you a lot of RAM.

- Julia provides several options for storing strings in collections, each with a slightly different performance and memory usage profile. This allows you to flexibly optimize your code against the structure of the data you process. Additionally, several standard Julia packages, like CSV.jl, will create nonstandard InlineStrings.jl strings or `PooledVector` automatically for you when reading in the data if they detect that they would be more efficient.

Handling time-series
data and missing values

7

This chapter covers

- Fetching data by using HTTP queries
- Parsing JSON data
- Working with dates
- Handling missing values
- Plotting data with missing values
- Interpolating missing values

This is the last chapter of part 1, which focuses on the Julia language. A motivating use case for the topics that we will cover in this chapter is working with financial asset prices. Imagine you want to analyze how the price of a certain stock or the exchange rate between two currencies evolves over time. To be able to handle these questions in Julia, you need to know how to work with time-series data. A frequent feature of real-life temporal data is that it contains missing data for some timestamps. Therefore, the second major topic of this chapter is handling missing values in Julia.

The problem we tackle in this chapter is analyzing the PLN/USD exchange rate that is published by the National Bank of Poland (NBP). The data is made available via a Web API, which is described at https://api.nbp.pl/en.html.

We will perform our task via the following steps:

1 Understand the format of the data that the Web API exposes.
2 Fetch the data by using HTTP GET requests for a specified range of dates.
3 Handle errors when the requested data is not available.
4 Extract the PLN/USD exchange rate from the obtained result of the query.
5 Perform simple statistical analysis of the fetched data.
6 Plot the fetched data with a proper handling of missing values.

To execute this sequence of steps, you will need to learn how to handle missing data in Julia, work with dates, and fetch data by using the HTTP requests, as well as parse information passed using the JSON format (https://www.json.org/json-en.html). To help you learn these topics one by one, this chapter is divided into four sections:

- In section 7.1, you will learn the JSON format of the exchange-rate data that NBP exposes via its Web API; you will see how to perform HTTP GET requests in Julia and how to parse JSON data.
- In section 7.2, you will learn how to handle missing values in Julia. This knowledge is required to understand how to process the data fetched from the NBP Web API since it contains missing values.
- In section 7.3, you will see how to handle a series of NBP Web API queries for data coming from different dates and process their results as a time series. You will learn how to work with dates in Julia.
- In section 7.4, you will analyze time-series data statistically and plot it. We'll pay special attention to handling missing data in both data analysis and visualization.

7.1 Understanding the NBP Web API

Before you can start analyzing the exchange-rate data, you need to learn how to fetch it from the NBP Web API. Also, as you will soon see, the NBP Web API exposes information about exchange rates in JSON format, so you will also see how to parse it. I have chosen this data source for this chapter because the JSON format is commonly used by many data sources, so it is worth learning how to work with it. Also, you can expect that in practice, you will often need to fetch data via various web APIs in your data science projects.

We start by visually inspecting the data that the NBP Web API exposes. We will be passing sample queries via a web browser. Next, you will learn how to perform this operation programmatically.

7.1.1 Getting the data via a web browser

The full specification of the Web API is available at https://api.nbp.pl/en.html. The API can be accessed both via a web browser and programmatically. We start by querying it using a web browser. For our purpose, it is enough to know one format of the request:

```
https://api.nbp.pl/api/exchangerates/rates/a/usd/YYYY-MM-DD/?format=json
```

In this request, you should replace the YYYY-MM-DD part with a specific date, first passing four digits of a year, then two digits for the month, and finally two digits for the day. Here is an example of getting data for June 1, 2020:

```
https://api.nbp.pl/api/exchangerates/rates/a/usd/2020-06-01/?format=json
```

When you run this query in your web browser, you should get the following response (depending on the browser you use, the layout of the response might be a bit different):

```
{
 "table":"A",
 "currency":"dolar amerykański",
 "code":"USD",
 "rates":[
          {
           "no":"105/A/NBP/2020",
           "effectiveDate":"2020-06-01",
           "mid":3.9680
          }
         ]
}
```

The result is returned in JSON format. You can find the format specification at www.json.org/json-en.html. Additionally, if you want to learn more about JSON, consider reading *JSON for Beginners: Your Guide to Easily Learn JSON Programming in 7 Days* by iCode Academy (White Flower Publishing, 2017) or going through the MDN Web Docs tutorial at http://mng.bz/DDKa. Here, I will concentrate on explaining how this specific JSON structure should be interpreted.

Figure 7.1 presents the explanation. The result contains one object with four fields: table, currency, code, and rates. The field that is interesting for us is rates, which contains an array holding a single object. This single object has three

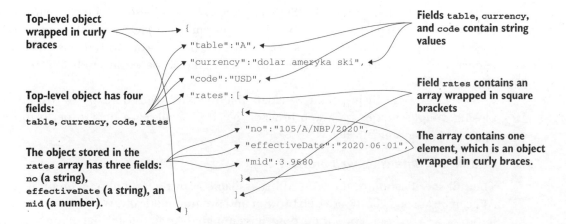

Figure 7.1 In this JSON data returned by a request to the NBP Web API, key-value fields are wrapped in curly braces, and arrays are wrapped in square brackets.

fields: `no`, `effectiveDate`, and `mid`. For us, the important field is `mid`, which stores the PLN/USD exchange rate for the day we have queried. For June 1, 2020, the exchange rate was 3.960 PLN/USD.

7.1.2   *Getting the data by using Julia*

Now that we understand the structure of the data, we switch to Julia. We will fetch the data from the NBP Web API by using the `HTTP.get` function from the HTTP.jl package. Next, we will parse this response by using the JSON reader provided by the function `JSON3.read` from the JSON3.jl package. The following listing presents how to execute these steps.

Listing 7.1   Executing the NBP Web API query and parsing the fetched JSON response

```
julia> using HTTP

julia> using JSON3
```
Defines a string with the URL we query
```
julia> query = "https://api.nbp.pl/api/exchangerates/rates/a/usd/" *
               "2020-06-01/?format=json"
"https://api.nbp.pl/api/exchangerates/rates/a/usd/2020-06-01/?format=json"

julia> response = HTTP.get(query)
```
Sends an HTTP GET request to the NBP Web API
```
HTTP.Messages.Response:
"""
HTTP/1.1 200 OK
Date: Mon, 06 Dec 2021 10:29:10 GMT
Cache-Control: no-cache
Pragma: no-cache
Content-Length: 134
Content-Type: application/json; charset=utf-8
Expires: -1
ETag: "cZimS9v8pROOFg78jX55w0AsnRyhsNg4/e6vNH+Nxos="
Set-Cookie: ee3la5eizeiY4Eix=ud5ahSho; path=/

{"table":"A","currency":"dolar amerykański","code":"USD",
"rates":[{"no":"105/A/NBP/2020",
"effectiveDate":"2020-06-01","mid":3.9680}]}"""
```
Parses the fetched response data as JSON
```
julia> json = JSON3.read(response.body)
JSON3.Object{Vector{UInt8}, Vector{UInt64}} with 4 entries:
  :table    => "A"
  :currency => "dolar amerykański"
  :code     => "USD"
  :rates    => JSON3.Object[{…
```

We pass the `query` string to the `HTTP.get` function and get the `response` object. We can see in the printed result message that the query is successful, as it has a `200 OK` status code. In the bottom of the response message, we see the same JSON data that we fetched using the web browser.

The `response` object has several fields, and the one that is important for us is body, which stores the vector of fetched bytes:

```
julia> response.body
134-element Vector{UInt8}:
 0x7b
 0x22
 0x74
    ⋮
 0x7d
 0x5d
 0x7d
```

We pass this vector of bytes to the JSON reader function `JSON3.read`. Before discussing this step, let me explain how you can efficiently inspect the contents of `response.body` as a string. You can simply use the `String` constructor:

```
julia> String(response.body)
"{\"table\":\"A\",\"currency\":\"dolar amerykański\",\"code\":\"USD\",
\"rates\":[{\"no\":\"105/A/NBP/2020\",
\"effectiveDate\":\"2020-06-01\",\"mid\":3.9680}]}"
```

This operation is efficient, which means that the string is wrapped around the passed vector of bytes, and no copying of data is performed. This has one side effect that we must bear in mind. Since we used the vector of bytes to create the `String` object, the `response.body` vector is emptied:

```
julia> response.body
UInt8[]
```

Calling the `String` constructor on `Vector{UInt8}` consumes the data stored in a vector. The benefit of this behavior is that the operation is very fast. The downside is that you can perform the conversion only once. After the operation, the `response.body` vector is empty, so calling `String(response.body)` again would produce an empty string (`""`).

The fact that the `String` constructor empties the `Vector{UInt8}` source that is passed to it is one of the rare cases in Julia when a function mutates an object passed to it that does not have the `!` suffix in its name. Therefore, it is important that you remember this exception. In our example, if you wanted to preserve the value stored in `response.body`, you should have copied it before passing it to the `String` constructor as follows: `String(copy(response.body))`.

Now that you understand how to work with the `response` object, let's turn to the `json` variable to which we have bound the return value of `JSON3.read(response.body)`. A nice feature of the `JSON3.read` function is that the object it returns can be queried just like any other object in Julia. Therefore, use the dot (.) to access its fields:

```
julia> json.table
"A"
```

```
julia> json.currency
"dolar amerykański"

julia> json.code
"USD"

julia> json.rates
1-element JSON3.Array{JSON3.Object, Vector{UInt8},
SubArray{UInt64, 1, Vector{UInt64}, Tuple{UnitRange{Int64}}, true}}:
 {
              "no": "105/A/NBP/2020",
   "effectiveDate": "2020-06-01",
             "mid": 3.968
}
```

Similarly, JSON arrays, like the one stored in the `json.rates` field, can be accessed using 1-based indexing, just like any vector in Julia. Therefore, to get the `mid` field of the first object stored in the `json.rates`, you can write this:

```
julia> json.rates[1].mid
3.968
```

Next, I'll introduce a useful function that can be used to ensure correctness of one specific use case of getting the data from the array in Julia. If we know and want to check that an array contains exactly one element, and we want to extract it, we can use the `only` function:

```
julia> only(json.rates).mid
3.968
```

An important property of the `only` function is that it will throw an error if our vector contains zero or more than one element:

```
julia> only([])
ERROR: ArgumentError: Collection is empty, must contain exactly 1 element

julia> only([1, 2])
ERROR: ArgumentError: Collection has multiple elements, must contain exactly
     1 element
```

The `only` function is quite useful when writing production code, as it allows you to easily catch bugs if your data does not meet the assumptions.

7.1.3 *Handling cases when an NBP Web API query fails*

Before we proceed to fetching data for a wider range of dates, let's discuss one more feature of the NBP Web API. The scenario I want to consider is what happens if we do not have data on the PLN/USD exchange rate for a given day. First, execute the following query in your browser:

```
https://api.nbp.pl/api/exchangerates/rates/a/usd/2020-06-06/?format=json
```

You should get the following response:

```
404 NotFound - Not Found - Brak danych
```

We see that in this case, the data has no date for June 6, 2020. Let's see how this scenario is handled when we try to execute the query programmatically in the next listing.

Listing 7.2   An example of a query that throws an exception

```julia
julia> query = "https://api.nbp.pl/api/exchangerates/rates/a/usd/" *
               "2020-06-06/?format=json"
"https://api.nbp.pl/api/exchangerates/rates/a/usd/2020-06-06/?format=json"

julia> response = HTTP.get(query)
ERROR: HTTP.ExceptionRequest.StatusError(404, "GET",
"/api/exchangerates/rates/a/usd/2020-06-06/?format=json",
HTTP.Messages.Response:
"""
HTTP/1.1 404 Not Found
Date: Mon, 06 Dec 2021 10:56:16 GMT
Cache-Control: no-cache
Pragma: no-cache
Content-Length: 38
Content-Type: text/plain; charset=utf-8
Expires: -1
Set-Cookie: ee3la5eizeiY4Eix=Naew5Ohp; path=/

404 NotFound - Not Found - Brak danych""")
```

The `HTTP.get` function throws an exception in this case with a 404 error, informing us that the requested page was not found. This is a new scenario that we have not encountered yet. Let's discuss how to handle it.

An *exception* means that an unexpected situation happened when executing the query, and the Julia program is immediately terminated without producing a result.

This behavior is useful when we encounter an unexpected situation. However, in this case, we could consider the situation expected. We do not want our program to halt when we do not get a proper query result. Alternatively, we would most likely want to get a result signaling that there was no data for a given day, as the PLN/USD exchange rate is missing for this day. Such a value in Julia is represented as `missing`, and section 7.2 details what it means and how it is used.

Let's discuss how to handle exceptions so that they do not terminate our program if we do not want them to. For this, we use the `try-catch-end` block.

The code in listing 7.3 does the following (see also figure 7.2):

- Tries to execute our query in the `try` part of the block
- If the query succeeds, returns its result
- If the query fails, executes the contents of the `catch` part of the block

Listing 7.3   Using the `try-catch-end` block to handle exceptions

```julia
julia> query = "https://api.nbp.pl/api/exchangerates/rates/a/usd/" *
               "2020-06-01/?format=json"
"https://api.nbp.pl/api/exchangerates/rates/a/usd/2020-06-01/?format=json"
```

```
julia> try
           response = HTTP.get(query)
           json = JSON3.read(response.body)
           only(json.rates).mid
       catch e
           if e isa HTTP.ExceptionRequest.StatusError
               missing
           else
               rethrow(e)
           end
       end
3.968
```

In the try part, we execute the code that should normally work.

Extracts the mid field of the only entry of the rates vector in the fetched request response

Checks if the error is caused by a status error of the HTTP server; in such a case, produces a missing value

If code we try to execute throws an error, stores the error information in variable e

If the error has another cause, rethrows it so that the programmer is informed that an unexpected situation happened

```
julia> query = "https://api.nbp.pl/api/exchangerates/rates/a/usd/" *
               "2020-06-06/?format=json"
"https://api.nbp.pl/api/exchangerates/rates/a/usd/2020-06-06/?format=json"

julia> try
           response = HTTP.get(query)
           json = JSON3.read(response.body)
           only(json.rates).mid
       catch e
           if e isa HTTP.ExceptionRequest.StatusError
               missing
           else
               rethrow(e)
           end
       end
missing
```

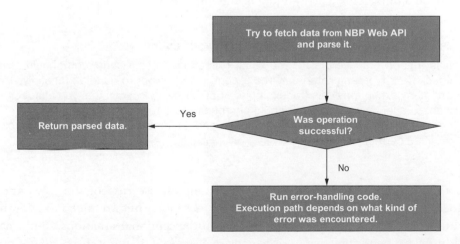

Figure 7.2   The logic of handling HTTP GET errors when using the NBP Web API. When fetching data from a remote location, errors often happen, so your code should be prepared for such a situation.

We can see that for the valid date of June 1, 2020, we get the parsed value 3.968, and for the invalid date of June 6, 2020, a missing value is produced.

Let's recap the structure of the `try-catch-end` block in the following pseudocode:

```
try
    <instructions that we try to execute>
catch
    <instructions executed if there is an exception in the try part>
end
```

Here, we are trying to perform three operations we have already discussed: fetching the data, parsing it in JSON format, and extracting the exchange rate.

Now look at the `catch` part of listing 7.3. First note the e after the `catch` keyword. This syntax means that we will bind the exception information with the variable called e.

Next, we use `e isa HTTP.ExceptionRequest.StatusError` to check whether the exception is indeed the problem with the HTTP request This is exactly the type of the exception that we saw in listing 7.2. If there's a problem with the HTTP request, we produce the `missing` value. However, we do this only if we get this kind of exception. In all other cases, we use the `rethrow` function to re-raise the same exception that we just caught.

You might ask why we do that. The reason is that we could have gotten an exception raised by, for example, the `only` function. As you already know, this function raises an exception if it gets an array that does not have exactly one element. If this were the case, we would not want to hide such a problem by producing `missing`, but rather prefer to explicitly warn the user that something unexpected happened (we expected a one-element array and got something else).

Do not blindly catch any exception in your code

It is a good practice that, if you catch exceptions in your code, you should always check their type and catch only the exceptions you want to handle gracefully. There are many exception types (for example, `OutOfMemoryError`) that you almost never want to silently hide and that could potentially be thrown in an arbitrary part of your code. For example, if a Julia program runs out of memory, it is most likely not able to proceed correctly.

In this section, I have discussed only the simplest use case of the `try-catch-end` block. I discuss this topic so late in the book because, while you need to know how to handle exceptions, they should be reserved for exceptional situations. In normal situations, it is a better practice to write code in a way that does not throw exceptions.

This recommendation is based on two reasons. First, handling exceptions is relatively slow, so having code that heavily uses the `try-catch-end` block might degrade its performance. Second, such code is usually more difficult to reason about.

If you would like to learn more about handling exceptions, check the "Exception Handling" section of the Julia Manual (http://mng.bz/lR9B).

7.2   Working with missing data in Julia

In our example in section 7.1, we decided to produce `missing` if the data on the PLN/USD exchange rate was missing in the NBP Web API. In this section, we will define the `missing` value and discuss why it is used in data science projects.

Learning to work with a `missing` value is important because most real-life data has quality issues. One of the most common cases you will need to handle in practice is when some features of the objects you want to analyze have not been collected. For example, imagine you're analyzing data about the body temperature of a patient in a hospital. You expect the measurement to be made every hour. However, sometimes the measurement is not made or not recorded. These cases are represented as `missing` in the data you will analyze.

7.2.1   Definition of the missing value

Let's start with the definition of the `missing` value from the Julia Manual (https://docs.julialang.org/en/v1/manual/missing/):

> *Julia provides support for representing missing values in the statistical sense, that is, for situations where no value is available for a variable in an observation, but a valid value theoretically exists.*

This situation is represented as a `missing` value having a `Missing` type. The Julia language (similarly to R, but unlike, for example, Python) is designed with a built-in concept of a missing value. In your code, you do not need to use sentinel values to represent the absence of data. You can easily check if a value is missing by using the `ismissing` function:

```
julia> ismissing(missing)
true

julia> ismissing(1)
false
```

Let's recall another value introduced in chapter 3: nothing (of type `Nothing`). How is nothing different? You should use nothing to indicate an objective absence of the value, whereas `missing` represents a value that exists but has not been recorded.

To make sure that the difference between `missing` and nothing is clear, let me give a nontechnical example. Assume we have a person, and we ask the brand of their car. We can have three situations:

- The person has a car, and we know the brand; then we just give it.
- We know that the person has a car, but we do not know the brand; then we should produce `missing` since objectively this brand name exists, but we do not know it.
- We know that the person does not have a car, and we produce nothing because the value is objectively absent.

Indeed, in some cases there is a thin line between using `missing` and `nothing` (as in the preceding example—what if we did not even know if the person had a car?). However, in practice it is quite easy to decide, given the context of the application, whether `missing` or `nothing` is more suitable. In the data science world, the `missing` value is predominantly encountered in source data when, for some reason, its recording failed.

7.2.2 Working with missing values

The definition of `missing` has an important influence on the design of the programming languages that natively support it (like Julia or R). In this section, we discuss the most important aspects of working with `missing` values.

PROPAGATING MISSING VALUES IN FUNCTIONS

The principle is that many functions silently propagate `missing`—that is, if they get `missing` as an input, they return `missing` in their output. Here are a few examples:

```julia
julia> 1 + missing
missing

julia> sin(missing)
missing
```

One important case of `missing` propagation is in the context of tests that should produce a `Bool` value:

```julia
julia> 1 == missing
missing

julia> 1 > missing
missing

julia> 1 < missing
missing
```

This behavior is often called *three-valued-logic* (http://mng.bz/o59Z), as you can get `true`, `false`, or `missing` from a logical operation.

Three-valued-logic is a logically consistent way of handling `missing` values. However, in the context of logical tests, we should be careful if we potentially have missing data. The reason is that passing `missing` as a condition to the conditional statement produces an error:

```julia
julia> if missing
           print("this is not printed")
       end
ERROR: TypeError: non-boolean (Missing) used in boolean context

julia> missing && true
ERROR: TypeError: non-boolean (Missing) used in boolean context
```

The design of handling `missing` in Julia requires you to explicitly decide whether `missing` should be treated as `true` or `false`. This is achieved with the `coalesce` function, which you might know from SQL (http://mng.bz/BZ1r). Its definition is simple: `coalesce` returns its first nonmissing positional argument, or `missing` if all its arguments are `missing`.

The use of `coalesce` is most common with handling logical conditions. If you write `coalesce(condition, true)`, you say that if the condition evaluates to `missing`, you want this `missing` to be treated as `true`. Similarly, `coalesce(condition, false)` means that you want to treat `missing` as `false`. Here is an example:

```
julia> coalesce(missing, true)
true

julia> coalesce(missing, false)
false
```

> **missing values in logical conditions**
>
> If your data potentially contains `missing` values that you might use in logical conditions, always make sure to wrap them in `coalesce` with the second argument being `true` or `false`, depending on how you want the `missing` to be treated in the condition.

USING COMPARISON OPERATORS GUARANTEEING A BOOLEAN RESULT

Sometimes, however, it is useful to treat `missing` values in comparisons like any other values, without special treatment featuring three-valued logic. If needed in your code, you can use the `isless` function for testing ordering and `isequal` for testing equality. These two functions are guaranteed to return either `true` or `false`, no matter what value is passed to them. Here are some examples:

```
julia> isequal(1, missing)
false

julia> isequal(missing, missing)
true

julia> isless(1, missing)
true

julia> isless(missing, missing)
false
```

As a special rule, in `isless` comparisons of `missing` against numbers, `missing` is always treated as greater than all numbers, so we have the following:

```
julia> isless(Inf, missing)
true
```

In `isequal` comparisons, `missing` is treated as equal only to itself.

In addition to the `isequal` function that guarantees to return a `Bool` value, Julia provides yet another way to compare values for equality that also always returns a `Bool` value. This comparison is performed using the `===` operator.

The difference between the `isequal` function and the `===` operator is that, for values that support the notion of equality, `isequal` is usually implemented to compare the values themselves, while `===` tests whether two values are technically identical (in the sense that no program could distinguish them). The distinction between comparing content versus technical identity is most often seen when working with mutable collections like vectors. Here is an example:

```julia
julia> a = [1]
1-element Vector{Int64}:
 1

julia> b = [1]
1-element Vector{Int64}:
 1

julia> isequal(a, b)
true

julia> a === b
false
```

The a and b vectors have the same contents, so the `isequal` test returns `true`. However, they are technically different, as they have a different memory location. Therefore, the `===` test returns `false`. You will see more examples of using the `===` operator in part 2. Finally, Julia has the `!==` operator, which always gives an opposite answer than `===`.

Relationship between ===, ==, and isequal

Here are the rules that govern how the `===` and `==` operators and the `isequal` function are related in Julia:

- The `===` operator always returns a `Bool` value and allows us to compare any values for identity (in the sense that no program could distinguish them).
- The `==` operator falls back by default to `===`. If a type supports a notion of equality in a logical sense (like numbers, strings, or arrays), it defines a special method for the `==` operator. For example, numbers are compared based on their numeric value, and arrays are compared based on their contents. Therefore, special methods for the `==` operator are implemented for them. When performing comparisons using the `==` operator, the user must remember the following special rules:
  - Comparison against a `missing` value using `==` always returns `missing`.
  - Comparison against floating-point `NaN` values always returns `false` (see chapter 2 for more examples of this rule).
  - Comparison of floating-point positive zero (`0.0`) and negative zero (`-0.0`) returns `true`.
- The `isequal` function behaves like the `==` operator except that it always returns a `Bool` value, and the special rules are defined differently for it:
  - Comparison against a `missing` value using `isequal` returns `false`, except if two `missing` values are compared, and then it returns `true`.

- Comparison against a floating-point NaN value returns `false`, except if two NaN values are compared, and then it returns `true`.
- Comparison of floating-point positive zero (`0.0`) and negative zero (`-0.0`) returns `false`.

isequal is used to compare keys in dictionaries

It is important to remember that when key-value pairs are stored in the `Dict` dictionary, equality of keys is determined using the `isequal` function. For example, since `0.0` is not equal to `-0.0` when compared with `isequal`, the dictionary `Dict(0.0 => "zero", -0.0 => "negative zero")` stores two key-value pairs, one corresponding to the `0.0` key and the other to the `-0.0` key.

The same rule applies to grouping and joining data frames (these topics are discussed in part 2).

REPLACING MISSING VALUES IN COLLECTIONS

Let's go back to another common usage of the `coalesce` function, which is missing data imputation. Assume you have a vector that has `missing` values, as shown in the following listing.

Listing 7.4 A vector containing `missing` values

```julia
julia> x = [1, missing, 3, 4, missing]
5-element Vector{Union{Missing, Int64}}:
 1
  missing
 3
 4
  missing
```

The x vector contains both integers and `missing` values, so its element type, as explained in chapter 3, is `Union{Missing, Int64}`. Assume we want to replace all `missing` values with `0`. This is easily done by broadcasting the `coalesce` function:

```julia
julia> coalesce.(x, 0)
5-element Vector{Int64}:
 1
 0
 3
 4
 0
```

SKIPPING MISSING VALUES IN COMPUTATIONS

The propagation of `missing` values is also sometimes undesirable if they are hidden in the collections (like the vector x from listing 7.4). Consider, for example, the `sum` function:

```julia
julia> sum(x)
missing
```

The result is logically correct. We have `missing` values we want to add, so the result is unknown. However, we might very commonly want to add all the nonmissing values in the vector. To do this, use the `skipmissing` function to create a wrapper around the x vector:

```
julia> y = skipmissing(x)
skipmissing(Union{Missing, Int64}[1, missing, 3, 4, missing])
```

Now the y variable is bound to a new object that stores the x vector inside it, but when y is iterated, it skips `missing` values stored in x. Now, if you run `sum` on y, you will get the expected result:

```
julia> sum(y)
8
```

Typically, you would write this:

```
julia> sum(skipmissing(x))
8
```

Now you might ask why in Julia we create a special object that skips `missing` values. In other languages, like R, functions usually take a keyword argument to let the user decide whether `missing` values should be skipped.

There are two considerations. First, writing `skipmissing(x)` is efficient. No copying is done here: it is just a way to make sure that no `missing` values will be passed to the function taking `skipmissing(x)` as an argument. The second reason is composability of the design. If we have a `skipmissing(x)` object, the functions that we write (like `sum`, `mean`, and `var`) do not have to explicitly handle `missing` values. They can have one implementation, and the user chooses what should be operated on by passing an appropriate argument.

Why is this a benefit? In other ecosystems, some functions have an appropriate keyword argument for handling `missing` values, while others do not, and in the latter case, the user has to manually handle this. In Julia, handling `missing` values is abstracted to a higher level.

ENABLING MISSING PROPAGATION IN A FUNCTION

One final scenario of `missing` propagation involves functions that do not propagate `missing` values by default because their designers have decided against it. Let's write a simple function that has this behavior:

```
julia> fun(x::Int, y::Int) = x + y
fun (generic function with 1 method)
```

This function accepts only Int values as arguments; it errors if it gets a `missing` value:

```
julia> fun(1, 2)
3
```

```
julia> fun(1, missing)
ERROR: MethodError: no method matching fun(::Int64, ::Missing)
```

However, in some scenarios, even if the function's designer has not envisioned that someone might want to pass missing to it, we want to create another function, based on the original one that propagates missing values. This feature is provided by the passmissing function from the Missings.jl package. Here is an example of its use:

```
julia> using Missings

julia> fun2 = passmissing(fun)
(::Missings.PassMissing{typeof(fun)}) (generic function with 2 methods)

julia> fun2(1, 2)
3

julia> fun2(1, missing)
missing
```

The idea is simple. The passmissing function takes a function as its argument and returns a new function. The returned function, fun2 in this case, returns missing if any of its positional arguments are missing. Otherwise, it calls fun with the passed arguments.

Now you know the basic functionalities of the Julia language that are built around the missing value. If you would like to learn more, refer to the Julia Manual (https://docs.julialang.org/en/v1/manual/missing/) or the documentation of the Missings.jl package (https://github.com/JuliaData/Missings.jl).

To wrap up, let me mention that allowing a missing value in collections (for example, Vector{Union{Missing, Int}}) has a small performance and memory-consumption overhead in comparison to the same collection type that does not allow a missing value (for example, Vector{Int}). However, in most cases, this is not noticeable.

> **EXERCISE 7.1** Given a vector v = ["1", "2", missing, "4"], parse it so that strings are converted to numbers and the missing value remains a missing value.

7.3 Getting time-series data from the NBP Web API

We are now ready to get back to our problem of analyzing the PLN/USD exchange rate. For this example, assume we want to get the data for all days of June 2020. Using what you learned in section 7.1, we will create a function that fetches the data from a single day and then apply it to all days in question. But how can we list all days in June 2020?

You need to learn how to work with dates in Julia first. After we are done with this, we will come back to our main task.

Time-series analysis is often needed in data science projects. To properly handle such data, you need to know how to add timestamps to observations. This can be conveniently achieved using the Dates module from the Julia standard library.

7.3.1   *Working with dates*

In this section, I will show you how to manipulate dates in Julia. The support for dates is provided by the `Dates` standard module. The easiest way to create a date object is to pass to the `Date` constructor a string in the `YYYY-MM-DD` format you saw in section 7.1. Here is an example:

```
julia> using Dates

julia> d = Date("2020-06-01")
2020-06-01
```

Now we can inspect the object bound to the variable `d`, first checking its type, and then extracting the year, month, and date parts:

```
julia> typeof(d)
Date

julia> year(d)
2020

julia> month(d)
6

julia> day(d)
1
```

In addition to natural functions like `year`, `month`, and `day`, Julia provides several more-advanced functions. Here, let me show you how to query a date for its day-of-the-week number and name in English:

```
julia> dayofweek(d)
1

julia> dayname(d)
"Monday"
```

You can find a complete list of available functions in the "API Reference" section of the Julia Manual (http://mng.bz/derv).

If you have strings containing dates that do not follow the `YYYY-MM-DD` format, you can use the `DateFormat` object to specify a custom date format. See the "Constructors" section of the Julia Manual (http://mng.bz/rn6e) for details.

Another common way of constructing the date is to pass the numbers representing the year, month, and day that make up the date:

```
julia> Date(2020, 6, 1)
2020-06-01
```

The last constructor gives us an easy way to create a vector of dates from June 2020, using broadcasting, as shown in the following listing.

Listing 7.5   Creating a vector of all dates in June 2020

```
julia> dates = Date.(2020, 6, 1:30)
30-element Vector{Date}:
 2020-06-01
 2020-06-02
 2020-06-03
 ⋮
 2020-06-28
 2020-06-29
 2020-06-30
```

This way of creating a sequence of date objects is easy, but only for dates spanning within one month. What if we want dates from May 20, 2020 to July 5, 2020? To solve this question, we need to use a duration measure. For our purpose, the `Day` duration is proper. For instance, `Day(1)` is an object representing a time interval equal to one day:

```
julia> Day(1)
1 day
```

Now the important thing is that you can add dates with durations to get new dates. For example, to get the next day after June 1, 2020, you can write this:

```
julia> d
2020-06-01

julia> d + Day(1)
2020-06-02
```

You might have guessed how we can write a range of dates separated by one day. You can achieve this by using a range. All dates from May 20, 2020 to July 5, 2020 inclusive are as follows:

```
julia> Date(2020, 5, 20):Day(1):Date(2020, 7, 5)
Date("2020-05-20"):Day(1):Date("2020-07-05")
```

You can check that this range produces the expected set of values by using the `collect` function on it to convert it into a `Vector`:

```
julia> collect(Date(2020, 5, 20):Day(1):Date(2020, 7, 5))
47-element Vector{Date}:
 2020-05-20
 2020-05-21
 2020-05-22
 ⋮
 2020-07-03
 2020-07-04
 2020-07-05
```

Other measures of time duration exist, such as `Week` and `Year`. You can learn more about them and the rules of date arithmetic in the "TimeType-Period Arithmetic" section of the Julia Manual (http://mng.bz/VyBW).

Finally, Julia also allows you to work with time and date-time objects. The details can be found in the "Dates" section of the Julia Manual (https://docs.julialang.org/en/v1/stdlib/Dates/).

EXERCISE 7.2   Create a vector containing the first day of each month in the year 2021.

7.3.2   *Fetching data from the NBP Web API for a range of dates*

Now that we've created a `dates` vector of dates for which we want to get the PLN/USD exchange rate data (in listing 7.5), let's write a function in the next listing that gets data for a specific date. We'll follow the steps explained in section 7.1 so that we can easily collect the data for all required dates.

Listing 7.6   Function for fetching the PLN/USD exchange rate data for a specific date

```
function get_rate(date::Date)
    query = "https://api.nbp.pl/api/exchangerates/rates/" *
            "a/usd/$date/?format=json"
    try
        response = HTTP.get(query)
        json = JSON3.read(response.body)
        return only(json.rates).mid
    catch e
        if e isa HTTP.ExceptionRequest.StatusError
            return missing
        else
            rethrow(e)
        end
    end
end
```

This function collects our code from section 7.1 with a few small changes. First, we accept `date` with a `Date` as its argument, so we are sure that the user does not call our `get_rate` function with an arbitrary value that would get interpolated into the `query` string. Also note that I define the `get_rate` function to accept only a scalar `Date`. This is the recommended style of defining functions in Julia, as I explained in chapter 5. Later we will broadcast this function over the `dates` vector to get a vector of PLN/USD exchange rates.

Next, to form the `query` string, we interpolate `date` into it. As we discussed in chapter 6, the interpolation is done by using the `$` character followed by the name of the interpolated variable. Here is an example:

```
julia> d
2020-06-01

julia> "d = $d"
"d = 2020-06-01"
```

To give one more example, here is a way to interpolate the first value from the `dates` vector that we defined in listing 7.5 (the interpolated parts are in bold):

```
julia> "https://api.nbp.pl/api/exchangerates/rates/" *
       "a/usd/$(dates[1])/?format=json"
"https://api.nbp.pl/api/exchangerates/rates/a/usd/2020-06-01/?format=json"
```

This time, as an example, we interpolate the expression dates[1], so to make sure it gets properly interpolated, we wrap it in parentheses. If we omitted the parentheses, the whole dates vector would get interpolated, followed by the [1] character sequence, which is not what we want (again the interpolated part is in bold):

```
julia> "https://api.nbp.pl/api/exchangerates/rates/" *
       "a/usd/$dates[1]/?format=json"
"https://api.nbp.pl/api/exchangerates/rates/a/usd/[Date(\"2020-06-01\"),
 Date(\"2020-06-02\"), Date(\"2020-06-03\"), Date(\"2020-06-04\"),
 Date(\"2020-06-05\"), Date(\"2020-06-06\"), Date(\"2020-06-07\"),
 Date(\"2020-06-08\"), Date(\"2020-06-09\"), Date(\"2020-06-10\"),
 Date(\"2020-06-11\"), Date(\"2020-06-12\"), Date(\"2020-06-13\"),
 Date(\"2020-06-14\"), Date(\"2020-06-15\"), Date(\"2020-06-16\"),
 Date(\"2020-06-17\"), Date(\"2020-06-18\"), Date(\"2020-06-19\"),
 Date(\"2020-06-20\"), Date(\"2020-06-21\"), Date(\"2020-06-22\"),
 Date(\"2020-06-23\"), Date(\"2020-06-24\"), Date(\"2020-06-25\"),
 Date(\"2020-06-26\"), Date(\"2020-06-27\"), Date(\"2020-06-28\"),
 Date(\"2020-06-29\"), Date(\"2020-06-30\")][1]/?format=json"
```

The final change is, following the rule I introduced in chapter 2, that we explicitly write the return keyword in two places in the code to make sure that the value that will be returned by the get_rate function is clearly visible.

Now we are all set to fetch the exchange PLN/USD exchange rates for June 2020 in the next listing.

Listing 7.7   Fetching the PLN/USD exchange rates for June 2020

```
julia> rates = get_rate.(dates)
30-element Vector{Union{Missing, Float64}}:
 3.968
 3.9303
 3.9121
 ⋮
  missing
 3.9656
 3.9806
```

We use the dot (.) after the get_rate function to apply it to all elements of the dates vector. Additionally, the result is a Vector having the element type Union{Float64, Missing}, which means that in the result, we have a mixture of missing values and floating-point numbers.

7.4   *Analyzing data fetched from the NBP Web API*

Having defined the dates variable in listing 7.5 and the rates variable in listing 7.7, let's analyze the data to understand its content. We want to do the following:

- Calculate basic summary statistics of the data: the mean and standard deviation of the rates vector

- Analyze for which days of the week we encounter missing data in our vector
- Display the PLN/USD exchange rate on a plot

The key new skill you will acquire is performing this analysis while considering the temporal nature of data and proper handling of `missing` values.

7.4.1   *Computing summary statistics*

First, we want to calculate the mean and standard deviation of the `rates` vector defined in listing 7.7. Our first attempt uses the `mean` and `std` functions from the `Statistics` module:

```julia
julia> using Statistics

julia> mean(rates)
missing

julia> std(rates)
missing
```

Unfortunately, this is not what we expect. As explained in section 7.2, we need to additionally use the `skipmissing` function:

```julia
julia> mean(skipmissing(rates))
3.9452904761904755

julia> std(skipmissing(rates))
0.022438959529396577
```

In the analyzed period, the PLN/USD exchange rate is just below 4 PLN/USD with a standard deviation of around 0.02.

7.4.2   *Finding which days of the week have the most missing values*

As discussed in section 7.3, the `dayname` function returns the English name of the given day. Therefore, we can use the `proptable` function that you learned in chapter 6 to get the desired result by cross-tabulating `dayname.(dates)` and `ismissing.(rates)`, as shown in the next listing.

> **Listing 7.8   Frequency table of proportions of days with missing data in `rates` vector**

```julia
julia> using FreqTables

julia> proptable(dayname.(dates), ismissing.(rates); margins=1)
7×2 Named Matrix{Float64}
Dim1 ╲ Dim2 │ false    true
────────────┼───────────────
Friday      │   1.0     0.0
Monday      │   1.0     0.0
Saturday    │   0.0     1.0
Sunday      │   0.0     1.0
Thursday    │  0.75    0.25
Tuesday     │   1.0     0.0
Wednesday   │   1.0     0.0
```

We can see that we always have missing data for Saturday and Sunday. For all other days, no data is missing except for Thursday. Let's find which Thursdays are problematic. For this, create a Boolean vector that finds the indices in our vector that meet both conditions using broadcasting:

```
julia> dayname.(dates) .== "Thursday" .&& ismissing.(rates)
30-element BitVector:
 0
 0
 0
 ⋮
 0
 0
 0
```

We can use this Boolean vector to find elements of the `dates` vector for which the condition is true, as the following listing shows.

Listing 7.9 Finding Thursdays on which the `rates` vector contains a `missing` value

```
julia> dates[dayname.(dates) .== "Thursday" .&& ismissing.(rates)]
1-element Vector{Date}:
 2020-06-11
```

We can see that a single day meets our condition. You could confirm that this date was a national holiday in Poland, so the result seems reasonable.

You'll learn more details in part 2 that are relevant to this example:

- In the table presented in listing 7.8, the days are ordered alphabetically. In part 2, you will learn that you can order the rows to follow the standard order of the days of the week by using the CategoricalArrays.jl package.
- In listing 7.9, the condition used looks a bit complex. In part 2, you will learn that you can make the selection more easily if you keep the `dates` and `rates` vectors in a `DataFrame`.

7.4.3 Plotting the PLN/USD exchange rate

As a final step, let's create a plot of the PLN/USD exchange rate. Start with the simplest approach, passing the `dates` and `rates` vectors to the `plot` function:

```
julia> using Plots

julia> plot(dates, rates;
            xlabel="day", ylabel="PLN/USD", legend=false, marker=:o)
```

Figure 7.3 shows the plot. It does not look very nice, as it contains gaps in places where we have `missing` values in the `rates` vector.

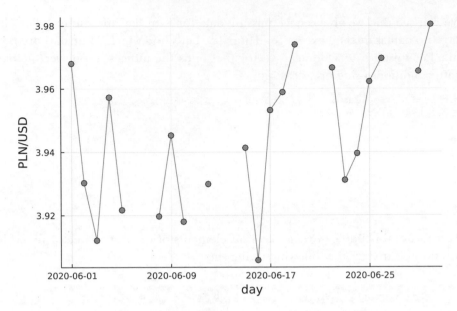

Figure 7.3   In this basic plot of `dates` against the `rates` vector, we have gaps in places where values in the vector are `missing`.

To fix the plot, let's skip the days in both `dates` and `rates` vectors in places where the `rates` vector contains `missing` values. We can again use the Boolean vector of valid indices. The syntax is slightly tricky:

```julia
julia> rates_ok = .!ismissing.(rates)
30-element BitVector:
 1
 1
 1
 ⋮
 0
 1
 1
```

How should we read it? For a single value passed, `!ismissing` is a negation of the return value produced by the `ismissing` function. Now we know that we need to prefix the bang (`!`) operator with a dot (`.`) to broadcast it, but we need to suffix the dot (`.`) to the `ismissing` part, which gives us the syntax that I have used.

Therefore, the plot with skipped missing values can be produced using the following command:

```julia
julia> plot(dates[rates_ok], rates[rates_ok];
            xlabel="day", ylabel="PLN/USD", legend=false, marker=:o)
```

Similarly to the note made at the end of section 7.4.2, this operation could have been done more cleanly if the data were stored in a `DataFrame`. We will discuss this topic in part 2.

Figure 7.4 shows the result you should get. Observe that on the plot's x-axis, the observations are properly spaced according to their dates. This effectively means that in figure 7.4, visually we have *linearly interpolated* the values for the days for which the data was missing in figure 7.3—that is, the dots in the plot are connected by straight lines.

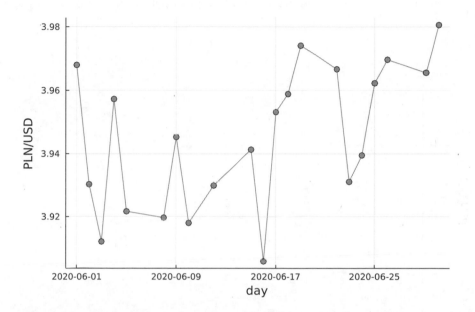

Figure 7.4   A plot of `dates` against the `rates` vector with skipped `missing` values. The plot, unlike in figure 7.3, is continuous.

You can perform linear interpolation of your data by using the `Impute.interp` function from the Impute.jl package. Given a vector, this function fills all `missing` values between two nonmissing values by using linear interpolation:

```julia
julia> using Impute

julia> rates_filled = Impute.interp(rates)
30-element Vector{Union{Missing, Float64}}:
 3.968
 3.9303
 3.9121
 ⋮
 3.9669666666666665
 3.9656
 3.9806
```

The Impute.jl package has many more features that facilitate handling of missing data. I recommend you check the package's repository (https://github.com/invenia/Impute.jl) for details.

To conclude our project, let's add a scatterplot of dates against the `rates_filled` vector to the plot shown in figure 7.4 to check that linear interpolation was indeed used there:

```julia
julia> scatter!(dates, rates_filled, markersize=3)
```

We use the `scatter!` function (with `!` at the end) to update the previous plot with additional data. Figure 7.5 shows the result of our operation.

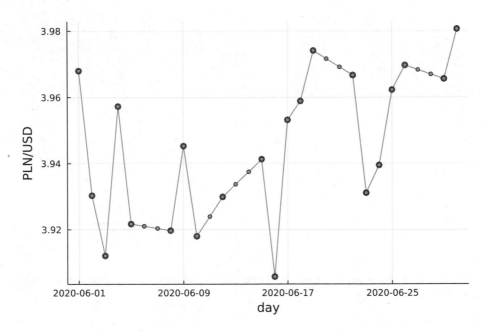

Figure 7.5   A plot of `dates` against the `rates` vector with skipped `missing` values and an added scatterplot of the `rates_filled` vector that holds missing data imputed using linear interpolation. The shape of the plot is the same as in figure 7.4.

If you would like to learn more about attributes that you can pass to plotting functions provided by the Plots.jl package, the "Attributes" section of its manual (https://docs.juliaplots.org/stable/attributes/) is a good starting point. In the context of plots presented in figures 7.3–7.5, you might, for example, find it useful to define custom ticks on the x-axis by using the `xticks` keyword argument so they use a different spacing or display format than the one used by default. Using this functionality, let's reproduce figure 7.4 with x-axis ticks for dates for which we have nonmissing data. Figure 7.6 presents the result we want.

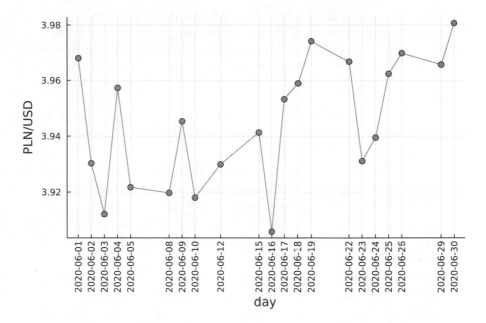

Figure 7.6 Adding x-axis ticks at dates for which we have data in a plot of `dates` against the `rates` vector with skipped `missing` values.

Figure 7.6, in comparison to figure 7.4, has three changes. First, we have x-axis ticks located at dates. We achieve this by adding the `xticks=dates[rates_ok]` keyword argument to the `plot` call. Second, since we now have a lot of ticks, we print them vertically, which is achieved by the `xrot=90` keyword argument. Third, now that the labels take up much more vertical space, we increase the bottom margin of the plot with the `bottommargin=5Plots.mm` keyword argument.

You might ask what `5Plots.mm` means. This expression defines a value that represents 5 millimeters. This functionality is provided by the Measures.jl package and is available in the Plots.jl package. We need to use the `Plots.` prefix, as Plots.jl does not export the `mm` constant. The capability to define dimensions of the plot in Plots.jl by using absolute measures of length (millimeters, in our case) is often useful when you want to create production-quality plots.

Here is the complete code producing figure 7.6:

```julia
julia> plot(dates[rates_ok], rates[rates_ok];
            xlabel="day", ylabel="PLN/USD", legend=false, marker=:o,
            xticks=dates[rates_ok], xrot=90, bottommargin=5Plots.mm)
```

To wrap up this chapter, try the following more advanced exercise.

EXERCISE 7.3 The NBP Web API allows you to get a sequence of rates for a period of dates. For example, the query `"https://api.nbp.pl/api/exchangerates/rates/a/usd/2020-06-01/2020-06-30/?format=json"`

returns a sequence of rates from June 2020 for dates when the rate is present—in other words, dates for which there is no rate are skipped. Your task is to parse the result of this query and confirm that the obtained result is consistent with the data we collected in the `dates` and `rates` vectors.

Summary

- JSON is a storage format often used to exchange data. It allows you to handle complex data structures, including both objects (providing key-value mapping) and arrays (storing sequences of values).

- The `HTTP.get` function from the HTTP.jl package can be used to send HTTP GET request messages. If the request fails, this function throws the `HTTP.ExceptionRequest.StatusError` exception.

- You can handle the exceptions thrown by Julia by using `try-catch-end` blocks. Use this functionality with care and catch only exceptions that you really want to handle.

- You can parse JSON data in Julia by using the `JSON3.read` function from the JSON3.jl package. The resulting value can be accessed using standard Julia syntax: object keys can be retrieved using the dot (`.`) syntax, and array elements using indexing.

- Julia provides the `missing` value for situations where no value is available for a variable in an observation, but a valid value theoretically exists. This special value was introduced in Julia since it is often needed, as real-life data is rarely complete.

- Many standard Julia functions propagate `missing` values: if they get `missing` as an argument, they return `missing` as a result. As a consequence, if you use these functions, you do not need to add any special code to handle missing data.

- Use the `coalesce` function to provide the default value for `missing` if you have a variable that might take this value. It is especially useful when writing logical conditions. You write `coalesce(x, false)` if you want the expression to produce `false` if x is `missing`, and leave the value of x otherwise.

- If you have a data collection that contains `missing` values, you can use the `skipmissing` wrapper to efficiently create (without copying data) another collection that has these missing values removed.

- If you have a function that does not accept `missing` values by default, you can wrap it with the `passmissing` function to turn it into a function that propagates `missing` values.

- The `Dates` standard module provides functionality for working with date, time, and date-time objects. You will likely use this module if you work with temporal data.

- You can use the `Date` object to represent instances of time as a date. Several objects (such as `Day` and `Month`) allow you to represent time periods. You can perform arithmetic operations on objects representing instances and periods of time. This built-in feature of the `Dates` standard module is useful as rules of arithmetic involving dates are complex, so you do not need to implement them yourself.

- Julia provides many convenience functions, such as `dayofweek` and `dayname`, that allow you to query `Date` objects. Such information is often needed when analyzing temporal data.

- When plotting data by using the `plot` function from the Plots.jl package, missing data is skipped. You need to take this into account when designing your plots.

- Plots.jl properly handles `Date` objects passed to it and ensures that spacing of points on the plot follows the distance between dates in the calendar. This is an important feature, as the distance on the plot is proportional to an interval between dates.

- If you want to perform linear interpolation of `missing` values in a time series of data, you can use the `Impute.interp` function from the Impute.jl package. Using this package saves you the effort of implementing the interpolation code yourself.

Part 2

Toolbox for data analysis

In part 1, you learned to load and analyze data by using data structures that are part of Base Julia, like vectors, matrices, dictionaries, and named tuples. I am sure you will find these skills useful in your projects. However, many standard data processing tasks are repeatedly needed by users—for example, reading data from a CSV file or aggregating data. Since you do not want to reimplement these tasks from scratch every time, a wide collection of Julia packages were designed to make doing them easy and efficient.

In this second part of the book, you will learn how to use DataFrames.jl and related packages to build complex data analysis pipelines. We'll cover a wide range of topics, starting from fetching and reading data, to data transformation, and finishing with building simple data analysis models and visualization.

You can expect that the topics covered in these chapters will gradually become more challenging from both data science and programming perspectives. I have selected the material in this part in a way that ensures that after learning, you will be ready to do data analysis projects and learn and use packages not covered in the book.

This part consists of seven chapters organized as follows:

- Chapter 8 teaches you how to create a data frame from a CSV file and perform basic operations on data frames. It also shows how to process data in the Apache Arrow and SQLite databases, work with compressed files, and do basic data visualization.
- Chapter 9 teaches you how to select rows and columns from a data frame. You will also learn how to build and visualize locally estimated scatterplot smoothing (LOESS) regression models.

- Chapter 10 covers various ways of creating new data frames and populating existing data frames with new data. It discusses the Tables.jl interface, an implementation-independent abstraction of a table concept. In this chapter, you will also learn how to integrate Julia with R and how to serialize Julia objects.

- Chapter 11 teaches you how to convert data frames into objects of other types. One fundamental type is the grouped data frame. You will also learn about the important general concepts of type-stable code and type piracy.

- Chapter 12 focuses on transformation and mutation of data frame objects—in particular, using the split-apply-combine strategy. Additionally, this chapter covers the basics of using the Graphs.jl package to work with graph data.

- Chapter 13 discusses advanced data frame transformation options provided by the DataFrames.jl package, as well as data frame sorting, joining, and reshaping. It also teaches you how to chain multiple operations in data processing pipelines. From a data science perspective, this chapter shows you how to work with categorical data and evaluate classification models in Julia.

- Chapter 14 shows how to build a web service in Julia that serves data produced by an analytical algorithm. Additionally, it shows how to implement Monte Carlo simulations and make them run faster by taking advantage of Julia's multithreading capabilities.

First steps with
data frames

This chapter covers

- Working with compressed files
- Reading and writing CSV files, Apache Arrow data, and SQLite databases
- Getting columns from a data frame
- Computing summary statistics of data frame contents
- Visualizing data distribution by using histograms

In this chapter, you will learn the basic principles of working with data frames in Julia provided by the DataFrames.jl package. *Data frame objects* are flexible data structures that allow you to work with tabular data. As I explained in chapter 1, tabular data in general, and a data frame in particular, is a two-dimensional structure consisting of cells. Each row has the same number of cells and provides information about one observation of the data. Each column has the same number of cells, stores information about the same feature across observations, and also has a name.

After reading part 1, you have acquired essential skills for working with Julia to analyze data. Starting with this chapter, you will learn how to efficiently perform data analysis tasks in Julia. We start with explaining how to work with tabular data, as most statistical data sets have this form. Therefore, essentially every ecosystem used for doing data science provides a data frame type. For example:

- Every relational database organizes data in one or more tables.
- In R, the `data.frame` object is a central concept built into the language. Over the years, alternative implementations of this concept were proposed in this ecosystem; two of the most popular are `tibble` and `data.table`.
- In Python, the pandas package is highly popular, and the `DataFrame` type is its pivotal component.

The goal of this chapter is to introduce you to working with data frames. We will achieve this goal by performing a simple data analysis task.

Many people like playing games. During the COVID-19 pandemic, playing chess online has become increasingly popular. Netflix additionally fueled this interest with its 2020 miniseries *The Queen's Gambit*. If you would like to read more about the recent growing interest in chess, you might want to check out the Chess.com blog post at http://mng.bz/O6Gj.

Many people practice playing chess by solving chess puzzles. Therefore, a natural question to ask is this: What makes a good chess puzzle? We will try to gain insight into this topic through the analysis we will perform in this chapter. Specifically, we will examine how the popularity of a puzzle is related to its difficulty. Maybe people like easy puzzles the most. Or maybe the opposite is true, and very hard puzzles that require finding ingenious moves are most attractive. My objective for this chapter and for chapter 9 is to show you how to find the answers to these questions.

As in any data science project, to gain insight into a problem, we need data that we can analyze. Fortunately, data on puzzles is freely available on the web. Lichess (https://lichess.org) is a free and open source chess server. One of its features is an option allowing its users to solve chess puzzles.

You can download the database of available puzzles from https://database .lichess.org. The data is distributed under the Creative Commons CC0 license. The file containing the puzzles is available as a bzip2 archive (http://mng.bz/YKgj). It contains information about more than two million puzzles, including the number of times a given puzzle was played, how hard the puzzle is, how much Lichess users like the puzzle, and what chess themes the puzzle features.

Our goal is to examine the relationship between the puzzle's degree of difficulty and whether users like it. We will perform this analysis in chapter 9. However, before we can get insights from data, we need to get it, load it, and perform its preliminary analysis. These preparatory steps are the objective of this chapter. Specifically, we will perform the following steps:

1 Download the compressed puzzle archive from the web.
2 Uncompress it.

3 Read its contents into a data frame.

4 Use histograms to analyze the distributions of selected features stored in this data set.

All these tasks need to be performed in virtually every data science project. Therefore, learning how to perform them efficiently is useful. To accomplish these objectives, I organized this chapter as follows:

- In section 8.1, you will learn how to work with bzip2 compressed data in Julia. Knowing how to programmatically handle compressed archives is often needed in practice, as data in many sources is typically compressed for storage.
- In section 8.2, I'll show you how to read a CSV file into a `DataFrame` object and quickly inspect its contents.
- Section 8.3 introduces you to the most basic way of getting data out of a data frame: by selecting a single column out of it.

The source data we work with in this chapter is in CSV format. To show you how to read and write data stored using different standards, in section 8.4 you will learn how to work with the Apache Arrow format and SQLite databases.

8.1 Fetching, unpacking, and inspecting the data

To work with the database of puzzles available on Lichess, we first need to download it from the web. Next, we will uncompress it so that later we can read it into a `Data-Frame`.

I will show you how to unpack data stored in the bzip2 archive. However, the same approach can be used to uncompress archives created in other formats. Data compression is often used, as it reduces storage size or transfer time, so knowing how to handle compressed data is useful in practice.

> **NOTE** In the GitHub repository containing the source code for this book, I have included the puzzles.csv.bz2 file that we use in this section to ensure reproducibility of the results presented in this chapter and chapter 9. The Lichess puzzle database is constantly updated, so if you choose to use its latest version instead of the one available on GitHub, you can expect slightly different results, and the code could require minor changes. For this reason, in the first step of the example code, we save the file as new_puzzles.csv.bz2 so that it does not overwrite the puzzles.csv.bz2 file that we use next in the analysis.

8.1.1 Downloading the file from the web

Since the downloaded file is large, we add a step that checks whether the file already exists locally to avoid fetching it again if this is not necessary:

```
julia> import Downloads                          Checks whether the file is
                                                 already present

julia> if isfile("new_puzzles.csv.bz2")  ⬏             If yes, prints the
           @info "file already present"        ⬏  information confirming it
```

```
        else
            @info "fetching file"
            Downloads.download("https://database.lichess.org/" *
                               "lichess_db_puzzle.csv.bz2",
                               "new_puzzles.csv.bz2")
        end
[ Info: file already present
```

> If not, informs the user that the data needs to be fetched from the web

We use the `@info` macro to print an appropriate status message. In the preceding printout, I showed that puzzles.csv.bz2 is already present in the working directory. In this case, the `isfile("new_puzzles.csv.bz2")` check produces `true`.

Creating logs of events in Julia

Julia is shipped with the `Logging` module, which allows you to log the progress of a computation as a log of events. The `@info` macro is part of this module and is used for logging informational messages. Other common event severity levels are supported via macros: `@debug`, `@warn`, and `@error`.

The `Logging` module allows you to flexibly decide which events get recorded and how. For example, you could decide you want to only log error messages and write them to a file. If you would like to learn more about how to configure logging in your Julia programs, refer to the "Logging" section of the Julia Manual (https://docs .julialang.org/en/v1/stdlib/Logging/) for details.

8.1.2 *Working with bzip2 archives*

The puzzles.csv.bz2 file that is stored in the GitHub repository and used in this chapter is compressed using the bzip2 algorithm (www.sourceware.org/bzip2/), which is indicated by the bz2 file extension. We will use the CodecBzip2.jl package to uncompress it. We first read the contents of the file as a vector of `UInt8` values (a single `UInt8` value is 1 byte), and then uncompress it to a vector of bytes by using the transcode function:

```
julia> using CodecBzip2

julia> compressed = read("puzzles.csv.bz2")
94032447-element Vector{UInt8}:
 0x42
 0x5a
 0x68
  ⋮
 0x49
 0x5f
 0x30
```

> Reads compressed data into a vector of bytes

```
julia> plain = transcode(Bzip2Decompressor, compressed)
366020640-element Vector{UInt8}:
 0x30
 0x30
 0x30
```

> Uncompresses the data using the Bzip2Decompressor codec

```
      ⋮
0x32
0x30
0x0a
```

The compressed data has 94,032,447 bytes, which after uncompression becomes 366,020,640 bytes. Thus, the compression ratio for this data set is around 4:

```
julia> length(plain) / length(compressed)
3.892492981704496
```

Understanding the transcode function

In our example, we use the `transcode` function to uncompress a vector of bytes. In Julia, this function is used in two contexts: changing string encoding and transcoding data streams.

The first use case is converting data between Unicode encodings. As you learned in chapter 6, strings in Julia are UTF-8 encoded. If you happen to have a source data stream encoded in UTF-16 or UTF-32, you can use the `transcode` function to convert it to UTF-8. Similarly, you can convert UTF-8-encoded data to UTF-16 or UTF-32.

The second situation for using the `transcode` function is to transcode data streams. In this scenario, you should provide as an input a codec you want to apply to this data and a vector of bytes. A *codec* is a program that changes encoding of data from its source format to another target. The most common usages of transcoding are data compression, uncompression, and changing data format. Here is a list of selected available codecs along with the packages that provide them:

- gzip, zlib, and deflate format compression and uncompression: CodecZlib.jl
- bzip2 format compression and uncompression: CodecBzip2.jl
- xz format compression and uncompression: CodecXz.jl
- zsdf format compression and uncompression: CodecZstd.jl
- base16, base32, and base64 decoding and encoding: CodecBase.jl

I leave out the details of all these formats and functionalities, as we will not need them in this book. If you would like to learn more about how to use the `transcode` function, refer to the documentation of the respective packages.

We most likely will want to get back to our uncompressed data several times. Let's write it to a puzzles.csv file.

In the code that saves the puzzles.csv file, we use the pattern involving the `open` function with the `do-end` block you have already seen in chapter 6. What is new is the use of the `write` function. It is used to write a binary representation of data to a file. In our case, since `plain` is `Vector{UInt8}`, we write its raw contents to the file. Before writing the uncompressed data stored in the `plain` vector, we write a string to this file by using the `println` function. This is needed because, as you will soon learn, the original CSV data does not have a header with column names. I have used column names given on the Lichess website (https://database.lichess.org/#puzzles):

```
julia> open("puzzles.csv", "w") do io
           println(io, "PuzzleId,FEN,Moves,Rating,RatingDeviation," *
                       "Popularity,NbPlays,Themes,GameUrl")
           write(io, plain)
       end
366020640
```

Writes to io the binary representation of the second passed argument

Writes to io the text representation of the second passed argument followed by a newline

8.1.3   Inspecting the CSV file

Let's quickly inspect the contents of the puzzles.csv file:

```
julia> readlines("puzzles.csv")
```

Running this command gives the following output in a terminal:

```
2132990-element Vector{String}:
 "PuzzleId,FEN,Moves,Rating,RatingDeviation,Popularity,NbPlays,Themes,GameUrl"
 "00008,r6k/pp2r2p/4Rp1Q/3p4/8/1N" ⋯ 118 bytes ⋯ "/lichess.org/787zsVup/black#48"
 "0000D,5rk1/1p3ppp/pq3b2/8/8/1P1" ⋯ 88 bytes ⋯ "https://lichess.org/F8M8OS71#53"
 "0009B,r2qr1k1/b1p2ppp/pp4n1/P1P" ⋯ 113 bytes ⋯ "/lichess.org/4MWQCxQ6/black#32"
 "000aY,r4rk1/pp3ppp/2n1b3/q1pp2B" ⋯ 108 bytes ⋯ "ttps://lichess.org/iihZGl6t#29"
 ⋮
 "zzzTs,r2qrk2/pb1n1ppQ/1p2p3/2pP" ⋯ 108 bytes ⋯ "/lichess.org/8SAGnBjb/black#32"
 "zzzUZ,r2qk2r/pp2ppbp/2n3pn/1B1p" ⋯ 107 bytes ⋯ "ttps://lichess.org/0YzF6l5X#19"
 "zzzco,5Q2/pp3R1P/1kpp4/4p3/2P1P" ⋯ 108 bytes ⋯ "ttps://lichess.org/hZWTYIAT#69"
 "zzzhI,r3kb1r/ppp2ppp/2n5/3q3b/3" ⋯ 112 bytes ⋯ "/lichess.org/NO92KH4f/black#20"
```

Indeed, the file looks like a properly formatted CSV file. This file format, which is a popular way to store tabular data, is specified as follows:

- The first line of the file contains column names separated by commas (,).
- Each of the following lines contains information about a single observation (record) of our data. In a single line, commas separate cells that refer to consecutive columns of our table. The number of columns in each row must be equal to the number of column names defined in the first row of data.

8.2   Loading the data to a data frame

Now that we have uncompressed the data, let's load it into a data frame. Our Lichess data is stored in the CSV format, and I have chosen this example intentionally because CSV is one of the most popular human-readable data formats used in practice. It can be easily read and written by spreadsheet editors. Therefore, knowing how to work with CSV files in Julia is worthwhile.

8.2.1   Reading a CSV file into a data frame

The DataFrame type defined in the DataFrames.jl library is one of the most popular options that you can use to store tabular data in memory in Julia. To read in the puzzles.csv file from disk to a `DataFrame`, use the `CSV.read` function from the CSV.jl package:

```
julia> using CSV

julia> using DataFrames

julia> puzzles = CSV.read("puzzles.csv", DataFrame);
```

In the last expression, I use the semicolon (`;`) to suppress printing the data frame contents to screen.

The `CSV.read` function can not only read data from a file whose name is passed as a string, but can also be directly passed a source that provides a sequence of bytes containing the data that should be read in. In our case, we have such a source, as it is a binary vector bound to the `plain` variable. Therefore, we could alternatively have created our data frame by writing this:

```
julia> puzzles2 = CSV.read(plain, DataFrame;
                    header=["PuzzleId", "FEN", "Moves",
                            "Rating", "RatingDeviation",
                            "Popularity", "NbPlays",
                            "Themes", "GameUrl"]);
julia> puzzles == puzzles2
true
```

Checks that puzzles and puzzles2 data frames are identical

Reads the data from the vector of bytes while passing column names using the header keyword argument

Note that in this case, we pass the `header` keyword argument to the `CSV.read` function, as our original data does not have column names. Next, we compare the two data frames by using the `==` operator to make sure they are identical.

Choosing how CSV.read reads the data from the source

In our example, we have seen that the `CSV.read` function allows passing the `header` keyword argument to supply column names to a created table. In the CSV.jl documentation (https://csv.juliadata.org/stable/reading.html), you can find a list of all options supported by the reader. I'll summarize several of the most often used keyword arguments and their functions:

- `header`—Controls how column names are treated when processing files. By default, it is assumed that the column names are the first row/line of the input.
- `limit`—Specifies the number of rows that should be read from the data. By default, all data is read.
- `misssingstring`—Controls how `missing` values are handled while parsing input data. By default, an empty string is considered to represent a `missing` value.
- `delim`—Argument that parsing looks for in the data input that separates distinct columns on each row. If no argument is provided (the default), parsing will try to detect the most consistent delimiter on the first 10 rows of the input,

(continued)

falling back to a single comma (,) if no other delimiter can be detected consistently.

- `ignorerepeated`—Used if parsing should ignore consecutive delimiters between columns. This option can be used to parse fixed-width data inputs. By default, it is set to `false`.
- `dateformat`—Controls how parsing detects date and time values in the data input. If no argument is provided (the default), parsing will try to detect time, date, and date and time columns.
- `decimal`—Used when parsing float values to indicate where the fractional portion of the float value begins. By default, a dot (.) is used.
- `stringtype`—Controls the type of string columns. By default, the Inline-String.jl package, discussed in chapter 6, is used for columns storing narrow strings, and the `String` type is used for wide columns holding strings.
- `pool`—Controls which columns will be returned as `PooledArray`. We discussed this type in chapter 6. By default, a column is pooled if it stores strings, the number of unique values stored is less than 20% of its length, and the number of unique values is less than 500.

Further, we will not need the values bound to the `compressed` and `plain` variables. Therefore, to allow Julia to free up memory allocated to these objects, we bind nothing to both variables:

```
julia> compressed = nothing

julia> plain = nothing
```

Freeing memory allocated to large objects

It is important to remember that if a large object is bound to a variable name that is reachable in the Julia program, the memory allocated to them will not be freed by Julia. To allow Julia to reclaim this memory, you must make sure that the object is not reachable.

In one common case, global variables are often created in interactive sessions. Since in Julia you cannot delete a variable name after it has been bound to a value (see http://mng.bz/G1GA), the solution is to change the binding of the variable name from pointing to a large object to `nothing`.

8.2.2   *Inspecting the contents of a data frame*

Let's have a peek at the `puzzles` data frame in the following listing.

> **Listing 8.1   Printing a sample data frame to the screen**

```
julia> puzzles
```

The output of listing 8.1 is cropped, as you can see here:

```
2132989×9 DataFrame
      Row │ PuzzleId  FEN                              Moves                            ⋯
          │ String7   String                           String                           ⋯
──────────┼────────────────────────────────────────────────────────────────────────────
        1 │ 00008     r6k/pp2r2p/4Rp1Q/3p4/8/1N1P2R1/P…  f2g3 e6e7 b2b1 b3c1 b1c1 h6c1  ⋯
        2 │ 0000D     5rk1/1p3ppp/pq3b2/8/8/1P1Q1N2/P4…  d3d6 f8d8 d6d8 f6d8
        3 │ 0009B     r2qr1k1/b1p2ppp/pp4n1/P1P1p3/4P1…  b6c5 e2g4 h3g4 d1g4
        ⋮ │    ⋮                    ⋮                                  ⋮                   ⋱
  2132987 │ zzzUZ     r2qk2r/pp2ppbp/2n3pn/1B1pP3/3P4/…  d2f3 d8a5 c1d2 a5b5
  2132988 │ zzzco     5Q2/pp3R1P/1kpp4/4p3/2P1P3/3PP2P…  f7f2 b2c2 c1b1 e2d1             ⋯
  2132989 │ zzzhI     r3kb1r/ppp2ppp/2n5/3q3b/3P1B2/5N…  c6d4 f1e1 e8d8 b1c3 d4f3 g2f3
                                                          6 columns and 2132983 rows omitted
```

Cropping is indicated by triple dots and the message at the bottom right of the print-out, where we learn that seven more columns and 2,123,983 rows were not fully printed. The exact output you get when you run this command on your computer depends on the window size where it is displayed.

When the `puzzles` data frame is printed, the header contains information about the names of the columns displayed and their element types. Each row in our data frame is a single puzzle description. Observe that the `PuzzleId` column uses five characters to encode the puzzle identifier. The `CSV.read` function automatically detects this fact and reads in this column by using the `String7` type to store the strings. On the other hand, the `FEN` and `Moves` columns are wider, and therefore the `String` type is used.

After reading in the data, it is a good practice to check whether the process produced the expected results in all columns. To get a quick view of the summary statistics for a data frame, use the `describe` function, as shown in the next listing.

> **Listing 8.2   Getting summary statistics of the data frame columns**

```julia
julia> show(describe(puzzles); truncate=14)
```

You can see the result here:

```
9×7 DataFrame
 Row │ variable       mean      min               median     max             nmissing  eltype
     │ Symbol         Union…    Any               Union…     Any             Int64     DataType
─────┼──────────────────────────────────────────────────────────────────────────────────────────
   1 │ PuzzleId                 00008                        zzzhI                  0  String7
   2 │ FEN                      1B1K4/2P5/4k3/…              rrqb2k1/3n2p1/…        0  String
   3 │ Moves                    a1a2 a3a2 b2a2…              h8h7 h6h7 g7h7…        0  String
   4 │ Rating         1533.54   511               1498.0     3001                   0  Int64
   5 │ RatingDeviation 94.9239  49                78.0       500                    0  Int64
   6 │ Popularity     81.7095   -100              89.0       123                    0  Int64
   7 │ NbPlays        891.27    0                 246.0      309831                 0  Int64
   8 │ Themes                   advancedPawn a…              opening                0  String
   9 │ GameUrl                  https://liches…              https://liches…        0  String
```

I wanted to show you the entire default result of the `describe` function. Therefore, this example also uses the `show` function to customize the data frame display. The `truncate` keyword argument allows you to specify a column's maximum display width for output before being truncated (you can learn about other keyword arguments that the `show` function supports by executing `?show` to check its documentation string).

The `describe` function returns a new data frame in which each row contains information about a single column of the original data frame. By default, `describe` produces the following statistics for each source column:

- `variable`—Name stored as a `Symbol`
- `mean`—Average of values if the column contains numeric data
- `min`—Minimum value if the column contains data that can have a defined order
- `median`—Median of values if the column contains numeric data
- `max`—Maximum value if the column contains data that can have a defined order
- `nmissing`—Number of `missing` values
- `eltype`—Type of values stored

The `describe` function allows you to additionally specify the statistics you want to compute (the ones listed here are the default) and select for which columns the summary statistics should be computed. Refer to the documentation (http://mng.bz/ 09wE) if you would like to learn the details.

Given the information presented in the summary statistics in listing 8.2, we are ready to give an interpretation of the columns stored in the `puzzles` data frame:

- `PuzzleId`—A unique identifier of the puzzle
- `FEN`—An encoding of a starting position of the puzzle
- `Moves`—Moves that are a solution to the puzzle
- `Rating`—Difficulty of the puzzle
- `RatingDeviation`—Accuracy of assessment of difficulty of the puzzle
- `Popularity`—How much the puzzle is liked by users (the higher, the better)
- `NbPlays`—Number of times a given puzzle was played
- `Themes`—Description of chess themes featured by the puzzle
- `GameUrl`—URL to the source game from which the puzzle was taken

Before we move forward, let's discuss three functions that are commonly used when working with data frames: the `ncol`, `nrow`, and `names` functions.

The `ncol` function returns the number of columns in a data frame:

```
julia> ncol(puzzles)
9
```

The nrow function returns the number of rows in a data frame:

```
julia> nrow(puzzles)
2132989
```

Finally, the names function returns a vector of column names in our data frame (this function has more features that we will discuss in chapter 9):

```
julia> names(puzzles)
9-element Vector{String}:
 "PuzzleId"
 "FEN"
 "Moves"
 "Rating"
 "RatingDeviation"
 "Popularity"
 "NbPlays"
 "Themes"
 "GameUrl"
```

8.2.3   Saving a data frame to a CSV file

Before we wrap up this section, let's see how to save a data frame back to a CSV file. You use the CSV.write function, where the first argument is the target filename, and the second argument is the table you want to save:

```
julia> CSV.write("puzzles2.csv", puzzles)
"puzzles2.csv"
```

In this code, we save the puzzles data frame to the puzzles2.csv file.

It would be interesting to check whether the original puzzles.csv and puzzles2.csv files are identical. To perform this test, we will use the read function, which when passed a file as a single argument, returns a Vector{UInt8} that contains bytes read from the file. Here is an example:

```
julia> read("puzzles2.csv")
386223179-element Vector{UInt8}:
 0x50
 0x75
 0x7a
    ⋮
 0x32
 0x30
 0x0a
```

Therefore, we can check whether the files puzzles.csv and puzzles2.csv are identical by comparing the result of the read function applied to them:

```
julia> read("puzzles2.csv") == read("puzzles.csv")
true
```

Indeed, both files contain identical data.

Choosing how CSV.write writes the data

Like the `CSV.read` function, the `CSV.write` function allows passing multiple keyword arguments to control the way the CSV data should be written. You can find all the options in the CSV.jl package documentation (https://csv.juliadata.org/stable/writing.html). Here are the most important ones:

- `delim`—A character or string to print out as the field delimiter. The default is a comma (`,`).
- `missingstring`—A string to print for `missing` values. By default, an empty string is used.
- `dateformat`—The date format string to use. The default is a format specified by the `Dates` module.
- `append`—Whether to append writing to an existing file. If `true`, it will not write column names; the default is `false`.
- `compress`—Controls whether the written output should be compressed using standard gzip compression. By default, `false` is used.
- `decimal`—Character to use as the decimal point when writing floating-point numbers. The default is a dot (`.`).

8.3   Getting a column out of a data frame

To be able to perform our analysis, we need to learn how to get data out of a data frame. The most common operation of this kind is extracting a single column. DataFrames.jl provides several options for how to do this. Let's investigate them one by one.

To keep the focus on a task of analysis of the Lichess puzzles data, we will specifically want to create histograms of the `Rating`, `RatingDeviation`, `Popularity`, and `NbPlays` columns from the `puzzles` data frame, as they will be used in our further analysis.

8.3.1   Understanding the data frame's storage model

Internally, a `DataFrame` object stores data as a collection of vectors. Each vector represents one column of a data frame and is assigned a name and a number. Let's visualize this in table 8.1.

Table 8.1   Structure of the `puzzles` data frame

Column #	Column name	Column vector
1	PuzzleId	["00008", "0000D", "0009B", "000aY", ...]
2	FEN	["r6k/pp2r2p/ ... /7K b - - 0 24", ...]
3	Moves	["f2g3 e6e7 b2b1 b3c1 b1c1 h6c1", ...]
4	Rating	[1765, 1525, 1102, 1320, 1560, 1039, ...]
5	RatingDeviation	[74, 74, 75, 74, 76, 80, 75, ...]
6	Popularity	[93, 97, 85, 92, 88, 85, 80, ...]

Table 8.1 Structure of the `puzzles` data frame *(continued)*

Column #	Column name	Column vector
7	NbPlays	[493, 9211, 503, 395, 441, 54, ...]
8	Themes	["crushing ... middlegame", ...]
9	GameUrl	["https://lichess.org/.../black#48", ...]

For example, internally, column number 4 has the name `Rating` and stores a vector of integers that represents the puzzle's difficulties: [1765, 1525, 1102, 1320, 1560, ...].

The storage layout of a data frame was chosen to ensure that operations that are performed on columns of a data frame are very fast. We will discuss multiple such operations in this book. Let's start with the simplest one: extracting a column from a data frame.

8.3.2 Treating a data frame column as a property

In chapter 4, you learned about the `NamedTuple` type and about composite types that are created using the `struct` keyword argument. We discussed the fact that you can access fields of `NamedTuple` or a composite type by using a dot (`.`) followed by a field name. The same syntax allows accessing columns of a data frame.

If you consider the `puzzles` data frame and want to extract out the `Rating` column from it, write this:

```
julia> puzzles.Rating
2132989-element Vector{Int64}:
 1765
 1525
 1102
    ⋮
  980
 1783
 2481
```

Earlier, in chapter 5, I said that the dot (`.`) allows the user to access the fields of a struct. How is it then possible that the `DataFrame` type allows the user to access its columns by using this syntax?

The reason is that Julia makes a distinction between *fields* of a `struct` object and its *properties*. When you use the dot (`.`) syntax, you get access to properties of an object. By default, properties of the object are the same as its fields, but it is possible to override this behavior (technically, you need to add appropriate methods to the `getproperty` function; see http://mng.bz/K0Bg for more information). This is exactly what is done for the `DataFrame` type. Instead of exposing its fields, it allows users to access its columns by using the dot (`.`) syntax since this is much more useful in practice.

Note that field names are part of a type definition, so every value having this type has the same fields. Conversely, if a type overrides the definition of properties, they can be different across values having the same type. For instance, all values having the

DataFrame type have the same fields, but their properties depend on the column names that a given data frame stores.

You can get the list of fields of the DataFrame type by using the fieldnames function. If you called fieldnames(DataFrame), you would get the tuple (:columns, :colindex) if you work with DataFrames.jl 1.3. (Which fields the DataFrame object stores is an implementation detail, and they may change with versions of DataFrames.jl.) The internal fields store the vectors constituting the DataFrame columns, as well as a mapping of column names and their numbers. If you wanted to extract the fields from a df variable of the DataFrame type, you could use the getfield function. For example, getfield(df, :columns) returns a vector of vectors stored in a data frame.

Figure 8.1 shows how the fields and properties of two sample data frames are related.

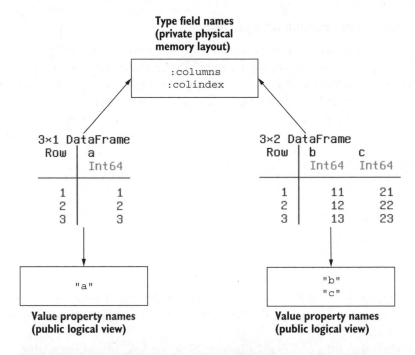

Figure 8.1   Because both data frames have the same type, they have the same field names. These field names are part of the definition of the DataFrame type. Conversely, since both data frames have different columns, their property names are different. DataFrame type properties are defined to correspond to column names of a given instance.

Although it is technically possible, you should never directly extract the fields from a data frame. The internal layout of the DataFrame type is considered private and might change in the future. I cover this topic only to make sure that you understand the distinction between fields and properties of objects in Julia.

Let's go back to the topic of this section and check how fast the operation of getting a column from a data frame is, using the `@btime` macro (recall from chapter 3 that we need to prefix the global variable `puzzles` with `$` to get proper benchmark results):

```
julia> using BenchmarkTools

julia>  @btime $puzzles.Rating;
  7.600 ns (0 allocations: 0 bytes)
```

The operation is very fast. It takes only a few nanoseconds because accessing a data frame's column this way is performed without copying the data. By writing `puzzles.Rating`, you get the same data that is referenced by the `puzzles` variable. The only operations that Julia needs to perform to get the column from a data frame are to retrieve from the `:colindex` private field the information that `Rating` has column number 4 and then extract it out from the `:columns` private field.

This behavior has a clear performance benefit. However, you might ask what to do if you want to get a copy of the vector. This is not a mundane question. In practice, you might later want to modify it without altering the original vector's data.

An established way to copy an object in Julia is to call the `copy` function on it, so by writing `copy(puzzles.Rating)`, you get a copy of the vector stored in the `puzzles` data frame. However, when you compare the `puzzles.Rating` and `copy(puzzles.Rating)`, you learn that they are equal:

```
julia> puzzles.Rating == copy(puzzles.Rating)
true
```

This shows us that using `==` to test two vectors for equality compares their contents, not their memory location. Is it possible to compare vectors in a way that would check if they were the same objects (in the sense that no Julia program could distinguish between them)? Indeed, there is. You can achieve this by using the `===` comparison discussed in chapter 7:

```
julia> puzzles.Rating === copy(puzzles.Rating)
false
```

We see that these two objects are not the same (although they have the same contents).

If we compare `puzzles.Rating` to `puzzles.Rating` by using `===`, we get `true`, as this time it is indeed the same object:

```
julia> puzzles.Rating === puzzles.Rating
true
```

On the other hand, two copies are different, as expected:

```
julia> copy(puzzles.Rating) === copy(puzzles.Rating)
false
```

You can also use a string literal after the dot (.) when getting the column from a data frame:

```julia
julia> puzzles."Rating"
2132989-element Vector{Int64}:
 1765
 1525
 1102
    ⋮
  980
 1783
 2481
```

The effect of this operation is the same as writing puzzles.Rating. You might ask, then, why puzzles."Rating" is useful. This syntax facilitates handling any special characters in a data frame's column name (for example, spaces). Then the double quotes (") make the column name's beginning and ending unambiguous. A small downside of writing puzzles."Rating" instead of puzzles.Rating is that it is a bit slower, as internally Julia needs to convert the string to a Symbol before getting the data from a data frame. However, this operation is still fast (nanoseconds).

> **EXERCISE 8.1** Using the BenchmarkTools.jl package, measure the performance of getting a column from a data frame by using the puzzles ."Rating" syntax.

8.3.3 *Getting a column by using data frame indexing*

Using the property access, like puzzles.Rating, to get a data frame's column is easy to type but has one drawback. What if the column name is stored in a variable like this?

```julia
julia> col = "Rating"
"Rating"
```

How can you get a column of the puzzles data frame that is referenced to by the col variable? And how do you get a column by its number, not by its name, from a data frame? Both questions are answered by using the indexing syntax.

The general form of indexing into a data frame is as follows:

```julia
data_frame_name[selected_rows, selected_columns]
```

As you can see, this is similar to matrices discussed in chapter 4. In this chapter, we will discuss various options for the accepted values of selected_rows and selected_columns, but in this section, we focus on what you should use to get a single column from a data frame.

To get a column from a data frame via copying, use a colon (:) as the row selector, and use a string, Symbol, or number as the column selector. Here are four equivalent ways of using copying to get the Rating column from the puzzles data frame:

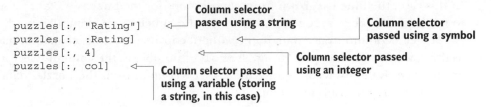

It is important to highlight that when referring to the column of a data frame, you can always use either a string or a `Symbol`. For user convenience, the data frame will accept both and treat them in the same way. Choose the style that is more convenient for you. If you are concerned about performance, using `Symbol` is a bit faster, but the time increase of using a string is negligible.

Note that in the last selector, `puzzles[:, col]`, we use the `col` variable bound to the `"Rating"` string. Allowing for this selection is the benefit of using indexing over property access.

Finally, you might ask how I have established that `Rating` is the fourth column in our data frame. This is easy to check using the `columnindex` function:

```julia
julia> columnindex(puzzles, "Rating")
4
```

If a certain column name is not found in the data frame, the `columnindex` function returns 0, as in this example:

```julia
julia> columnindex(puzzles, "Some fancy column name")
0
```

In DataFrames.jl, columns are numbered starting with 1 (just as in standard arrays), so if you get a 0 value from the `columnindex` function, you know that such a column name is not present in the data frame.

You can also test whether a data frame contains a certain column name by using the `hasproperty` function:

```julia
julia> hasproperty(puzzles, "Rating")
true
```

```julia
julia> hasproperty(puzzles, "Some fancy column name")
false
```

Note that in both `columnindex` and `hasproperty`, we could have used a `Symbol` instead of a string to pass a column name if we preferred.

Getting a column from a data frame by copying is more expensive than a noncopying operation:

```julia
julia> @btime $puzzles[:, :Rating];
  2.170 ms (2 allocations: 16.27 MiB)
```

In this case, the time has grown from nanoseconds for the puzzles.Rating selector to milliseconds for puzzles[:, :Rating]. Also, much more memory is used.

To get a column from a data frame without copying, use an exclamation mark (!) as the row selector, and use a string, Symbol, or number as the column selector. Here are four equivalent ways of getting the Rating column from the puzzles data frame without copying by using indexing:

```
puzzles[!, "Rating"]
puzzles[!, :Rating]
puzzles[!, 4]
puzzles[!, col]
```

Note that writing puzzles[!, "Rating"] is equivalent to writing puzzles.Rating. Recall that if you used : instead of ! (like this: puzzles[:, "Rating"]), you would get a copy of the Rating column.

> ### Be cautious with noncopying access to the data frame's columns
>
> In many applications, users are tempted to use the noncopying access to columns of a data frame, by, for example, writing puzzles.Rating or puzzles[!, "Rating"]. This approach has merit, as access is faster. However, noncopying access has a serious drawback if you mutate the obtained vector. The experience of DataFrames.jl users shows that this type of access can occasionally lead to hard-to-catch bugs.
>
> Therefore, as a rule of thumb, always access columns of a data frame with copying—that is, like puzzles[:, "Rating"]—unless you are 100% sure you are not going to mutate the column, or your operation needs to be performed very fast (for example, it is inside a loop that is executed millions of times).

8.3.4   *Visualizing data stored in columns of a data frame*

Now that you have learned how to get a column from a data frame, we are ready to create the desired plots. The following code uses the histogram function from the Plots.jl package to produce four histograms of the columns Rating, Rating-Deviation, Popularity, and NbPlays:

```
julia> using Plots

julia> plot(histogram(puzzles.Rating; label="Rating"),
            histogram(puzzles.RatingDeviation; label="RatingDeviation"),
            histogram(puzzles.Popularity; label="Popularity"),
            histogram(puzzles.NbPlays; label="NbPlays"))
```

You can see the result in figure 8.2. All these variables are significantly skewed. We discuss how to handle this issue and analyze the relationship between puzzle rating and popularity in chapter 9.

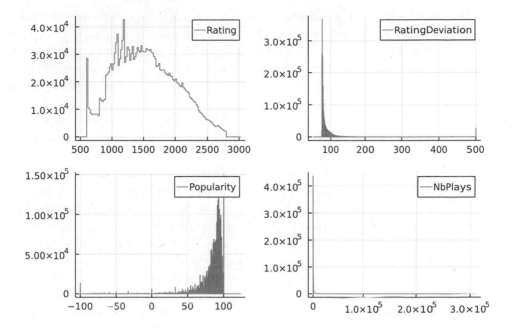

Figure 8.2 In these histograms of the columns `Rating`, `RatingDeviation`, `Popularity`, and `NbPlays` from the `puzzles` data frame, all the analyzed variables are skewed.

However, before moving to the next chapter, let's write the code generating the plot in an alternative way as an exercise:

```
julia> plot([histogram(puzzles[!, col]; label=col) for
            col in ["Rating", "RatingDeviation",
                "Popularity", "NbPlays"]]...)
```

The three dots (...) at the end of the code are the splatting operation that you learned about in chapter 4. We need it because the `plot` function expects that the histograms we create are passed as consecutive positional arguments. This code shows how you can leverage the fact that you can pass a variable instead of an explicit column name when indexing a data frame. Note that in this case, I used noncopying access to the data (by applying `!` as a row selector) because I am sure that I will not modify or store the extracted column (the values are used only to produce a plot).

8.4 *Reading and writing data frames using different formats*

In this chapter, you have learned how to read and write CSV files with Julia. However, many other data storage formats are used in data science projects. You will often want to use these formats when working with data frames in Julia.

Here are some in alphabetical order (in the parentheses, I give names of Julia packages that support them): Apache Arrow (Arrow.jl), Apache Avro (Avro.jl), Apache Parquet (Parquet.jl), Microsoft Excel (XLSX.jl), JSON (JSON3.jl), MySQL

(MySQL.jl), PostgreSQL (LibPQ.jl), and SQLite (SQLite.jl). In this section, I'll show you the Arrow.jl and SQLite.jl packages.

Apache Arrow format is a language-independent columnar memory format, organized for efficient analytic operations. This format is gaining popularity because it allows data to be transferred between different systems at little or no cost, regardless of the programming language used. Apart from these advantages, I picked this format to show how Julia allows you to handle data stored in a non-native memory format in a transparent manner. You can learn more about this standard at https://arrow .apache.org/.

As a second example, we will use a SQLite database. It is, in my opinion, one of the easiest databases to set up and use. It is also, therefore, one of the most popular databases used in practice; it is reported that more than one trillion (10^{12}) SQLite databases are in active use (www.sqlite.org/mostdeployed.html).

For both data formats, I will give you a minimal introduction to how to save and load back the `puzzles` data frame that we worked with in this chapter.

8.4.1 Apache Arrow

We start with saving a data frame in Apache Arrow format. As discussed in chapter 1, it is supported by such popular frameworks as Apache Parquet, PySpark, and Dask. The task is relatively easy; just use the `Arrow.write` function, passing it the filename and data frame you want to save:

```
julia> using Arrow

julia> Arrow.write("puzzles.arrow", puzzles)
"puzzles.arrow"
```

A more interesting process is related to reading the data stored in the Apache Arrow format. You first need to create an `Arrow.Table` object that is then passed to the `DataFrame` constructor. In the code, we check that the object we read back is the same as the original `puzzles` data frame:

```
julia> arrow_table = Arrow.Table("puzzles.arrow")      ⟵  Creates the Arrow.Table
Arrow.Table with 2329344 rows, 9 columns, and schema:      object that holds a reference
 :PuzzleId          String                                 to the source data on disk
 :FEN               String
 :Moves             String
 :Rating            Int64
 :RatingDeviation   Int64
 :Popularity        Int64
 :NbPlays           Int64
 :Themes            String
 :GameUrl           String

julia> puzzles_arrow = DataFrame(arrow_table);      ⟵  Constructs a DataFrame
                                                        from Arrow.Table

julia> puzzles_arrow == puzzles      ⟵  Checks that the data frame we've
true                                     created has the same contents as
                                         the source data frame we used
```

A distinguishing aspect of the `Arrow.Table` object is that the columns it stores use Apache Arrow format. Also, importantly, the columns in an `Arrow.Table` are views into the original arrow memory.

This has a significant advantage. When creating an `Arrow.Table` object, the operating system does not actually load the entire file contents into RAM at the same time. Instead, the file is partially swapped into RAM as different regions of the file are requested. This allows for support for working with Apache Arrow data that is larger than available RAM. Also, if you need to process only a portion of the source table, the process of reading it is much faster, as you fetch only the data required.

This design has one downside, however, since this implies that the columns having Apache Arrow data format are read-only. Here is an example:

```
julia> puzzles_arrow.PuzzleId
2329344-element Arrow.List{String, Int32, Vector{UInt8}}:
 "00008"
 "0000D"
 ⋮
 "zzzco"
 "zzzhI"

julia> puzzles_arrow.PuzzleId[1] = "newID"
ERROR: setindex! not defined for Arrow.List{String, Int32, Vector{UInt8}}
```

Note that the `puzzles_arrow.PuzzleId` column has a nonstandard `Arrow.List` type, and not, for example, a `Vector` type. This nonstandard vector type is read-only. We check this by trying to change an element of such a vector, and we get an error.

In many applications, having columns of a source data frame that are read-only is not a problem, since we might only want to read data from them. However, sometimes you might want to mutate vectors stored in a data frame created from an Apache Arrow source.

In such a case, just copy the data frame. By doing this, you will materialize the Apache Arrow columns in RAM and change their types to standard Julia types that are mutable. Here is an example:

```
julia> puzzles_arrow = copy(puzzles_arrow);

julia> puzzles_arrow.PuzzleId
2329344-element Vector{String}:
 "00008"
 "0000D"
 ⋮
 "zzzco"
 "zzzhI"
```

After performing a `copy` operation of a data frame, the `:PuzzleId` column now has a standard `Vector` type.

8.4.2 SQLite

For Apache Arrow data, we will first create an SQLite database on disk. Next, we will store the `puzzles` data frame in it. Finally, we will read it back using the SQL `SELECT` query.

First, we create an SQLite database that is backed up by a file on disk. Use the `SQLite.DB` function, passing it a filename as an argument:

```
julia> using SQLite

julia> db = SQLite.DB("puzzles.db")
SQLite.DB("puzzles.db")
```

Next, we store the `puzzles` data frame in it by using the `SQLite.load!` function. We pass the table we want to store in the database, the connection to a database where we want to store it, and the table name in the target database as three positional arguments:

```
julia> SQLite.load!(puzzles, db, "puzzles")
"puzzles"
```

Let's check to see if we have successfully created a table in our database. We first use the `SQLite.tables` function to list all tables stored in the database, followed by the `SQLite.columns` function to get more detailed information on columns stored in a given table:

```
julia> SQLite.tables(db)
1-element Vector{SQLite.DBTable}:
 SQLite.DBTable("puzzles", Tables.Schema:
 :PuzzleId          Union{Missing, String}
 :FEN               Union{Missing, String}
 :Moves             Union{Missing, String}
 :Rating            Union{Missing, Int64}
 :RatingDeviation   Union{Missing, Int64}
 :Popularity        Union{Missing, Int64}
 :NbPlays           Union{Missing, Int64}
 :Themes            Union{Missing, String}
 :GameUrl           Union{Missing, String})

julia> SQLite.columns(db, "puzzles")
(cid = [0, 1, 2, 3, 4, 5, 6, 7, 8],
 name = ["PuzzleId", "FEN", "Moves", "Rating", "RatingDeviation",
         "Popularity", "NbPlays", "Themes", "GameUrl"],
 type = ["TEXT", "TEXT", "TEXT", "INT", "INT",
         "INT", "INT", "TEXT", "TEXT"],
 notnull = [1, 1, 1, 1, 1, 1, 1, 1, 1],
 dflt_value = [missing, missing, missing, missing, missing,
               missing, missing, missing, missing],
 pk = [0, 0, 0, 0, 0, 0, 0, 0, 0])
```

We see that there is now one `puzzles` table in our database. The metadata about columns of this table matches the structure of the source `puzzles` data frame.

Finally, we read back the `puzzles` table into a data frame. As an important first step, we need to create a query. We use the `DBInterface.execute` function, to which we pass a connection to a database and a string containing the SQL query we want to run. Importantly, this operation is lazy and does not materialize the query.

The data is fetched only when we need it. In our example, we perform this materialization by creating a data frame using the results of the query.

Also, note that we are using a generic `execute` function that is not SQLite specific. It is defined in the interface package DBInterface.jl that is automatically loaded by SQLite.jl. If we used another database backend, we would also use the `DBInterface` `.execute` to run SQL queries against it in the same way. After creating the data frame, we check that the obtained result is the same as the original `puzzles` data frame:

```julia
julia> query = DBInterface.execute(db, "SELECT * FROM puzzles")
SQLite.Query(SQLite.Stmt(SQLite.DB("puzzles.db"), 7),
Base.RefValue{Int32}(100), [:PuzzleId, :FEN, :Moves, :Rating,
:RatingDeviation, :Popularity, :NbPlays, :Themes, :GameUrl],
Type[Union{Missing, String}, Union{Missing, String},
Union{Missing, String}, Union{Missing, Int64}, Union{Missing, Int64},
Union{Missing, Int64}, Union{Missing, Int64}, Union{Missing, String},
Union{Missing, String}], Dict(:NbPlays => 7, :Themes => 8, :GameUrl => 9,
:Moves => 3, :RatingDeviation => 5, :FEN => 2, :Rating => 4,
:PuzzleId => 1, :Popularity => 6), Base.RefValue{Int64}(0))

julia> puzzles_db = DataFrame(query);

julia> puzzles_db == puzzles
true
```

This time, unlike with the Apache Arrow case, the columns of a data frame are standard Julia vectors. Let's check it for the `:PuzzleId` column:

```julia
julia> puzzles_db.PuzzleId
2329344-element Vector{String}:
 "00008"
 "0000D"
 ⋮
 "zzzco"
 "zzzhI"
```

After we are done using the SQLite database, we close it:

```julia
julia> close(db)
```

To learn more about how to work with the Arrow.jl and SQLite.jl packages discussed in this section, visit their respective repositories at https://github.com/apache/arrow-julia and https://github.com/JuliaDatabases/SQLite.jl.

Summary

- DataFrames.jl is a package that allows you to work with tabular data in Julia. The most important type it defines is `DataFrame`, whose rows typically represent observations and whose columns typically represent features of those observations.
- You can use the CodecBzip2.jl package to uncompress bzip2 archives. Similar functionality is available in Julia as well as for other compression formats, because in real-life applications, you will often need to work with compressed data.

- The `CSV.read` function from the CSV.jl package can be used to read data stored in CSV files into a `DataFrame`. Similarly, the `CSV.write` function can be used to save tabular data to a CSV file. The CSV format is one of the most popular human-readable ones, and you can expect to use it often when doing data analysis.

- You can use the `describe` function to get summary information about a data frame. In this way, you can quickly inspect whether the data stored in a data frame follows your expectations.

- The `nrow` and `ncol` functions give you information about the number of rows and columns of a data frame. Since these functions return a value, they are often used when writing code that operates on data frame objects.

- The `names` function can be used to get a list of column names in a data frame; it additionally accepts a column selector argument that allows you to pass conditions specifying the column names you want to get. This feature is especially useful when you work with very wide data frames with thousands of columns.

- Internally, `DataFrame` objects store data in columns. Every column of a data frame is a vector. This ensures that extracting columns from a data frame is very fast.

- You can get a column from a data frame by using the property access syntax (for example, `puzzles.Rating` returns the `Rating` column). This is one of the most performed operations, as it is convenient to type and read.

- When referring to columns of a data frame, you can use either strings or symbols; therefore, both `puzzles."Rating"` and `puzzles.Rating` are valid. Using strings is especially useful if your column name contains characters not allowed in identifiers in Julia (for example, spaces).

- You can use the `histogram` function from the Plots.jl package to plot histograms of your data. This is a useful way to inspect the distribution of your data.

- The Arrow.jl package allows you to work with data stored in the Apache Arrow format. This is often useful when you want to interchange data between different data analysis ecosystems or want to work with data that is too large to fit into RAM.

- The SQLite.jl package provides an interface to the SQLite database engine. The SQLite database is one of the most popular formats for storing, sharing, and archiving your data.

Getting data from a data frame

This chapter covers

- Subsetting rows of a data frame
- Selecting columns of a data frame
- Creating local linear regression (LOESS) models
- Visualizing LOESS predictions

In chapter 8, you learned the basic principles of working with data frames in Julia provided by the DataFrames.jl package, and we started to analyze the Lichess chess puzzle data. Recall that our objective was to identify the relationship between puzzle difficulty and popularity.

In section 8.3, we stopped our investigation by concluding that we would like to clean the original data before performing its final analysis (in figure 9.1, I reproduce the histograms we used in chapter 8 to conclude that the original data is significantly skewed). The simplest form of data cleaning is removing the unwanted observations. Therefore, in this chapter, you will learn how to get data from a data frame by subsetting its rows and selecting columns.

Our goal in this chapter is to check the relationship between the puzzle difficulty and how much users like it. To perform this analysis, we will take the following steps:

1 Subset the data set to concentrate only on columns and rows that we want to analyze later.

2 Aggregate data about the relationship between puzzle difficulty and popularity in a data frame and plot it.

3 Build a local linear regression (LOESS) to obtain better summary information about relationships present in the data.

Through this analysis, the key skill that you will obtain after studying this chapter is learning various ways for indexing into a data frame.

Data frame *indexing*—selecting some of its columns or subsetting rows—is one of the most often needed operations in practice. Therefore, learning how to index into a data frame is a good starting point in your journey with DataFrames.jl.

To accomplish this goal, and at the same time show you how to perform the analysis of the Lichess puzzle, I organized this chapter as follows:

- In section 9.1, I discuss in depth multiple ways to index into a data frame by subsetting its rows and/or selecting columns.
- To reinforce your learning, in section 9.2, I do not introduce any new concepts but show how knowledge introduced in chapter 8 and section 9.1 can be combined in a more complex scenario. As a final step in this section, we will build a LOESS model to understand the relationship between puzzle difficulty and popularity in the Lichess database.

9.1   Advanced data frame indexing

In this section, you will learn how to perform column selection and row subsetting in a data frame. This is one of the most common operations when working with data frames.

Figure 8.2, reproduced here as figure 9.1 for your convenience, shows that the data we are working with is significantly skewed.

Before continuing with the analysis of the relationship of the `Rating` and `Popularity` columns, let's apply the following conditions to our data frame to create a new one that we will use later in the analysis:

- We want to keep only the `Rating` and `Popularity` columns, as these are the only columns we will need for the analysis.
- We want to drop rows representing puzzles that we do not want to include in the analysis.

Let's now discuss the conditions that the puzzle must meet to be included in our analysis.

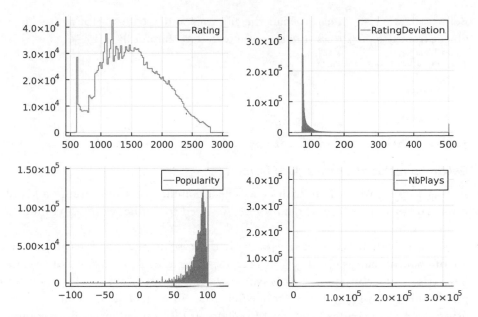

Figure 9.1 These histograms of the `Rating`, `RatingDeviation`, `Popularity`, and `NbPlays` columns from the `puzzles` data frame show that all the analyzed variables are skewed.

First, we want to keep puzzles that were played enough times. Therefore, we focus on those puzzles for which the number of plays, `NbPlays`, is greater than the median of that column. This condition will eliminate 50% of puzzles. In this way, we remove puzzles that were not played much, as they might not have a stable value for their rating or popularity.

Second, we want to drop puzzles with low or very high difficulty ratings. This removes easy puzzles, which are most likely evaluated by inexperienced players, as well as very hard puzzles for which typical players might not have enough experience to fairly evaluate them. We will consider puzzles having ratings less than 1500 as too easy to be included. I chose 1500 as a threshold since this is the starting rating of any puzzle. In listing 8.2, you can see that the median and mean of ratings are around 1500. To indicate a very high rating, we use the 99th percentile (we will drop 1% of the hardest puzzles).

This section is organized as follows. In section 9.1.1, I show you how to perform the exact operation that we want to do to analyze the Lichess puzzle data. In this way, you will get an idea of how these operations work. Next, in subsection 9.1.2, I will give you a complete list of allowed column selectors, and in subsection 9.1.3, we will discuss a complete list of allowed row-subsetting options.

NOTE Before working with code from this chapter, follow the instructions in section 8.1 to make sure that you have the puzzles.csv file present in your working directory.

Before we start, we need to load the libraries and create the `puzzles` data frame object from the puzzles.csv file that we created in chapter 8:

```julia
julia> using DataFrames

julia> using CSV

julia> using Plots

julia> puzzles = CSV.read("puzzles.csv", DataFrame);
```

9.1.1 *Getting a reduced puzzles data frame*

In this section, you will learn how to select columns of a data frame and subset its rows. To get our processed data frame, we need to define a proper column selector and row selector.

We start with the column selector, as in this case, it is simple. We can just pass a vector of column names like this: `["Rating", "Popularity"]`. Alternatively, we could have passed the column names as symbols, `[:Rating, :Popularity]`, or, for example, as integers `[4, 6]`. (Remember that you can easily check a column number by using the `columnindex` function.) In section 9.1.2, you will learn more column selector options that DataFrames.jl offers.

To define a proper row-subsetting operation, we will use the *indicator vector*. This vector must have as many elements as we have rows in our data frame and must contain `Bool` values. Rows corresponding to `true` values in the indicator vector are kept, and the `false` values are dropped.

First, we create an indicator vector of rows with the number of plays less than the median by using the `median` function from the `Statistics` module:

```julia
julia> using Statistics

julia> plays_lo = median(puzzles.NbPlays)
246.0

julia> puzzles.NbPlays .> plays_lo
2132989-element BitVector:
 1
 1
 1
 ⋮
 1
 1
 0
```

Note that we use broadcasting when we write `.>` to compare the `NbPlays` column to a scalar value of a computed median. If we were to omit the dot (`.`), we would get an error:

```julia
julia> puzzles.NbPlays > plays_lo
ERROR: MethodError: no method matching isless(::Float64, ::Vector{Int64})
```

In a similar way, let's create an indicator vector of puzzles whose rating is between 1500 and the 99th percentile. For the second condition, we use the `quantile` function from the `Statistics` module:

```
julia> rating_lo = 1500
1500

julia> rating_hi = quantile(puzzles.Rating, 0.99)
2658.0

julia> rating_lo .< puzzles.Rating .< rating_hi
2132989-element BitVector:
 1
 1
 0
 ⋮
 0
 1
 1
```

We have used broadcasting again to get the desired result. Finally, let's combine both conditions by using the broadcasted `&&` operator:

```
julia> row_selector = (puzzles.NbPlays .> plays_lo) .&&
                      (rating_lo .< puzzles.Rating .< rating_hi)
2132989-element BitVector:
 1
 1
 0
 ⋮
 0
 1
 0
```

In this expression, I could have omitted the parentheses, but my personal preference leads me to always explicitly show how operations should be grouped together when working with complex conditions.

Let's check how many rows we selected. We can use either the `sum` or the `count` function:

```
julia> sum(row_selector)
513357

julia> count(row_selector)
513357
```

The difference between the `sum` and the `count` functions is that `count` requires that the data passed to it is Boolean and counts the number of `true` values, while `sum` can process any data for which addition is meaningfully defined. Since in Julia, `Bool` values are treated as numbers, as you learned in chapter 2, you can add them. In such an addition, `true` is considered to be 1 and `false` to be 0.

We are now ready to create our desired data frame in the next listing. We'll call it good.

Listing 9.1   Selecting rows and columns of a data frame by using indexing

```julia
julia> good = puzzles[row_selector, ["Rating", "Popularity"]]
513357×2 DataFrame
    Row │ Rating  Popularity
        │ Int64   Int64
────────┼────────────────────
      1 │   1765          93
      2 │   1525          97
      3 │   1560          88
      ⋮ │   ⋮           ⋮
 513356 │   2069          92
 513357 │   1783          90
             513352 rows omitted
```

We can see that the good data frame has 513,357 rows and two columns as expected. Let's create the histograms of the selected columns (figure 9.2) to see if they have a better distribution now:

```julia
julia> plot(histogram(good.Rating; label="Rating"),
            histogram(good.Popularity; label="Popularity"))
```

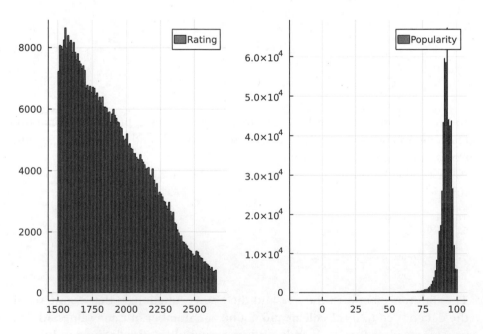

Figure 9.2   In these histograms of the columns Rating and Popularity from the good data frame, the distributions of both variables follow the expectations, and we will use this data in our further analysis.

The rating distribution is now roughly decreasing; we have fewer difficult puzzles than easy puzzles. For the distribution of popularity, we do not have peaks at –100 and 100 as in figure 8.2, which were most likely caused by puzzles that have not been played much. Please check this hypothesis as an exercise.

> **EXERCISE 9.1** Calculate summary statistics of the NbPlays column under two conditions. In the first, select only puzzles that have popularity equal to 100, and in the second, select puzzles that have popularity equal to –100. To calculate the summary statistics of a vector, use the summarystats function from the StatsBase.jl package.

9.1.2 Overview of allowed column selectors

In practice, you might want to select columns of a data frame by using different conditions—for example, keep all columns except several that you do not want, or keep all columns whose name matches a particular pattern. In this section, you will learn that DataFrames.jl provides a rich set of column selectors that allow you to easily accomplish such tasks.

You learned in section 8.3 that passing a string, a Symbol, or an integer as a column selector extracts a column from a data frame. These three column selectors are called *single-column selectors*. The type of the obtained result depends on the row selector used. If it is a single integer, you get the value stored in the cell of a data frame:

```
julia> puzzles[1, "Rating"]
1765
```

If a row selector picks multiple rows, you get a vector. Let's repeat an example you already saw in section 8.3:

```
julia> puzzles[:, "Rating"]
2132989-element Vector{Int64}:
 1765
 1525
 1102
    ⋮
  980
 1783
 2481
```

All other selectors we will discuss select multiple columns. The type of the obtained result again depends on the row-subsetting value used. If you pick a single row, you get an object called DataFrameRow:

```
julia> row1 = puzzles[1, ["Rating", "Popularity"]]
DataFrameRow
 Row │ Rating  Popularity
     │ Int64   Int64
─────┼────────────────────
   1 │   1765          93
```

You can think of `DataFrameRow` as a `NamedTuple` containing the selected cells. The only difference is that `DataFrameRow` retains a link to the data frame it was taken from. Technically, it is a view. Therefore, when the data frame is updated, it is reflected in the `DataFrameRow`. Conversely, if you update the `DataFrameRow`, the underlying data frame would also be updated (we will discuss mutation of data frames in detail in chapter 12).

Some users are surprised that using normal indexing creates a view in this case. However, this design choice, after a hot debate, was made to ensure that getting a row of a data frame is a fast operation, as typically you pick many consecutive rows of a data frame in a loop and only read data from them.

For now, as I have said, you can think of `DataFrameRow` as a single-dimensional object. Therefore, you can get data from it exactly as from a data frame, but just using a single index if you use indexing. Here are the ways to get a `Rating` value from the row1 object:

```
julia> row1["Rating"]
1765

julia> row1[:Rating]
1765

julia> row1[1]
1765

julia> row1.Rating
1765

julia> row1."Rating"
1765
```

On the other hand, if you select multiple rows and multiple columns, you get a `Data-Frame`. You have already seen this kind of selection in listing 9.1:

```
julia> good = puzzles[row_selector, ["Rating", "Popularity"]]
513357×2 DataFrame
    Row │ Rating  Popularity
        │ Int64   Int64
────────┼────────────────────
      1 │   1765          93
      2 │   1525          97
      3 │   1560          88
    ⋮   │   ⋮         ⋮
 513356 │   2069          92
 513357 │   1783          90
          513352 rows omitted
```

Table 9.1 summarizes the possible output types of data frame indexing.

Table 9.1 Output types of data frame indexing, depending on the row subsetting value and column selector

	Single-column selector	Multiple-column selector
Single-row subsetting	good[1, "Rating"] Value stored in a cell	good[1, :] DataFrameRow
Multiple-row subsetting	good[:, "Rating"] A vector	good[:, :] DataFrame

Now that you now know the output types that you can expect, given different column selectors, we are ready to dive into the available multiple column selectors. We have a lot of them, as many rules exist for selecting columns. I will list them one by one with examples, referring to our `puzzles` data frame.

I'll first show you the list of available options so that you have a brief reference to them. Next, I explain how you can check which columns are selected by each of them, using the `names` function. We start with the list:

- *A vector of string,* `Symbol`, *or integer values*—You have already seen this style in section 8.3: `["Rating", "Popularity"]`, `[:Rating, :Popularity]`, `[4, 6]`.
- *A vector of Boolean values that has a length equal to the data frame's number of columns*—Here, to select the columns `Rating` and `Popularity`, an appropriate vector would be the following (note that it has length 9 and has a `true` value in positions 4 and 6):

```
julia> [false, false, false, true, false, true, false, false, false]
9-element Vector{Bool}:
 0
 0
 0
 1
 0
 1
 0
 0
 0
```

- *A regular expression*—This selects columns matching the passed expression (we discussed regular expressions in chapter 6). For example, passing an `r"Rating"` regular expression would pick columns `Rating` and `RatingDeviation`.
- *A* `Not` *expression*—This negates the passed selector. For example, `Not([4, 6])` would select all columns except columns 4 and 6; similarly, `Not(r"Rating")` would pick all columns except `Rating` and `RatingDeviation` that match the `r"Rating"` regular expression.
- A `Between` expression—An example is `Between("Rating", "Popularity")`, which fetches consecutive columns starting from `Rating` and ending with `Popularity`, so in our case, it would be `Rating`, `RatingDeviation`, and `Popularity`.

- A colon (:) or All() selector—This selects all columns.
- A Cols selector—This has two forms. In the first one, you can pass multiple selectors as arguments and select their union; for example, Cols(r"Rating", "NbPlays") would select columns Rating, RatingDeviation, and NbPlays. In the second form, you pass a function as an argument to Cols; then this function should accept a string that is the name of the column and return a Boolean value. As a result, you will get the list of columns for which the passed function returns true. For example, if you use the Cols(startswith ("P")) selector, you would get PuzzleId and Popularity columns, as these are the only columns in the puzzles data frame whose names start with P.

This was exhausting. Fortunately, as I have hinted, there is an easy way to test all of these examples.

Do you remember the names function discussed in section 8.2? It returns the column names stored in the data frame. Often you need to pick column names from a data frame without performing data frame indexing. The nice thing about the names function is that it can take any column selector as its second argument and will return the names of the selected columns. Let's try the names function with all the examples in the preceding list:

```julia
julia> names(puzzles, ["Rating", "Popularity"])
2-element Vector{String}:
 "Rating"
 "Popularity"

julia> names(puzzles, [:Rating, :Popularity])
2-element Vector{String}:
 "Rating"
 "Popularity"

julia> names(puzzles, [4, 6])
2-element Vector{String}:
 "Rating"
 "Popularity"

julia> names(puzzles,
             [false, false, false, true, false, true, false, false, false])
2-element Vector{String}:
 "Rating"
 "Popularity"

julia> names(puzzles, r"Rating")
2-element Vector{String}:
 "Rating"
 "RatingDeviation"

julia> names(puzzles, Not([4, 6]))
7-element Vector{String}:
 "PuzzleId"
 "FEN"
 "Moves"
 "RatingDeviation"
```

```
  "NbPlays"
  "Themes"
  "GameUrl"

julia> names(puzzles, Not(r"Rating"))
7-element Vector{String}:
 "PuzzleId"
 "FEN"
 "Moves"
 "Popularity"
 "NbPlays"
 "Themes"
 "GameUrl"

julia> names(puzzles, Between("Rating", "Popularity"))
3-element Vector{String}:
 "Rating"
 "RatingDeviation"
 "Popularity"

julia> names(puzzles, :)
9-element Vector{String}:
 "PuzzleId"
 "FEN"
 "Moves"
 "Rating"
 "RatingDeviation"
 "Popularity"
 "NbPlays"
 "Themes"
 "GameUrl"

julia> names(puzzles, All())
9-element Vector{String}:
 "PuzzleId"
 "FEN"
 "Moves"
 "Rating"
 "RatingDeviation"
 "Popularity"
 "NbPlays"
 "Themes"
 "GameUrl"

julia> names(puzzles, Cols(r"Rating", "NbPlays"))
3-element Vector{String}:
 "Rating"
 "RatingDeviation"
 "NbPlays"

julia> names(puzzles, Cols(startswith("P")))
2-element Vector{String}:
 "PuzzleId"
 "Popularity"
```

This is not everything that the names function has in its store.

First, instead of writing names(puzzles, Cols(startswith("P"))), you can omit the Cols wrapper. The call to names(puzzles, startswith("P")), where you pass a function taking a string and returning a Boolean value, will produce the same result.

The final feature is that you can pass a type as a second argument to the names function. You will get columns whose element type is a subtype of the passed type. For example, to get all columns that store real numbers in our puzzles data frame, you can write this:

```julia
julia> names(puzzles, Real)
4-element Vector{String}:
 "Rating"
 "RatingDeviation"
 "Popularity"
 "NbPlays"
```

And to get all columns holding strings, write this:

```julia
julia> names(puzzles, AbstractString)
5-element Vector{String}:
 "PuzzleId"
 "FEN"
 "Moves"
 "Themes"
 "GameUrl"
```

Note that the last two forms accepted in names (passing a function and passing a type) are not accepted in indexing. Therefore, to select all columns storing real numbers from the puzzles data frame, write puzzles[:, names(puzzles, Real)].

You now have all the power of flexible selection of data frame columns at your fingertips. We can move on to row selectors, which are a bit simpler.

9.1.3   *Overview of allowed row-subsetting values*

In this section, you will learn the options for performing row subsetting of a data frame. In subsection 9.1.2, we discussed passing a single integer as a row-subsetting value. You get either a value of a single cell (if a single-column selector is used) or a DataFrameRow (if a multiple-column selector is used).

When you select multiple rows, you get either a vector (when a single column is picked) or a data frame (when multiple columns are selected). Which multiple-row selectors are allowed? Here is a complete list:

- *A vector of integers*—For example, [1, 2, 3] will pick rows corresponding to the passed-in numbers.
- *A vector of Boolean values*—Its length must be equal to the number of rows in a data frame, and in the result, you get rows for which the vector contains true. You saw this selector in section 8.3; for example, in the expression puzzles[row_selector, ["Rating", "Popularity"]] in listing 9.1, the row_selector is a Boolean vector.

- *A* Not *expression*—This works in the same way as for columns. Writing Not([1, 2, 3]) will pick all rows except rows 1, 2, and 3.
- *A colon* (:)—This picks all rows from a data frame with copying.
- *An exclamation mark* (!)—This picks all rows from a data frame without copying (remember the warning in section 8.2 that you should use this option with care, as it can lead to hard-to-catch bugs).

First, let's look at a comparison of integer, Boolean, and Not selectors on a small data frame. In the example, we first create the df_small data frame with a single column named :id and values in the range from 1 to 4 (we will discuss this and other ways to create a data frame in detail in chapter 10). Next, we subset this data frame by using various row selectors:

```
julia> df_small = DataFrame(id=1:4)
4×1 DataFrame
 Row │ id
     │ Int64
─────┼───────
   1 │     1
   2 │     2
   3 │     3
   4 │     4

julia> df_small[[1, 3], :]
2×1 DataFrame
 Row │ id
     │ Int64
─────┼───────
   1 │     1
   2 │     3

julia> df_small[[true, false, true, false], :]
2×1 DataFrame
 Row │ id
     │ Int64
─────┼───────
   1 │     1
   2 │     3

julia> df_small[Not([2, 4]), :]
2×1 DataFrame
 Row │ id
     │ Int64
─────┼───────
   1 │     1
   2 │     3

julia> df_small[Not([false, true, false, true]), :]
2×1 DataFrame
 Row │ id
     │ Int64
─────┼───────
   1 │     1
   2 │     3
```

In the example, all indexing operations keep rows number 1 and 3 from the df_small data frame.

Next, let's look at an example comparing the : and ! row selectors. Let's compare the following selection operations:

```julia
julia> df1 = puzzles[:, ["Rating", "Popularity"]];

julia> df2 = puzzles[!, ["Rating", "Popularity"]];
```

Both df1 and df2 pick all rows and two columns from the puzzles data frame. We can check whether they store the same data:

```julia
julia> df1 == df2
true
```

Although df1 and df2 share the same contents, they are not identical. The difference is that df1 has copied the Rating and Popularity columns, while df2 reuses the Rating and Popularity columns from the puzzles data frame. We can easily check it by using the === comparison:

```julia
julia> df1.Rating === puzzles.Rating
false

julia> df1.Popularity === puzzles.Popularity
false

julia> df2.Rating === puzzles.Rating
true

julia> df2.Popularity === puzzles.Popularity
true
```

Therefore, mutating the df2 data frame later could affect the data stored in the puzzles data frame, which is unsafe. Again, the benefit of using ! over : is speed and memory consumption, as we can see in the following benchmark:

```julia
julia> using BenchmarkTools

julia> @btime $puzzles[:, ["Rating", "Popularity"]];
  4.370 ms (27 allocations: 32.55 MiB)

julia> @btime $puzzles[!, ["Rating", "Popularity"]];
  864.583 ns (21 allocations: 1.70 KiB)
```

As a wrap-up, I'll summarize the available options again. Remember that passing an integer like 1 selects a single row or column, while passing a vector wrapping it like [1] selects multiple rows or columns (which happen to be 1 in this case). Therefore, we have four options for indexing to a data frame, differing in the obtained result:

- Passing single-element selectors for both row and column indices returns the contents of a single cell of a data frame:

```
julia> puzzles[1, 1]
"00008"
```

- Passing a multirow subsetting value and a single-column selector returns a vector:

```
julia> puzzles[[1], 1]
1-element Vector{String7}:
 "00008"
```

- Passing a single-row subsetting value and a multicolumn selector returns a `DataFrameRow`:

```
julia> puzzles[1, [1]]
DataFrameRow
 Row │ PuzzleId
     │ String7
─────┼──────────
   1 │ 00008
```

- Passing a multirow subsetting value and a multicolumn selector returns a `DataFrame`:

```
julia> puzzles[[1], [1]]
1×1 DataFrame
 Row │ PuzzleId
     │ String7
─────┼──────────
   1 │ 00008
```

Data frame row names

You might have noticed that DataFrames.jl does not support providing row names for your `DataFrame` objects. The only way to refer to a data frame's row is by its number.

However, it is easy to add a column to your data frame that stores row names. Row names are often used in other ecosystems to provide a way to perform a fast row lookup. In chapters 11, 12, and 13, you will learn that DataFrames.jl delivers this functionality by using an alternative approach based on the `groupby` function.

9.1.4 *Making views of data frame objects*

In chapter 4, you learned that you can use the `@view` macro to create views into arrays that avoid copying the data. The same mechanism is supported in DataFrames.jl. If you pass any indexing expression to a `@view` macro, you get a view.

The benefit of creating a view is that it is, in general, faster and uses less memory than the standard indexing discussed in section 9.1.3. However, this benefit comes at a cost. A view shares data with the parent object, which can lead to hard-to-catch bugs in your code, especially if you modify the data that the view references.

You have four options for making a view of a data frame, depending on whether row and column selectors pick one or multiple rows, as discussed in subsection 9.1.3:

- Passing single-element selectors for both row and column indices returns a view to the contents of a single cell of a data frame (technically, as you can see, it is considered a zero-dimensional object; if you want to learn more about these, refer to the "Frequently Asked Questions" section of the Julia manual at http://mng.bz/9VKq):

```
julia> @view puzzles[1, 1]
0-dimensional view(::Vector{String7}, 1) with eltype String7:
"00008"
```

- Passing a multirow selector and single column selector returns a view into a vector:

```
julia> @view puzzles[[1], 1]
1-element view(::Vector{String7}, [1]) with eltype String7:
 "00008"
```

- Passing a single-row selector and multicolumn selector returns a `DataFrame-Row` (so there is no difference from `puzzles[1, [1]]`, as normal indexing already produces a view; see the discussion in subsection 9.1.2):

```
julia> @view puzzles[1, [1]]
DataFrameRow
 Row │ PuzzleId
     │ String7
─────┼──────────
   1 │ 00008
```

- Passing a multirow and multicolumn selector returns a `SubDataFrame`:

```
julia> @view puzzles[[1], [1]]
1×1 SubDataFrame
 Row │ PuzzleId
     │ String7
─────┼──────────
   1 │ 00008
```

Out of these options, the most frequently used one is creating a `SubDataFrame`. You use a view of a data frame when you want to save memory and time, and you accept that your resulting object will reuse the memory with its parent.

As an example, let's compare the performance of the operation `puzzles[row_selector, ["Rating", "Popularity"]]` that we did in listing 9.1 against the same operation creating a view:

```
julia> @btime $puzzles[$row_selector, ["Rating", "Popularity"]];
  4.606 ms (22 allocations: 11.75 MiB)

julia> @btime @view $puzzles[$row_selector, ["Rating", "Popularity"]];
  1.109 ms (12 allocations: 3.92 MiB)
```

Creating a view is faster and uses less memory. The biggest allocations that we see when creating a view of a data frame are for storing information about the selected rows and columns. You can retrieve the indices of the source data frame that are picked by a SubDataFrame by using the `parentindices` function:

```
julia> parentindices(@view puzzles[row_selector, ["Rating", "Popularity"]])
([1, 2, 5, 8 … 2132982, 2132983, 2132984, 2132988], [4, 6])
```

What is a data frame?

You now know that DataFrames.jl defines the `DataFrame` and `SubDataFrame` types. These two types have a common supertype: `AbstractDataFrame`. The `AbstractDataFrame` represents a general concept of a data frame in Data-Frames.jl, independent of its underlying representation in memory.

Most of the functions in DataFrames.jl work with `AbstractDataFrame` objects, so they accept both the `DataFrame` and `SubDataFrame` types In these cases. In this book, I write that we work with a data frame. For example, the indexing that we used in this chapter works in the same way for all data frames.

However, in some cases, it is important that we work with a concrete type. For example, the `DataFrame` constructor always returns a `DataFrame`. Also, in chapter 11, we will discuss adding rows to a `DataFrame` in place by using the `push!` function. This operation is not supported by `SubDataFrame` objects since they are views.

9.2 Analyzing the relationship between puzzle difficulty and popularity

As promised in the chapter introduction, in this section, we'll use the skills that you have acquired in a more complex context to understand the relationship between puzzle difficulty and popularity. We'll do it in two steps. In section 9.2.1, we'll calculate the mean popularity of puzzles by their rating. Next, in section 9.2.2, we'll fit a LOESS regression to this data.

9.2.1 Calculating mean puzzle popularity by its rating

In this section, you'll learn how to aggregate data in a data frame by using functionalities from Base Julia. Aggregation is one of the most common operations needed for data analysis.

We will use the `good` data frame that we created in listing 9.1. The approach that we use in this section is intended to show you how to use indexing into a data frame. However, this is not the most efficient way to perform the analysis. At the end of this chapter, I will show you the code that accomplishes the required operation faster but requires learning more advanced features of the DataFrames.jl package related to the `groupby` function (these are discussed in chapters 11, 12, and 13). First, let's recall the contents of the `good` data frame:

```
julia> describe(good)
2×7 DataFrame
 Row │ variable    mean      min    median    max    nmissing  eltype
     │ Symbol      Float64    Int64  Float64   Int64  Int64     DataType
─────┼────────────────────────────────────────────────────────────────
   1 │ Rating      1900.03    1501   1854.0    2657         0   Int64
   2 │ Popularity    91.9069   -17     92.0     100         0   Int64
```

For each unique value in the `Rating` column, we will want to calculate the average of the `Popularity` column. We will perform this task in two steps:

1 Create a dictionary, mapping a given rating value to a vector of rows in the data frame where it can be found.

2 Use this dictionary to compute the average popularity per each unique value of rating.

We start with the first task, creating a dictionary and mapping a rating to data frame rows where it can be found:

```
julia> rating_mapping = Dict{Int, Vector{Int}}()    ⟵  Creates an empty dictionary that
Dict{Int64, Vector{Int64}}()                             will be used to store the mapping

julia> for (i, rating) in enumerate(good.Rating)    ⟵  Iterates all elements of the
             if haskey(rating_mapping, rating)              good.Rating vector and keeps
                 push!(rating_mapping[rating], i)    ⟵     track of both the index and
             else                                           value of the iterated element
                 rating_mapping[rating] = [i]        ⟵
             end
       end
```

Checks whether we have already encountered a given rating value

If we have not seen a given rating value, creates a new entry in the dictionary

If we have seen a given rating value, appends its index to an existing entry in the dictionary

```
julia> rating_mapping
Dict{Int64, Vector{Int64}} with 1157 entries:
  2108 => [225, 6037, 6254, 7024, 8113, 8679, 8887, 131…
  2261 => [361, 2462, 5276, 6006, 6409, 6420, 9089, 101…
  1953 => [655, 984, 1290, 1699, 2525, 2553, 3195, 3883…
  2288 => [864, 1023, 2019, 3475, 4164, 9424, 9972, 123…
  1703 => [68, 464, 472, 826, 1097, 1393, 2042, 2110, 4…
  ⋮   => ⋮
```

Let's review key parts of this code. The `enumerate(good.Rating)` expression used in a `for` loop yields `(i, rating)` tuples, where `i` is a counter starting at 1 and rating is the i-th value from the `good.Rating` vector. Using `enumerate` is useful when you need not only the values `rating` over which you are iterating, but also the number of iterations so far.

Next, we check whether the `rating` we get was seen previously. If we already have it in the `rating_mapping` dictionary, we retrieve the vector of indices mapped to this rating value and append at the end of this vector the row number i using the `push!` function. On the other hand, if we have not seen a given `rating` yet, we create a new entry in the dictionary that maps `rating` to a vector holding a single integer i.

Let's try to get the rows of the `good` data frame for indices stored in the `rating_mapping` dictionary for a rating equal to 2108:

```
julia> good[rating_mapping[2108], :]
457×2 DataFrame
 Row │ Rating  Popularity
     │ Int64   Int64
─────┼───────────────────
   1 │   2108          95
   2 │   2108          90
   3 │   2108          90
   ⋮ │    ⋮           ⋮
 456 │   2108          91
 457 │   2108          92
          452 rows omitted
```

It seems we get only rows with the 2108 rating. We can make sure that this is the case by using the `unique` function:

```
julia> unique(good[rating_mapping[2108], :].Rating)
1-element Vector{Int64}:
 2108
```

Indeed, only the 2108 value is in the `Rating` column in our selection.

> **EXERCISE 9.2** Make sure that the values stored in the `rating_mapping` dictionary add up to represent all row indices of our `good` data frame. To do this, check whether the sum of lengths of these vectors is equal to the number of rows in the `good` data frame.

Computing the mean rating of our `Popularity` column for a 2108 rating is now easy:

```
julia> using Statistics

julia> mean(good[rating_mapping[2108], "Popularity"])
91.64989059080963
```

Now we have all the pieces ready to create a plot, showing the relationship between rating and popularity of puzzles. First, create a vector of unique rating values by using the `unique` function again:

```
julia> ratings = unique(good.Rating)
1157-element Vector{Int64}:
 1765
 1525
 1560
    ⋮
 2616
 2619
 2631
```

Next, we compute mean popularity per unique rating value:

```
julia> mean_popularities = map(ratings) do rating
           indices = rating_mapping[rating]
           popularities = good[indices, "Popularity"]
           return mean(popularities)
       end
```

```
1157-element Vector{Float64}:
 92.6219512195122
 91.7780580075662
 91.79565772669221
  ⋮
 88.87323943661971
 89.56140350877193
 89.34782608695652
```

If you would like to refresh your understanding of how the map function works with the do-end block, see chapter 2. To get the desired result, we could have used comprehension instead of the map function. It would be the following expression:

```
[mean(good[rating_mapping[rating], "Popularity"]) for rating in ratings]
```

However, I prefer the solution using the map function as, in my opinion, the code is easier to understand.

Finally, we can perform the desired plot:

```
julia> using Plots

julia> scatter(ratings, mean_popularities;
               xlabel="rating", ylabel="mean popularity", legend=false)
```

Figure 9.3 shows the result.

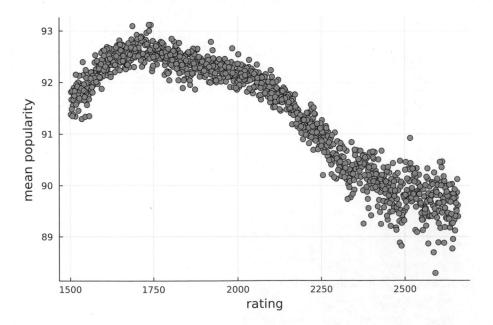

Figure 9.3 Plotting the relationship between a puzzle rating and its popularity shows that puzzles with a rating of around 1750 have the highest mean popularity.

9.2.2 *Fitting LOESS regression*

In this section, you will learn how to fit the LOESS regression to your data and make predictions using the fitted model.

The relationship presented in figure 9.3 shows that the results have some noise. Let's create a plot showing a smoothed relationship between rating and mean popularity. For this, we will use a popular local regression model called LOESS.

> **LOESS regression**
>
> The locally estimated scatterplot smoothing (LOESS) model was originally developed for scatterplot smoothing. You can find more information about this method in "Computational Methods for Local Regression" by William S. Cleveland and E. Grosse (https://doi.org/10.1007/BF01890836).
>
> In Julia, the Loess.jl package allows you to build LOESS regression models.

We'll create a LOESS model, make a prediction using it, and add a line to our plot. First prepare the predictions:

```julia
julia> using Loess

julia> model = loess(ratings, mean_popularities);

julia> ratings_predict = float(sort(ratings))
1157-element Vector{Float64}:
 1501.0
 1502.0
 1503.0
    ⋮
 2655.0
 2656.0
 2657.0

julia> popularity_predict = predict(model, ratings_predict)
1157-element Vector{Float64}:
 91.78127959282982
 91.78699303591367
 91.7926814281816
    ⋮
 89.58061736598427
 89.58011426583589
 89.57962657070658
```

Note that to make a prediction, we first sort ratings by using the `sort` function. This is done to make a final plot look nice, as we want the points to be ordered on the x-axis. (As an alternative to sorting data, you can pass the `serisetype=:line` keyword argument to the `plot` function.) Additionally, we use the `float` function on the resulting vector. The reason is that the `predict` function accepts only vectors of floating-point numbers, and our original `ratings` vector contains integers, not floats.

You can check which arguments the `predict` function accepts by running the `methods` function with `predict` as its argument:

```
julia> methods(predict)
# 3 methods for generic function "predict":
[1] predict(model::Loess.LoessModel{T}, z::T)
    where T<:AbstractFloat in Loess at …
[2] predict(model::Loess.LoessModel{T}, zs::AbstractVector{T})
    where T<:AbstractFloat in Loess at ...
[3] predict(model::Loess.LoessModel{T}, zs::AbstractMatrix{T})
    where T<:AbstractFloat in Loess at ...
```

As you can see, the `predict` function has three methods. Each takes a trained model as a first argument, and the second argument can be a scalar, a vector, or a matrix. In all three methods, the restriction is that the elements of the second argument must be a subtype of `AbstractFloat`.

We are now ready to add a smoothed line to our plot:

```
julia> plot!(ratings_predict, popularity_predict; width=5, color="black")
```

Note that we use `plot!` to add an additional line to the already existing plot. The result is shown in figure 9.4.

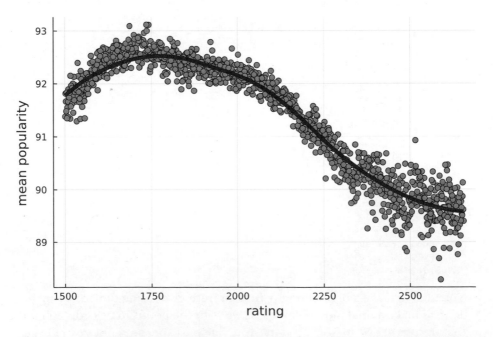

Figure 9.4 Adding a local regression plot to the relationship between a puzzle rating and its popularity confirms that the puzzles with the highest mean popularity have a rating of around 1750.

From figure 9.4, we can see that the most popular puzzles have a rating of around 1750, so if the puzzle is either too easy or too hard, its popularity is lower.

From a data science perspective, this analysis is, of course, a bit simplified:

- I have omitted that both ratings are measured with uncertainty (the `Rating-Deviation` column measures it).
- Popularity is also based on only a sample of users' responses.
- For different ratings, we have a different number of puzzles.
- I have not optimized the smoothing in the LOESS model (this can be done using the `span` keyword argument in the `Loess.loess` function; see https://github.com/JuliaStats/Loess.jl).

A more careful analysis could have taken all these factors into account, but I decided to omit such analysis to keep the example simple and concentrate on the topic of indexing that we cover in this chapter.

> **EXERCISE 9.3** Check the consequences of changing the value of the `span` keyword argument in the `loess` function. By default, this argument has the value 0.75. Set it to 0.25 and add another prediction line to the plot presented in figure 9.4. Make the line yellow with its width equal to 5.

As a last example in this chapter, as promised previously, let's see how we could have used more advanced features of DataFrames.jl to aggregate the data for our analysis to get popularity means by rating:

```julia
julia> combine(groupby(good, :Rating), :Popularity => mean)
1157×2 DataFrame
  Row │ Rating  Popularity_mean
      │ Int64   Float64
──────┼─────────────────────────
    1 │  1501           91.3822
    2 │  1502           91.8164
    3 │  1503           91.6671
    ⋮ │   ⋮              ⋮
 1156 │  2656           89.6162
 1157 │  2657           89.398
              1152 rows omitted
```

The exact rules for the meaning of this code and its execution are explained in chapters 11, 12, and 13. I decided to show this code here to make it clear to you that the calculations using a dictionary in section 9.2.1 are not an idiomatic way to perform data aggregation in DataFrames.jl. Still, I wanted to present the low-level approach in that section as I believe it nicely explains how you can write more-complex data processing code using loops, dictionaries, and data frame indexing, as you might occasionally need to write such low-level code.

Summary

- Indexing into a data frame always requires passing both a row selector and column selector and has the general form `data_frame[row_selector, column_selector]`. This approach ensures that the person reading your code will immediately see what output to expect.

- DataFrames.jl defines a wide range of accepted column selectors that can be integers, strings, symbols, vectors, regular expressions, or `:`, `Not`, `Between`, `Cols`, or `All` expressions. This flexibility is needed as users often want to use complex patterns for column selection. Note that the `1` and `[1]` selectors are not equivalent. Although both refer to the first column, the first one extracts it from a data frame, while the second creates a data frame with this single column.

- To select rows of a data frame, you can use integers, vectors, and `Not`, `:`, and `!` expressions. Similarly, column selectors `1` and `[1]` are not equivalent. The first one creates a `DataFrameRow`, while the second creates a data frame.

- Both `:` and `!` select all rows from a data frame. The difference between them is that `:` performs a copy of the vectors stored in the data frame, while `!` reuses the vectors stored in the source data frame. Using `!` is faster and uses less memory but can lead to hard-to-catch bugs, so I discourage it unless the user's code is performance sensitive.

- You can make views of `DataFrame` objects by using the `@view` macro exactly as you can for arrays. It is important to remember that views share memory with the parent object. Therefore, they are fast to create and do not use much memory, but at the same time, you need to be careful when mutating their contents. In particular, if you select a single row and multiple columns of a data frame, you get a `DataFrameRow` object that is a view into a single row of a data frame.

- The `==` infix operator compares the contents of containers like vectors or data frames. The `===` operator can be used to check whether the compared objects are the same (in the most common case of mutable containers, this checks whether they are stored in the same memory location).

- You can use dictionaries to help you with aggregation of data. This approach allows you to process data independent of the type of container storing your data. However, if you are using DataFrames.jl, you can alternatively use the `groupby` function to achieve the same result. The details of this functionality are explained in chapters 11, 12, and 13.

- The Loess.jl package can be used to build local regression models. These models are used when your data has nonlinear relationships between the feature and target variable.

Creating data frame objects

10

This chapter covers

- Creating data frames
- Using RCall.jl to integrate with the R language
- Understanding the Tables.jl interface
- Plotting a correlation matrix
- Constructing a data frame iteratively by adding rows to it
- Serializing Julia objects

In chapter 8, I introduced you to working with data frames, using sample data loaded from a CSV file. In this chapter, I'll show you more ways to convert values of different types to and from a DataFrame object. You need to have this fundamental knowledge so you can use the DataFrames.jl package efficiently. You must be prepared for source data to come in various formats, and you need to know how to convert that data to a DataFrame.

Since the topic of creating DataFrame objects is broad, in this chapter, I use several small tasks as examples of applying the concepts you learn. Following one complex example (as we did with the Lichess puzzle data in chapters 8 and 9) would not allow me to show all the options that are useful in practice. To ensure that this chapter, apart from teaching you how to create data frames, also gives you useful recipes for data analysis, we will create a plot of a correlation matrix of data stored in a data frame.

I divided the chapter into two sections to help you easily navigate the available options and concentrate on the scenarios that are most relevant in your day-to-day work:

- In section 10.1, you'll learn various ways to create a data frame from an object of a different type holding the source data. You will need to do such operations if you already have data that you want to store in a data frame.
- In section 10.2, you'll learn to create a data frame iteratively by adding new rows to it as new data becomes available. You will use this approach to create data frame objects if the data you want to store in a data frame is generated when your program is running (for example, if you collect results of a simulation experiment).

In section 10.1.2, we will use the RCall.jl package that provides integration between Julia and R. Running the examples in that section requires having a properly configured R installation on your computer. Therefore, make sure to follow the environment setup instructions in appendix A.

10.1 *Reviewing the most important ways to create a data frame*

In this section, you'll learn the three most common ways to create a data frame from source data that has a different type than `DataFrame`. This is an essential skill you need to master because your source might have various formats. However, to use the functionalities that the DataFrames.jl package offers, you first need to create an object that has the `DataFrame` type.

In this section, I illustrate the most common scenarios by using the Anscombe's quartet data that we worked with in chapter 4. In these scenarios, we create a data frame via the following:

- A matrix
- A collection of vectors
- The Tables.jl interface

In addition, you will learn how to use RCall.jl to integrate Julia with the R language and how to create a plot of a correlation matrix of data stored in a data frame. Before we can start creating data frame objects, we first need to re-create the `aq` matrix with the Anscombe's quartet data that we used in chapter 4:

```
julia> aq = [10.0    8.04   10.0   9.14   10.0    7.46    8.0    6.58
              8.0    6.95    8.0   8.14    8.0    6.77    8.0    5.76
             13.0    7.58   13.0   8.74   13.0   12.74    8.0    7.71
              9.0    8.81    9.0   8.77    9.0    7.11    8.0    8.84
             11.0    8.33   11.0   9.26   11.0    7.81    8.0    8.47
             14.0    9.96   14.0   8.1    14.0    8.84    8.0    7.04
              6.0    7.24    6.0   6.13    6.0    6.08    8.0    5.25
              4.0    4.26    4.0   3.1     4.0    5.39   19.0   12.50
```

```
       12.0   10.84   12.0   9.13   12.0   8.15   8.0   5.56
        7.0    4.82    7.0   7.26    7.0   6.42   8.0   7.91
        5.0    5.68    5.0   4.74    5.0   5.73   8.0   6.89];
```

First, make sure to load the DataFrames.jl package:

```
julia> using DataFrames
```

10.1.1 Creating a data frame from a matrix

In this section, you will learn how to create a data frame from a matrix since matrices are commonly used to store data that you might want to analyze.

One of the differences between a `Matrix` and a `DataFrame` in Julia is that a `Matrix` does not support column names. Therefore, when we pass a `Matrix` to a `DataFrame` constructor, we need to provide column names. These names can be given as either a vector of strings or a vector of symbols. I show both options in the following listing.

Listing 10.1 Creating the `aq1` data frame

```
julia> aq1 = DataFrame(aq, ["x1", "y1", "x2", "y2", "x3", "y3", "x4", "y4"])     Uses a
11×8 DataFrame                                                                   vector of
 Row │ x1       y1       x2       y2       x3       y3       x4       y4         strings as
     │ Float64  Float64  Float64  Float64  Float64  Float64  Float64  Float64     column
─────┼───────────────────────────────────────────────────────────────────────    names
   1 │    10.0     8.04     10.0     9.14     10.0     7.46      8.0     6.58
   2 │     8.0     6.95      8.0     8.14      8.0     6.77      8.0     5.76
   3 │    13.0     7.58     13.0     8.74     13.0    12.74      8.0     7.71
   4 │     9.0     8.81      9.0     8.77      9.0     7.11      8.0     8.84
   5 │    11.0     8.33     11.0     9.26     11.0     7.81      8.0     8.47
   6 │    14.0     9.96     14.0      8.1     14.0     8.84      8.0     7.04
   7 │     6.0     7.24      6.0     6.13      6.0     6.08      8.0     5.25
   8 │     4.0     4.26      4.0      3.1      4.0     5.39     19.0    12.5
   9 │    12.0    10.84     12.0     9.13     12.0     8.15      8.0     5.56
  10 │     7.0     4.82      7.0     7.26      7.0     6.42      8.0     7.91
  11 │     5.0     5.68      5.0     4.74      5.0     5.73      8.0     6.89
```

Uses a vector of symbols as column names

```
julia> DataFrame(aq, [:x1, :y1, :x2, :y2, :x3, :y3, :x4, :y4])
11×8 DataFrame
 Row │ x1       y1       x2       y2       x3       y3       x4       y4
     │ Float64  Float64  Float64  Float64  Float64  Float64  Float64  Float64
─────┼───────────────────────────────────────────────────────────────────────
   1 │    10.0     8.04     10.0     9.14     10.0     7.46      8.0     6.58
   2 │     8.0     6.95      8.0     8.14      8.0     6.77      8.0     5.76
   3 │    13.0     7.58     13.0     8.74     13.0    12.74      8.0     7.71
   4 │     9.0     8.81      9.0     8.77      9.0     7.11      8.0     8.84
   5 │    11.0     8.33     11.0     9.26     11.0     7.81      8.0     8.47
   6 │    14.0     9.96     14.0      8.1     14.0     8.84      8.0     7.04
   7 │     6.0     7.24      6.0     6.13      6.0     6.08      8.0     5.25
   8 │     4.0     4.26      4.0      3.1      4.0     5.39     19.0    12.5
   9 │    12.0    10.84     12.0     9.13     12.0     8.15      8.0     5.56
  10 │     7.0     4.82      7.0     7.26      7.0     6.42      8.0     7.91
  11 │     5.0     5.68      5.0     4.74      5.0     5.73      8.0     6.89
```

When we convert a `Matrix` to a `DataFrame`, columns of the `Matrix` become columns in a `DataFrame`. For convenience, you can ask the `DataFrame` constructor to create column names automatically by passing the `:auto` argument instead of a vector of column names:

```
julia> DataFrame(aq, :auto)
11×8 DataFrame
 Row │ x1       x2       x3       x4       x5       x6       x7       x8
     │ Float64  Float64  Float64  Float64  Float64  Float64  Float64  Float64
─────┼────────────────────────────────────────────────────────────────────────
   1 │    10.0     8.04     10.0     9.14     10.0     7.46      8.0     6.58
   2 │     8.0     6.95      8.0     8.14      8.0     6.77      8.0     5.76
   3 │    13.0     7.58     13.0     8.74     13.0    12.74      8.0     7.71
   4 │     9.0     8.81      9.0     8.77      9.0     7.11      8.0     8.84
   5 │    11.0     8.33     11.0     9.26     11.0     7.81      8.0     8.47
   6 │    14.0     9.96     14.0      8.1     14.0     8.84      8.0     7.04
   7 │     6.0     7.24      6.0     6.13      6.0     6.08      8.0     5.25
   8 │     4.0     4.26      4.0      3.1      4.0     5.39     19.0    12.5
   9 │    12.0    10.84     12.0     9.13     12.0     8.15      8.0     5.56
  10 │     7.0     4.82      7.0     7.26      7.0     6.42      8.0     7.91
  11 │     5.0     5.68      5.0     4.74      5.0     5.73      8.0     6.89
```

When we use the `:auto` option, the generated column names consist of an x character followed by the column number.

Similarly to a `Matrix` argument, the `DataFrame` constructor accepts a `Vector` of vectors as a first argument and column names as a second argument. Let's first create a `Vector` of vectors from our `aq` matrix (recall that we discussed the `collect` and `eachcol` functions in chapter 4):

```
julia> aq_vec = collect(eachcol(aq))
8-element Vector{SubArray{Float64, 1, Matrix{Float64},
                 Tuple{Base.Slice{Base.OneTo{Int64}}, Int64}, true}}:
 [10.0, 8.0, 13.0, 9.0, 11.0, 14.0, 6.0, 4.0, 12.0, 7.0, 5.0]
 [8.04, 6.95, 7.58, 8.81, 8.33, 9.96, 7.24, 4.26, 10.84, 4.82, 5.68]
 [10.0, 8.0, 13.0, 9.0, 11.0, 14.0, 6.0, 4.0, 12.0, 7.0, 5.0]
 [9.14, 8.14, 8.74, 8.77, 9.26, 8.1, 6.13, 3.1, 9.13, 7.26, 4.74]
 [10.0, 8.0, 13.0, 9.0, 11.0, 14.0, 6.0, 4.0, 12.0, 7.0, 5.0]
 [7.46, 6.77, 12.74, 7.11, 7.81, 8.84, 6.08, 5.39, 8.15, 6.42, 5.73]
 [8.0, 8.0, 8.0, 8.0, 8.0, 8.0, 8.0, 19.0, 8.0, 8.0, 8.0]
 [6.58, 5.76, 7.71, 8.84, 8.47, 7.04, 5.25, 12.5, 5.56, 7.91, 6.89]
```

The way to create a `DataFrame` from the `aq_vec` object is to either pass the column names as the second argument

```
julia> DataFrame(aq_vec, ["x1", "y1", "x2", "y2", "x3", "y3", "x4", "y4"])
11×8 DataFrame
 Row │ x1       y1       x2       y2       x3       y3       x4       y4
     │ Float64  Float64  Float64  Float64  Float64  Float64  Float64  Float64
─────┼────────────────────────────────────────────────────────────────────────
   1 │    10.0     8.04     10.0     9.14     10.0     7.46      8.0     6.58
   2 │     8.0     6.95      8.0     8.14      8.0     6.77      8.0     5.76
   3 │    13.0     7.58     13.0     8.74     13.0    12.74      8.0     7.71
   4 │     9.0     8.81      9.0     8.77      9.0     7.11      8.0     8.84
   5 │    11.0     8.33     11.0     9.26     11.0     7.81      8.0     8.47
```

```
 6 │    14.0    9.96    14.0    8.1     14.0    8.84     8.0    7.04
 7 │     6.0    7.24     6.0    6.13     6.0    6.08     8.0    5.25
 8 │     4.0    4.26     4.0    3.1      4.0    5.39    19.0   12.5
 9 │    12.0   10.84    12.0    9.13    12.0    8.15     8.0    5.56
10 │     7.0    4.82     7.0    7.26     7.0    6.42     8.0    7.91
11 │     5.0    5.68     5.0    4.74     5.0    5.73     8.0    6.89
```

or pass the `:auto` keyword argument:

```
julia> DataFrame(aq_vec, :auto)
11×8 DataFrame
 Row │ x1       x2       x3       x4       x5       x6       x7       x8
     │ Float64  Float64  Float64  Float64  Float64  Float64  Float64  Float64
─────┼────────────────────────────────────────────────────────────────────────
   1 │    10.0     8.04    10.0     9.14    10.0     7.46     8.0     6.58
   2 │     8.0     6.95     8.0     8.14     8.0     6.77     8.0     5.76
   3 │    13.0     7.58    13.0     8.74    13.0    12.74     8.0     7.71
   4 │     9.0     8.81     9.0     8.77     9.0     7.11     8.0     8.84
   5 │    11.0     8.33    11.0     9.26    11.0     7.81     8.0     8.47
   6 │    14.0     9.96    14.0     8.1     14.0     8.84     8.0     7.04
   7 │     6.0     7.24     6.0     6.13     6.0     6.08     8.0     5.25
   8 │     4.0     4.26     4.0     3.1      4.0     5.39    19.0    12.5
   9 │    12.0    10.84    12.0     9.13    12.0     8.15     8.0     5.56
  10 │     7.0     4.82     7.0     7.26     7.0     6.42     8.0     7.91
  11 │     5.0     5.68     5.0     4.74     5.0     5.73     8.0     6.89
```

10.1.2 *Creating a data frame from vectors*

You will often want to convert objects that store columns as vectors to a `DataFrame`. Vectors, like the matrices discussed in section 10.1.1, are a common format in which your source data might originally be stored. For example, in listing 4.2, we used the following `NamedTuple` to store the Anscombe's quartet data:

```
julia> data = (set1=(x=aq[:, 1], y=aq[:, 2]),
               set2=(x=aq[:, 3], y=aq[:, 4]),
               set3=(x=aq[:, 5], y=aq[:, 6]),
               set4=(x=aq[:, 7], y=aq[:, 8]));
```

In the `data` NamedTuple, we have stored the columns of our data frame as vectors. For example, recall from chapter 4 that you can retrieve the x column from the `set1` data set as follows:

```
julia> data.set1.x
11-element Vector{Float64}:
 10.0
  8.0
 13.0
  9.0
 11.0
 14.0
  6.0
  4.0
 12.0
  7.0
  5.0
```

CONSTRUCTOR USING KEYWORD ARGUMENTS

We can pass vectors to a DataFrame constructor in two ways. The first is to use the keyword arguments:

```
julia> DataFrame(x1=data.set1.x, y1=data.set1.y,
                 x2=data.set2.x, y2=data.set2.y,
                 x3=data.set3.x, y3=data.set3.y,
                 x4=data.set4.x, y4=data.set4.y)
11×8 DataFrame
 Row │ x1       y1       x2       y2       x3       y3       x4       y4
     │ Float64  Float64  Float64  Float64  Float64  Float64  Float64  Float64
─────┼────────────────────────────────────────────────────────────────────────
   1 │    10.0     8.04     10.0     9.14     10.0     7.46      8.0     6.58
   2 │     8.0     6.95      8.0     8.14      8.0     6.77      8.0     5.76
   3 │    13.0     7.58     13.0     8.74     13.0    12.74      8.0     7.71
   4 │     9.0     8.81      9.0     8.77      9.0     7.11      8.0     8.84
   5 │    11.0     8.33     11.0     9.26     11.0     7.81      8.0     8.47
   6 │    14.0     9.96     14.0     8.1      14.0     8.84      8.0     7.04
   7 │     6.0     7.24      6.0     6.13      6.0     6.08      8.0     5.25
   8 │     4.0     4.26      4.0     3.1       4.0     5.39     19.0    12.5
   9 │    12.0    10.84     12.0     9.13     12.0     8.15      8.0     5.56
  10 │     7.0     4.82      7.0     7.26      7.0     6.42      8.0     7.91
  11 │     5.0     5.68      5.0     4.74      5.0     5.73      8.0     6.89
```

Using this style, we pass a column name followed by a vector that we want to store in this column. Note that we take advantage of the fact that keyword arguments in Julia do not require any additional decorators (like a : prefix in the case of Symbol); see the discussion of keyword arguments in section 2.4.

In this example, we have unnested the data object that held four data sets into eight columns. In section 10.1.3, you will see another way to convert the data object to a data frame that relies on the Tables.jl interface.

CONSTRUCTOR USING PAIRS

Another way you can create the same data frame is by using positional arguments with the Pair notation column_name => column_data:

```
julia> DataFrame(:x1 => data.set1.x, :y1 => data.set1.y,
                 :x2 => data.set2.x, :y2 => data.set2.y,
                 :x3 => data.set3.x, :y3 => data.set3.y,
                 :x4 => data.set4.x, :y4 => data.set4.y)
11×8 DataFrame
 Row │ x1       y1       x2       y2       x3       y3       x4       y4
     │ Float64  Float64  Float64  Float64  Float64  Float64  Float64  Float64
─────┼────────────────────────────────────────────────────────────────────────
   1 │    10.0     8.04     10.0     9.14     10.0     7.46      8.0     6.58
   2 │     8.0     6.95      8.0     8.14      8.0     6.77      8.0     5.76
   3 │    13.0     7.58     13.0     8.74     13.0    12.74      8.0     7.71
   4 │     9.0     8.81      9.0     8.77      9.0     7.11      8.0     8.84
   5 │    11.0     8.33     11.0     9.26     11.0     7.81      8.0     8.47
   6 │    14.0     9.96     14.0     8.1      14.0     8.84      8.0     7.04
   7 │     6.0     7.24      6.0     6.13      6.0     6.08      8.0     5.25
   8 │     4.0     4.26      4.0     3.1       4.0     5.39     19.0    12.5
   9 │    12.0    10.84     12.0     9.13     12.0     8.15      8.0     5.56
```

```
10 |    7.0    4.82    7.0    7.26    7.0    6.42    8.0    7.91
11 |    5.0    5.68    5.0    4.74    5.0    5.73    8.0    6.89
```

Again, instead of symbols, we could have used strings, which can be handy when you want your columns to contain nonstandard characters like spaces.

An additional feature of the notation using `Pair` is that instead of passing multiple positional arguments, we can pass a vector of these pairs to get the same result (I omit printing it to save space since the output is the same as in the preceding example):

```
julia> DataFrame([:x1 => data.set1.x, :y1 => data.set1.y,
                  :x2 => data.set2.x, :y2 => data.set2.y,
                  :x3 => data.set3.x, :y3 => data.set3.y,
                  :x4 => data.set4.x, :y4 => data.set4.y]);
```

What is the benefit of such an approach? It is useful because it is then easy to traverse the `data` `NamedTuple` with a comprehension. Let's do this step by step. First, create a vector iterating data set numbers (from 1 to 4) and columns (`:x` and `:y`):

```
julia> [(i, v) for i in 1:4 for v in [:x, :y]]
8-element Vector{Tuple{Int64, Symbol}}:
 (1, :x)
 (1, :y)
 (2, :x)
 (2, :y)
 (3, :x)
 (3, :y)
 (4, :x)
 (4, :y)
```

Note that in this comprehension, we use a double `for` loop, which produces a vector of tuples. Next, we can convert these values to column names by using the `string` function that concatenates its passed arguments into a string:

```
julia> [string(v, i) for i in 1:4 for v in [:x, :y]]
8-element Vector{String}:
 "x1"
 "y1"
 "x2"
 "y2"
 "x3"
 "y3"
 "x4"
 "y4"
```

We are almost done. Next, using a comprehension, create a vector with pairs mapping each column name to a column value from the `data` object:

```
julia> [string(v, i) => getproperty(data[i], v)
        for i in 1:4 for v in [:x, :y]]
8-element Vector{Pair{String, Vector{Float64}}}:
"x1" => [10.0, 8.0, 13.0, 9.0, 11.0, 14.0, 6.0, 4.0, 12.0, 7.0, 5.0]
"y1" => [8.04, 6.95, 7.58, 8.81, 8.33, 9.96, 7.24, 4.26, 10.84, 4.82, 5.68]
"x2" => [10.0, 8.0, 13.0, 9.0, 11.0, 14.0, 6.0, 4.0, 12.0, 7.0, 5.0]
"y2" => [9.14, 8.14, 8.74, 8.77, 9.26, 8.1, 6.13, 3.1, 9.13, 7.26, 4.74]
```

```
"x3" => [10.0, 8.0, 13.0, 9.0, 11.0, 14.0, 6.0, 4.0, 12.0, 7.0, 5.0]
"y3" => [7.46, 6.77, 12.74, 7.11, 7.81, 8.84, 6.08, 5.39, 8.15, 6.42, 5.73]
"x4" => [8.0, 8.0, 8.0, 8.0, 8.0, 8.0, 8.0, 19.0, 8.0, 8.0, 8.0]
"y4" => [6.58, 5.76, 7.71, 8.84, 8.47, 7.04, 5.25, 12.5, 5.56, 7.91, 6.89]
```

In this code, you see the call to the getproperty function. You can use this function to get a property of a NamedTuple using a variable. Therefore, writing data.set1 is equivalent to writing getproperty(data, :set1).

Now that we have a vector of pairs of column names and column values, we can pass it to the DataFrame constructor (I omit the output again as it is identical to the earlier cases):

```
julia> DataFrame([string(v, i) => getproperty(data[i], v)
                  for i in 1:4 for v in [:x, :y]]);
```

CONSTRUCTOR USING A DICTIONARY

Relatedly, when you collect dictionaries in Julia by using the collect function, you get a vector of pairs mapping their keys to values. For example:

```
julia> data_dict = Dict([string(v, i) => getproperty(data[i], v)
                         for i in 1:4 for v in [:x, :y]])
Dict{String, Vector{Float64}} with 8 entries:
"y3" => [7.46, 6.77, 12.74, 7.11, 7.81, 8.84, 6.08, 5.39, 8.15, 6.42, 5.73]
"x1" => [10.0, 8.0, 13.0, 9.0, 11.0, 14.0, 6.0, 4.0, 12.0, 7.0, 5.0]
"y1" => [8.04, 6.95, 7.58, 8.81, 8.33, 9.96, 7.24, 4.26, 10.84, 4.82, 5.68]
"y4" => [6.58, 5.76, 7.71, 8.84, 8.47, 7.04, 5.25, 12.5, 5.56, 7.91, 6.89]
"x4" => [8.0, 8.0, 8.0, 8.0, 8.0, 8.0, 8.0, 19.0, 8.0, 8.0, 8.0]
"x2" => [10.0, 8.0, 13.0, 9.0, 11.0, 14.0, 6.0, 4.0, 12.0, 7.0, 5.0]
"y2" => [9.14, 8.14, 8.74, 8.77, 9.26, 8.1, 6.13, 3.1, 9.13, 7.26, 4.74]
"x3" => [10.0, 8.0, 13.0, 9.0, 11.0, 14.0, 6.0, 4.0, 12.0, 7.0, 5.0]

julia> collect(data_dict)
8-element Vector{Pair{String, Vector{Float64}}}:
"y3" => [7.46, 6.77, 12.74, 7.11, 7.81, 8.84, 6.08, 5.39, 8.15, 6.42, 5.73]
"x1" => [10.0, 8.0, 13.0, 9.0, 11.0, 14.0, 6.0, 4.0, 12.0, 7.0, 5.0]
"y1" => [8.04, 6.95, 7.58, 8.81, 8.33, 9.96, 7.24, 4.26, 10.84, 4.82, 5.68]
"y4" => [6.58, 5.76, 7.71, 8.84, 8.47, 7.04, 5.25, 12.5, 5.56, 7.91, 6.89]
"x4" => [8.0, 8.0, 8.0, 8.0, 8.0, 8.0, 8.0, 19.0, 8.0, 8.0, 8.0]
"x2" => [10.0, 8.0, 13.0, 9.0, 11.0, 14.0, 6.0, 4.0, 12.0, 7.0, 5.0]
"y2" => [9.14, 8.14, 8.74, 8.77, 9.26, 8.1, 6.13, 3.1, 9.13, 7.26, 4.74]
"x3" => [10.0, 8.0, 13.0, 9.0, 11.0, 14.0, 6.0, 4.0, 12.0, 7.0, 5.0]
```

Therefore, you could write DataFrame(collect(data_dict)) to create a data frame from the data_dict dictionary. However, in this case, it is unnecessary. The DataFrame constructor automatically handles this, and you can just pass a dictionary to it to get a data frame:

```
julia> DataFrame(data_dict)
11x8 DataFrame
Row │ x1       y1       x2       y2       x3       y3       x4       y4
    │ Float64  Float64  Float64  Float64  Float64  Float64  Float64  Float64
────┼────────────────────────────────────────────────────────────────────────
  1 │    10.0     8.04     10.0     9.14     10.0     7.46      8.0     6.58
  2 │     8.0     6.95      8.0     8.14      8.0     6.77      8.0     5.76
```

```
 3 |    13.0     7.58    13.0     8.74    13.0    12.74     8.0     7.71
 4 |     9.0     8.81     9.0     8.77     9.0     7.11     8.0     8.84
 5 |    11.0     8.33    11.0     9.26    11.0     7.81     8.0     8.47
 6 |    14.0     9.96    14.0     8.1     14.0     8.84     8.0     7.04
 7 |     6.0     7.24     6.0     6.13     6.0     6.08     8.0     5.25
 8 |     4.0     4.26     4.0     3.1      4.0     5.39    19.0    12.5
 9 |    12.0    10.84    12.0     9.13    12.0     8.15     8.0     5.56
10 |     7.0     4.82     7.0     7.26     7.0     6.42     8.0     7.91
11 |     5.0     5.68     5.0     4.74     5.0     5.73     8.0     6.89
```

In the common case of the `Dict` dictionary, as shown in the example, the columns of the resulting data frame are sorted by their names, as `Dict` has an undefined order of iteration (see chapter 4 for a discussion of this topic).

When creating a data frame, an important consideration is memory management. You have two options here:

- Make the `DataFrame` constructor copy the data passed to it so that the columns of a data frame are freshly allocated.
- Make the `DataFrame` constructor reuse the data passed to it so that the columns of a data frame are not allocated.

THE COPYCOLS KEYWORD ARGUMENT

By default, a `DataFrame` constructor copies data. This is a safe approach that leads to code that is less error prone. However, if you are concerned about memory usage or performance, you can turn off copying by passing the `copycols=false` keyword argument to the `DataFrame` constructor.

Let's compare these options. First, check that the columns are copied by default:

```julia
julia> df1 = DataFrame(x1=data.set1.x)
11×1 DataFrame
 Row | x1
     | Float64
─────┼─────────
   1 |    10.0
   2 |     8.0
   3 |    13.0
   4 |     9.0
   5 |    11.0
   6 |    14.0
   7 |     6.0
   8 |     4.0
   9 |    12.0
  10 |     7.0
  11 |     5.0

julia> df1.x1 === data.set1.x
false
```

Now let's investigate the noncopying behavior:

```julia
julia> df2 = DataFrame(x1=data.set1.x; copycols=false)
11×1 DataFrame
```

```
Row │ x1
    │ Float64
────┼────────
  1 │    10.0
  2 │     8.0
  3 │    13.0
  4 │     9.0
  5 │    11.0
  6 │    14.0
  7 │     6.0
  8 │     4.0
  9 │    12.0
 10 │     7.0
 11 │     5.0

julia> df2.x1 === data.set1.x
true
```

EXERCISE 10.1 Compare the performance of creating a data frame holding a single random vector of one million elements with and without copying of a source vector. You can generate this vector by using the `rand(10^6)` command.

RULES OF HANDLING NONSTANDARD ARGUMENTS

Before wrapping up the discussion of creating a `DataFrame` from vectors, I'll comment on a convenience feature of the `DataFrame` constructor. As you know from chapter 5, by default, Julia never implicitly vectorizes your code. Instead, you are required to use explicit broadcasting.

In DataFrames.jl, an exception to this rule is made for user convenience. If you pass a scalar (for example, a number or a string) to a `DataFrame` constructor, this scalar is automatically repeated as many times as required to match the length of the vectors passed in the constructor. This behavior is called *pseudo broadcasting*. Here is an example:

```
julia> df = DataFrame(x=1:3, y=1)
3×2 DataFrame
 Row │ x      y
     │ Int64
─────┼────────────
   1 │    1      1
   2 │    2      1
   3 │    3      1
```

The scalar `1` is repeated three times to match the length of the `1:3` range.

Another convenience feature is that the `DataFrame` constructor always collects ranges (like `1:3` passed in the preceding example) to a `Vector`. You can check it by writing this:

```
julia> df.x
3-element Vector{Int64}:
 1
 2
 3
```

The rationale behind such a rule is that most of the time, if you store a column in a `Data-Frame`, you want this column to be mutable—that is, to allow adding elements to it or changing the values stored in them. Ranges, on the other hand, are read-only objects. This is the reason the `DataFrame` constructor always converts them to a `Vector`.

Finally, pseudo broadcasting applies only to scalars. If you pass vectors of different lengths to the `DataFrame` constructor, you will get an error:

```
julia> DataFrame(x=[1], y=[1, 2, 3])
ERROR: DimensionMismatch("column :x has length 1 and column :y has length 3")
```

This behavior might be surprising to R users, who are allowed to pass to a data frame constructor vectors of different lengths if the least common denominator of these lengths is equal to the length of the longest passed vector. For example, if you use vectors having lengths 6, 2, and 3, you will get a data frame with six rows.

INTEGRATION OF JULIA WITH R

To show this feature of R, I will use the RCall.jl package and explain how you can convert R data frame objects to a `DataFrame` object from DataFrames.jl. Knowing how to use the RCall.jl package is useful, as you might already have code written in R that you want to run as a part of your Julia program:

```
julia> using RCall
```

```
julia> r_df = R"data.frame(a=1:6, b=1:2, c=1:3)"    ◁── Executes an R command by
RObject{VecSxp}                                          prefixing the string containing
  a b c                                                  R code with the R character
1 1 1 1
2 2 2 2
3 3 1 3
4 4 2 1
5 5 1 2
6 6 2 3
```

```
julia> julia_df = rcopy(r_df)    ◁── Converts an R data frame into a
6×3 DataFrame                         DataFrame by using the rcopy function
 Row │ a      b      c
     │ Int64  Int64  Int64
─────┼─────────────────────
   1 │     1      1      1
   2 │     2      2      2
   3 │     3      1      3
   4 │     4      2      1
   5 │     5      1      2
   6 │     6      2      3
```

After loading the RCall.jl package, we first create the `r_df` object that is an R data frame. One of the ways you can execute any R command is by writing it in a string prefixed by the R character. Next, using the `rcopy` function, I convert the R data frame to a `DataFrame` object defined in DataFrames.jl.

The example shows us that R recycles the `1:2` and `1:3` vectors when creating a data frame to have their lengths match the `1:6` vector. As I have explained, this behavior is not allowed in DataFrames.jl since it could lead to hard-to-catch bugs in production code.

The RCall.jl package

This section presented a minimal example showing how to use Julia and R together with the RCall.jl package. If you would like to learn more about the available features, consult the package documentation (https://juliainterop.github.io/RCall.jl/stable/). Here, let's discuss the most important aspects of using the RCall.jl package.

First, you need to have R installed to work with it. In some computing environments, installing the RCall.jl package might not automatically detect your R installation. In this case, consult the Installing RCall.jl manual (http://mng.bz/jAy8) for instructions explaining how to resolve the problem.

In our example code, we used a string prefixed by the R character to execute R code. Additionally, the RCall.jl package offers you an R REPL mode in which you can execute R code in your terminal directly. When you are in the Julia REPL and press the $ (dollar) key, the prompt will switch from `julia>` to `R>`, and the R mode will be activated. You exit this mode by pressing Backspace. The R REPL mode is useful in interactive sessions.

You can find a more detailed explanation of how to use the R REPL mode, as well as a description of additional features of the RCall.jl package that I have not described here, in the "Getting Started" section of the package manual (http://mng.bz/WM7l).

10.1.3 *Creating a data frame using a Tables.jl interface*

In this subsection, we discuss the Tables.jl package, which provides simple yet powerful interface functions for working with all kinds of *tabular data*—data that has observations stored in rows and variables stored in columns. The Tables.jl package is needed because in many analytical tasks, you get a table-like object that is not a `DataFrame`.

For example, if you solve a differential equation by using the DifferentialEquations.jl package, you might want to store the solution as a data frame, as shown in the package documentation (http://mng.bz/82l5). The point is that it is enough that DifferentialEquations.jl implements a proper interface that allows for such a conversion; it does not need to have DataFrames.jl as its dependency. As discussed in chapter 1, such composability is one of the strengths of Julia.

`DataFrame` is an example of a type that supports the table interface provided by the Tables.jl package. If you have an object that supports the Tables.jl interface, you can pass it as a single argument to the `DataFrame` constructor and get a `DataFrame` as a result.

The list of packages that support integration with Tables.jl is extensive (http://mng.bz/E0xX). In this section, we will concentrate on two of the most common object types that support this interface and are defined in Base Julia:

- A `NamedTuple` of vectors
- An iterator of `NamedTuple` objects

Iterators in Julia

You learned in chapter 4 about various types of collections that Julia supports. These include arrays, tuples, named tuples, and dictionaries.

Many of the Julia collections can be iterated. You can think of this as follows. If a collection c is iterable, you can write a for loop like this to sequentially retrieve all elements of the collection c in this loop (note that this code is not runnable):

```
for v in c
    # loop body
end
```

Also, many functions, like map, rely on a collection being iterable. Types that support this form of usage are said to implement the iteration interface. If you define your own type that you want to support this interface, you can check the Julia Manual (http://mng.bz/82w2) to learn how to do that.

You can find a list of standard Julia collections that support an iteration interface in the "Iteration" section of the Julia Manual (http://mng.bz/N5xv).

In the first case of a NamedTuple of vectors, the interpretation is intuitive. The field names of a NamedTuple become column names of a data frame, and the vectors become its columns. Remember that these vectors must have the same length for the operation to work. Here is an example using the data.set1 NamedTuple:

```
julia> data.set1
(x = [10.0, 8.0, 13.0, 9.0, 11.0, 14.0, 6.0, 4.0, 12.0, 7.0, 5.0],
 y = [8.04, 6.95, 7.58, 8.81, 8.33, 9.96, 7.24, 4.26, 10.84, 4.82, 5.68])

julia> DataFrame(data.set1)
11×2 DataFrame
 Row │ x        y
     │ Float64  Float64
─────┼──────────────────
   1 │    10.0     8.04
   2 │     8.0     6.95
   3 │    13.0     7.58
   4 │     9.0     8.81
   5 │    11.0     8.33
   6 │    14.0     9.96
   7 │     6.0     7.24
   8 │     4.0     4.26
   9 │    12.0    10.84
  10 │     7.0     4.82
  11 │     5.0     5.68
```

The second scenario occurs when an iterator of NamedTuple objects is passed. Then we assume that each NamedTuple has the same set of fields (the field names from the first NamedTuple are used), and each NamedTuple is used to create one row of data.

Let's start with a minimal example to make sure that the rules I describe are clear, and then we will move to a more advanced case of the data NamedTuple:

```
julia> DataFrame([(a=1, b=2), (a=3, b=4), (a=5, b=6)])
3×2 DataFrame
 Row │ a      b
     │ Int64  Int64
─────┼──────────────
   1 │     1      2
   2 │     3      4
   3 │     5      6
```

In this case, we pass a vector (which is iterable) to the `DataFrame` constructor. This vector contains three elements, and each is a `NamedTuple` having fields a and b. Thus, as a result, we get a data frame with three rows and two columns: a and b.

Let's turn to the `data` object. It is a `NamedTuple` of `NamedTuple` objects:

```
julia> data
(set1 = (x = [10.0, 8.0, 13.0, 9.0, 11.0, 14.0, 6.0, 4.0, 12.0, 7.0, 5.0],
  y = [8.04, 6.95, 7.58, 8.81, 8.33, 9.96, 7.24, 4.26, 10.84, 4.82, 5.68]),
 set2 = (x = [10.0, 8.0, 13.0, 9.0, 11.0, 14.0, 6.0, 4.0, 12.0, 7.0, 5.0],
  y = [9.14, 8.14, 8.74, 8.77, 9.26, 8.1, 6.13, 3.1, 9.13, 7.26, 4.74]),
 set3 = (x = [10.0, 8.0, 13.0, 9.0, 11.0, 14.0, 6.0, 4.0, 12.0, 7.0, 5.0],
  y = [7.46, 6.77, 12.74, 7.11, 7.81, 8.84, 6.08, 5.39, 8.15, 6.42, 5.73]),
 set4 = (x = [8.0, 8.0, 8.0, 8.0, 8.0, 8.0, 8.0, 19.0, 8.0, 8.0, 8.0],
  y = [6.58, 5.76, 7.71, 8.84, 8.47, 7.04, 5.25, 12.5, 5.56, 7.91, 6.89]))
```

If `data` were a `NamedTuple` of vectors, we would get a data frame with four columns, set1, set2, set3, and set4. However, this `NamedTuple` stores named tuples, so this rule does not apply to it. Since `NamedTuple` is iterable and it stores named tuples, each value is treated as a row in the created `DataFrame`. Since each of the internal named tuples contains fields x and y, we will get a `DataFrame` with two columns x and y and four rows representing the four data sets we work with. Let's see if this is the case in the next listing.

Listing 10.2   Creating the `aq2` data frame

```
julia> aq2 = DataFrame(data)
4×2 DataFrame
 Row │ x                               y
     │ Array…                          Array…
─────┼────────────────────────────────────────────────────────────────
   1 │ [10.0, 8.0, 13.0, 9.0, 11.0, 14.…   [8.04, 6.95, 7.58, 8.81, 8.33, 9…
   2 │ [10.0, 8.0, 13.0, 9.0, 11.0, 14.…   [9.14, 8.14, 8.74, 8.77, 9.26, 8…
   3 │ [10.0, 8.0, 13.0, 9.0, 11.0, 14.…   [7.46, 6.77, 12.74, 7.11, 7.81, …
   4 │ [8.0, 8.0, 8.0, 8.0, 8.0, 8.0, 8…   [6.58, 5.76, 7.71, 8.84, 8.47, 7…
```

We get a vector of four vectors, both in columns x and y. Note that in listing 10.2, you can see that columns of a `DataFrame` can store any objects; in this case, the columns store vectors.

10.1.4   *Plotting a correlation matrix of data stored in a data frame*

In this section, we will plot the correlation matrix of data stored in the `aq1` data frame that we created in section 10.1. Recall that this data frame stores the Anscombe's data:

```
julia> aq1
11×8 DataFrame
Row │ x1       y1       x2       y2       x3       y3       x4       y4
    │ Float64  Float64  Float64  Float64  Float64  Float64  Float64  Float64
────┼────────────────────────────────────────────────────────────────────────
  1 │    10.0     8.04     10.0     9.14     10.0     7.46      8.0     6.58
  2 │     8.0     6.95      8.0     8.14      8.0     6.77      8.0     5.76
  3 │    13.0     7.58     13.0     8.74     13.0    12.74      8.0     7.71
  4 │     9.0     8.81      9.0     8.77      9.0     7.11      8.0     8.84
  5 │    11.0     8.33     11.0     9.26     11.0     7.81      8.0     8.47
  6 │    14.0     9.96     14.0      8.1     14.0     8.84      8.0     7.04
  7 │     6.0     7.24      6.0     6.13      6.0     6.08      8.0     5.25
  8 │     4.0     4.26      4.0      3.1      4.0     5.39     19.0    12.5
  9 │    12.0    10.84     12.0     9.13     12.0     8.15      8.0     5.56
 10 │     7.0     4.82      7.0     7.26      7.0     6.42      8.0     7.91
 11 │     5.0     5.68      5.0     4.74      5.0     5.73      8.0     6.89
```

First, we create a correlation matrix of this data frame's columns, and then we plot it. To compute the correlation matrix, we use the `pairwise` function from the StatsBase.jl package.

This function takes two arguments. The first argument is the function we want to apply—in our case, the `cor` function from the `Statistics` module that computes the Pearson correlation. The second argument is a collection of vectors for which we want to compute the correlation. Since our data is stored in a data frame, we get this collection by using the `eachcol` function:

```
julia> using Statistics

julia> using StatsBase

julia> cor_mat = pairwise(cor, eachcol(aq1))
8×8 Matrix{Float64}:
  1.0       0.81642  1.0       0.81624  1.0       0.81629  -0.5      -0.31405
  0.81642   1.0      0.81642   0.75001  0.81642   0.46872  -0.52909  -0.48912
  1.0       0.81642  1.0       0.81624  1.0       0.81629  -0.5      -0.31405
  0.81624   0.75001  0.81624   1.0      0.81624   0.58792  -0.71844  -0.47810
  1.0       0.81642  1.0       0.81624  1.0       0.81629  -0.5      -0.31405
  0.81629   0.46872  0.81629   0.58792  0.81629   1.0      -0.34466  -0.15547
 -0.5      -0.52909 -0.5      -0.71844 -0.5      -0.34466   1.0       0.81652
 -0.31405  -0.48912 -0.31405  -0.47810 -0.31405  -0.15547   0.81652   1.0
```

Next, we plot the `cor_mat` matrix by using the `heatmap` function from Plots.jl. As a first and second argument to this function, we pass names of variables, which we get using the `names(aq1)` call. The third argument is the `cor_mat` correlation matrix.

We additionally pass `aspect_ratio=:equal` and `size=(400,400)` keyword arguments to make sure that each cell in our correlation matrix is a square. Without passing these keyword arguments, the correlation matrix would not be square, but would be wider horizontally than vertically. Additionally, we pass `right-margin=5Plots.mm` to make sure that the annotation of the color bar is not cropped; we already discussed adding extra padding when we plotted figure 7.6 in chapter 7:

```
julia> using Plots

julia> heatmap(names(aq1), names(aq1), cor_mat;
               aspect_ratio=:equal, size=(400, 400),
               rightmargin=5Plots.mm)
```

Figure 10.1 shows the resulting plot. We can see that pairs of matching variables—
(:x1, :y1), (:x2, :y2), (:x3, :y3), and (:x4, :y4)—have similar Pearson correlation coefficients.

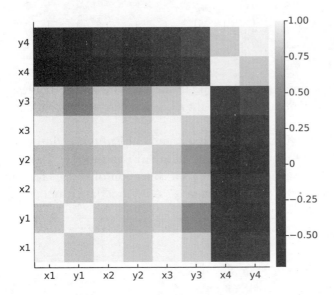

Figure 10.1   **In plotting the correlation matrix of the** `aq1` **data frame, light squares indicate positive correlation and dark squares indicate negative correlation.**

10.2 *Creating data frames incrementally*

In many cases, you will want to create a data frame incrementally—for example, by
adding new rows of data to an existing data frame. One of the most common scenarios in which this is useful is when you generate data in your program and want to store
it in a data frame. I will show an example in subsection 10.2.3, where we will discuss a
simulation of a two-dimensional random walk.

This section covers the three most common operations allowing you to add rows to
a data frame:

- Vertical concatenation of several data frames into one new data frame
- Appending a data frame to an existing data frame in place
- Adding a new row to an existing data frame in place

10.2.1 *Vertically concatenating data frames*

In this section, you will learn how to combine multiple data frames into one by vertically concatenating them. This operation is often needed when you have data coming
from several sources but want to store it in one data frame.

We start by creating several data frames that we will vertically concatenate. In section 10.1, you learned that by writing `DataFrame(data.set1)`, you can create a data frame from a `NamedTuple` of vectors. In this section, we start by creating four data frames for each of the four data sets contained in the `data` object. Next, we will vertically concatenate these four data frames.

In the next listing, we will use the `map` function to create four source data frames from four fields of the `data` `NamedTuple`.

> **Listing 10.3 Creating multiple data frames by using the `map` function**

```
julia> data_dfs = map(DataFrame, data)
(set1 = 11×2 DataFrame
 Row │ x        y
     │ Float64  Float64
─────┼──────────────────
   1 │    10.0     8.04
   2 │     8.0     6.95
   3 │    13.0     7.58
   4 │     9.0     8.81
   5 │    11.0     8.33
   6 │    14.0     9.96
   7 │     6.0     7.24
   8 │     4.0     4.26
   9 │    12.0    10.84
  10 │     7.0     4.82
  11 │     5.0     5.68, set2 = 11×2 DataFrame
 Row │ x        y
     │ Float64  Float64
─────┼──────────────────
   1 │    10.0     9.14
   2 │     8.0     8.14
   3 │    13.0     8.74
   4 │     9.0     8.77
   5 │    11.0     9.26
   6 │    14.0     8.1
   7 │     6.0     6.13
   8 │     4.0     3.1
   9 │    12.0     9.13
  10 │     7.0     7.26
  11 │     5.0     4.74, set3 = 11×2 DataFrame
 Row │ x        y
     │ Float64  Float64
─────┼──────────────────
   1 │    10.0     7.46
   2 │     8.0     6.77
   3 │    13.0    12.74
   4 │     9.0     7.11
   5 │    11.0     7.81
   6 │    14.0     8.84
   7 │     6.0     6.08
   8 │     4.0     5.39
   9 │    12.0     8.15
  10 │     7.0     6.42
```

```
11  |     5.0       5.73, set4 = 11×2 DataFrame
Row |  x         y
    |  Float64   Float64
    |----------------------
 1  |     8.0       6.58
 2  |     8.0       5.76
 3  |     8.0       7.71
 4  |     8.0       8.84
 5  |     8.0       8.47
 6  |     8.0       7.04
 7  |     8.0       5.25
 8  |    19.0      12.5
 9  |     8.0       5.56
10  |     8.0       7.91
11  |     8.0       6.89)
```

We create the `data_dfs` NamedTuple by storing four data frames corresponding to four data sets in the `data` object. We would now like to vertically concatenate (stack) these data frames. You can do this in Julia by using the `vcat` function:

```
julia> vcat(data_dfs.set1, data_dfs.set2, data_dfs.set3, data_dfs.set4)
44×2 DataFrame
Row |  x         y
    |  Float64   Float64
    |----------------------
 1  |    10.0       8.04
 2  |     8.0       6.95
 3  |    13.0       7.58
 :  |     :         :
42  |     8.0       5.56
43  |     8.0       7.91
44  |     8.0       6.89
            38 rows omitted
```

The result of the operation is a single data frame with the source data frames stacked one over the other. The only problem is that we do not see which rows come from which source data frame. You can fix this by passing the `source` keyword argument to `vcat`. If you pass a column name as `source`, this column will store the number of the data frame from which a given row originates:

```
julia> vcat(data_dfs.set1, data_dfs.set2, data_dfs.set3, data_dfs.set4;
            source="source_id")
44×3 DataFrame
Row |  x         y         source_id
    |  Float64   Float64   Int64
    |--------------------------------
 1  |    10.0       8.04          1
 2  |     8.0       6.95          1
 3  |    13.0       7.58          1
 :  |     :         :             :
42  |     8.0       5.56          4
43  |     8.0       7.91          4
44  |     8.0       6.89          4
                38 rows omitted
```

After the operation, the `source_id` column contains numbers from 1 to 4 showing from which source data frame a given row was taken. If you would like to use custom names for source data frames, pass as a `source` keyword argument a `Pair` holding the source column name and the identifiers assigned to passed data frames. Here is an example:

```
julia> vcat(data_dfs.set1, data_dfs.set2, data_dfs.set3, data_dfs.set4;
            source="source_id"=>string.("set", 1:4))
44×3 DataFrame
 Row │ x        y        source_id
     │ Float64  Float64  String

   1 │    10.0     8.04  set1
   2 │     8.0     6.95  set1
   3 │    13.0     7.58  set1
   :  │     :        :      :
  42 │     8.0     5.56  set4
  43 │     8.0     7.91  set4
  44 │     8.0     6.89  set4
                      38 rows omitted
```

If you have a lot of data frames stored in a vector, listing them one by one in the `vcat` call might be inconvenient. We can use the `reduce` function, passing it a `vcat` as a first argument followed by a vector of data frames, and, if needed, appropriate keyword arguments. In this case, we can turn the `data_dfs` `NamedTuple` into a vector of data frame objects by using the `collect` function so we can use this pattern. Here is an example:

```
julia> reduce(vcat, collect(data_dfs);
              source="source_id"=>string.("set", 1:4))
44×3 DataFrame
 Row │ x        y        source_id
     │ Float64  Float64  String

   1 │    10.0     8.04  set1
   2 │     8.0     6.95  set1
   3 │    13.0     7.58  set1
   :  │     :        :      :
  42 │     8.0     5.56  set4
  43 │     8.0     7.91  set4
  44 │     8.0     6.89  set4
                      38 rows omitted
```

The reduce function

The `reduce` function is not specific to DataFrames.jl. In general, if you write `reduce(op, collection)`, a reduction of the passed `collection` with a given operator `op` is performed; see the Julia Manual at tinyurl.com/3pbhaw84 for more details.

For example, if you write `reduce(*, [2, 3, 4])`, you get 24, as it is a product of the numbers stored in the vector `[2, 3, 4]`.

In vertical concatenation operations I have shown up until now, all data frames have the same column names. However, in practice, you might want to vertically concatenate data frames that do not meet this condition. We use the `cols=:union` keyword argument to create a union of columns from the passed data frames. Columns that are not present in some data frames are filled with `missing` where necessary. The following listing shows a simple example.

Listing 10.4 Vertically concatenating data frames whose column names do not match

```
julia> df1 = DataFrame(a=1:3, b=11:13)
3×2 DataFrame
 Row │ a      b
     │ Int64  Int64
─────┼──────────────
   1 │     1     11
   2 │     2     12
   3 │     3     13

julia> df2 = DataFrame(a=4:6, c=24:26)
3×2 DataFrame
 Row │ a      c
     │ Int64  Int64
─────┼──────────────
   1 │     4     24
   2 │     5     25
   3 │     6     26

julia> vcat(df1, df2)
ERROR: ArgumentError: column(s) c are missing from argument(s) 1,
and column(s) b are missing from argument(s) 2

julia> vcat(df1, df2; cols=:union)
6×3 DataFrame
 Row │ a      b        c
     │ Int64  Int64?   Int64?
─────┼─────────────────────────
   1 │     1       11  missing
   2 │     2       12  missing
   3 │     3       13  missing
   4 │     4  missing       24
   5 │     5  missing       25
   6 │     6  missing       26
```

You can see that `vcat(df1, df2)` throws an error because the passed data frames have nonmatching column names. On the other hand, `vcat(df1, df2; cols= :union)` works and keeps a union of columns passed in the source data frames. Note that since column `c` is not present in `df1`, its first three elements are filled with `missing` in the resulting data frame. Similarly, column `b` is not present in `df2`, so its last three elements are filled with `missing` in the resulting data frame.

Options for the cols keyword argument in vcat

The `cols` keyword argument in `vcat` can take the following values:

- `:setequal`—Requires all data frames to have the same column names, disregarding order. If they appear in different orders, the order of the first provided data frame is used.
- `:orderequal`—Requires all data frames to have the same column names and in the same order.
- `:intersect`—Only the columns present in all provided data frames are kept. If the intersection is empty, an empty data frame is returned.
- `:union`—Columns present in at least one of the provided data frames are kept. Columns not present in some data frames are filled with `missing` where necessary.

By default, the `cols` keyword argument takes the `:setequal` value.

EXERCISE 10.2 Check the result of `vcat` on the data frames `df1=Data-Frame(a=1, b=2)` and `df2=DataFrame(b=2, a=1)`. Next, verify the result of the operation if we additionally pass the `cols=:orderequal` keyword argument.

10.2.2 Appending a table to a data frame

In section 10.2.1, you learned how to create a new data frame from several source data frames. Next, we'll discuss a similar operation that updates the data frame instead. I will show you how to append tabular data to an existing data frame in place. The difference is that appending does not create a new data frame but mutates an existing one.

You can append data to an existing data frame by using the `append!` function. Let's start with an example. We will create an empty data frame and then append to it the `data_dfs.set1` and `data_dfs.set2` data frames, as the next listing shows.

Listing 10.5 Appending a data frame to a data frame

```julia
julia> df_agg = DataFrame()
0×0 DataFrame

julia> append!(df_agg, data_dfs.set1)
11×2 DataFrame
 Row │ x        y
     │ Float64  Float64
─────┼──────────────────
   1 │    10.0     8.04
   2 │     8.0     6.95
   3 │    13.0     7.58
   4 │     9.0     8.81
   5 │    11.0     8.33
   6 │    14.0     9.96
```

```
 7 |      6.0      7.24
 8 |      4.0      4.26
 9 |     12.0     10.84
10 |      7.0      4.82
11 |      5.0      5.68
```

```
julia> append!(df_agg, data_dfs.set2)
22×2 DataFrame
 Row │ x        y
     │ Float64  Float64
─────┼──────────────────
   1 │    10.0     8.04
   2 │     8.0     6.95
   3 │    13.0     7.58
   4 │     9.0     8.81
   5 │    11.0     8.33
   6 │    14.0     9.96
   7 │     6.0     7.24
   8 │     4.0     4.26
   9 │    12.0    10.84
  10 │     7.0     4.82
  11 │     5.0     5.68
  12 │    10.0     9.14
  13 │     8.0     8.14
  14 │    13.0     8.74
  15 │     9.0     8.77
  16 │    11.0     9.26
  17 │    14.0     8.1
  18 │     6.0     6.13
  19 │     4.0     3.1
  20 │    12.0     9.13
  21 │     7.0     7.26
  22 │     5.0     4.74
```

Apart from updating the passed data frame in place, the append! function has similar mechanics to vcat with the following differences:

- You are allowed to append to a data frame any table that follows the Tables.jl interface (vcat requires all arguments to be data frames).

- append! does not support the source keyword argument. If you want to have a column representing the source of a given row when using append!, you should add it to the source data frames before appending them.

- append! supports the cols keyword argument like vcat does. For :setequal, :orderequal, and :union values of this argument, the behavior is the same. For the :intersect value, the behavior is a bit different; for this option, the appended table contains more columns than the target data frame, but all column names that are present in the target data frame must be present in the appended data frame, and only these are used. Additionally, the :subset value, which behaves like :intersect, is supported, but if a column is missing in the appended data frame, then missing values are pushed to the target data frame for that column. As presented in listing 10.5, you can always, independent of the value of the `cols` keyword argument, append data to a data frame that has no columns (`DataFrame()` object), and similarly, `DataFrame()` can always be appended.

- `append!` supports the `promote` keyword argument that is not needed in `vcat`. This argument determines what should happen if the values stored in the appended data frame cannot be stored in the columns of the target data frame. If `promote=false`, an error is thrown. If `promote=true`, then in the target data frame, the column types are changed so that the `append!` operation can be successfully completed. By default, `promote=false` except if the `cols` keyword argument is `:union` or `:subset`; then `promote=true`.

Let's look at examples of the first and last points from the preceding list, as they demonstrate the biggest differences between `append!` and `vcat`.

We start by examining how to append a Tables.jl table that is not a data frame to a data frame. As discussed in section 10.1, a `NamedTuple` of vectors is a Tables.jl table. Therefore, `data.set1` and `data.set2` are such tables. As a result, the following code produces a result that's identical to the result of listing 10.5 (I omit the output to save space):

```
df_agg = DataFrame()
append!(df_agg, data.set1)
append!(df_agg, data.set2)
```

The `promote` keyword of the `append!` function is most often needed when you have data that potentially contains `missing` values. Consider the following example:

```
julia> df1 = DataFrame(a=1:3, b=11:13)
3×2 DataFrame
 Row │ a      b
     │ Int64  Int64
─────┼──────────────
   1 │     1     11
   2 │     2     12
   3 │     3     13
julia> df2 = DataFrame(a=4:6, b=[14, missing, 16])
3×2 DataFrame
 Row │ a      b
     │ Int64  Int64?
─────┼────────────────
   1 │     4        14
   2 │     5   missing
   3 │     6        16

julia> append!(df1, df2)
? Error: Error adding value to column :b.
```

We get an error because column `b` in the `df1` data frame does not allow storing `missing` values in it. You can resolve this issue by passing the `promote=true` keyword argument to `append!`:

```
julia> append!(df1, df2; promote=true)
6×2 DataFrame
```

```
Row │ a      b
    │ Int64  Int64?
────┼───────────────
  1 │ 1         11
  2 │ 2         12
  3 │ 3         13
  4 │ 4         14
  5 │ 5      missing
  6 │ 6         16
```

This time, the operation succeeds, and, as you can see, the b column element type is promoted to Union{Int, Missing} as its element type is displayed as Int64?.

10.2.3 *Adding a new row to an existing data frame*

The append! function adds a table to a data frame in place. Often, however, you need to add a single row to a data frame. This operation can be performed using the push! function. This function works exactly the same way as append!, including the allowed keyword arguments. The only difference is that instead of accepting whole tables, push! accepts a single row. The values of the following types are valid rows:

- DataFrameRow, NamedTuple, and dictionary—The column names contained in the pushed row are checked and are matched to the target data frame column names following the cols keyword argument rules
- AbstractArray and Tuple—The pushed collection must have the same number of elements as there are columns in the target data frame.

Let's look at two minimal examples of both options, and then we will switch to a practical case study of this functionality.

We'll start with an example of pushing data that has column names defined using NamedTuples to represent rows:

```
julia> df = DataFrame()
0×0 DataFrame

julia> push!(df, (a=1, b=2))
1×2 DataFrame
 Row │ a      b
     │ Int64  Int64
─────┼──────────────
   1 │     1      2

julia> push!(df, (a=3, b=4))
2×2 DataFrame
 Row │ a      b
     │ Int64  Int64
─────┼──────────────
   1 │     1      2
   2 │     3      4
```

Next, we push a vector to a data frame:

```
julia> df = DataFrame(a=Int[], b=Int[])
0×2 DataFrame
```

```julia
julia> push!(df, [1, 2])
1×2 DataFrame
 Row │ a      b
     │ Int64  Int64
─────┼──────────────
   1 │     1      2

julia> push!(df, [3, 4])
2×2 DataFrame
 Row │ a      b
     │ Int64  Int64
─────┼──────────────
   1 │     1      2
   2 │     3      4
```

Note that in this case, since the vector does not carry information about column names, we have to initialize the columns of the data frame with `DataFrame (a=Int[], b=Int[])` before pushing rows to it. When we push `NamedTuples` to a data frame, it is enough to initialize it with `DataFrame()`, as column names can be inferred from the pushed `NamedTuples`.

10.2.4 *Storing simulation results in a data frame*

Pushing rows to a data frame is useful when performing computer simulation studies. The reason a data frame is a good object to store simulation results is twofold. First, simulations usually produce data that has a fixed structure, so consecutive simulation results can easily be stored as rows in a data frame. Second, after you finish doing your simulation, you usually want to analyze the produced data, and DataFrames.jl provides many functions that make this part of your task easy.

In this section, I use an example of a random walk simulation to show you how this is done.

DEFINITION OF A TWO-DIMENSIONAL RANDOM WALK

Let's create a simple simulation of a two-dimensional random walk (http://mng.bz/E0Zl). We will call the first dimension x and the second y.

Assume that an object starts its journey at point (0, 0) and in one step, can move left (decrease its x location by 1), right (increase its x location by 1), down (decrease its y location by 1), or up (increase its y location by 1). Each direction is picked randomly with the same probability. We want to visualize a sample of 10 steps of this simulation. Figure 10.2 depicts a single step of this process.

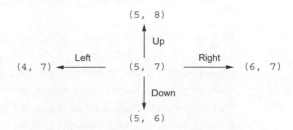

Figure 10.2 Possible changes of coordinates of the point in a single step of a two-dimensional random walk. Each direction is picked with the same probability.

In our implementation, we will not try to provide the most efficient way to perform this simulation. Rather, our goal is to learn how to work with data frames.

First, we create a function that generates one random step of our simulation:

```
function sim_step(current)                                  | Randomly samples one of
    dx, dy = rand(((1,0), (-1,0), (0,1), (0,-1)))    ◁──┘   the four accepted directions
    return (x=current.x + dx, y=current.y + dy)   ◁──┐  Returns a NamedTuple
end                                                   |  with an updated location
```

The `step` function assumes that the `current` value passed to it has x and y properties that give information about the location of the object in the first and second dimension, respectively. It returns a `NamedTuple` with an updated location of the object.

It is worth paying attention to the `rand(((1,0), (-1,0), (0,1), (0,-1)))` operation. The `rand` function gets passed a tuple containing four tuples `((1,0), (-1,0), (0,1), (0,-1))`. Since this tuple is a four-element collection, the `rand` function returns one of its elements picked with equal probability. An important feature of this syntax is that we are not allocating any memory to perform it, since we are using tuples (see chapter 4 for an explanation of the differences between tuples and vectors). Therefore, it is fast:

```
julia> using BenchmarkTools

julia> @btime rand(((1,0), (-1,0), (0,1), (0,-1)));
  5.200 ns (0 allocations: 0 bytes)
```

Next, note that the `dx, dy = ...` syntax performs an *iterator destructuring*. The first element of the tuple returned by the `rand` function gets assigned to `dx`, and the second to the `dy` variable—for example:

```
julia> dx, dy = (10, 20)
(10, 20)

julia> dx
10

julia> dy
20
```

Before moving forward, let's quickly check by simulation that indeed the `rand(((1,0), (-1,0), (0,1), (0,-1)))` operation returns each of the four tuples with equal probability by running 10 million (10^7) random draws. In the code, I use _ as the variable name in the `for _ in 1:10^7` expression. This approach can be used when a variable name is required by Julia's syntax, but you do not plan to use the value of that variable in your code:

```
julia> using FreqTables

julia> using Random
```

```
julia> Random.seed!(1234);

julia> proptable([rand(((1,0), (-1,0), (0,1), (0,-1))) for _ in 1:10^7])
4-element Named Vector{Float64}
Dim1    |
────────┼─────────
(-1, 0) | 0.249893
(0, -1) | 0.250115
(0, 1)  | 0.250009
(1, 0)  | 0.249983
```

We see that all four values have approximately a one-in-four chance of being observed as expected. We already used the `Random.seed!` and `proptable` functions in chapter 6.

A SIMPLE SIMULATOR OF A RANDOM WALK

We are now ready to run our simulation in the next listing.

Listing 10.6   A sample simulation of the two-dimensional random walk

```
julia> using Random

julia> Random.seed!(6);

julia> walk = DataFrame(x=0, y=0)        ◁──┐  Initializes the data frame with the
1×2 DataFrame                                │  starting point of the simulation
 Row │ x      y
     │ Int64  Int64
─────┼──────────────
   1 │     0      0
                                         ┌── Uses the underscore (_) as the name
julia> for _ in 1:10                     │   of the variable for the iteration, as
           current = walk[end, :]    ◁───┘   we will not need it later
           push!(walk, sim_step(current))  ◁──┐ Gets the current location of the object
       end                                     │ as a DataFrameRow representing the
                                               │ last row of the walk data frame
                         Adds a new row to the end
julia> walk             of the walk data frame │
11×2 DataFrame
 Row │ x      y
     │ Int64  Int64
─────┼──────────────
   1 │     0      0    ◁──┐ In instance 1, the object
   2 │     0      1       │ is at point (0, 0).
   3 │     0      2
   4 │     0      3
   5 │     1      3
   6 │     1      4
   7 │     1      5
   8 │     1      6
   9 │     0      6
  10 │     0      7    ┌── In instance 11, after 10 moves,
  11 │     0      8    ◁── the object is at point (0, 8).
```

Let's plot the result of our simulation:

```julia
julia> using Plots

julia> plot(walk.x, walk.y;
            legend=false,
            series_annotations=1:11,
            xticks=range(extrema(walk.x)...),
            yticks=range(extrema(walk.y)...))
```

Adds text annotations to data points on the plot

Makes ticks on the plot integers in the range of observed values

Figure 10.3 shows the result of the simulation.

Figure 10.3   In this visualization of our `walk` data frame, each number on the plot indicates in which instance the object was present in a given location. For this run of the simulation, the points on the grid are visited only once.

The object was at point (0,0) in instance 1 and then moved 10 times to end up in location (0, 8) in instance 11.

This example shows you some more advanced options that can be used in the `plots` function:

- The `series_annotations` keyword argument allows you to pass labels that should be used as text annotations on the drawn points.
- The `xticks` and `yticks` keyword arguments govern how x- and y-axis ticks should be located.

Note that I wanted the ticks to be integers in the range of values present in a given dimension in the `walk` data frame. Let's look at how the `range(extrema(walk.y)...))` expression works step by step. First, we run the `extrema` function:

```julia
julia> extrema(walk.y)
(0, 8)
```

It produces a tuple with a minimum and maximum value observed in the `walk.y` vector. Next, we use the `range` function to create a range of values from minimal to maximal value with the step equal to 1. Note that normally the `range` function expects to get two positional arguments for our case; for example:

```julia
julia> range(1, 5)
1:5
```

Since the `extrema` function returns a two-element tuple, we need to splat it by using the `...` notation.

ANALYSIS OF SIMULATION OUTPUT

Let's go back to figure 10.3. What might catch your attention is that all the points on this figure are distinct. In each instance from 1 to 11, the point has a different location. Should this fact surprise us? I would argue yes. (I have carefully chosen the seed of the random number generator to achieve this effect.)

Note that the chance that locations in instances 1 and 3 are different is 3/4. The reason is that no matter how we move from instance 1 to instance 2, there is exactly one way to get back to the position we had in instance 1 when we are in instance 3. Therefore, the chance that we will not get back is 3/4 (only one direction out of four possible supports this event). A similar reasoning applies to instances 2 and 4, 3 and 5, ..., and finally instances 9 and 11 (in total, nine events, each happening with 3/4 probability). Since all nine events are independent, following the laws of probability, the probability of having all unique points is at most a product of these nine individual probabilities:

```julia
julia> (3/4)^9
0.07508468627929688
```

We expect this probability to be smaller in practice, because in the preceding calculation, we considered hitting the same spot only two steps ahead, and in general, we might get back to the position we had in instance 1 in instance 5 (without visiting it in instance 3)—for example, after the sequence of moves (0, 1), (1, 0), (0, –1), (–1, 0).

Let's use a simulation to approximate this probability of having all unique points in the next listing.

> **Listing 10.7 Code checking the probability of having a walk with all unique points**

```julia
julia> function walk_unique()          ⬅  Defines a function running
           walk = DataFrame(x=0, y=0)      a whole simulation once
           for _ in 1:10
               current = walk[end, :]
               push!(walk, sim_step(current))
           end
           return nrow(unique(walk)) == nrow(walk)   ⬅  Checks if all rows in the
       end                                              walk data frame are unique
walk_unique (generic function with 1 method)
```

```
julia> Random.seed!(2);

julia> proptable([walk_unique() for _ in 1:10^5])
2-element Named Vector{Float64}
Dim1   |
───────┼────────
false  | 0.95744
true   | 0.04256
```

We observe that the probability that our 10-step walk consists of all unique points is 4.2%, which is less than 7.5%, as expected.

The new element of the walk_unique function in comparison to the code from listing 10.6 is the nrow(unique(walk)) == nrow(walk) expression. It compares the number of rows of the original walk data frame and the unique(walk) data frame. The unique function, when applied to a data frame object, retains only distinct rows stored in it.

> ### The unique function
>
> The unique function allows you to de-duplicate rows of a data frame. Additionally, it can optionally be passed any column selector that is accepted by a data frame (these selectors were explained in chapter 9) as a second positional argument. In that case, the de-duplication is performed only on the selected columns. For example, unique(walk, "x") would ensure that there are no duplicates in the x column of the walk data frame.
>
> If you would like to avoid allocating a new data frame when removing duplicates, you have two options. First, you could pass the view=true keyword argument to the unique function. Instead of allocating a new data frame, a view of the source data frame is returned. Second, you could use the unique! function instead, which works the same as unique but drops the rows of the passed data frame in place.
>
> The unique function is not only defined for data frames; it is available without loading any packages and returns an array containing unique values of a collection as determined by the isequal function. We already discussed the unique function in chapter 4.

EXERCISE 10.3   Change the code from listing 10.7 so that we perform only two-steps-ahead verification if the random walk visits the same point again. Verify that under such a definition, the probability that we do not have duplicate visits of the same point is around 7.5%.

SERIALIZATION OF JULIA OBJECTS

In chapter 11, we will use the walk data frame that we created in this section. Therefore, before we finish our discussion, let's save it to disk. We could use the CSV.jl package for this, as you learned in chapter 8. However, I would like to show you another persistent storage option that Julia offers.

The `Serialization` module offers functionality to save Julia objects in binary format to disk. This is a similar functionality to `pickle` in Python or `save` and `load` functions in R. The two functions you need to learn are `serialize`, which writes an object to disk, and `deserialize`, which reads it from disk into memory:

```
julia> using Serialization

julia> serialize("walk.bin", walk)   ◁── The first argument is the file we want
                                          to write the object to, and the
                                          second is the object we want to save.

julia> deserialize("walk.bin") == walk  ◁──
true                                         The deserialize function takes a single
                                             argument, which is the file where we
                                             have stored the data we want to read in.
```

In the code, I have checked that serializing and deserializing the `walk` data frame produces the same value. Please do not erase the walk.bin file we have created, as we will use it in chapter 11.

Limitations of object serialization

Serialization of Julia objects is designed as functionality for short-term storage. Therefore, serialization and deserialization can safely be done only by the same version of Julia with the same loaded packages in the same versions.

Summary

- You can construct `DataFrame` objects from a wide variety of source values, including matrices, vectors of vectors, a list of vectors, a `NamedTuple` of vectors, an iterator of named tuples, and a dictionary with vectors as keys. You can pass any object supporting the table interface defined in the Tables.jl package to the `DataFrame` constructor. This flexibility means that you can easily create `Data-Frame` objects in your code.
- When constructing data frames from matrices, you either need to pass column names as a second argument or request automatic generation of column names. You can have full control of the constructed data frame, while retaining convenience when you do not care about exact names of the columns.
- You can construct data frames by passing the column name and column value to the `DataFrame` constructor. This is one of the most often used ways of constructing a data frame.
- You can easily convert any object that supports the Tables.jl interface into a data frame. This often significantly simplifies your code, as dozens of Julia packages define types supporting the Tables.jl interface.
- The `DataFrame` constructor supports the `copycols` keyword argument that takes a Boolean value and allows you to decide whether the passed data should be copied. Having such control is useful in practice. By default, data is copied, so you do not run into the risk of having data aliases spread around your code.

However, if you need performance, or your computations are memory bound, you can use `copycols=false` to avoid copying.

- You can integrate Julia with R by using the RCall.jl package. This is useful when you have R installed on your machine and would like to use R code in your Julia project.

- The `pairwise` function from StatsBase.jl can be used to compute values of a function taking all possible pairs of entries of a passed collection. It is often used to create a correlation matrix of a data frame's columns, in which case the `cor` function is used. We obtain a collection of data frame columns by using the `eachcol` function.

- You can plot a heatmap of a matrix by using the `heatmap` function from the Plots.jl package. This function is often used to display a correlation matrix.

- You can vertically concatenate data frames by using the `vcat` function. This operation is often needed in practice when you want to combine several source data frames into one.

- If you collect your data incrementally, you can use the `append!` and `push!` functions to add rows to your data frame dynamically. The `append!` function appends whole tables to a data frame, while `push!` adds a single row. These functions are often used when you want to store results of a simulation in a data frame.

- Sometimes you want to combine data that has different columns or different types of values in the columns. For this reason, `vcat`, `append!`, and `push!` support the `cols` keyword argument that governs how situations in which you do not have matching columns should be handled. Additionally, the `append!` and `push!` functions take the `promote` keyword argument that allows you to perform column type promotion in case you want to add to your data frame some data that does not have a type matching the element type of a column in a target data frame. These options are often used when working with real-life data that is of low quality and requires cleaning.

- You can use the `unique` function to de-duplicate rows of a data frame. This function is often used when cleaning data.

- You can serialize and deserialize Julia objects by using the `Serialization` module. This is a convenient method for short-term persistent storage of Julia objects.

Converting and grouping data frames

This chapter covers

- Converting data frames to other Julia types
- Writing type-stable code
- Understanding type piracy
- Grouping data frame objects
- Working with grouped data frames

In chapter 10, we reviewed various ways that `DataFrame` objects can be constructed from different data sources. In this chapter, we discuss the reverse process and show how you can create other objects from a data frame (recall from chapter 9 that a data frame can be a `DataFrame` or its view, that is, a `SubDataFrame`). You might want to perform such an operation in two scenarios.

In the first scenario, you need to perform analytical tasks provided by functions that do not accept a data frame as input, but instead accept another type, so you'd need to convert a data frame to the expected target format. An example is conversion of a data frame to a matrix that you want to use later in linear algebra operations.

In the second scenario, you want to change the way the data stored in the data frame is interpreted. The most important operation of this kind is grouping a data frame. You can group a data frame by using the `groupby` function on it to produce the `GroupedDataFrame` object. Both dplyr in R and pandas in Python also have grouping functionality. The most important application of grouped objects is making it possible for users to perform split-apply-combine transformations (see www.jstatsoft .org/article/view/v040i01). This data analysis task is performed often. We will discuss these operations in the remaining chapters.

However, `GroupedDataFrame` objects are more functional than just a support for split-apply-combine. They also make it possible for you to efficiently perform such operations as group iteration, lookup, reordering, and subsetting. All these tasks are often performed in practice; let's look at a few examples.

Assume you have a large database of students in a university. You want to efficiently perform the following operations after grouping students by field of study (by *efficiently*, I mean without having to scan or move the source data, as it might be large):

- Finding all students of mathematics (without having to perform a full table scan)
- Arranging fields of studies by the number of students enrolled in them (without having to sort the source data frame)
- Removing all fields of study with fewer than 10 students (without changing the source data frame)

You can perform these tasks by using `GroupedDataFrame` objects. We will discuss how to do them in this chapter. I divided this chapter into two sections:

- Section 11.1 shows how to convert a data frame to values of other types that are often used in Julia.
- Section 11.2 explains how to create a `GroupedDataFrame` from a source data frame using the `groupby` function, as well as how to work with it.

While discussing how to convert a data frame object to other types, we examine two important concepts that you need to learn when working with Julia: *type stability* of code and *type piracy*. I explain both topics in section 11.1.

11.1 *Converting a data frame to other value types*

In this section, you'll learn how to convert a data frame into other value types. This operation is often needed when you have a function that does not accept a data frame as its argument, but you have data you want to pass to this function stored in a data frame.

The most frequently encountered target types to which data frame objects get converted are as follows:

- Matrix
- `NamedTuple` of vectors

- Vector of `NamedTuple`
- Iterator of columns of a data frame
- Iterator of rows of a data frame

In the examples of conversions, we will use the `walk` data frame we created in chapter 10. Therefore, we first need to read it in from the walk.bin file by using the `deserialize` function:

```julia
julia> using DataFrames

julia> using Serialization

julia> walk = deserialize("walk.bin");
```

A note on the meaning of conversion in Julia

In this chapter, I have used *convert* several times, meaning to take an object of one type and create an object of another type from it. For instance, I say that we convert a data frame to a `NamedTuple` of vectors. This meaning is consistent with an intuitive understanding of this word and is often encountered in practice. That is why I decided to use it.

However, in Julia, if we want to be precise, *conversion* has a narrower meaning. Julia defines the `convert` function, and Julia language purists might argue that conversion happens only if you use this function either explicitly or implicitly. An implicit use of the `convert` function happens when you perform an assignment of a value to an array. Consider the following operation:

```julia
julia> x = [1.5]
1-element Vector{Float64}:
 1.5

julia> x[1] = 1
1

julia> x
1-element Vector{Float64}:
 1.0
```

The x variable is a vector of `Float64`. However, in the `x[1] = 1` operation, we assign an integer to the first element of this vector. As you can see, the `1` integer gets implicitly converted to `1.0` float without us asking for it.

Therefore, strictly speaking, conversion of an object to a type is different from construction of a value of this type. If you would like to learn more about the details of the distinction between conversion and construction, refer to the Julia Manual (http://mng.bz/KOZ4).

In this book, for convenience and where this does not introduce ambiguity, I use the term *convert* in a loose sense (meaning we create a new object of a certain type, either when the `convert` method is invoked or when a type constructor is used).

11.1.1 *Conversion to a matrix*

In this section, you will learn how to convert a data frame to a matrix. You might need to perform this conversion if, for example, your data frame contains numeric values only, and you want to process them using linear algebra functions to check if the columns of a matrix are linearly independent.

To convert a data frame to a matrix, pass it to a `Matrix` constructor:

```
julia> Matrix(walk)
11×2 Matrix{Int64}:
 0  0
 0  1
 0  2
 0  3
 1  3
 1  4
 1  5
 1  6
 0  6
 0  7
 0  8
```

The appropriate element type of the resulting matrix will automatically be detected. Optionally, you could specify it yourself by passing it as a parameter to the constructor:

```
julia> Matrix{Any}(walk)
11×2 Matrix{Any}:
 0  0
 0  1
 0  2
 0  3
 1  3
 1  4
 1  5
 1  6
 0  6
 0  7
 0  8
```

Although passing the element type of a matrix is possible, it is rarely needed. Typically, it is better to rely on automatic type detection as it ensures that the operation will succeed. If you pass an incorrect element type to the constructor, you will get an error:

```
julia> Matrix{String}(walk)
ERROR: MethodError: Cannot `convert` an object of type Int64
to an object of type String
```

The conversion to a matrix allocates new memory for the resulting matrix, but apart from this, it is quite fast. It is useful when, in your analyses, you need to pass a matrix to a function. Let's look at an example. If you pass a matrix to the `plot` function from Plots.jl, it draws several lines on a single plot. However, passing a data frame to the plot function is not supported:

```
julia> using Plots

julia> plot(walk)
ERROR: Cannot convert DataFrame to series data for plotting
```

Instead, you can plot Matrix(walk):

```
julia> plot(Matrix(walk); labels=["x" "y"] , legend=:topleft)
```

Figure 11.1 shows the resulting plot. We have drawn two series of data.

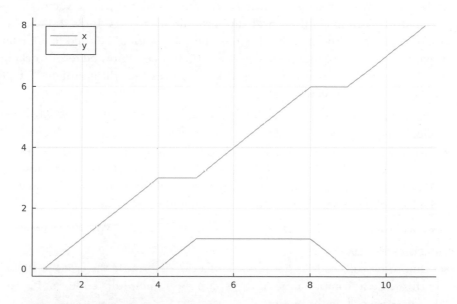

Figure 11.1 Visualization of the `walk` data frame using two series of data. Note that we have moved the legend to the top-left corner of the plot (by default, the legend is shown in the top-right corner and would overlap with the graph).

We have used two keyword arguments of the `plot` function here. The first is `labels`, which accepts a one-row matrix of series labels—in our case, `["x" "y"]`. Note that it is not a vector (which would be written as `["x", "y"]`). We have only put space between `"x"` and `"y"`. The second keyword argument is `legend`, which allows us to specify the legend location. In this case, I have chosen to put it in the top-left corner of the plot.

11.1.2 *Conversion to a named tuple of vectors*

In this section, you will learn how to convert a data frame to a named tuple of vectors. This is sometimes done in practice because it can improve the performance of your code. In this section, you will see an example of when doing this might help. Additionally, such a conversion is cheap.

The conversion itself is simple. Just call the following:

```julia
julia> Tables.columntable(walk)
(x = [0, 0, 0, 0, 1, 1, 1, 1, 0, 0, 0],
 y = [0, 1, 2, 3, 3, 4, 5, 6, 6, 7, 8])
```

The operation does not copy the vectors stored in the source data frame and retains column names. Recall that conversion to a matrix, which we discussed in section 11.1.1, loses information about column names in the source data frame and allocates new memory.

At this point, you can see that `DataFrame` and a `NamedTuple` of vectors seem similar. Both store data in columns and support column names. Let's discuss the most important reasons why both are useful and when they should be used. Understanding this topic is one of the fundamental pieces of advanced knowledge of working with tabular data in Julia. It is related to two key features that differentiate `DataFrame` from a `NamedTuple` of vectors:

- `DataFrame` is a type-unstable object, while a `NamedTuple` of vectors is type stable. This distinction is related to the performance of both container types.
- `DataFrame` is a type defined in the DataFrames.jl package, while the `Named-Tuple` type is defined in Julia without loading any packages. Maintainers of the DataFrames.jl package have much greater flexibility in defining the behavior of `DataFrame` objects. This distinction is related to *type piracy*.

Next, we will first discuss the type stability issue and then the type piracy issue.

TYPE STABILITY IN JULIA

We say that some Julia code is *type stable* if Julia can determine the types of all variables used in this code at compile time. If this condition is met, Julia code can be executed quickly. Otherwise, it might be slow.

I explain the consequence of type stability with an example of the `DataFrame` object, as this is the core topic of this book. If you would like to learn more about related performance considerations, see the "Performance Tips" section of the Julia Manual (http://mng.bz/9Vda).

From the point of view of the Julia compiler, every column of a `DataFrame` is an `AbstractVector`. If you extract a column from a data frame, the compiler is not able to infer its concrete type. As a consequence, the operations on that column will be slow.

Here is an example. We want to manually compute a sum of elements of a single column of a data frame. In the example, when I write the `1_000_000` literal, Julia ignores the underscores, which makes it easier to read this number:

```julia
julia> using BenchmarkTools

julia> function mysum(table)
           s = 0
           for v in table.x
               s += v
           end
```

Assumes we sum integers ◁─┘

Assumes the table has the property x that is its column ◁─┘

```
            return s
        end
mysum (generic function with 1 method)

julia> df = DataFrame(x=1:1_000_000);

julia> @btime mysum($df)
  87.789 ms (3998948 allocations: 76.28 MiB)
500000500000
```

We see that the operation has made a lot of allocations, but assessing whether the time is good or bad is initially hard. However, let's create a `NamedTuple` of vectors from our `df` data frame and benchmark its performance:

```
julia> tab = Tables.columntable(df);

julia> @btime mysum($tab)
  153.600 μs (0 allocations: 0 bytes)
500000500000
```

We see no allocations and a much faster execution time, so running this code on the `df` data frame is not a good choice from a performance perspective.

What is the difference between the `df` and `tab` objects? As I have said, all columns of a `DataFrame` are seen by the compiler as `AbstractVector`. Since `Abstract-Vector` is an abstract container (recall the discussion of the difference between abstract versus concrete types in chapter 3), the Julia compiler does not know the actual memory layout of a value having this type and is forced to use generic (and thus slow) code that handles it. In the `tab` object, the Julia compiler knows that column `x` has the `Vector{Int64}` type. This type is concrete, so Julia can generate optimal machine code for doing the computations.

This can be confirmed by running the `@code_warntype` macro on the `mysum(df)` function call:

```
julia> @code_warntype mysum(df)
MethodInstance for mysum(::DataFrame)
  from mysum(table) in Main at REPL[32]:1
Arguments
  #self#::Core.Const(mysum)
  table::DataFrame
Locals
  @_3::Any
  s::Any
  v::Any
Body::Any
1 ─       (s = 0)
│   %2  = Base.getproperty(table, :x)::AbstractVector
│         (@_3 = Base.iterate(%2))
│   %4  = (@_3 === nothing)::Bool
│   %5  = Base.not_int(%4)::Bool
└──       goto #4 if not %5
```

```
2 ... %7  = @_3::Any
   |          (v = Core.getfield(%7, 1))
   |    %9  = Core.getfield(%7, 2)::Any
   |          (s = s + v)
   |          (@_3 = Base.iterate(%2, %9))
   |   %12  = (@_3 === nothing)::Bool
   |   %13  = Base.not_int(%12)::Bool
   └──         goto #4 if not %13
3 -           goto # 2
4 ...     return s
```

The @code_warntype macro tells us how the compiler sees our function call. You do not need to understand all the details of this printout. It is enough to check that the compiler gets a proper idea of which data types it is processing. In general, if something is problematic, you will see it highlighted in red (bold in this book). We can see that the column x of our data frame is seen as AbstractVector, which is printed in red, and you have several Any values also printed in red. This is a signal that the code will not run fast.

Let's check the @code_warntype macro call on the mysum(tab) object:

```
julia> @code_warntype mysum(tab)
MethodInstance for mysum(::NamedTuple{(:x,), Tuple{Vector{Int64}}})
  from mysum(table) in Main at REPL[32]:1
Arguments
  #self#::Core.Const(mysum)
  table::NamedTuple{(:x,), Tuple{Vector{Int64}}}
Locals
  @_3::Union{Nothing, Tuple{Int64, Int64}}
  s::Int64
  v::Int64
Body::Int64
1 -       (s = 0)
   |    %2  = Base.getproperty(table, :x)::Vector{Int64}
   |          (@_3 = Base.iterate(%2))
   |    %4  = (@_3 === nothing)::Bool
   |    %5  = Base.not_int(%4)::Bool
   └──         goto #4 if not %5
2 ... %7  = @_3::Tuple{Int64, Int64}
   |          (v = Core.getfield(%7, 1))
   |    %9  = Core.getfield(%7, 2)::Int64
   |          (s = s + v)
   |          (@_3 = Base.iterate(%2, %9))
   |   %12  = (@_3 === nothing)::Bool
   |   %13  = Base.not_int(%12)::Bool
   └──         goto #4 if not %13
3 -           goto # 2
4 ...     return s
```

This time, nothing is printed in red, and we see that Julia identifies types of all values. This means that we can expect mysum(tab) to be executed fast.

Why is it possible for Julia to do proper type inference on the tab object? The reason is that names and types of the columns stored in it are encoded in its type:

```
julia> typeof(tab)
NamedTuple{(:x,), Tuple{Vector{Int64}}}
```

We have just seen a benefit of this fact: the operations working with the `tab` object are fast. However, downsides must exist, as DataFrames.jl developers decided not to make the `DataFrame` object type stable. There are two problems:

- Since column names and types are part of the `tab` object's type definition, they cannot be changed dynamically. You cannot add, remove, change the type of, or rename columns of a `NamedTuple` of vectors (as you learned in chapter 4, `NamedTuple` is immutable).
- Compiling a `NamedTuple` of vectors that contains many columns is expensive. As a rule of thumb, over 1,000 columns is problematic, and you should avoid such operations.

> **EXERCISE 11.1** Measure the time required to create a data frame having 1 row and 10,000 columns consisting of only 1s. Use the matrix created by `ones(1, 10_000)` as a source, along with automatic column names. Next, measure the time required to create a `NamedTuple` of vectors from this data frame.

For these reasons, the design of the `DataFrame` object starts to make sense; it is much more flexible and Julia-compiler-friendly than a `NamedTuple` of vectors. However, there is one issue: how to overcome type instability of objects having a `DataFrame` type.

We can use one simple trick, called a *function-barrier method* (http://mng.bz/jAXy), to accomplish this. Extracting a column from a data frame within a function is slow, but if you pass this extracted column next to another function, the compiler will properly identify the column type in this inner function, and things will be fast. You can think of it as follows: every time you enter a function, the compiler performs a type check of its arguments. Here is an example of solving the type instability problem of the `mysum` function:

```
julia> function barrier_mysum2(x)
           s = 0
           for v in x
               s += v
           end
           return s
       end
barrier_mysum2 (generic function with 1 method)

julia> mysum2(table) = barrier_mysum2(table.x)
mysum2 (generic function with 1 method)

julia> @btime mysum2($df)
  161.500 µs (1 allocation: 16 bytes)
500000500000
```

We have a very fast execution time now, like `mysum(tab)`. We see only one allocation. It is related to the `table.x` operation, which is type unstable. However, once we are inside the `barrier_mysum2` function, everything is type stable as the Julia compiler correctly identifies the type of its argument `x`. It is crucial to understand that the type of `table.x` is not known in the `mysum2` function, but once it gets passed to the `barrier_mysum2` function, it becomes known inside it.

As you can see, the solution is relatively simple. For many operations that we will discuss in the remaining chapters, DataFrames.jl automatically creates such kernel functions, so in practice, most of the time, you do not even have to think about it.

In summary, the design of the `DataFrame` object combined with the functionalities built into DataFrames.jl bring you the flexibility of mutating and low compilation cost of the `DataFrame` object, as well as fast execution time of computations by using the function-barrier method.

Nevertheless, sometimes the standard methods provided by DataFrames.jl do not give you the expected performance (these cases are rare in my experience). Then you might want to create a temporary `NamedTuple` of vectors for analysis of your data if you have a data frame with only a few columns and you know you do not want to mutate it.

TYPE PIRACY IN JULIA

The second reason we need a special `DataFrame` type is related to *type piracy*.

> **NOTE** You can skip this section on the first reading of this book, as this topic is a bit more advanced. However, understanding type piracy is essential if you want to create a Julia package on your own in the future.

The Julia manual defines *type piracy* as *the practice of extending or redefining methods in Base or other packages on types that you have not defined* (http://mng.bz/WMEx). I explain what this means and the potential consequences through examples.

As you have seen in this chapter, the `DataFrame` type supports many standard functions defined in Base Julia, including `push!`, `append!`, `vcat`, `unique`, and `unique!`. DataFrames.jl developers can safely define methods for these functions for the `DataFrame` type since it is defined in DataFrames.jl. There is no risk that we will break existing code by making our custom definitions.

Now imagine we start to define a special method for `unique` on a `NamedTuple` of vectors. Remember that running `unique` on a data frame object de-duplicates its rows:

```
julia> df = DataFrame(a=[1, 1, 2], b=[1, 1, 2])
3×2 DataFrame
 Row │ a      b
     │ Int64  Int64
─────┼──────────────
   1 │     1      1
   2 │     1      1
   3 │     2      2
```

```
julia> unique(df)
2×2 DataFrame
 Row │ a      b
     │ Int64  Int64
─────┼──────────────
   1 │     1      1
   2 │     2      2
```

Now check what happens if we run `unique` on a `NamedTuple` of vectors:

```
julia> tab = Tables.columntable(df)
(a = [1, 1, 2], b = [1, 1, 2])

julia> unique(tab)
1-element Vector{Vector{Int64}}:
 [1, 1, 2]
```

Instead of de-duplicating rows, we get unique columns of `tab`. This is the default behavior of `unique` when it is passed a `NamedTuple` built into Base Julia. Therefore, we must not create a custom `unique` definition for a `NamedTuple` of vectors, even if we want to, because it could break existing code that relies on the way `unique` works by default on `NamedTuple` objects.

In conclusion, since we define our own `DataFrame` type, we are free to define the way functions work on it in any way we like (even functions from Base Julia). On the other hand, if you have a type and a function defined in Base Julia, you are not allowed to do this, as this would be type piracy. DataFrames.jl developers can define the behavior of values of the `DataFrame` type in the way that is most user-friendly without being constrained by the default behaviors defined in Base Julia.

Selected packages that offer type-stable table-like objects

The Julia ecosystem has several implementations of table-like types that are type stable, as opposed to the `DataFrame` type defined in DataFrames.jl. Here is a list of selected packages that provide such functionality.

The TypedTables.jl package provides the `Table` type. To the user, a `Table` presents itself as an array of named tuples. Each row of the table is represented as a `NamedTuple`. Internally, a `Table` stores a named tuple of arrays and is a convenient structure for column-based storage of tabular data.

Another similar package is TupleVectors.jl, which defines the `TupleVector` type. Again, to the user, it looks like a vector of named tuples, but it is stored internally as a `NamedTuple` of vectors. An interesting feature of this package is that it supports column nesting; see https://github.com/cscherrer/TupleVectors.jl for details.

Finally, the StructArrays.jl package provides the `StructArray` type. This type is an `AbstractArray` whose elements are any `struct` objects, like, for example, `NamedTuple` (see chapter 4 for a discussion of `struct` types). However, its internal memory layout is column based (each field of the struct is stored in a separate `Array`).

(continued)

Which package should you pick for your data analysis? In my experience, Data-Frames.jl will most often be the best choice. It is currently the most feature-rich package. Also, a benefit of `DataFrame` being type unstable is that you can effortlessly process very wide tables and can mutate tables in place. However, you might hit a performance bottleneck when working with DataFrames.jl. It might happen, for example, when you process millions of tables containing very few rows and columns. In such a case, you can consider using a `NamedTuple` of vectors (recall from this section that you can use `Tables.columntable` to create it from a data frame) or using one of the packages I have listed (TypedTables.jl, TupleVectors.jl, or StructArrays.jl) to improve the execution speed of your code.

11.1.3 *Other common conversions*

I'll finish this section by summarizing some more common conversions that are often used in practice. Apart from conversion to a `Matrix` and to a `NamedTuple` of vectors that we already discussed, I list other common conversions in table 11.1. In the following subsections, I discuss them, also explaining when and why you might want to use them. In the examples, we will keep using the `walk` data frame that we deserialized at the beginning of this section.

Table 11.1   Selected conversion methods of data frame objects. In all example code, I assume that `df` is a data frame.

Output value	Meaning	Example code	Allocates memory for data	Type stable
`Matrix`	Columns of the matrix are columns of data.	`Matrix(df)`	Yes	Yes or no
`NamedTuple` of vectors	Each element of the named tuple is a column of data.	`Tables.columntable(df)`	No	Yes
`Vector` of `NamedTuple`	Each element of the vector is one row of data.	`Tables.rowtable(df)`	Yes	Yes
Iterator of `NamedTuple`	Each iterated element is one row of data.	`Tables.namedtupleiterator(df)`	No	Yes
Collection of `DataFrameRow`	Each element of the collection is one row of data.	`eachrow(df)`	No	No
Collection of data frame columns	Each element of the collection is one column of data.	`eachcol(df)`	No	No
Vector of data frame columns	Each element of the vector is one column of data.	`identity.(eachcol(df))`	No	Yes or no

VECTOR OF NAMEDTUPLE

We start with creating a `Vector` of `NamedTuple`. This conversion is useful if you later want to process the data row by row:

```julia
julia> Tables.rowtable(walk)
11-element Vector{NamedTuple{(:x, :y), Tuple{Int64, Int64}}}:
 (x = 0, y = 0)
 (x = 0, y = 1)
 (x = 0, y = 2)
 (x = 0, y = 3)
 (x = 1, y = 3)
 (x = 1, y = 4)
 (x = 1, y = 5)
 (x = 1, y = 6)
 (x = 0, y = 6)
 (x = 0, y = 7)
 (x = 0, y = 8)
```

The benefit of this object is that it is type stable and can be worked with later, just like any other vector. The downside is that for wide tables, it is expensive to compile and allocates memory.

ITERATOR OF NAMEDTUPLE

If you want to avoid memory allocation, use an iterator of `NamedTuple`. The downside is that you cannot work with this object as you can with vectors. You can only iterate it:

```julia
julia> nti = Tables.namedtupleiterator(walk)
Tables.NamedTupleIterator{Tables.Schema{(:x, :y), Tuple{Int64, Int64}},
Tables.RowIterator{NamedTuple{(:x, :y), Tuple{Vector{Int64},
Vector{Int64}}}}}(Tables.RowIterator{NamedTuple{(:x, :y),
Tuple{Vector{Int64}, Vector{Int64}}}}(
(x = [0, 0, 0, 0, 1, 1, 1, 1, 0, 0, 0],
 y = [0, 1, 2, 3, 3, 4, 5, 6, 6, 7, 8]), 11))

julia> for v in nti
           println(v)
       end
(x = 0, y = 0)
(x = 0, y = 1)
(x = 0, y = 2)
(x = 0, y = 3)
(x = 1, y = 3)
(x = 1, y = 4)
(x = 1, y = 5)
(x = 1, y = 6)
(x = 0, y = 6)
(x = 0, y = 7)
(x = 0, y = 8)
```

TYPE-UNSTABLE ITERATORS OF ROWS AND COLUMNS OF A DATA FRAME

If we accept that we work with type-unstable collections, we can call `eachrow` and `eachcol` to get iterable and indexable objects producing rows (as `DataFrameRow`) and columns (as vectors) from the source data frame, respectively:

```
julia> er = eachrow(walk)
11×2 DataFrameRows
 Row │ x      y
     │ Int64  Int64
─────┼──────────────
   1 │     0      0
   2 │     0      1
   3 │     0      2
   4 │     0      3
   5 │     1      3
   6 │     1      4
   7 │     1      5
   8 │     1      6
   9 │     0      6
  10 │     0      7
  11 │     0      8

julia> er[1]
DataFrameRow
 Row │ x      y
     │ Int64  Int64
─────┼──────────────
   1 │     0      0

julia> er[end]
DataFrameRow
 Row │ x      y
     │ Int64  Int64
─────┼──────────────
  11 │     0      8

julia> ec = eachcol(walk)
11×2 DataFrameColumns
 Row │ x      y
     │ Int64  Int64
─────┼──────────────
   1 │     0      0
   2 │     0      1
   3 │     0      2
   4 │     0      3
   5 │     1      3
   6 │     1      4
   7 │     1      5
   8 │     1      6
   9 │     0      6
  10 │     0      7
  11 │     0      8

julia> ec[1]
11-element Vector{Int64}:
 0
 0
 0
 0
 1
```

```
 1
 1
 1
 0
 0
 0

julia> ec[end]
11-element Vector{Int64}:
 0
 1
 2
 3
 3
 4
 5
 6
 6
 7
 8
```

Collections produced by `eachrow` and `eachcol`, called with a data frame argument, do not copy data and have a low compilation cost at the expense of being slower because the compiler can't generate optimal code when working with them. This issue is especially important for `eachrow` if we work with a data frame that has millions of rows. To efficiently handle such cases, the nonallocating `Tables.namedtupleiterator` function was introduced (you must remember not to pass to it very wide tables, as then its compilation cost gets very high).

VECTOR OF VECTORS

The last conversion option we will discuss is a vector of data frame columns created with `identity.(eachcol(df))`, as shown in table 6.1. You might be wondering why we are broadcasting the `identity` function over columns of a data frame. This operation achieves two goals: it changes the `DataFrameColumns` collection returned by the `eachcol` function to a `Vector`, and if columns of the passed data frame have the same type, this type will be correctly identified as an element type of the returned vector. Therefore, for a cost of allocating the outer vector (which should typically be low), the returned value will be fast to work with later:

```
julia> identity.(eachcol(walk))
2-element Vector{Vector{Int64}}:
 [0, 0, 0, 0, 1, 1, 1, 1, 0, 0, 0]
 [0, 1, 2, 3, 3, 4, 5, 6, 6, 7, 8]
```

In this case, you see that the element type of the produced vector is correctly identified as `Vector{Int64}`, as all columns of the passed data frame have the same element type.

Note that this would not hold if we passed a data frame having heterogeneous column types:

```
julia> df = DataFrame(x=1:2, b=["a", "b"])
2×2 DataFrame
 Row │ x      b
     │ Int64  String
─────┼───────────────
   1 │     1  a
   2 │     2  b

julia> identity.(eachcol(df))
2-element Vector{Vector}:
 [1, 2]
 ["a", "b"]
```

This time, the element type of the produced vector is Vector (which is not a concrete type, as explained in chapter 5). Therefore, code that worked later with a value having the Vector{Vector} type would not be type stable. For this reason, table 6.1 indicates that identity.(eachcol(df)) can be type stable or not, depending on which types have columns stored in the source data frame.

11.2 Grouping data frame objects

In this section, we discuss how to create a GroupedDataFrame object from a data frame and work with it. The GroupedDataFrame object is a wrapper around a source data frame and is useful when you want to perform operations on your data in groups.

As discussed in the introduction to this chapter, grouping data is the first step in performing split-apply-combine transformations. These transformations are useful if you want to work with grouped data by performing such operations as group lookup or group reordering. In this section, we concentrate on how to work with Grouped-DataFrame objects directly, while in the remaining chapters, you will learn how to use them to perform split-apply-combine transformations.

11.2.1 Preparing the source data frame

In this section, we will create a data frame that we will use in the examples of data frame grouping. I have chosen the data set that I use in the JuliaAcademy course on DataFrames.jl (https://github.com/JuliaAcademy/DataFrames). It shows the amount of rainfall in two towns over several days of 2020. It has only 10 rows so that it will be easier to understand the consequences of operations we perform. We start by reading in the data into a DataFrame:

```
julia> using CSV

julia> raw_data = """
       city,date,rainfall
       Olecko,2020-11-16,2.9
       Olecko,2020-11-17,4.1
       Olecko,2020-11-19,4.3
       Olecko,2020-11-20,2.0
       Olecko,2020-11-21,0.6
       Olecko,2020-11-22,1.0
       Ełk,2020-11-16,3.9
       Ełk,2020-11-19,1.2
```

```
        Ełk,2020-11-20,2.0
        Ełk,2020-11-22,2.0
        """;

julia> rainfall_df = CSV.read(IOBuffer(raw_data), DataFrame)
10×3 DataFrame
 Row │ city     date        rainfall
     │ String7  Date        Float64
─────┼───────────────────────────────
   1 │ Olecko   2020-11-16       2.9
   2 │ Olecko   2020-11-17       4.1
   3 │ Olecko   2020-11-19       4.3
   4 │ Olecko   2020-11-20       2.0
   5 │ Olecko   2020-11-21       0.6
   6 │ Olecko   2020-11-22       1.0
   7 │ Ełk      2020-11-16       3.9
   8 │ Ełk      2020-11-19       1.2
   9 │ Ełk      2020-11-20       2.0
  10 │ Ełk      2020-11-22       2.0
```

This time, we store the source CSV data in a `raw_data` string. Next, we use the
`IOBuffer` function on it to create an in-memory file-like object that can be read in by
the `CSV.read` function. Note that if we (incorrectly, in this case) had passed a string
to the `CSV.read` function as a first argument, the function would treat the argument
as a filename, which is not what we want.

The `rainfall_df` data frame that we created stores information about the rainfall in millimeters in two cities (Olecko and Ełk) for several days in November 2020.

11.2.2 Grouping a data frame

In this section, you will learn how to group a data frame by using the `groupby` function. We start our analysis by grouping the data by city name and storing the result in
the `gdf_city` GroupedDataFrame:

```
julia> gdf_city = groupby(rainfall_df, "city")
GroupedDataFrame with 2 groups based on key: city
First Group (6 rows): city = "Olecko"
 Row │ city     date        rainfall
     │ String7  Date        Float64
─────┼───────────────────────────────
   1 │ Olecko   2020-11-16       2.9
   2 │ Olecko   2020-11-17       4.1
   3 │ Olecko   2020-11-19       4.3
   4 │ Olecko   2020-11-20       2.0
   5 │ Olecko   2020-11-21       0.6
   6 │ Olecko   2020-11-22       1.0
⋮
Last Group (4 rows): city = "Ełk"
 Row │ city     date        rainfall
     │ String7  Date        Float64
─────┼───────────────────────────────
   1 │ Ełk      2020-11-16       3.9
   2 │ Ełk      2020-11-19       1.2
   3 │ Ełk      2020-11-20       2.0
   4 │ Ełk      2020-11-22       2.0
```

When we print the `gdf_city` object, we first get the information that it consists of two groups and that the grouping key is the column `city`. Then the contents of the first and last group are displayed.

You can pass any column selector (we discussed column selectors in chapter 9) to specify the columns used to group your data frame. For example, to group the `rainfall_df` data frame on all columns except `rainfall`, write this:

```
julia> gdf_city_date = groupby(rainfall_df, Not("rainfall"))
GroupedDataFrame with 10 groups based on keys: city, date
First Group (1 row): city = "Olecko", date = Dates.Date("2020-11-16")
 Row │ city    date          rainfall
     │ String7 Date          Float64
─────┼──────────────────────────────────
   1 │ Olecko  2020-11-16        2.9
⋮
Last Group (1 row): city = "Ełk", date = Dates.Date("2020-11-22")
 Row │ city    date          rainfall
     │ String7 Date          Float64
─────┼──────────────────────────────────
   1 │ Ełk     2020-11-22        2.0
```

This time, our data is split into 10 groups by unique combinations of values stored in the `city` and `date` columns.

Available options during grouping of a data frame

The `groupby` function has two keyword arguments, `sort` and `skipmissing`, that you can optionally pass to change the way the resulting `GroupedDataFrame` is created.

The `sort` keyword argument defines the order of groups in the returned `Grouped-DataFrame`. By default (`sort=nothing`), this order is undefined. In this case, you ask `groupby` to group the data by using the fastest algorithm that it supports. Use this option if you care about grouping operation speed when working with large data frames. If you pass `sort=true`, groups are ordered according to the values of the grouping columns. If you pass `sort=false`, groups are created in the order of their appearance in the source data frame.

The `skipmissing` keyword argument takes Boolean values. By default, it is set to `false`, which means that all groups present in the source data frame are kept in the result. If you pass `skipmissing=true` instead, groups with `missing` values in one of the grouping columns will be dropped from the result.

11.2.3 *Getting group keys of a grouped data frame*

In this section, you will learn how to check the grouping keys corresponding to each group in a `GroupedDataFrame`. This information is useful when you want to learn what groups your `GroupedDataFrame` stores.

When you work with large `GroupedDataFrame` objects, it is often hard to understand which groups it holds. For example, we know that `gdf_city_date` has 10 groups, but we do not see all of them since this would take too much space. To get this information, you can use the keys function:

```
julia> keys(gdf_city_date)
10-element DataFrames.GroupKeys{GroupedDataFrame{DataFrame}}:
 GroupKey: (city = "Olecko", date = Dates.Date("2020-11-16"))
 GroupKey: (city = "Olecko", date = Dates.Date("2020-11-17"))
 GroupKey: (city = "Olecko", date = Dates.Date("2020-11-19"))
 GroupKey: (city = "Olecko", date = Dates.Date("2020-11-20"))
 GroupKey: (city = "Olecko", date = Dates.Date("2020-11-21"))
 GroupKey: (city = "Olecko", date = Dates.Date("2020-11-22"))
 GroupKey: (city = "Ełk", date = Dates.Date("2020-11-16"))
 GroupKey: (city = "Ełk", date = Dates.Date("2020-11-19"))
 GroupKey: (city = "Ełk", date = Dates.Date("2020-11-20"))
 GroupKey: (city = "Ełk", date = Dates.Date("2020-11-22"))
```

The keys function returns a vector storing `GroupKey` objects that behave like named tuples holding the values of the grouping columns for a given group. You can easily convert the `GroupKey` object to a tuple, named tuple, or dictionary if you wanted to later use such objects in your code. Here is an example of such a conversion for the first group:

```
julia> gk1 = keys(gdf_city_date)[1]
GroupKey: (city = "Olecko", date = Dates.Date("2020-11-16"))

julia> g1_t = Tuple(gk1)
("Olecko", Dates.Date("2020-11-16"))

julia> g1_nt = NamedTuple(gk1)
(city = "Olecko", date = Dates.Date("2020-11-16"))

julia> g1_dict = Dict(gk1)
Dict{Symbol, Any} with 2 entries:
  :date => Date("2020-11-16")
  :city => "Olecko"
```

11.2.4   *Indexing a grouped data frame with a single value*

In this section, you will learn how to use indexing to get a single group from a grouped data frame. This is a fundamental operation you need to learn for working with `GroupedDataFrame` objects.

You now know how to get information about group keys for a `GroupedDataFrame`. Let's turn to getting the data stored in the groups. Fortunately, this is easy since `GroupedDataFrame` objects support indexing, just like vectors.

Importantly, you can index into a `GroupedDataFrame` by using normal vector indexing with integers, but you also can pass a `GroupKey`, `Tuple`, `NamedTuple`, or dictionary to select the group you would like to pick.

Let's look at an example. The following are equivalent ways to extract the first group from our gdf_city_date object:

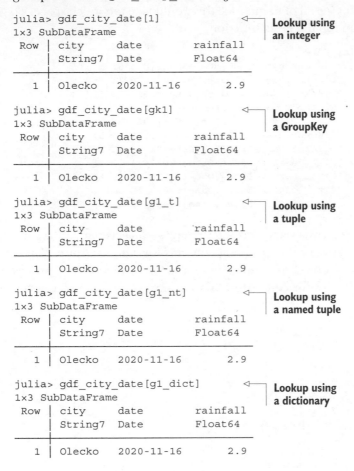

```
julia> gdf_city_date[1]                    ◁───┐ Lookup using
1×3 SubDataFrame                                │ an integer
 Row │ city     date        rainfall
     │ String7  Date        Float64
─────┼──────────────────────────────
   1 │ Olecko   2020-11-16       2.9

julia> gdf_city_date[gk1]                  ◁───┐ Lookup using
1×3 SubDataFrame                                │ a GroupKey
 Row │ city     date        rainfall
     │ String7  Date        Float64
─────┼──────────────────────────────
   1 │ Olecko   2020-11-16       2.9

julia> gdf_city_date[g1_t]                 ◁───┐ Lookup using
1×3 SubDataFrame                                │ a tuple
 Row │ city     date        rainfall
     │ String7  Date        Float64
─────┼──────────────────────────────
   1 │ Olecko   2020-11-16       2.9

julia> gdf_city_date[g1_nt]                ◁───┐ Lookup using
1×3 SubDataFrame                                │ a named tuple
 Row │ city     date        rainfall
     │ String7  Date        Float64
─────┼──────────────────────────────
   1 │ Olecko   2020-11-16       2.9

julia> gdf_city_date[g1_dict]              ◁───┐ Lookup using
1×3 SubDataFrame                                │ a dictionary
 Row │ city     date        rainfall
     │ String7  Date        Float64
─────┼──────────────────────────────
   1 │ Olecko   2020-11-16       2.9
```

In all five indexing scenarios in the code, we obtain a data frame that stores rows from our original rainfall_df data frame. The returned object is a SubDataFrame, which means, as you learned in chapter 9, that this is a view. This design choice was made to ensure that getting a single group from a GroupedDataFrame is fast, as it does not involve copying the source data.

To see one more example of group lookup, let's extract a group corresponding to the city Olecko from the gdf_city object (recall that gdf_city is grouped by a single column, city):

```
julia> gdf_city[("Olecko",)]               ◁───┐ Indexing using
6×3 SubDataFrame                                │ a tuple
 Row │ city     date        rainfall
     │ String7  Date        Float64
─────┼──────────────────────────────
   1 │ Olecko   2020-11-16       2.9
   2 │ Olecko   2020-11-17       4.1
```

```
   3 | Olecko    2020-11-19       4.3
   4 | Olecko    2020-11-20       2.0
   5 | Olecko    2020-11-21       0.6
   6 | Olecko    2020-11-22       1.0
```

```
julia> gdf_city[(city="Olecko",)]      ◄    Indexing using
6×3 SubDataFrame                             a named tuple
 Row | city      date          rainfall
     | String7   Date          Float64
─────┼────────────────────────────────────
   1 | Olecko    2020-11-16       2.9
   2 | Olecko    2020-11-17       4.1
   3 | Olecko    2020-11-19       4.3
   4 | Olecko    2020-11-20       2.0
   5 | Olecko    2020-11-21       0.6
   6 | Olecko    2020-11-22       1.0
```

As you can see, it is easy to look up a concrete group when you know which key values you are interested in.

You might ask why it is required to pass values identifying groups in collections like `Tuple` or `NamedTuple`. In general, you can group a data frame by multiple columns, so DataFrames.jl needs to accept collections of values to identify groups. As we discussed, the only exception is passing an integer as an index, in which case it is interpreted as a group number.

11.2.5 Comparing performance of indexing methods

In this section, we compare the speed of the indexing methods discussed in section 11.2.4. But before we continue, let's look at a simple benchmark comparing the lookup speed in a large grouped data frame. In all the following lines, I suppress printing of the values produced by the expressions to make the timing results easier to follow.

> **WARNING**   These tests were run on a machine with 32 GB of RAM. If you have less RAM and would like to reproduce these tests, please decrease the number of rows in the `bench_df` data frame to, for example, 10^7.

```
julia> using BenchmarkTools

julia> bench_df = DataFrame(id=1:10^8);

julia> bench_gdf = groupby(bench_df, :id);

julia> @btime groupby($bench_df, :id);       ◄    Timing of creation of a
  248.141 ms (88 allocations: 858.31 MiB)         grouped data frame

julia> bench_i = 1_000_000;

julia> bench_gk = keys(bench_gdf)[bench_i];

julia> bench_t = Tuple(bench_gk);

julia> bench_nt = NamedTuple(bench_gk);
```

```
julia> bench_dict = Dict(bench_gk);

julia> @btime $bench_gdf[$bench_i];
  283.544 ns (7 allocations: 176 bytes)
```
Timing of lookup using an integer

```
julia> @btime $bench_gdf[$bench_gk];
  336.406 ns (9 allocations: 208 bytes)
```
Timing of lookup using a GroupKey

```
julia> @btime $bench_gdf[$bench_t];
  483.505 ns (10 allocations: 224 bytes)
```
Timing of lookup using a tuple

```
julia> @btime $bench_gdf[$bench_nt];
  575.691 ns (12 allocations: 256 bytes)
```
Timing of lookup using a named tuple

```
julia> @btime $bench_gdf[$bench_dict];
  678.912 ns (15 allocations: 304 bytes)
```
Timing of lookup using a dictionary

I have the following comments about these benchmarks:

- When grouping by integer column, the groupby operation for 100 million rows is performed in several hundred milliseconds, which I consider fast.
- All indexing operations are performed on the order of several hundreds of nanoseconds, which should be fast enough in most practical applications.
- Integer indexing is fastest, followed by GroupKey indexing and Tuple indexing. Next is NamedTuple indexing, which is more expensive than tuple indexing because it additionally checks column names. Using dictionary indexing is slowest as dictionaries are mutable, and working with mutable objects is usually slower than with immutable objects in Julia.
- Although not visible in these benchmarks, if you use Tuple, NamedTuple, or dictionary indexing, then the first time you perform the lookup, it is slower than consecutive operations. To make the amortized cost of Tuple, Named-Tuple, or dictionary lookup low, DataFrames.jl lazily creates a helper data structure inside a GroupedDataFrame object. This operation is done lazily because in situations when you would perform lookup using only integers or GroupKeys, such a helper data structure is not needed, so DataFrames.jl avoids its creation by default.

11.2.6 *Indexing a grouped data frame with multiple values*

In this section, you will use indexing to select several groups from a GroupData-Frame.

You now know that to perform a single group lookup in a GroupDataFrame object, you need to index it with a single value. As a natural extension of this rule, if you pass multiple values when indexing a GroupedDataFrame, you get a Grouped-DataFrame with only the selected groups kept. Here are two examples:

```
julia> gdf_city[[2, 1]]
GroupedDataFrame with 2 groups based on key: city
First Group (4 rows): city = "Ełk"
```
Changes the order of groups in the gdf_city grouped data frame

```
Row │ city      date         rainfall
    │ String7   Date         Float64
────┼─────────────────────────────────
  1 │ Ełk       2020-11-16        3.9
  2 │ Ełk       2020-11-19        1.2
  3 │ Ełk       2020-11-20        2.0
  4 │ Ełk       2020-11-22        2.0
⋮
Last Group (6 rows): city = "Olecko"
Row │ city      date         rainfall
    │ String7   Date         Float64
────┼─────────────────────────────────
  1 │ Olecko    2020-11-16        2.9
  2 │ Olecko    2020-11-17        4.1
  3 │ Olecko    2020-11-19        4.3
  4 │ Olecko    2020-11-20        2.0
  5 │ Olecko    2020-11-21        0.6
  6 │ Olecko    2020-11-22        1.0
```

```
julia> gdf_city[[1]]
GroupedDataFrame with 1 group based on key: city      ◁──┐  Creates a grouped data frame
First Group (6 rows): city = "Olecko"                     │  having a single group
Row │ city      date         rainfall
    │ String7   Date         Float64
────┼─────────────────────────────────
  1 │ Olecko    2020-11-16        2.9
  2 │ Olecko    2020-11-17        4.1
  3 │ Olecko    2020-11-19        4.3
  4 │ Olecko    2020-11-20        2.0
  5 │ Olecko    2020-11-21        0.6
  6 │ Olecko    2020-11-22        1.0
```

As you can see, the indexing rules are the same as you would expect them to be after learning general indexing rules in Julia. For example, passing a one-element vector as an index in the gdf_city[[1]] expression returns a grouped data frame with a single group. This example uses integer numbers to index into a grouped data frame, but could have also used vectors of GroupKey, Tuple, NamedTuple, or dictionary.

Let me highlight here, again, that GroupedDataFrame indexing does not involve copying of the source data stored in the rainfall_df data frame, so all such operations are fast.

In summary, using GroupedDataFrame indexing, you can easily perform the following three operations that are often useful when preparing data for further manipulation:

- Group lookup, returning a data frame if you pass a single group index when indexing
- Reordering of groups, returning a grouped data frame if you pass a permutation of group indices when indexing
- Subsetting of groups, returning a grouped data frame if you pass a vector of a subset of group indices when indexing

11.2.7 *Iterating a grouped data frame*

In this section, I will show you how to iterate groups of a `GroupedDataFrame`. This operation is useful if you want to perform the same operation on all groups of a `GroupedDataFrame`.

Since `GroupedDataFrame` objects support indexing, it is natural to expect that they also follow the iteration interface discussed in chapter 10. Indeed, this is the case, and such iteration produces data frames representing consecutive groups. You can therefore use it in a comprehension. Here is an example showing how to determine the number of rows in each group of the `gdf_city` grouped data frame:

```julia
julia> [nrow(df) for df in gdf_city]
2-element Vector{Int64}:
 6
 4
```

While this iteration is often useful, it has one problem. When iterating the values, we do not see which keys correspond to them. We can resolve this issue by wrapping the `gdf_city` object with the `pairs` function. This function returns an iterator of `GroupKey` and data frame pairs. Here is a simple example printing these pairs:

```julia
julia> for p in pairs(gdf_city)
           println(p)
       end
GroupKey: (city = "Olecko",) => 6×3 SubDataFrame
 Row │ city    date        rainfall
     │ String7 Date        Float64
─────┼──────────────────────────────
   1 │ Olecko  2020-11-16       2.9
   2 │ Olecko  2020-11-17       4.1
   3 │ Olecko  2020-11-19       4.3
   4 │ Olecko  2020-11-20       2.0
   5 │ Olecko  2020-11-21       0.6
   6 │ Olecko  2020-11-22       1.0
GroupKey: (city = "Ełk",) => 4×3 SubDataFrame
 Row │ city    date        rainfall
     │ String7 Date        Float64
─────┼──────────────────────────────
   1 │ Ełk     2020-11-16       3.9
   2 │ Ełk     2020-11-19       1.2
   3 │ Ełk     2020-11-20       2.0
   4 │ Ełk     2020-11-22       2.0
```

Let's now use the `pairs` function to produce a dictionary mapping each city name to the number of rows of observations for this city:

```julia
julia> Dict(key.city => nrow(df) for (key, df) in pairs(gdf_city))
Dict{String7, Int64} with 2 entries:
  "Ełk"    => 4
  "Olecko" => 6
```

This time, the code is a bit more complex, so I'll explain it step by step (you learned all this syntax in part 1). The `(key, df) in pairs(gdf_city)` part of our code performs destructuring of the `Pair` object, and in each iteration assigns the first element, which is a `GroupKey`, to the `key` variable, and assigns the second element, which is a data frame, to the `df` variable. The `key.city` part extracts the city name from the `GroupKey` object.

The `nrow(df)` function produces the number of rows in a data frame representing a given group. Finally, we feed the iterator of `key.city => nrow(df)` pairs to the dictionary constructor.

The pairs function

In this section, we used the `pairs` function to produce `key => value` pairs when iterating `GroupedDataFrame` objects.

The `pairs` function can also be used with different collections. For example, if you pass a `Vector` to it, you get an iterator of `element index => element value` pairs. The general rule is that the `pairs` function returns an iterator over `key => value` pairs for any collection that maps a set of keys to a set of values.

Now you know all the fundamental concepts related to working with grouped data frames. In the remaining chapters, you will learn to use grouped data frames to perform split-apply-combine operations. However, since the example of counting the number of observations per group is a simple split-apply-combine operation, I'll show you how you could have performed it by using the `combine` function (we will discuss this in detail in the remaining chapters):

```
julia> combine(gdf_city, nrow)
2×2 DataFrame
 Row │ city     nrow
     │ String7  Int64
─────┼────────────────
   1 │ Olecko       6
   2 │ Ełk          4
```

In my opinion, this code has the following advantages over the manual aggregation of a grouped data frame into a dictionary that we performed earlier:

- It is shorter and easier to read.
- It produces a data frame, so we could use other functionalities of the DataFrames.jl package if we wanted to further process this data.

EXERCISE 11.2   Using the `gdf_city` grouped data frame, compute the mean temperature in each city by using the `mean` function from the `Statistics` module. Store the result as a dictionary in which keys are city names and values are corresponding mean temperatures. Compare your result with the output of the following call: `combine(gdf_city, :rainfall => mean)`. We will discuss the exact syntax of such expressions in chapters 12 and 13.

Summary

- You can easily convert a data frame to a wide variety of other types. Some of the most common conversions are to a `Matrix`, `NamedTuple` of vectors, and `Vector` of `NamedTuple`. Such conversions are commonly needed when you have a function that does not accept a `DataFrame` but requires a value of another type as an input.
- We call Julia code type stable if Julia can infer during compilation the types of all used variables. Type-stable code is typically faster than type-unstable code.
- The `DataFrame` object and the objects returned by the `eachrow` and `eachcol` functions called on a data frame are not type stable. This has benefits, as it does not incur significant compilation time and allows changing columns of a data frame. However, it also has the downside that the function-barrier method needs to be used to ensure that operations on data stored in them are fast.
- Type piracy in Julia happens if you extend or redefine methods in Base Julia or other packages on types that you have not defined. Writing code that does type piracy is discouraged, as it can break existing code.
- You can create an iterator of data frame columns by using the `eachcol` function. It is used when you want to iteratively perform operations on consecutive columns of a data frame.
- You can create an iterator of data frame rows by using the `eachrow` function or `Tables.namedtupleiterator` function. They are used when you want to iteratively perform operations on consecutive rows of a data frame.
- You can create `GroupedDataFrame` objects from a data frame by using the `groupby` function. Grouped data frames are useful when you want to process your data frame grouped by values stored in one or more columns of the data frame. Such processing of data is often needed in practice, for example, when performing split-apply-combine operations.
- `GroupedDataFrame` objects are indexable and iterable. You can easily perform group lookup and reorder or subset groups in a grouped data frame. These operations are needed when you analyze data stored in `GroupedDataFrame`.
- You can index into `GroupedDataFrame` objects by using an integer value, `GroupKey`, `Tuple`, `NamedTuple`, or dictionary. Having such a wide selection of possibilities is useful as it allows you to choose the one that corresponds best to your needs.
- Indexing of `GroupedDataFrame` objects is fast because source data stored in the parent data frame is not copied when such an operation is performed. Therefore, you can efficiently work with grouped data frames that have even a very large number of groups.

12

Mutating and transforming data frames

This chapter covers

- Extracting data from ZIP archives
- Adding and mutating columns of a data frame
- Performing split-apply-combine transformations of data frames
- Working with graphs and analyzing their properties
- Creating complex plots

In chapters 8–11, you learned to create data frames and extract data from them. It is time to discuss ways in which data frames can be mutated. By *data frame mutation*, I mean creating new columns by using data from existing columns. For example, you might have a date column in a data frame and want to create a new column that stores the year extracted from this date. In DataFrames.jl, you can achieve this objective in two ways:

- Update the source data frame in place by adding a new column to it.
- Create a new data frame storing only the columns that you will later need in your data analysis pipeline.

This chapter covers both approaches. Data frame mutation is a fundamental step in all data science projects. As discussed in chapter 1, after ingesting the source data, you need to prepare it before it can be analyzed for insights. This data preparation process typically involves such tasks as data cleaning and transforming, which are usually achieved by mutating existing columns of a data frame.

The problem we solve in this chapter is a classification of GitHub developers. The data we will use is taken from the work of Benedek Rozemberczki et al. presented in "Multi-Scale Attributed Node Embedding" (https://github.com/benedekrozember czki/MUSAE). The shared data set is licensed under GPL-3.0.

The task of classifying GitHub developers is a typical data science project from the field of mining complex networks. A practical business application of these techniques is predicting types of products that your customers might be interested in buying by investigating what their friends purchase.

In our source data, each developer is classified as either a web or a machine learning expert. Additionally, we have information on which developers are connected. Two developers are defined as *connected* if they mutually follow each other on GitHub.

It is natural to assume that web developers are mostly connected to other web developers; similarly, machine learning developers are probably working with other machine learning developers. Our goal in this chapter is to check whether our source data confirms these hypotheses.

As usual in this book, I present a full example of a data science project. Therefore, apart from this chapter's core topic of data frame mutation, you will learn new things in all areas of data analysis: getting, transforming, and analyzing the data. We will discuss how to integrate DataFrames.jl, which makes it possible for you to work with tabular data, with the Graphs.jl package, which provides functionalities you can use to analyze graph data. The point of such integration is that some data transformations, as you will see in this chapter, are expressed more naturally when data is in tabular form, while others are easier to do when you represent data using a graph structure.

12.1 Getting and loading the GitHub developers data set

In this section, you will download and extract from the ZIP archive the GitHub developers data set. You will store the information about developers in two data frames and additionally learn how to update the columns in a data frame. All these tasks are commonly performed when doing virtually any data analysis project.

The GitHub developers data set is available for download on Stanford University's Large Network Dataset Collection website (https://snap.stanford.edu/data/github -social.html). This data set contains information about GitHub developers' social networks. The observational unit in this data is a GitHub developer. For each developer, we have information about their specialization, which is either machine learning or web development. Additionally, for each pair of developers, we know whether they mutually follow each other. In data science, this kind of data structure is called a *graph*.

12.1.1   *Understanding graphs*

In this section, you'll learn what a graph is and how to represent GitHub developer data by using a graph. A *graph* is a collection of *nodes*, and some pairs of nodes may be connected by *undirected edges*. In our data, a single GitHub developer is a node, and a connection between two developers is an edge. When visualized, nodes are typically represented as points, and edges as lines connecting these points. Figure 12.1 shows an example of a small graph representing five developers, taken from the GitHub developers' social network.

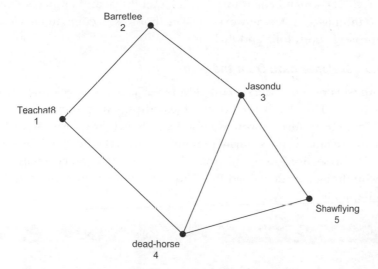

Figure 12.1   In this graph of five GitHub developers, each developer is a numbered node (point), and each connection between developers is an edge (line).

This graph consists of five nodes. For each node, I present the GitHub name of the developer. In the Graphs.jl package, nodes are assigned numbers. In Julia, we use 1-based indexing (see chapter 4 for details), so nodes are numbered from 1 to 5.

   Nodes in a graph are connected by edges. In this example, edges are drawn as lines connecting nodes. Typically, an edge is described by a pair of numbers indicating the nodes they're connected to; for example, edge (1, 2) means that nodes 1 and 2 are connected by an edge. We have six edges in our graph: (1, 2), (1, 4), (2, 3), (3, 4), (3, 5), and (4, 5).

   When analyzing a graph, we often talk about a set of neighbors of a particular node. *Neighbors* of a node are defined as nodes that are connected by an edge to the analyzed node. For example, in figure 12.1, node 4 is connected by an edge to nodes 1, 3, and 5, so the set {1, 3, 5} is the neighborhood of node 4. Additionally, for each node, we define its *degree* as the number of edges connected to it. In the case of node 4, its degree is 3.

   Going back to our problem involving the GitHub developer graph, we want to see if, by inspecting the neighborhood of a node (GitHub developer), we will be able to predict whether this developer is a machine learning or web specialist. For example, in figure 12.1, node 4 (dead-horse GitHub user) is connected to nodes 1, 3, and 5 (Teachat8, Jasondu, and Shawflying GitHub users), which are its neighborhood. We want to check if, by learning whether nodes 1, 3, and 5 represent web or machine learning developers, we can predict the type of node 4.

The problem I just described is a standard task in the graph-mining domain called *node classification.* In this chapter, I will show you how to do a simple analysis of this problem, focusing mostly on processing data by using DataFrames.jl. If you would like to explore analyzing graph data in more detail, you can check out *Mining Complex Networks* (CBC Press, 2021), which I coauthored with Paweł Prałat and François Théberge (www.ryerson.ca/mining-complex-networks/). The book is accompanied by source code for all examples in both Julia and Python.

12.1.2 *Fetching GitHub developer data from the web*

In this section, we will download the GitHub developer data and check that the downloaded file is correct. This time, the source file (https://snap.stanford.edu/data/git_web_ml.zip) is a ZIP archive, so you will also learn how to work with this file type. Since ZIP archives are binary, for security reasons, we will validate the SHA-256 hash (explained later in this section) of the file to make sure it is fetched correctly.

In the following listing, we download the data by using the functions described in more detail in chapter 6.

Listing 12.1   Downloading and checking the git_web_ml.zip file

```
julia> import Downloads

julia> using SHA

julia> git_zip = "git_web_ml.zip"
"git_web_ml.zip"

julia> if !isfile(git_zip)              Downloads the file only if it is not
           Downloads.download("https://snap.stanford.edu/data/" *
                              "git_web_ml.zip",
                              git_zip)
       end

julia> isfile(git_zip)              Makes sure the file has
true                                been successfully downloaded

julia> open(sha256, git_zip) == [0x56, 0xc0, 0xc1, 0xc2,
                                 0xc4, 0x60, 0xdc, 0x4c,
                                 0x7b, 0xf8, 0x93, 0x57,
                                 0xb1, 0xfe, 0xc0, 0x20,
                                 0xf4, 0x5e, 0x2e, 0xce,
                                 0xba, 0xb8, 0x1d, 0x13,
                                 0x1d, 0x07, 0x3b, 0x10,
                                 0xe2, 0x8e, 0xc0, 0x31]
true
```

Annotations:
- Downloads the file only if it is not present in the current working directory
- Makes sure the file has been successfully downloaded
- Applies the sha256 function to the downloaded file to compute its SHA-256 hash and compare it to a reference vector that I have computed on my machine

Let's focus on the open(sha256, git_zip) operation. It is a short piece of code but does a lot underneath. In this pattern, we pass two arguments to the open function. The first is the function that we want to apply to the file, and the second is the filename we want to work with. Figure 12.2 lists the steps that Julia performs when executing this operation.

The function that is passed as a first argument to the open function must accept the handle to the newly opened file as its only argument. This is the case with the sha256 function, which can accept this file handle and compute the SHA-256 hash value for data read in from it. Notably, this calculation is done without having to read the whole file into RAM, which allows processing of very large files. Additionally, it is important to know that if the open function gets a function as its first argument, then open returns the value returned by that function and automatically closes the stream that it opened. This behavior is useful because the programmer does not have to remember to manually close the stream.

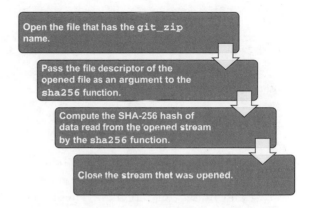

Figure 12.2   Steps performed by the open(sha256, git_zip) operation. The open function, when passed the sha256 function as a first argument, guarantees to close the opened stream when the operation finishes and to return the value produced by the sha256 function.

SHA-256 hash

SHA-256 is a cryptographic hash function designed by the US National Security Agency. The SHA-256 algorithm takes a stream of bytes and returns its 256-bit representation. The idea is that if you have two different source streams, it is highly unlikely that they will have the same SHA-256 representation. Additionally, the algorithm is called *one-way*, which means that if you have 256-bit representation of data, it is hard to come up with input data whose SHA-256 hash matches the one you have. If you would like to learn more about this topic, check out *Real-World Cryptography* by David Wong (Manning, 2021; www.manning.com/books/real-world-cryptography).

One common use of SHA-256 hashing is verifying that data fetched from the web is correctly downloaded. If you have the data's expected SHA-256 hash and it matches the hash you compute on the fetched data, the data is likely not corrupted.

In Julia, the sha256 function from the SHA module returns a 32-element Vector {UInt8} that contains the result of applying the SHA-256 algorithm to the passed data.

12.1.3   *Implementing a function that extracts data from a ZIP file*

Now that we have downloaded the git_web_ml.zip archive, we can read the data we want to later work with into a data frame. In this section, we will create a function that performs this operation.

As a first step, we open the ZIP archive by using the ZipFile.jl package:

```
julia> import ZipFile

julia> git_archive = ZipFile.Reader(git_zip)
ZipFile.Reader for IOStream(<file git_web_ml.zip>) containing 6 files:

uncompressedsize method  mtime            name
---------------------------------------------
             0 Store   2019-10-03 21-49 git_web_ml/
       3306139 Deflate 2019-09-20 22-39 git_web_ml/musae_git_edges.csv
       4380176 Deflate 2019-09-20 22-39 git_web_ml/musae_git_features.json
        676528 Deflate 2019-09-20 22-39 git_web_ml/musae_git_target.csv
           485 Deflate 2019-10-03 21-44 git_web_ml/citing.txt
           881 Deflate 2019-10-03 21-49 git_web_ml/README.txt
```

The `git_archive` variable is bound to an object that allows us to read data from the archive. We can see five files in the archive. We are interested in musae_git_edges.csv and musae_git_target.csv. These are CSV files, so we will read them in by using the CSV.jl package.

Before we continue, let's look at the structure of `ZipFile.Reader`. Every Zip-File.Reader object has a `files` property that is a `Vector` of files stored in it. Let's investigate this property for our `git_archive` variable:

```
julia> git_archive.files
6-element Vector{ZipFile.ReadableFile}:
 ZipFile.ReadableFile(name=git_web_ml/, method=Store,
     uncompresssedsize=0, compressedsize=0, mtime=1.57013214e9)
   ⋮
 ZipFile.ReadableFile(name=git_web_ml/README.txt, method=Deflate,
     uncompresssedsize=881, compressedsize=479, mtime=1.57013214e9)
```

In this case, we have elements: one directory and five files. Each stored file has several properties. We are interested in the `name` property that stores the name of the file. Let's check for the second file stored in `git_archive`:

```
julia> git_archive.files[2].name
"git_web_ml/musae_git_edges.csv"
```

First, we write a helper function that creates a `DataFrame` from a CSV file stored in an archive. In listing 12.2, the `ingest_to_df` function takes two arguments. The first is `archive`, which should be an open `ZipFile.Reader` object, just like the one bound to the `git_archive` variable. The second argument is `filename`, which is the name of the file that we want to extract from the archive. This name includes a full path to the file so all files in the archive are uniquely identified.

Listing 12.2   Function extracting a CSV file from the ZIP archive to a data frame

```
function ingest_to_df(archive::ZipFile.Reader, filename::AbstractString)
    idx = only(findall(x -> x.name == filename, archive.files))
    return CSV.read(read(archive.files[idx]), DataFrame)
end
```

Let's look at what this function does step by step. The `findall(x -> x.name ==` `filename, archive.files)` call finds all files whose name matches the `filename` variable and returns them as a vector. The `findall` function takes two arguments. The first is a function specifying a condition we want to check (in this case, whether the name of the file matches `filename`). The second argument is a collection; from this collection, we want to find elements for which the function passed as the first argument returns `true`.

The `findall` function returns a vector of indices to the collection for which the checked condition is satisfied. Here are two examples of `findall` calls:

```
julia> findall(x -> x.name == "git_web_ml/musae_git_edges.csv",
               git_archive.files)
1-element Vector{Int64}:
 2

julia> findall(x -> x.name == "", git_archive.files)
Int64[]
```

In the first call to `findall`, we learn that at index 2, we have a file whose name is `git_web_ml/musae_git_edges.csv`. In the second call, we find that no files have a name matching `""`.

In the `ingest_to_df` function, we expect that the passed `filename` matches exactly one file in our archive. Therefore, we use the `only` function to get the index of this file as an integer. If we do not have exactly one match, an error is thrown:

```
julia> only(findall(x -> x.name == "git_web_ml/musae_git_edges.csv",
                    git_archive.files))
2

julia> only(findall(x -> x.name == "", git_archive.files))

ERROR: ArgumentError: Collection is empty, must contain exactly 1 element
```

Using `only` in combination with `findall` is a common pattern that provides a safe way to check whether exactly one element in a collection meets a certain condition.

In the `ingest_to_df` function, we store the index of the file found in the `idx` variable. Next, we call `read(archive.files[idx])` to uncompress the file to a `Vector{UInt8}` object. It is important to remember that reading the data from the archive consumes it. If we were to call the `read` function on the same file object, we would get the empty vector `UInt8[]`. This is the same pattern as discussed in chapter 7, when we were converting the result of the `HTTP.get` query to `String`.

Next, this `Vector{UInt8}` object is passed to the `CSV.read` function that parses the passed data as a CSV and returns a data frame. Note that earlier we used the `CSV.read` function, passing it a string that contains the name of the file to be parsed. This time, we pass it a vector of bytes directly, and it gets correctly handled. This approach is useful because we do not have to save the unpacked CSV file to disk before reading it to a data frame.

12.1.4 *Reading the GitHub developer data into a data frame*

In this section, using the `ingest_to_df` function defined in listing 12.2, we will read the data into a data frame.

CREATING THE DATA FRAMES

In listing 12.3, we create two data frames. The first is `edges_df`. With the calls to the `summary` and `describe` functions, we learn that this data frame has 289,003 rows and two columns: `id_1` and `id_2`. The rows of this data frame represent edges in our GitHub developer graph. The second data frame is `classes_df`. It has 37,700 rows and three columns: `id`, `name`, and `ml_target`. One row of this data frame represents information about one developer.

The key node feature we are interested in is stored in the `ml_target` column. It takes two values, `0` and `1`, where `0` indicates a web developer and `1` indicates a machine learning developer. Observe that only roughly 25% of developers in the data set are machine learning specialists.

Listing 12.3 Constructing edge and node attribute data frames

```
julia> using CSV

julia> using DataFrames

julia> edges_df = ingest_to_df(git_archive,
                    "git_web_ml/musae_git_edges.csv");
```
Data frame containing the edges of the GitHub developer graph

```
julia> classes_df = ingest_to_df(git_archive,
                    "git_web_ml/musae_git_target.csv");
```
Data frame containing the targets for our classification problem

```
julia> close(git_archive)
```
Closes the ZipFile.Reader object after we are done getting data from it

```
julia> summary(edges_df)
"289003×2 DataFrame"

julia> describe(edges_df, :min, :max, :mean, :nmissing, :eltype)
2×6 DataFrame
 Row │ variable   min    max    mean      nmissing   eltype
     │ Symbol     Int64  Int64  Float64   Int64      DataType
─────┼──────────────────────────────────────────────────────────
   1 │ id_1           0  37694  14812.6          0   Int64
   2 │ id_2          16  37699  23778.8          0   Int64
julia> summary(classes_df)
"37700×3 DataFrame"
```
Passes a list of summary statistics we are interested in

```
julia> describe(classes_df, :min, :max, :mean, :nmissing, :eltype)     #D
3×6 DataFrame
 Row │ variable    min           max       mean       nmissing  eltype
     │ Symbol      Any           Any       Union…     Int64     DataType
─────┼──────────────────────────────────────────────────────────────────
   1 │ id          0             37699     18849.5           0  Int64
   2 │ name        007arunwilson timqian                     0  String31
   3 │ ml_target   0             1         0.258329          0  Int64
```

Before we continue our analysis, let's look at the describe call. I introduced this function in chapter 8, where you learned that it can be passed more arguments than only the data frame we want to describe. In this example, I have limited the computed statistics to only those that we're interested in for the analysis: min, max, mean, number of missing values, and column's element type. If you want to see all default column statistics, you can call describe(edges_df) and describe(classes_df).

At this point, if you have a GitHub account, you might be curious about whether you are included in the database that we analyze. You can check by using the findall function that we used previously in this chapter. Here, we use my bkamins name on GitHub:

```
julia> findall(n -> n == "bkamins", classes_df.name)
Int64[]
```

The returned vector is empty, which means that my name is not included in this data. Now let's look for StefanKarpinski (one of the creators of the Julia language):

```
julia> findall(n -> n == "StefanKarpinski", classes_df.name)
1-element Vector{Int64}:
 1359
```

```
julia> classes_df[findall(n -> n == "StefanKarpinski", classes_df.name), :]
1×3 DataFrame
 Row │ id     name             ml_target
     │ Int64  String31         Int64
─────┼───────────────────────────────────
   1 │  1358  StefanKarpinski          1
```

This time, the check succeeds. Note that the id of StefanKarpinski is 1358, but it is row number 1359 in our data frame. Let's fix this off-by-one issue.

USING BROADCASTING TO UPDATE THE CONTENTS OF DATA FRAMES

An important feature we learn from listing 12.3 is that the developer's identifier (columns id_1 and id_2 in edges_df and column id in classes_df) starts indexing with 0. Let's increase all the indices by 1 so that they start from 1. This is needed because in section 12.2, we will use these edges to create a graph with the Graphs.jl package, and in this package, nodes in a graph use 1-based indexing, just like standard arrays in Julia. We accomplish the update by using broadcasting:

```
julia> edges_df .+= 1
289003×2 DataFrame
```

```
     Row │ id_1     id_2
         │ Int64    Int64
   ──────┼────────────────
       1 │     1    23978
       2 │     2    34527
       3 │     2     2371
       ⋮ │    ⋮        ⋮
  289001 │ 37645     2348
  289002 │ 25880     2348
  289003 │ 25617     2348
        288997 rows omitted

julia> classes_df.id .+= 1
37700-element SentinelArrays.ChainedVector{Int64, Vector{Int64}}:
     1
     2
     3
     ⋮
 37698
 37699
 37700
```

The edges_df .+= 1 example shows that when broadcasting a data frame as a whole, it is treated as a two-dimensional object. Therefore, in this case, the operation gives the same result as we would get if we had a matrix instead of a data frame: we have incremented each cell in the data frame by 1.

The classes_df.id .+= 1 example shows that if you get a single column from a data frame, you can update it exactly as you update a vector—in this case, by also incrementing all its elements by 1.

A rule to remember is that broadcasting data frames works in the same way as for other arrays. Therefore, everything that you learned about broadcasting in Julia in general (covered in chapter 5) applies to data frame objects.

Let's look at a few more examples using a smaller df data frame (not related to our GitHub example) because is easier to follow visually:

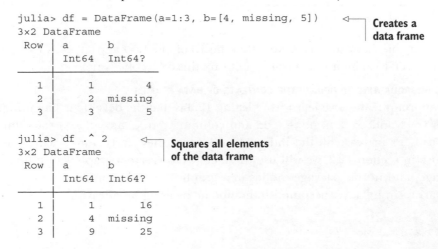

```
julia> df = DataFrame(a=1:3, b=[4, missing, 5])     ⟵┐ Creates a
3×2 DataFrame                                        │ data frame
 Row │ a      b
     │ Int64  Int64?
 ────┼───────────────
   1 │     1        4
   2 │     2  missing
   3 │     3        5

julia> df .^ 2          ⟵┐ Squares all elements
3×2 DataFrame            │ of the data frame
 Row │ a      b
     │ Int64  Int64?
 ────┼───────────────
   1 │     1       16
   2 │     4  missing
   3 │     9       25
```

```
julia> coalesce.(df, 0)
3×2 DataFrame
 Row │ a      b
     │ Int64  Int64
─────┼──────────────
   1 │     1      4
   2 │     2      0
   3 │     3      5
```

Replaces all missing elements in the data frame by 0 (the coalesce function was explained in chapter 5)

```
julia> df .+ [10, 11, 12]
3×2 DataFrame
 Row │ a      b
     │ Int64  Int64?
─────┼─────────────────
   1 │    11        14
   2 │    13   missing
   3 │    15        17
```

Adds a vector [10 11, 12] to each column of the data frame

```
julia> df .+ [10 11]
3×2 DataFrame
 Row │ a      b
     │ Int64  Int64?
─────┼─────────────────
   1 │    11        15
   2 │    12   missing
   3 │    13        16
```

Adds a one-row matrix [10 11] to each row of the data frame

Going back to the GitHub example, our developer identifiers now start from 1. There is more to it. All developers have unique numbers, and the classes_df data frame stores them in sorted order, starting from developer 1 and ending with developer 37700. We can easily check this by using the axes function you learned about in chapter 4:

```
julia> classes_df.id == axes(classes_df, 1)
true
```

The previous classes_df.id .+= 1 example showed how you can update the existing column of a data frame by using broadcasting. However, instead of using classes_df.id, you could have written classes_df[:, :id] .+= 1 or classes _df[!, :id] .+= 1. You could also use "id" here instead of :id. A natural question is whether there is a difference between using : and ! as a row selector in these two assignments. Indeed, there is a subtle one. The classes_df[:, :id] .+= 1 operation updates the :id column in place, while classes_df[!, :id] .+= 1 allocates a new column in the data frame.

If you are wondering in which cases this choice makes a difference, consider the following example. Again, I use a new, small df data frame not related to the GitHub case study to make it easier to check the result of the operations we perform:

```
julia> df = DataFrame(a=1:3, b=1:3)
3×2 DataFrame
```

```
Row │ a      b
    │ Int64  Int64
────┼─────────────
  1 │   1      1
  2 │   2      2
  3 │   3      3

julia> df[!, :a] .= "x"
3-element Vector{String}:
 "x"
 "x"
 "x"

julia> df[:, :b] .= "x"
ERROR: MethodError: Cannot `convert` an object of type String
to an object of type Int64

julia> df
3×2 DataFrame
Row │ a       b
    │ String  Int64
────┼───────────────
  1 │ x          1
  2 │ x          2
  3 │ x          3
```

In this example, we see that df[!, :a] .= "x" works because it replaces the column with new data (the df.a .= "x" call would be equivalent). However, df[:, :a] .= "x" fails because it tries to update the existing column in place, and we cannot assign strings to a vector of integers.

The same patterns as we discussed for broadcasting an assignment (.= operator) to a column of a data frame apply also to a standard assignment (= operator) to an existing column. Here is an example:

```
julia> df = DataFrame(a=1:3, b=1:3, c=1:3)
3×3 DataFrame
Row │ a      b      c
    │ Int64  Int64  Int64
????????????????????????????????
  1 │   1      1      1
  2 │   2      2      2
  3 │   3      3      3

julia> df[!, :a] = ["x", "y", "z"]
3-element Vector{String}:
 "x"
 "y"
 "z"

julia> df[:, :b] = ["x", "y", "z"]
ERROR: MethodError: Cannot `convert` an object of type String
to an object of type Int64
```

```
julia> df[:, :c] = [11, 12, 13]
3-element Vector{Int64}:
 11
 12
 13

julia> df
3×3 DataFrame
 Row │ a       b      c
     │ String  Int64  Int64
─────┼──────────────────────
   1 │ x           1     11
   2 │ y           2     12
   3 │ z           3     13
```

In this example, we can see that the df[!, :a] = ["x", "y", "z"] operation (or, equivalently, df.a = ["x", "y", "z"]) works because it replaces the column. The df[:, :b] = ["x", "y", "z"] assignment fails because it is an in-place operation into an existing column, and we cannot convert a string to an integer. However, df[:, :c] = [11, 12, 13] works since we assign a vector of integers to the c column.

12.2 Computing additional node features

In this section, you will learn how to integrate tabular data stored in a data frame with a graph by using the SimpleGraph type defined in the Graphs.jl package. We will create a graph from a list of edges stored in the edges_df data frame. Next, using the Graphs.jl package, we will compute several features of the graph's nodes and add them as new columns to the classes_df data frame. If you will ever work with social media data, knowing how to analyze it by using the Graphs.jl package will be useful.

Graphs.jl package

This section presents only a limited set of functionalities provided by the Graphs.jl package. If you want to learn more about working with graphs in Julia, refer to the package documentation (https://juliagraphs.org/Graphs.jl/dev/). Here, I will just comment that it supports all typical functionalities that are useful when working with graphs, including graph traversal, computing node distances, and centrality measures.

12.2.1 Creating a SimpleGraph object

In this section, we will create a Graph object. This object is useful because the Graphs.jl package offers multiple functions that will later allow you to efficiently query such an object about its properties—for example, neighbors of a particular node—from this graph.

In listing 12.4, we use the Graphs.jl package to work with graphs. First, we create an empty graph with the SimpleGraph function and then iterate rows of the edges_df data frame to add edges to it by using the add_edge! function. Next, we check the number of edges and nodes in the graph. They are consistent with the number of rows in `edges_df` and `classes_df` data frames, respectively, as expected. In Graphs.jl, nodes are always numbered with consecutive integers, starting with 1.

Listing 12.4   Creating a graph from a list of edges

```
julia> using Graphs

julia> gh = SimpleGraph(nrow(classes_df))        ◁─┐ Creates a graph with 37,700
{37700, 0} undirected simple Int64 graph            │ nodes and no edges

julia> for (srt, dst) in eachrow(edges_df)       ◁─┐ Adds edges to the graph by iterating
           add_edge!(gh, srt, dst)                  │ rows of the edges_df data frame
       end

julia> gh
{37700, 289003} undirected simple Int64 graph

julia> ne(gh)     ◁─┐ Gets the number of
289003              │ edges in the graph

julia> nv(gh)     ◁─┐ Gets the number of nodes (also
37700              │ called vertices) in the graph
```

Let's look at the `for (src, dst) in eachrow(edges_df)` expression. Recall that `edges_df` has two columns. This means that each row of this data frame is a `Data-FrameRow` that has two elements (we discussed `DataFrameRow` objects in chapter 9). When we iterate these two element objects, we can automatically destructure them into two variables (we discussed destructuring in chapter 10) by using a tuple syntax. In this case, these variables are `src` and `dst` (they need to be wrapped in parentheses). In the code, I use `src` and `dst` variable names because they are internally used in the Graphs.jl package. However, please keep in mind that our graph is undirected, so no orientation is applied to the edge.

Here's one more example of an iteration using a matrix instead of a data frame (to show that this is a general pattern that you can use):

```
julia> mat = [1 2; 3 4; 5 6]
3×2 Matrix{Int64}:
 1  2
 3  4
 5  6

julia> for (x1, x2) in eachrow(mat)
           @show x1, x2
       end
(x1, x2) = (1, 2)
(x1, x2) = (3, 4)
(x1, x2) = (5, 6)
```

Indeed, we see that the `x1` and `x2` variables get the first and the second elements of iterated rows of a matrix. This example uses the `@show` macro, which is useful in debugging as it shows the expression passed to it and its value.

12.2.2 Computing features of nodes by using the Graphs.jl package

In this section, using the `gh` graph, we will use the functionalities of the Graphs.jl
library to compute some features of its nodes. We start with node degrees that can be
obtained using the `degree` function:

```
julia> degree(gh)
37700-element Vector{Int64}:
   1
   8
   1
   ⋮
   4
   3
   4
```

We can see that the first node has one neighbor, the second node has eight neighbors,
and so forth. Let's create the `deg` column in the `classes_df` data frame that stores
this node degree information:

```
julia> classes_df.deg = degree(gh)
37700-element Vector{Int64}:
   1
   8
   1
   ⋮
   4
   3
   4
```

We can perform this assignment because we are sure that the `classes_df` data frame
stores developers in increasing order, starting from 1 and ending with 37700. If this
were not the case, we would have to perform a join operation to properly match developers to their features. We discuss joins in chapter 13.

   The syntax for creating columns is the same as the syntax for updating existing columns. Therefore, you could also have written `classes_df[!, :deg] = degree(gh)`
or `classes_df[:, :deg] = degree(gh)` to add a column to a data frame. As with
updating columns, there is a difference between using the `!` and `:` row selectors. The
`!` row selector stores the passed vector in the data frame without copying (the same
happens when we update an existing column). The `:` row selector creates a copy of
the passed vector. Here is an example showing this difference:

```
julia> df = DataFrame()
0×0 DataFrame

julia> x = [1, 2, 3]
3-element Vector{Int64}:
 1
 2
 3
```

```
julia> df[!, :x1] = x
3-element Vector{Int64}:
 1
 2
 3

julia> df[:, :x2] = x
3-element Vector{Int64}:
 1
 2
 3

julia> df
3×2 DataFrame
 Row │ x1     x2
     │ Int64  Int64
─────┼──────────────
   1 │     1      1
   2 │     2      2
   3 │     3      3

julia> df.x1 === x
true

julia> df.x2 === x
false

julia> df.x2 == x
true
```

The x1 column is created without copying, so it stores the same vector as the x vector. The x2 column is created with copying, so it stores a vector that has the same contents but a different location in memory. Therefore, if we later changed the contents of the x vector, the contents of the x1 column would change, but the contents of the x2 column would not be affected.

For completeness of the exposition, let me mention that you can also create columns by using broadcasting assignment. Here's one example using the df data frame created in the preceding example:

```
julia> df.x3 .= 1
3-element Vector{Int64}:
 1
 1
 1

julia> df
3×3 DataFrame
 Row │ x1     x2     x3
     │ Int64  Int64  Int64
─────┼─────────────────────
   1 │     1      1      1
   2 │     2      2      1
   3 │     3      3      1
```

12.2.3 *Counting a node's web and machine learning neighbors*

In this section, we'll compute two more features of the GitHub developers data frame. We want to compute the number of neighbors of a node that are web developers and the number of neighbors that are machine learning developers. This operation is slightly more complex than what we've typically performed in this book, and it uses many features of the Julia language that you have already learned.

ITERATING EDGES OF A GRAPH

Before we perform this operation, let's look at the `edges` function from the Graphs.jl library that returns an iterator of the edges of a graph:

```julia
julia> edges(gh)
SimpleEdgeIter 289003
```

Let's inspect its first element:

```julia
julia> e1 = first(edges(gh))
Edge 1 => 23978

julia> dump(e1)
Graphs.SimpleGraphs.SimpleEdge{Int64}
  src: Int64 1
  dst: Int64 23978

julia> e1.src
1

julia> e1.dst
23978
```

We can see that the `e1` object represents a single edge in the graph. Using the `dump` function, we inspect its structure and learn that it has two fields, `src` and `dst`, and we next check that they can be accessed using the property access syntax.

We know how to work with edges of the `gh` graph, so let's turn to the function that computes the number of neighbors of a node that are web developers and the number that are machine learning developers.

DEFINING A FUNCTION THAT COUNTS NEIGHBORS OF A NODE

In listing 12.5, the `deg_class` function takes two arguments: a `gh` graph and the 0–1 vector `class` that indicates whether a developer works with machine learning or the web.

Using the `zeros` function, we create vectors in which we will store the number of neighbors that are machine learning and web developers, respectively. These vectors are initialized with integer zeros, indicated by the `Int` argument, and have a length equal to the number of developers we have in our data, which is the length of the `class` vector.

Next, we iterate edges of the graph. For a single edge, we store the numbers assigned to developers that are its ends in `a` and `b` variables. Next, we check whether the b developer is working with machine learning by using the class[b] == 1 condition. If this is the case, we increase the number of machine learning neighbors of developer a by one; otherwise, we do the same for the number of web developers for developer a. Then we do the same operation but check the type of developer a and update the neighbor count information for developer b. Finally, we return a tuple consisting of both vectors we have created.

Listing 12.5   The function that counts neighbors of a node

```
function deg_class(gh, class)
    deg_ml = zeros(Int, length(class))      Initializes the vectors
    deg_web = zeros(Int, length(class))     with integer zeros
    for edge in edges(gh)
        a, b = edge.src, edge.dst           Assigns to the a and b variables
        if class[b] == 1                     the ends of the iterated edge
            deg_ml[a] += 1                   Updates the number of
        else                                 neighbors of node a
            deg_web[a] += 1
        end
        if class[a] == 1
            deg_ml[b] += 1                   Updates the number of
        else                                 neighbors of node b
            deg_web[b] += 1
        end
    end
    return (deg_ml, deg_web)
end
```

Iterates edges of the graph → points to `for edge in edges(gh)`

Let's see the deg_class function in action:

```
julia> classes_df.deg_ml, classes_df.deg_web =
       deg_class(gh, classes_df.ml_target)
([0, 0, 0, 3, 1, 0, 0, 0, 1, 2  …  2, 0, 12, 1, 0, 1, 0, 0, 1, 0],
 [1, 8, 1, 2, 1, 1, 6, 8, 7, 5  …  213, 3, 46, 3, 20, 0, 2, 4, 2, 4])
```

We add two columns to the classes_df data frame in one operation in one assignment. As previously discussed, in Julia, we can destructure an iterator from the right-hand side of the assignment (a tuple returned by the deg_class function in our case) to multiple variables passed on its left-hand side.

APPLYING THE FUNCTION-BARRIER TECHNIQUE

One more feature of the deg_class function that is important to highlight is that it will be fast. We are using the function-barrier technique that you learned in chapter 11 by passing the classes_df.ml_target vector to it. So, although the classes_df data frame is not type stable inside the deg_class function, Julia is able to identify the types of all variables and thus generate efficient code for its execution. Let's check that the deg_class function is efficient with the @time and @code_warntype macros:

```
julia> @time deg_class(gh, classes_df.ml_target);
  0.007813 seconds (5 allocations: 589.250 KiB)
```

```
julia> @code_warntype deg_class(gh, classes_df.ml_target)
MethodInstance for deg_class(::SimpleGraph{Int64},
    ::SentinelArrays.ChainedVector{Int64, Vector{Int64}})
  from deg_class(gh, class) in Main at REPL[106]:1
Arguments
  #self#::Core.Const(deg_class)
  gh::SimpleGraph{Int64}
  class::SentinelArrays.ChainedVector{Int64, Vector{Int64}}
Locals
  @_4::Union{Nothing, Tuple{Graphs.SimpleGraphs.SimpleEdge{Int64},
    Tuple{Int64, Int64}}}
  deg_web::Vector{Int64}
  deg_ml::Vector{Int64}
  edge::Graphs.SimpleGraphs.SimpleEdge{Int64}
  b::Int64
  a::Int64
Body::Tuple{Vector{Int64}, Vector{Int64}}
    ⋮
```

In the timing produced by the @time macro, the most important information is that the code performs five allocations. The number of allocations does not grow proportionally to the number of iterations of the for edge in edges(gh) loop in the function (remember that we have almost 300,000 edges in the graph). This is a good signal indirectly indicating that the function is type stable.

We get a confirmation of this when we inspect the output of the @code_warntype macro. I have truncated the preceding output, as it is quite long, but no types are presented in red (bold), and they are all concrete (recall the discussion of concrete types in chapter 5).

Looking at the time that the operation takes, we can determine that even if all developers in our graph were connected by an edge (a complete graph), we could process it in a few seconds (on my laptop). Note that such a graph would be quite big, as it would have 710,626,150 edges (which can be computed by using the formula $37700(37700-1)/2$ for the number of two-element subsets of a set containing 37,700 elements).

> **EXERCISE 12.1**   Using the complete_graph(37700) call, create a complete graph on 37,700 nodes (the number of nodes we have in the gh graph). But beware: if you have less than 32 GB RAM on your machine, use a smaller graph size, as this exercise is memory intensive. Next, using the Base .summarysize function, check how much memory this graph takes. Finally, using the @time function, check how long the deg_class function would take on this graph to finish, using the classes_df.ml_target vector as the vector of developer types.

INTERPRETING THE RESULTS OF THE ANALYSIS

Let's check the summary statistics of our classes_df data frame after adding the columns with additional graph features:

```
julia> describe(classes_df, :min, :max, :mean, :std)
6×5 DataFrame
```

Row	variable	min	max	mean	std
	Symbol	Any	Any	Union…	Union…
1	id	1	37700	18850.5	10883.2
2	name	007arunwilson	timqian		
3	ml_target	0	1	0.258329	0.437722
4	deg	1	9458	15.3317	80.7881
5	deg_ml	0	1620	2.22981	13.935
6	deg_web	0	8194	13.1019	69.9712

Observe that the average node degree in a graph is a bit over 15. We can cross-check this value by using the ne and nv functions. Since each edge contributes to the degree of two nodes, the average degree of the node in the whole graph should be two times the number of edges in the graph divided by the number of nodes in the graph:

```julia
julia> 2 * ne(gh) / nv(gh)
15.331724137931035
```

We have obtained the same value as by averaging over degrees of individual nodes, as expected.

Also note that, on average, developers have more links to web developers than to machine learning developers. This is not surprising, as in the graph, almost 75% of nodes are web developers. From the summary, we also learn from the information about the maximum and standard deviation columns that significant variability exists in node degrees of the graph (we will have to take this observation into account when analyzing the data later).

Before moving forward, let's check that for each node, the sum of the number of web neighbors and machine learning neighbors of a node is equal to its total degrees (as each neighbor of a node is either a web or machine learning developer):

```julia
julia> classes_df.deg_ml + classes_df.deg_web == classes_df.deg
true
```

Indeed, this is the case.

PERFORMING OBJECT CONSISTENCY CHECKS IN DATAFRAMES.JL

Performing data consistency checks is important when developing more complex solutions. For example, in DataFrames.jl, consistency checks of the DataFrame object are run when you execute selected operations on data frame objects. Here's an example of when such a consistency check is triggered:

```julia
julia> df = DataFrame(a=1, b=11)
1×2 DataFrame
 Row │ a      b
     │ Int64  Int64
─────┼──────────────
   1 │     1     11

julia> push!(df.a, 2)
2-element Vector{Int64}:
 1
 2
```

```
julia> df
Error showing value of type DataFrame:
ERROR: AssertionError: Data frame is corrupt: length of column :b (1)
does not match length of column 1 (2). The column vector has likely been
resized unintentionally (either directly or because it is shared with
another data frame).
```

This code creates a data frame with one row and two columns. Next, we add an element to only one of its columns with the push!(df.a, 2) operation (recall from chapter 10 that if you want to add a row to a data frame, you should use push! on the whole data frame). If we try to show this data frame next, we get an error indicating that the data frame is corrupted since all columns in a data frame must have the same number of elements. Don't try to work with corrupted data frames. Instead, locate the part of the code that caused this problem and fix it.

12.3 Using the split-apply-combine approach to predict the developer's type

In this section, we will check whether we can predict the type of a node by learning the number of its web and machine learning neighbors. Intuitively, we expect machine learning developers to have more connections with other machine learning developers. Similarly, we expect that web developers connect to web developers. You are going to learn how to apply the split-apply-combine strategy in DataFrames.jl, create complex plots using Plots.jl, and fit logistic regression with GLM.jl.

12.3.1 Computing summary statistics of web and machine learning developer features

In this section, we will check the average of the deg_ml and deg_web variables for web and machine learning developers separately.

APPROACH USING INDEXING

First, let's perform this computation by using the indexing syntax we learned in chapter 9:

```
julia> using Statistics

julia> for type in [0, 1], col in ["deg_ml", "deg_web"]
           println((type, col,
                    mean(classes_df[classes_df.ml_target .== type, col])))
       end
(0, "deg_ml", 1.5985122134401488)
(0, "deg_web", 16.066878866993314)
(1, "deg_ml", 4.042304138001848)
(1, "deg_web", 4.589382893520895)
```

In the loop, we iterate over the developer type (which is 0 or 1) and column name (which is deg_ml or deg_web) and print the conditional mean of the column. We see that web developers (encoded by 0) have many more web friends than machine learning friends on average. For machine learning developers, the number of web and machine learning contacts is comparable.

The preceding code works but is verbose, is not very readable, and produces output to the screen only. There must be a nicer way to perform these computations. Indeed, there is: the split-apply-combine pattern.

Described in "The Split-Apply-Combine Strategy for Data Analysis" by Hadley Wickham (www.jstatsoft.org/article/view/v040i01), this pattern is implemented in frameworks supporting data frame operations in many languages. If you know pandas in Python or dplyr in R, the concepts will be familiar. Figure 12.3 depicts this approach.

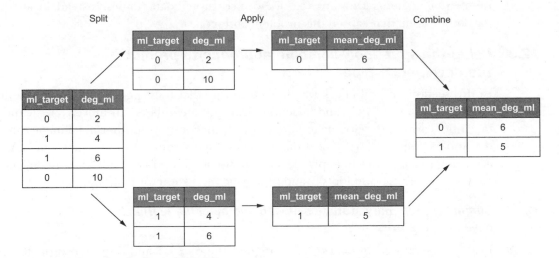

Figure 12.3 In the split-apply-combine strategy, we split the source data frame by the `ml_target` column into two groups, apply the mean function to the `deg_ml` column, and combine the results back into a single data frame.

OPERATION SPECIFICATION SYNTAX

In this section, I explain the split-apply-combine pattern in DataFrames.jl through an example. Chapter 13 covers the details of this topic.

If you want to aggregate data by groups in DataFrames.jl, you need to use two functions:

- `groupby`—Splits a data frame; you learned about this function in chapter 11
- `combine`—Takes a `GroupedDataFrame` object and performs its aggregation

We first group the `classes_ml` data frame by the `ml_target` column and then compute the means of the `deg_ml` and `deg_web` columns by group:

```
julia> gdf = groupby(classes_df, :ml_target)
GroupedDataFrame with 2 groups based on key: ml_target
First Group (27961 rows): ml_target = 0
```

| Row | id | name | ml_target | deg | deg_ml | deg_web |
	Int64	String31	Int64	Int64	Int64	Int64
1	1	Eiryyy	0	1	0	1
2	2	shawflying	0	8	0	8
3	4	SuhwanCha	0	5	3	2
:	:	:	:	:	:	:
27959	37697	kris-ipeh	0	2	0	2
27960	37698	qpautrat	0	4	0	4
27961	37700	caseycavanagh	0	4	0	4

27955 rows omitted

⋮

Last Group (9739 rows): ml_target = 1

| Row | id | name | ml_target | deg | deg_ml | deg_web |
	Int64	String31	Int64	Int64	Int64	Int64
1	3	JpMCarrilho	1	1	0	1
2	5	sunilangadi2	1	2	1	1
3	33	city292	1	2	2	0
:	:	:	:	:	:	:
9737	37694	chengzhongkai	1	4	1	3
9738	37696	shawnwanderson	1	1	1	0
9739	37699	Injabie3	1	3	1	2

9733 rows omitted

We can see that, as expected, we have two groups in our `gdf` object. The first corresponds to the value of the `ml_target` column equal to 0 (web developers), and the second to 1 (machine learning developers). When we pass the `GroupedDataFrame` object to the `combine` function, it performs data aggregation operations groupwise. Here's the syntax, which I'll explain next:

```julia
julia> combine(gdf,
               :deg_ml => mean => :mean_deg_ml,
               :deg_web => mean => :mean_deg_web)
2×3 DataFrame
```

| Row | ml_target | mean_deg_ml | mean_deg_web |
	Int64	Float64	Float64
1	0	1.59851	16.0669
2	1	4.0423	4.58938

> **The specification of the operation in the combine function has three parts linked by the => operator: source column name, the function that should be applied to this column, and the target column name.**

As a result of the `combine` function, we obtain a data frame whose first column is the variable on which we have grouped the `gdf` data frame (`ml_target`), and the following columns are the results of aggregations that we performed. We see that the numbers are the same as those we computed before using the `for` loop.

The crucial element to understand in this example is the syntax of the single operation specification that the `combine` function accepts. Let's focus on the `:deg_ml =>` `mean => :mean_deg_ml` operation. This syntax tells the `combine` function that it should take the `:deg_ml` column, pass it to the `mean` function, and store the result in the `:mean_deg_ml` column. Since we have passed a `GroupedDataFrame` object to the combine function, these operations are applied groupwise. Figure 12.4 explains this syntax further.

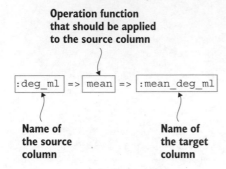

Figure 12.4 In this operation-specification syntax accepted by the combine function, you pass the source data for the computation, the operation that should be applied to the source data, and the target column name where the results of the computations should be stored.

This operation specification syntax is designed to be flexible and easy to use programmatically (that is, any of the components of the operation specification could have been passed as a variable). In chapter 13, we will discuss more options that this syntax provides.

DATAFRAMESMETA.JL DOMAIN-SPECIFIC LANGUAGE

If you are a dplyr user from R, you might wonder if you can achieve the same result by using the assignment syntax. This is possible with the DataFramesMeta.jl package:

```
julia> using DataFramesMeta

julia> @combine(gdf,
                :mean_deg_ml = mean(:deg_ml),
                :mean_deg_web = mean(:deg_web))
2×3 DataFrame
 Row │ ml_target   mean_deg_ml   mean_deg_web
     │ Int64       Float64       Float64

   1 │         0      1.59851        16.0669
   2 │         1      4.0423          4.58938
```

In this syntax, you write @combine instead of combine, and then you can use assignment to specify operations. In the operations, we use symbols to refer to the column names of the data frame, so we use the : prefix in front of the names. This convenience comes at the cost that the :mean_deg_ml = mean(:deg_ml) expression is not valid Julia code. In computer science parlance, we call such code a *domain-specific language*. For this reason, in the DataFrames.jl ecosystem, two high-level APIs are provided for specifying operations when, for example, aggregating data:

- *A standard evaluation API provided by DataFrames.jl*—This uses the => syntax described in figure 12.4. This syntax is more verbose but easier to use programmatically and is valid Julia code.

■ *A nonstandard evaluation API provided by the DataFramesMeta.jl package*—This uses
the assignment operator. This syntax is shorter at the cost of relying on nonstandard evaluation of code. It is often preferred by users when working interactively with data frames.

12.3.2 Visualizing the relationship between the number of web and machine learning neighbors of a node

Now that we've investigated the aggregate relationship between the type of the developer and the number of their machine learning and web neighbors, we can analyze it in more detail visually. Start with the following plot, which is shown in figure 12.5:

```
julia> using Plots

julia> scatter(classes_df.deg_ml, classes_df.deg_web;
               color=[x == 1 ? "black" : "yellow"
                      for x in classes_df.ml_target],
               xlabel="degree ml", ylabel="degree web", labels=false)
```

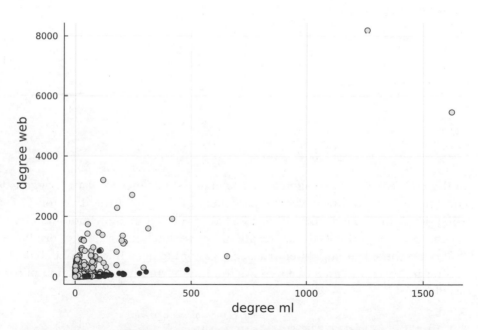

Figure 12.5   In this scatterplot of the node's number of machine learning and web neighbors, developer type is indicated by point color: black indicates a machine learning developer, and yellow (gray in the printed book) indicates a web developer.

Unfortunately, this plot is not very informative for the following key reasons:

■ The distribution of the number of neighbors is highly skewed. (We already saw this when computing summary statistics of the data.)

- Many developers have the same number of web and machine learning neighbors, so points representing that data overlap.

We will solve these problems by using the following techniques:

- Plot data aggregated by the combination of the number of web and machine learning neighbors of a developer. In this way, we will have a single point on the plot for a single combination of these values.
- Manually change the axis of the plots to be in logarithmic scale. In this way, we will visually decompress the low-degree part of the plot.
- Add jitter (random noise) to the displayed data to further reduce the problems caused by many points on the plot.

We'll start with aggregation of the data. We want to have a data frame that, for each unique combination of values stored in the deg_ml and deg_web columns, gives us information about a fraction of web developers:

```
julia> agg_df = combine(groupby(classes_df, [:deg_ml, :deg_web]),
                        :ml_target => (x -> 1 - mean(x)) => :web_mean)
2103x3 DataFrame
  Row | deg_ml  deg_web  web_mean
      | Int64   Int64    Float64
──────┼──────────────────────────────
    1 |      0        1  0.755143
    2 |      0        8  0.952104
    3 |      3        2  0.148148
    : |      :        :         :
 2101 |     41       14  0.0
 2102 |    101       18  0.0
 2103 |      2      213  1.0
                 2097 rows omitted
```

In this code we group and aggregate data in one shot. Since we want to aggregate data conditionally on two variables, we pass them as the two-element vector [:deg_ml, :deg_web] to groupby. In this case, we have to define an anonymous function x -> 1 - mean(x) that performs the aggregation. The reason is that mean(x) produces a fraction of machine learning developers, and we want to get a fraction of web developers.

It is important to note that we have to wrap the anonymous function in parentheses like this:

```
julia> :ml_target => (x -> 1 - mean(x)) => :web_mean
:ml_target => (var"#27#28"() => :web_mean)
```

If we were to omit the parentheses, we would get the following result:

```
julia> :ml_target => x -> 1 - mean(x) => :web_mean
:ml_target => var"#29#30"()
```

As you can see, because of Julia operator precedence rules, the target column name gets interpreted as a part of our anonymous function definition, which is not our intention.

Before we move forward, take a look at the DataFramesMeta.jl syntax for the same operation:

```
julia> @combine(groupby(classes_df, [:deg_ml, :deg_web]),
               :web_mean = 1 - mean(:ml_target))
2103×3 DataFrame
  Row │ deg_ml  deg_web  web_mean
      │ Int64   Int64    Float64
──────┼───────────────────────────
    1 │      0        1  0.755143
    2 │      0        8  0.952104
    3 │      3        2  0.148148
    ⋮ │   ⋮        ⋮        ⋮
 2101 │     41       14  0.0
 2102 │    101       18  0.0
 2103 │      2      213  1.0
                  2097 rows omitted
```

This is, in my opinion, easier to read than the syntax using the `=>` operator. Now that we have our aggregated data, let's check its summary statistics:

```
julia> describe(agg_df)
3×7 DataFrame
  Row │ variable  mean      min   median   max   nmissing  eltype
      │ Symbol    Float64   Real  Float64  Real  Int64     DataType
──────┼───────────────────────────────────────────────────────────
    1 │ deg_ml    19.1992      0      9.0  1620         0  Int64
    2 │ deg_web   98.0314      0     40.0  8194         0  Int64
    3 │ web_mean   0.740227  0.0      1.0   1.0         0  Float64
```

What is important for plotting is that we have a minimum value for each axis equal to 0. We cannot apply a standard logarithmic rescaling of axes (which could be done in Plots.jl using the `xscale=:log` and `yscale=:log` keyword arguments). Therefore, we will implement a custom axis transformation using the `log1p` function. This function calculates the natural logarithm of 1 plus its argument. Therefore, when passed 0, it returns 0:

```
julia> log1p(0)
0.0
```

In listing 12.6, we apply the `log1p` transformation to the data, also jittering it, and define custom ticks for the plot axes to match the performed transformation. In the `gen_ticks` function, we define ticks at 0 and consecutive powers of 2 up to a rounded value of the maximum number to be plotted; the function returns a tuple consisting of the tick location and tick label.

> ### Listing 12.6 Plotting the scatterplot of aggregated web developer data

```
julia> function gen_ticks(maxv)
           max2 = round(Int, log2(maxv))        ◁─── Function generating
           tick = [0; 2 .^ (0:max2)]                 custom ticks for the plot
           return (log1p.(tick), tick)
```

```
        end
gen_ticks (generic function with 1 method)

julia> log1pjitter(x) = log1p(x) - 0.05 + rand() / 10
log1pjitter (generic function with 1 method)

julia> using Random

julia> Random.seed!(1234);

julia> scatter(log1pjitter.(agg_df.deg_ml),
               log1pjitter.(agg_df.deg_web);
               zcolor=agg_df.web_mean,
               xlabel="degree ml", ylabel="degree web",
               markersize=2,
               markerstrokewidth=0.5,
               markeralpha=0.8,
               legend=:topleft, labels="fraction web",
               xticks=gen_ticks(maximum(classes_df.deg_ml)),
               yticks=gen_ticks(maximum(classes_df.deg_web)))
```

Applies a log1p transformation to a value and adds a random jitter to it in the [-0.05,0.05] range

Sets a seed for the random number generator to ensure reproducibility of the results

Gives a color to each point plotted on the scatterplot corresponding to the fraction of web developers

Sets the size of each point

Sets the width of the stroke of each point

Sets the transparency of each point

Sets custom ticks for the plot, ensuring that they span up to a maximum value to be plotted on each axis

Figure 12.6 shows the resulting plot. We can see several relationships. In general, as the number of web neighbors increases for a node, the probability that the neighbor is a web developer increases. Similarly, as the number of machine learning neighbors

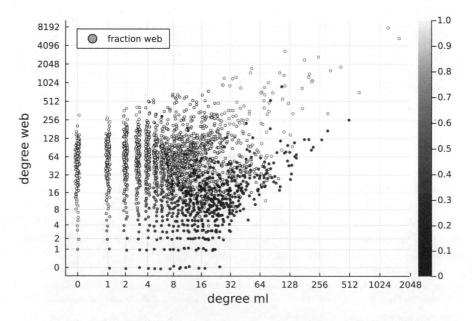

Figure 12.6   In this scatterplot of a fraction of a node's machine learning and web neighbors, the darker the point, the lower the fraction of web developers for a given number of machine learning and web neighbors.

of a node increases, the probability that the neighbor is a machine learning developer increases.

Additionally, we see that there is no point at the (0, 0) coordinate since each node in our graph has a positive degree. Finally, in general, a positive correlation seems to exist between the number of web and machine learning neighbors of a node. If a developer has many web neighbors, chances increase that they have also many machine learning neighbors. This relationship is especially visible for developers with a high degree.

Now, let's consider a few technical aspects related to figure 12.6 and the code generating it. First, observe that jitter is indeed useful in this plot. If we omitted it, we would see all the points with a machine learning degree equal to 0 in one line, and they most likely would overlap. Second, the `gen_ticks` function takes one argument that is a maximum value that we want to plot on an axis. Then, with `round(Int, log2(maxv))`, we compute the power to which we need to raise the number 2 that is nearest to this number.

Notice that this works nicely on our plot. For the x-axis, the largest machine learning degree is 1620, so we stop at 2048 (and not 1024). For the y-axis, the largest web degree is 8194, so we stop at 8192 (and not at 16384). Next, with `[0; 2 .^ (0:max2)]`, we produce ticks starting with 0 and then at consecutive powers of 2. Finally, with `(log1p.(tick), tick)`, we return a tuple of locations of the ticks transformed with the `log1p` function and the tick labels.

Making plots, like the one in figure 12.6, can be quite time-consuming if you want to really make sure they are informative. The big advantage of the Plots.jl package is that it provides many options for customizing your plot. In the Plots.jl documentation (https://docs.juliaplots.org/stable/attributes/), you can find an extensive list of available plotting options.

> **EXERCISE 12.2** Check to see how the plot in figure 12.6 will look if you remove jittering from it.

12.3.3 Fitting a logistic regression model predicting developer type

In this section, we create a logistic regression model for checking the relationship between the `ml_target` variable and the `deg_ml` and `deg_web` variables. If you do not have experience with logistic regression models, you can find introductory information on this topic at http://mng.bz/G1ZV.

We will use the GLM.jl package to estimate the model parameters and, as usual, I will show you some of the GLM.jl features that are useful in practice:

```julia
julia> using GLM

julia> glm(@formula(ml_target~log1p(deg_ml)+log1p(deg_web)),
           classes_df, Binomial(), LogitLink())
StatsModels.TableRegressionModel{GeneralizedLinearModel{
GLM.GlmResp{Vector{Float64}, Binomial{Float64}, LogitLink},
GLM.DensePredChol{Float64, LinearAlgebra.Cholesky{Float64,
Matrix{Float64}}}}, Matrix{Float64}}
```

```
ml_target ~ 1 + :(log1p(deg_ml)) + :(log1p(deg_web))

Coefficients:
─────────────────────────────────────────────────────────────────────────
                 Coef.    Std. Error      z   Pr(>|z|)  Lower 95%  Upper 95%
─────────────────────────────────────────────────────────────────────────
(Intercept)     0.30205   0.0288865   10.46   <1e-24    0.245433   0.358666
log1p(deg_ml)   1.80476   0.0224022   80.56   <1e-99    1.76085    1.84866
log1p(deg_web) -1.63877   0.0208776  -78.49   <1e-99   -1.67969   -1.59785
─────────────────────────────────────────────────────────────────────────
```

First, let's interpret the obtained result. All estimated coefficients are highly significant, which is indicated by very small values in the `Pr(>|z|)` column in the output. The positive `log1p(deg_ml)` coefficient means that as the number of machine learning neighbors of the node increases, the probability predicted by our model that this node represents a machine learning developer increases. Similarly, since the `log1p(deg_web)` coefficient is negative, we conclude that as the number of web neighbors of the node increases, the predicted probability that it represents a machine learning node decreases. Chapter 13 explains how such a model can be used to make predictions for new data.

Now, let's turn to implementing the model. To fit the logistic regression model, we use the `glm` function. In this case, we pass four arguments to it. The first is the model formula. Here, notably, observe that we can conveniently pass the variable transformations within the formula. In this case, since the data has a significant right skewness, we fit the model with features transformed using the `log1p` function. The `@formula` macro automatically identifies such transformations if we pass them and creates appropriate anonymous functions:

```
julia> @formula(ml_target~log1p(deg_ml)+log1p(deg_web))
FormulaTerm
Response:
  ml_target(unknown)
Predictors:
  (deg_ml)->log1p(deg_ml)
  (deg_web)->log1p(deg_web)
```

Second, to fit the logistic regression, we need to inform `glm` that our target feature is binary (follows the binomial distribution) by passing the `Binomial()` argument. Finally, since we can fit multiple possible models to binary data, we choose logistic regression via the `LogitLink()` argument. If, for example, you want to fit a probit model (www.econometrics-with-r.org/11-2-palr.html), use `ProbitLink()` instead.

> **EXERCISE 12.3** Fit a probit model instead of a logit model to predict the `ml_target` variable. Use the `ProbitLink()` argument to the `glm` function.

In this chapter, I show an example of how the GLM.jl package can be used to fit prediction models. If you would like more details about features of this package, refer to the package manual (https://juliastats.org/GLM.jl/stable/).

12.4 Reviewing data frame mutation operations

The key options that DataFrames.jl offers for mutating data frames are as follows:

- *A low-level API using assignment or broadcasted assignment*—An example operation using this API is df.x .= 1, setting the column x to 1 using broadcasting assignment. This API is sometimes referred to as *imperative* since you explicitly specify the way an operation should be performed.
- *A high-level API using data frame mutation functions*—This API is sometimes referred to as *declarative* since you specify only the operation you want to have performed and delegate to DataFrames.jl the decision of how to execute it most efficiently. The high-level API is useful when you want to perform a split-apply-combine operation. Two flavors of this high-level API are available:
  - *Using standard evaluation*—This is provided by DataFrames.jl and relics on operations specified using the pair (=>) notation. You have learned about the combine function that supports this API.
  - *Using nonstandard evaluation*—This is provided by the DataFramesMeta.jl package and allows you to use the assignment (=) notation. I have shown you the @combine macro that supports this API.

This chapter focused on explaining how the low-level (imperative) API works. Chapter 13 presents a more detailed discussion of the high-level (declarative) API.

The DataFrames.jl ecosystem provides these three options for working with data frame objects because different developers have different preferences for structuring their code. In this book, I discuss all three alternatives so you can pick the one that best matches your needs.

12.4.1 Performing low-level API operations

You can use the low-level API to update a data frame's columns in the following seven ways:

- Create a new column in a data frame without copying.
- Create a new column in a data frame via copying.
- Create a new column in a data frame by using broadcasting.
- Update an existing column in a data frame by replacing it.
- Update an existing column in a data frame in place.
- Update an existing column in a data frame by using broadcasting to replace it.
- Update an existing column in a data frame in place by using broadcasting.

We'll take a look at each option next.

CREATE A NEW COLUMN IN A DATA FRAME WITHOUT COPYING

To assign a vector v to a new column a in a data frame df without copying, write one of the following:

```
df.a = v
df[!, "a"] = v
```

CREATE A NEW COLUMN IN A DATA FRAME VIA COPYING

To copy a vector v to a new column a in a data frame df, write this:

```
df[:, "a"] = v
```

CREATE A NEW COLUMN IN A DATA FRAME BY USING BROADCASTING

To broadcast a scalar or vector s to a new column a in a data frame df (allocating this new column), write one of the following:

```
df.a .= s
df[!, "a"] .= s
df[:, "a"] .= s
```

UPDATE AN EXISTING COLUMN IN A DATA FRAME BY REPLACING IT

To assign a vector v to an existing column a in a data frame df without copying (by replacing the existing column), write one of the following:

```
df.a = v
df[!, "a"] = v
```

UPDATE AN EXISTING COLUMN IN A DATA FRAME IN PLACE

To assign a vector v to an existing column a in a data frame df in place (by updating data in the existing column), write this:

```
df[:, "a"] = v
```

The same rule can be used to update only selected rows r from the data frame (note that : is just a special kind of row selector):

```
df[r, "a"] = v
```

UPDATE AN EXISTING COLUMN IN A DATA FRAME BY USING BROADCASTING TO REPLACE IT

To assign a scalar or vector s to an existing column a in a data frame df and replace it by using broadcasting, write this:

```
df[!, "a"] .= s
```

UPDATE AN EXISTING COLUMN IN A DATA FRAME IN PLACE BY USING BROADCASTING

To assign a scalar or vector s to an existing column a in a data frame df in place (by updating data in the existing column) by using broadcasting, write this:

```
df[:, "a"] .= s
```

The same rule can be used to update only selected rows r from the data frame (an example of such a selector could be the 1:3 range; note that : is just a special kind of row selector):

```
df[r, "a"] .= s
```

In the preceding options, I have included only the operations that are most used. You can find a full list of operations supported by the low-level API in the DataFrames.jl documentation (http://mng.bz/z58r). Be warned that the list is extensive and might be hard to learn by heart. As a rule of thumb, you can assume the following:

- Most of the time, the operations I have listed will be sufficient for your needs.
- The DataFrames.jl API was designed to support every kind of operation you could possibly want in terms of behavior related to copying, or avoiding copying, data.

Therefore, if, in the future, you need to perform a special operation not covered here, you can refer to the documentation.

Comparison of ! and : row selector behavior

It is useful to highlight the difference between how `!` and `:` row selectors work. Assume that column `a` is present in data frame `df`.

Let's first start with reading the data from a data frame. If you use `df[!, "a"]` to get a column `a` from a data frame, then this operation returns a column stored in this data frame without making a copy, while `df[:, "a"]` returns a copy of this column.

A different situation is when you use the same syntax on the left hand of the assignment. In this case, if you write `df[:, "a"] = v` or `df[:, "a"] .= s`, then the operation is in-place, that is, the data from the right side is written to an existing column. If you write `df[!, "a"] = v`, then column `a` is replaced by vector `v` without copying. Finally, writing `df[!, "a"] .= s` allocates a new vector and replaces column `a` with it.

EXERCISE 12.4   Create an empty data frame. Add a column `a` to it, storing values `1`, `2`, and `3` without copying. Next, create another column in the data frame, called `b`, that is the same vector as column `a` (without copying). Check that columns `a` and `b` store the same vector. Storing two identical columns in a data frame is unsafe, so in column `b`, store its copy. Now check that columns `a` and `b` store the same data but are different objects. Update in place the first two elements of column `a` by 10.

12.4.2 *Using the insertcols! function to mutate a data frame*

In this section, before I finish the review of data frame mutation operations, you will learn about the `insertcols!` function. This function is used to add new columns to a data frame. It has a similar syntax to the `DataFrame` constructor, where you pass a pair `column_name => value` to add a column to a data frame.

The special feature of the `insertcols!` function is that it allows you to add a column in any location in a data frame and checks whether the passed column name already exists in the target data frame (to avoid accidental overwriting of a column). You can find more details about the `insertcols!` function in the DataFrames.jl documentation (http://mng.bz/09Gm).

Here I will present a few examples of how it works. Start with the most basic pattern, inserting a column at the end of the data frame:

```
julia> df = DataFrame(x=1:2)
```

```
3×1 DataFrame
 Row │ x
     │ Int64
─────┼──────
   1 │     1
   2 │     2
```

```
julia> insertcols!(df, :y => 4:5)
3×2 DataFrame
 Row │ x      y
     │ Int64  Int64
─────┼──────────────
   1 │     1      4
   2 │     2      5
```

◁─┐ **Inserts a new column to a data frame at its end**

```
julia> insertcols!(df, :y => 4:5)
ERROR: ArgumentError: Column y is already present in the data frame
which is not allowed when `makeunique=true`
```

◁─┐ **Trying to insert a duplicate column name is an error by default.**

```
julia> insertcols!(df, :z => 1)
3×3 DataFrame
 Row │ x      y      z
     │ Int64  Int64  Int64
─────┼─────────────────────
   1 │     1      4      1
   2 │     2      5      1
```

◁─┐ **Scalars are automatically broadcasted as in the DataFrame constructor.**

Let's continue this example by inserting a new column at a certain position in the data frame. To do this, we pass a second argument, specifying the position where the column should be added:

```
julia> insertcols!(df, 1, :a => 0)
3×4 DataFrame
 Row │ a      x      y      z
     │ Int64  Int64  Int64  Int64
─────┼────────────────────────────
   1 │     0      1      4      1
   2 │     0      2      5      1
```

◁─┐ **Inserts a new column in the first position in the data frame**

```
julia> insertcols!(df, :x, :pre_x => 2)
3×5 DataFrame
 Row │ a      pre_x  x      y      z
     │ Int64  Int64  Int64  Int64  Int64
─────┼───────────────────────────────────
   1 │     0      2      1      4      1
   2 │     0      2      2      5      1
```

◁─┐ **Inserts a new column before the x column in the data frame**

```
julia> insertcols!(df, :x, :post_x => 3; after=true)
3×6 DataFrame
 Row │ a      pre_x  x      post_x  y      z
     │ Int64  Int64  Int64  Int64   Int64  Int64
─────┼──────────────────────────────────────────
   1 │     0      2      1       3      4      1
   2 │     0      2      2       3      5      1
```

◁─┐ **Inserts a new column after the x column in the data frame, which is signaled by the after=true keyword argument**

> **Use of the => operator in DataFrames.jl**
>
> The `=>` operator is used in two contexts in DataFrames.jl that should not be confused.
>
> The first context is the `DataFrame` constructor and the `insertcols!` function, where the syntax has the form `column_name => value`. This form does not involve any data manipulation. It is used to put new data into a data frame. It is consistent with the way dictionaries are populated in Julia.
>
> The second context is operation syntax supported by the `combine` function (in chapter 13, you will learn that the same operation syntax is supported by other functions: `select`, `select!`, `transform`, `transform!`, `subset`, and `subset!`). The operation syntax is used for manipulation of data already present in the data frame. Its general structure, described in figure 12.4, is `source_column => operation_function => target_column_name`.

Summary

- A graph is a data structure that consists of nodes and edges connecting nodes. You can work with graphs in Julia by using the Graphs.jl package. You will need to work with graphs if you analyze data from social media, like Twitter or Facebook, where nodes represent users and edges represent the relationships between them.

- The SHA module provides functions that allow you to compute hash values of data you work with. One of these often-used algorithms is SHA-256, available via the `sha256` function. You can use it to validate that data you download from the web is not corrupted.

- The ZipFile.jl package provides tools for working with ZIP archives. It is often used in data science projects, as in many cases, your data sources will be compressed in this format.

- You can perform broadcasting operations on data frame objects just as you would on matrices. Broadcasting allows you to conveniently transform values stored in data frames.

- DataFrames.jl provides a low-level API for mutating the contents of the data frame that is based on indexing syntax. You can use both assignment (= operator) and broadcasted assignment (.= operator) syntaxes when you perform such operations. In general, operations of the form `df[:, column] =` are performed in place, and operations of the form `df[!, column] =` or `df.column =` replace columns. This API was designed to provide the developer with full control over the way the operation should be performed.

- The Graphs.jl package defines the `SimpleGraph` type that can be used to represent graphs in Julia, as well as multiple functions that allow you to analyze the properties of graphs (for example, listing neighbors of a node). This package is useful when, in your analysis, you have data that has a network structure.

- In the `SimpleGraph` type, graph nodes are represented as consecutive integers, starting with 1, and graph edges are represented as pairs of integers indicating the nodes they connect. Thanks to this representation, it is easy to keep node metadata in Julia collections that use 1-based indexing (for example, data frames).

- You can perform split-apply-combine operations on data frame objects by using the `groupby` and `combine` functions that are part of the high-level API in DataFrames.jl (more related functions are discussed in chapter 13). The `combine` function is used to perform aggregation operations per group. The split-apply-combine operation is often useful when summarizing data.

- The `combine` function performs aggregations of data based on the passed operation specification syntax. Its general structure is as follows: `source_column => operation_function => target_column_name`. For example, `:a => mean => :a_mean` indicates that data from column `:a` should be passed to the `mean` function, and the result of the computation should be stored in the `:a_mean` column. Operation specification syntax is especially convenient when used programmatically, as it is formed from valid Julia code.

- You can use the DataFramesMeta.jl package to simplify the specification of aggregation operations in the `@combine` macro. In this syntax, you write operations by using an assignment form; for example, the `:a_mean = mean(:a)` form is equivalent to `:a => mean => :a_mean` in a standard operation specification syntax. The syntax accepted by `@combine` is more convenient to write and read, but relies on a nonstandard evaluation.

- The Plots.jl package provides a rich list of options allowing you to flexibly shape plots you create. The list of available plot attributes can be found at https://docs.juliaplots.org/stable/attributes/. In practice, creating a customized plot that highlights the important aspects of data you analyze is often a key ingredient of success in data science projects.

- Using the GLM.jl package, you can fit logistic or probit regressions. These models are used when your target variable is binary.

- The `insertcols!` function can be used to add columns to a data frame in place. This function allows you to add a column in any location in the source data frame.

13
Advanced transformations of data frames

This chapter covers

- Performing advanced transformations of data frames and grouped data frames
- Chaining transformation operations to create data processing pipelines
- Sorting, joining, and reshaping data frames
- Working with categorical data
- Evaluating classification models

In chapter 12, you learned how to perform basic transformations of data frames by using operation specification syntax with the `combine` function. In this chapter, you will learn more advanced scenarios for using this syntax, along with more functions that accept it: `select`, `select!`, `transform`, `transform!`, `subset`, and `subset!`. With these functions, you can conveniently perform any operation you need on columns. At the same time, these functions are optimized for speed, and optionally can use multiple threads to perform computations. As in chapter 12, I also show you how to specify these transformations by using the DataFramesMeta.jl domain-specific language.

In this chapter, you will also learn to combine multiple tables by using join operations. DataFrames.jl has an efficient implementation for all standard joins: inner joins, left and right joins, outer joins, semi and anti joins, and cross joins. Similarly, I will show you how to reshape data frames with the `stack` and `unstack` functions.

The combination of advanced data transformation capabilities and support for joining and reshaping data frames makes DataFrames.jl a complete ecosystem for creating complex data analysis pipelines. Creating these pipelines is greatly simplified by the ability to chain multiple operations together. This can be achieved using the `@chain` macro that you will learn about in this chapter.

Additionally, you will learn to work with categorical data (known as *factors* by R users) by using the CategoricalArrays.jl package. This functionality is often needed when performing statistical analysis of data.

As usual in this book, I present all these concepts on a real-life data set. This time, we will use the Stanford Open Policing Project data, which is available under the Open Data Commons Attribution License. In this data set, each observation is one police stop, and it holds information about multiple features of the event. Our goal is to understand which features influence the probability that an arrest is made during a police stop in Owensboro, Kentucky. In the process, we will focus on performing feature engineering by using DataFrames.jl to prepare data that can be used to create a predictive model.

Since we are nearing the end of the book, expect the material in this chapter to be more advanced than in earlier chapters. The chapter covers many functionalities of DataFrames.jl, so it is relatively long. Therefore, in the descriptions, I concentrate on explaining new material.

13.1 Getting and preprocessing the police stop data set

In this section, we'll perform preparatory operations for our analysis. This material should be familiar to you from chapter 12, as the steps are the same (getting a ZIP archive from the web, checking its SHA, extracting a CSV file from the archive, and loading its contents to a data frame).

The difference is that I will show you how to pipe multiple operations by using the `@chain` macro. Creating pipelines combining several operations is a feature that many data scientists, especially those experienced with the `%>%` operator in R, enjoy and often use. At the end of this section, I'll show you how to drop columns from a data frame in place by using the `select!` function.

13.1.1 Loading all required packages

A common practice in Julia is to start analysis by loading all packages we are going to use in our project. I've added comments for packages that we have not used yet in this book:

```
julia> using CSV

julia> using CategoricalArrays    ◁──┐  Package allowing you to work with
                                       categorical data (factors in R)
```

```
julia> using DataFrames

julia> using DataFramesMeta

julia> using Dates

julia> using Distributions          ⟵⎯  Package providing support for working
                                           with various statistical distributions
julia> import Downloads

julia> using FreqTables

julia> using GLM

julia> using Plots

julia> using Random

julia> using ROCAnalysis            ⟵⎯  Package supplying functionalities for
                                           evaluation of classification models
julia> using SHA

julia> using Statistics

julia> import ZipFile
```

13.1.2 Introducing the @chain macro

The @chain macro provides functionality similar to the pipe (%>%) operator in R. We imported it in the preceding section by using the DataFramesMeta.jl package (which is originally provided by the Chain.jl package and re-exported by DataFramesMeta.jl). By using the @chain macro, you can conveniently perform multistep processing of your data.

> **Basic rules for how the @chain macro works**
>
> The @chain macro takes a starting value and a begin-end block of expressions, where typically one expression is one line of code. The basic rules of how this macro works are as follows:
>
> - By default, the result of the previous expression is used as the first argument in the current expression, and this argument is omitted when you specify the current expression.
> - As an exception, if at least one underscore (_) is present in the current expression, the first rule does not apply. Instead, every underscore is replaced with the result of the previous expression.

You can find a complete list of rules that the @chain macro follows at the Chain.jl GitHub page (https://github.com/jkrumbiegel/Chain.jl). The following are several code examples of its use. Start with the following expression:

```
julia> sqrt(sum(1:8))
6.0
```

This can be equivalently written using the @chain macro as follows:

```julia
julia> @chain 1:8 begin
           sum
           sqrt
       end
6.0
```

In this example, the sum and sqrt functions take one argument, so we do not have to use the underscore to indicate placement of the previous expression's result, and we can even drop the parentheses after the functions. The 1:8 start value is passed to the sum function, and then the result is passed to the sqrt function. Figure 13.1 illustrates this process. The var1 and var2 variable names are chosen only for illustrative purposes, as in practice, the @chain macro generates variable names that are guaranteed to not conflict with existing identifiers.

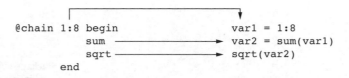

Figure 13.1   In this @chain macro, each operation is a function taking one argument. Arrows show how each part of the macro call is rewritten using temporary variables.

If you wanted to use the _ explicitly, you could write our example code in the following way:

```julia
julia> @chain 1:8 begin
           sum(_)
           sqrt(_)
       end
6.0
```

Now let's consider a more complex example:

```julia
julia> string(3, string(1, 2))
"312"
```

This can be equivalently written as follows:

```julia
julia> @chain 1 begin
           string(2)
           string(3, _)
       end
"312"
```

In this case, 1 is sent as the first argument to form the string(1, 2) call since the string(2) expression has no underscore. The result of this operation, which is a "12" string, is passed to the string(3, _) expression. Since in this expression the underscore is present, it is turned into string(3, "12") and produces "312" as its result. Figure 13.2 depicts this process.

```
                    ┌──────────────────────┐
                    │                      ▼
@chain 1 begin                  var1 = 1
    string(2)      ───────────▶ var2 = string(var1, 2)
    string(3, _)   ───────────▶ string(3, var2)
end
```

Figure 13.2   Evaluating the @chain macro when each operation is a function taking two arguments

13.1.3   Getting the police stop data set

We are now ready to download, uncompress, and load to a data frame the police stop data from Owensboro, Kentucky. In the process, we will use the @chain macro, which you learned about in section 13.1.2:

```julia
julia> url_zip = "https://stacks.stanford.edu/file/druid:yg821jf8611/" *
                 "yg821jf8611_ky_owensboro_2020_04_01.csv.zip";
```
URL of the file we want to fetch

```julia
julia> local_zip = "owensboro.zip";
```
Name of the file we want to save locally

```julia
julia> isfile(local_zip) || Downloads.download(url_zip, local_zip)
true
```
Fetches the file only if it is not present yet; true is printed if the file is already present

```julia
julia> isfile(local_zip)
true
```
Checks if the file is indeed present

```julia
julia> open(sha256, local_zip) == [0x14, 0x3b, 0x7d, 0x74,
                                    0xbc, 0x15, 0x74, 0xc5,
                                    0xf8, 0x42, 0xe0, 0x3f,
                                    0x8f, 0x08, 0x88, 0xd5,
                                    0xe2, 0xa8, 0x13, 0x24,
                                    0xfd, 0x4e, 0xab, 0xde,
                                    0x02, 0x89, 0xdd, 0x74,
                                    0x3c, 0xb3, 0x5d, 0x56]
true
```
Makes sure that the content of the file is correct by checking its SHA-256

```julia
julia> archive = ZipFile.Reader(local_zip)
ZipFile.Reader for IOStream(<file owensboro.zip>) containing 1 files:

uncompressedsize method  mtime            name
------------------------------------------------------
        1595853 Deflate 2020-04-01 07-58 ky_owensboro_2020_04_01.csv
```
Opens the ZIP archive and visually inspects its contents

```julia
julia> owensboro = @chain archive begin
           only(_.files)
           read
           CSV.read(DataFrame; missingstring="NA")
       end;
```
Extracts the CSV file from the archive and loads it into a DataFrame; treats NA values as missing by using the @chain

```julia
julia> close(archive)
```
Closes the ZIP archive after we are done reading it

In this example, the expression using the `@chain` macro is equivalent to the following line of code:

```
CSV.read(read(only(archive.files)), DataFrame; missingstring="NA");
```

In my opinion, the version using the `@chain` macro is easier to read and modify, if needed.

We have created the `owensboro` data frame. I have suppressed printing its contents because it is large. Instead, let's get its summary information by using the `summary` and `describe` functions that we used in chapter 12:

```
julia> summary(owensboro)
"6921×18 DataFrame"

julia> describe(owensboro, :nunique, :nmissing, :eltype)
18×4 DataFrame
 Row │ variable                  nunique  nmissing  eltype
     │ Symbol                    Union…    Int64    Type
─────┼──────────────────────────────────────────────────────────────────
   1 │ raw_row_number                            0  Int64
   2 │ date                      726             0  Date
   3 │ time                      1352            0  Time
   4 │ location                  4481            0  String
   5 │ lat                                       0  Float64
   6 │ lng                                       9  Union{Missing, Float64}
   7 │ sector                    10             10  Union{Missing, String15}
   8 │ subject_age                               3  Union{Missing, Int64}
   9 │ subject_race              4              18  Union{Missing, String31}
  10 │ subject_sex               2               0  String7
  11 │ officer_id_hash           87              0  String15
  12 │ type                      2              42  Union{Missing, String15}
  13 │ violation                 1979            0  String
  14 │ arrest_made                               0  Bool
  15 │ citation_issued                           0  Bool
  16 │ outcome                   2               0  String15
  17 │ vehicle_registration_state 35            55  Union{Missing, String3}
  18 │ raw_race                  4              18  Union{Missing, String31}
```

Our data set has almost 7,000 observations and 18 columns. I have presented the information about the number of unique values in text columns, the number of missing values recorded, and the element type of each column. In this chapter, we will not work with all columns of the data frame. Instead, we will concentrate on the following features:

- `date`—Gives information on when the event happened.
- `type`—Indicates who was stopped by the police (vehicle or pedestrian). This column has 42 missing observations.
- `arrest_made`—Shows whether an arrest was made. This will be our target column.
- `violation`—Provides a text description of the type of violation recorded.

We will look in more detail at data contained in these columns in the following sections. First, we'll drop the columns we do not need by using the `select!` function in the next listing.

```
julia> select!(owensboro, :date, :type, :arrest_made, :violation);

julia> summary(owensboro)
"6921×4 DataFrame"

julia> describe(owensboro, :nunique, :nmissing, :eltype)
4×4 DataFrame
 Row │ variable     nunique   nmissing   eltype
     │ Symbol       Union...   Int64     Type
─────┼──────────────────────────────────────────────────────────
   1 │ date         726              0   Date
   2 │ type         2               42   Union{Missing, String15}
   3 │ arrest_made                  0   Bool
   4 │ violation    1979             0   String
```

Updates the data frame in place and keeps only the listed columns in it

13.1.4   Comparing functions that perform operations on columns

In listing 13.1, we see the `select!` function, which is one of the five functions provided by DataFrames.jl for performing operations on data frame columns. You have already seen another, the `combine` function, in chapter 12, when working with `GroupedDataFrame` objects. Now, let's look at all available functions:

- `combine`—Performs column transformations following operation specification syntax, allowing for changing the number of rows in the source (typically, combining multiple rows into one row—that is, aggregating them)
- `select`—Performs column transformations following operation specification syntax with the restriction that the result will have the same number of rows and in the same order as the source
- `select!`—The same as `select`, but updates the source in place
- `transform`—The same as `select`, but always keeps all columns from the source
- `transform!`—The same as `transform`, but updates the source in place

Since in listing 13.1 we use the `select!` function, it updates the owensboro data frame in place by keeping only the columns whose names we pass.

All the functions I have listed allow passing several operation specifications in one call, as shown in listing 13.1. Also, all of them work with both data frames and grouped data frames. In the latter case, these functions process the data groupwise, as you learned in chapter 12 regarding `combine`. For `select`, `select!`, `transform`, and `transform!`, if they are applied to the `GroupedDataFrame`, the same rule applies: the result must have the same number of rows and in the same order as the source.

The following listing compares `combine` and `transform` on a minimal example. Figures 13.3 and 13.4 also illustrate these functions, since the differences between the options are important to remember.

Listing 13.2 Comparing the `combine`, `select`, and `transform` operations

```julia
julia> df = DataFrame(id=[1, 2, 1, 2], v=1:4)
4×2 DataFrame
 Row │ id     v
     │ Int64  Int64
─────┼──────────────
   1 │     1      1
   2 │     2      2
   3 │     1      3
   4 │     2      4
```

⟵ **Rows of df are combined into a single value 10, which is a sum of column v.**

```julia
julia> combine(df, :v => sum => :sum)
1×1 DataFrame
 Row │ sum
     │ Int64
─────┼───────
   1 │    10
```

⟵ **transform keeps columns from the source. As all rows from the source are kept, value 10 is pseudo broadcasted to all rows (see chapter 10 for an explanation of pseudo broadcasting).**

```julia
julia> transform(df, :v => sum => :sum)
4×3 DataFrame
 Row │ id     v      sum
     │ Int64  Int64  Int64
─────┼─────────────────────
   1 │     1      1     10
   2 │     2      2     10
   3 │     1      3     10
   4 │     2      4     10
```

⟵ **Same as transform, but the columns from the source data frame df are not kept**

```julia
julia> select(df, :v => sum => :sum)
4×1 DataFrame
 Row │ sum
     │ Int64
─────┼───────
   1 │    10
   2 │    10
   3 │    10
   4 │    10
```

```julia
julia> gdf = groupby(df, :id)
GroupedDataFrame with 2 groups based on key: id
First Group (2 rows): id = 1
 Row │ id     v
     │ Int64  Int64
─────┼──────────────
   1 │     1      1
   2 │     1      3
⋮
Last Group (2 rows): id = 2
 Row │ id     v
     │ Int64  Int64
─────┼──────────────
   1 │     2      2
   2 │     2      4
```

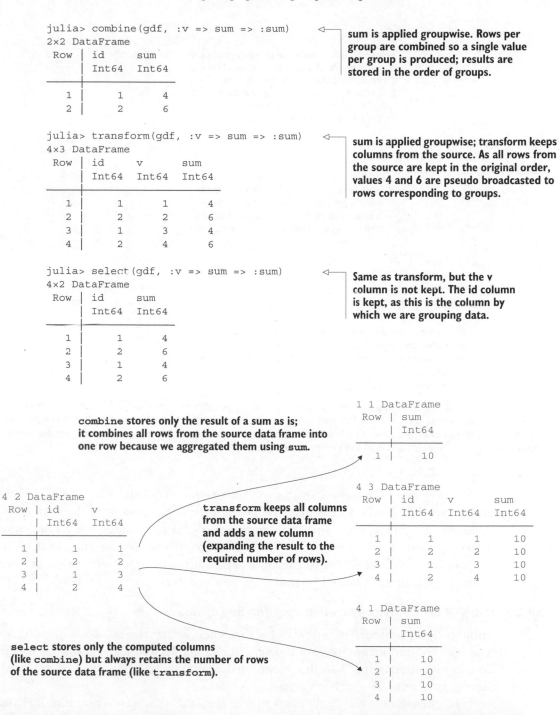

```
julia> combine(gdf, :v => sum => :sum)
2×2 DataFrame
 Row │ id     sum
     │ Int64  Int64
─────┼──────────────
   1 │     1      4
   2 │     2      6
```
◁— **sum is applied groupwise. Rows per group are combined so a single value per group is produced; results are stored in the order of groups.**

```
julia> transform(gdf, :v => sum => :sum)
4×3 DataFrame
 Row │ id     v      sum
     │ Int64  Int64  Int64
─────┼─────────────────────
   1 │     1      1      4
   2 │     2      2      6
   3 │     1      3      4
   4 │     2      4      6
```
◁— **sum is applied groupwise; transform keeps columns from the source. As all rows from the source are kept in the original order, values 4 and 6 are pseudo broadcasted to rows corresponding to groups.**

```
julia> select(gdf, :v => sum => :sum)
4×2 DataFrame
 Row │ id     sum
     │ Int64  Int64
─────┼──────────────
   1 │     1      4
   2 │     2      6
   3 │     1      4
   4 │     2      6
```
◁— **Same as transform, but the v column is not kept. The id column is kept, as this is the column by which we are grouping data.**

combine stores only the result of a sum as is; it combines all rows from the source data frame into one row because we aggregated them using sum.

```
1 1 DataFrame
 Row │ sum
     │ Int64
─────┼──────
   1 │    10
```

```
4 2 DataFrame
 Row │ id     v
     │ Int64  Int64
─────┼──────────────
   1 │     1      1
   2 │     2      2
   3 │     1      3
   4 │     2      4
```

transform keeps all columns from the source data frame and adds a new column (expanding the result to the required number of rows).

```
4 3 DataFrame
 Row │ id     v      sum
     │ Int64  Int64  Int64
─────┼─────────────────────
   1 │     1      1     10
   2 │     2      2     10
   3 │     1      3     10
   4 │     2      4     10
```

```
4 1 DataFrame
 Row │ sum
     │ Int64
─────┼──────
   1 │    10
   2 │    10
   3 │    10
   4 │    10
```

select stores only the computed columns (like combine) but always retains the number of rows of the source data frame (like transform).

Figure 13.3 Result of performing the :v => sum => :sum operation on a data frame using the combine, transform, and select functions. The transform function is the only one that always keeps all columns from the source. The combine function is the only one that allows for changing the number of rows of its result in comparison to the source data frame.

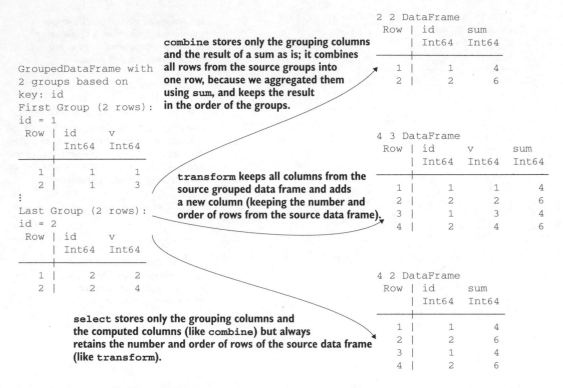

Figure 13.4   Result of performing the `:v => sum => :sum` operation on a grouped data frame using the combine, transform, and select functions. The `transform` function is the only one that always keeps all columns from the source. The `combine` function is the only one that allows for changing the number and order of rows of its result in comparison to the source data frame.

In summary, the most important thing to understand about the way `transform` and `select` work in listing 13.2 is that they guarantee that all rows from the source data frame `df` are kept in the result and that their order is not changed. If an operation returns a scalar, it is pseudo broadcasted to fill all required rows (see chapter 10 for an explanation of pseudo broadcasting). The difference between `select` and `transform` is that the latter keeps all columns from the source data frame.

13.1.5 *Using short forms of operation specification syntax*

Another thing to notice in listing 13.1 is that when we use the `select!` function, we pass only column names we want to keep. In chapter 12, you learned that the operation specification syntax uses this general pattern: `source_column => operation_function => target_column_name`.

Using this syntax, you might think that to keep the `:date` column without changing its name in listing 13.1, you would need to write `:date => identity => :date`. But this is not needed, as the `operation_function` and `target_column_name` parts are optional in the operation specification syntax. The following listing, which uses the df data frame defined in listing 13.2, shows the consequences of dropping the second and third components of operation specification syntax.

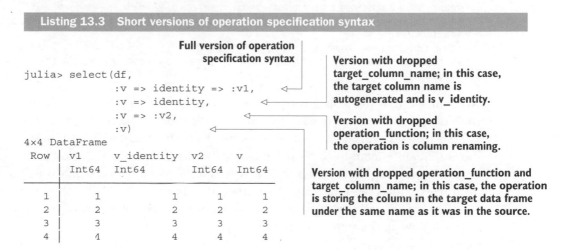

Listing 13.3 Short versions of operation specification syntax

Here, all four operations produce the same output vector but give different names to the column. Observe that both the operation_function and target_column_name parts can be dropped in the operation specification syntax. Dropping operation_function is the same as asking to not perform any transformation of the column, and dropping target_column_name leads to automatic generation of the target column name.

In listing 13.1, we dropped unwanted columns from the owensboro data frame. Let's now move to transforming these columns.

13.2 Investigating the violation column

We start by investigating the :violation column. It is a text column, so we need to perform text processing to understand its contents. In this section, you will learn how to do that. Analyzing the contents of data frame columns storing text data is a common operation, so practicing these operations is worthwhile.

13.2.1 Finding the most frequent violations

First, take a quick peek at the contents of the :violation column:

```
julia> owensboro.violation
6921-element SentinelArrays.ChainedVector{String, Vector{String}}:
 "POSS CONT SUB 1ST DEG, 1ST OFF " ⋯ 18 bytes ⋯ " DRUG PARAPHERLIA -
BUY/POSSESS"
 "FAILURE TO ILLUMITE HEAD LAMPS;" ⋯ 20 bytes ⋯ "LICENSE; NO REGISTRATION
PLATES"
 "NO TAIL LAMPS; OPER MTR VEHICLE" ⋯ 136 bytes ⋯ "EC, 1ST OFF; VIOLATION
UNKNOWN"
 "OPER MTR VEH U/INFLU ALC/DRUGS/" ⋯ 49 bytes ⋯ " LICENSE - 1ST OFF (AGG
CIRCUM)"
```

```
"OPERATING ON SUS OR REV OPER LICENSE"
⋮
"SPEEDING 10 MPH OVER LIMIT; FAILURE TO WEAR SEAT BELTS"
"SPEEDING 11 MPH OVER LIMIT; NO REGISTRATION RECEIPT"
"SPEEDING 17 MPH OVER LIMIT; FAI" ⋯ 127 bytes ⋯ "LATES; NO REGISTRATION
RECEIPT"
"SPEEDING 13 MPH OVER LIMIT"
"FAILURE OF NON-OWNER OPERATOR T" ⋯ 37 bytes ⋯ "THER STATE REGISTRATION
RECEIPT"
```

We can see that the violation types are codified using standard text, and if multiple violations happen, their descriptions are separated by a semicolon (;).

To structure this data, we want to extract from this column the indicators of violations that are encountered most frequently. In this analysis, we will additionally aggregate all speeding violations into one type since we can see that they differ only in number of miles per hour (mph) over the speed limit.

To achieve this goal, we first need to learn the types of the most frequent violations, following the steps in table 13.1.

Table 13.1   Steps taken to find the most frequent violations

#	Step description	Simplified example output
	Input data.	`["a1; b;c ","b; a2","a3"]`
1	Split each observation by using ; as a delimiter, and strip leading and trailing whitespace characters.	`[["a1","b","c"],["b","a2"],["a3"]]`
2	Vertically concatenate all individual observation vectors into a single vector.	`["a1","b","c","b","a2","a3"]`
3	Change all elements containing the substring "a" into a string "a" (for actual data, this string is "SPEEDING").	`["a","b","c","b","a","a"]`
4	Count occurrences of different strings in the vector and present them sorted by frequency in descending order.	`"a"` | 3 `"b"` | 2 `"c"` | 1

The following listing shows an implementation of these steps without DataFrames.jl, using functions you learned in part 1.

Listing 13.4   Finding the most frequent violations by using Base Julia

```
julia> violation_list = [strip.(split(x, ";"))
                            for x in owensboro.violation]          ◁
6921-element Vector{Vector{SubString{String}}}:
 ["POSS CONT SUB 1ST DEG, 1ST OFF (METHAMPHETAMINE)", "DRUG PARAPHERLIA -
BUY/POSSESS"]
 ⋮
```

> **Splits each violation description into a vector and removes leading and trailing whitespace from it**

Vertically concatenates all individual vectors into one vector by using the reduce function (see chapter 10 for a discussion of this function)

```
["SPEEDING 13 MPH OVER LIMIT"]
["FAILURE OF NON-OWNER OPERATOR TO MAINTAIN REQ INS/SEC, 1ST OFF", "NO
 OTHER STATE REGISTRATION RECEIPT"]

julia> violation_flat = reduce(vcat, violation_list)
13555-element Vector{SubString{String}}:
 "POSS CONT SUB 1ST DEG, 1ST OFF (METHAMPHETAMINE)"
 "DRUG PARAPHERLIA - BUY/POSSESS"
 ⋮
 "SPEEDING 13 MPH OVER LIMIT"
 "FAILURE OF NON-OWNER OPERATOR TO MAINTAIN REQ INS/SEC, 1ST OFF"
 "NO OTHER STATE REGISTRATION RECEIPT"

julia> violation_flat_clean = [contains(x, "SPEEDING") ?
                               "SPEEDING" : x for x in violation_flat]
13555-element Vector{AbstractString}:
 "POSS CONT SUB 1ST DEG, 1ST OFF (METHAMPHETAMINE)"
 "DRUG PARAPHERLIA - BUY/POSSESS"
 ⋮
 "SPEEDING"
 "FAILURE OF NON-OWNER OPERATOR TO MAINTAIN REQ INS/SEC, 1ST OFF"
 "NO OTHER STATE REGISTRATION RECEIPT"
```

Replaces all violations that contain "SPEEDING" in their text with "SPEEDING"

```
julia> sort(freqtable(violation_flat_clean), rev=true)
245-element Named Vector{Int64}
Dim1                                              │
──────────────────────────────────────────────────┼─────────
"FAILURE TO WEAR SEAT BELTS"                      │   2689
"NO REGISTRATION PLATES"                          │   1667
"FAILURE TO PRODUCE INSURANCE CARD"               │   1324
SPEEDING                                          │   1067
 ⋮                                                │    ⋮
"WANTON ENDANGERMENT-1ST DEGREE-POLICE OFFICER"   │      1
"WANTON ENDANGERMENT-2ND DEGREE-POLICE OFFICER"   │      1
```

Finds the counts of various violations and sorts them in descending order by using rev=true

In the results, we see that the most frequent violations are as follows:

- Failure to wear seat belts
- No registration plates
- Failure to produce insurance card
- Speeding

Later, we will investigate how these violation types influence the probability of being arrested. In the analysis in listing 13.4, we used the contains function, which checks whether the string passed as its first argument contains the string passed as its second argument.

Now, let's rewrite this code using DataFrames.jl and piping. The following listing presents the result. Again, we follow the steps described in table 13.1.

Listing 13.5   Finding the most frequent violations by using DataFrames.jl

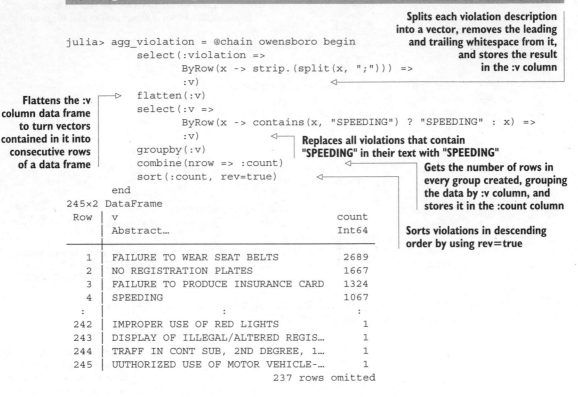

Splits each violation description into a vector, removes the leading and trailing whitespace from it, and stores the result in the :v column

```
julia> agg_violation = @chain owensboro begin
           select(:violation =>
               ByRow(x -> strip.(split(x, ";"))) =>
                   :v)
           flatten(:v)
           select(:v =>
               ByRow(x -> contains(x, "SPEEDING") ? "SPEEDING" : x) =>
                   :v)
           groupby(:v)
           combine(nrow => :count)
           sort(:count, rev=true)
       end
245×2 DataFrame
 Row │ v                                count
     │ Abstract…                        Int64
─────┼────────────────────────────────────────
   1 │ FAILURE TO WEAR SEAT BELTS        2689
   2 │ NO REGISTRATION PLATES            1667
   3 │ FAILURE TO PRODUCE INSURANCE CARD 1324
   4 │ SPEEDING                          1067
   ⋮ │              ⋮                      ⋮
 242 │ IMPROPER USE OF RED LIGHTS           1
 243 │ DISPLAY OF ILLEGAL/ALTERED REGIS…    1
 244 │ TRAFF IN CONT SUB, 2ND DEGREE, 1…    1
 245 │ UUTHORIZED USE OF MOTOR VEHICLE-…    1
                                 237 rows omitted
```

Flattens the :v column data frame to turn vectors contained in it into consecutive rows of a data frame

Replaces all violations that contain "SPEEDING" in their text with "SPEEDING"

Gets the number of rows in every group created, grouping the data by :v column, and stores it in the :count column

Sorts violations in descending order by using rev=true

I selected this example to teach you more features of DataFrames.jl that I discuss in the following sections.

13.2.2 *Vectorizing functions by using the ByRow wrapper*

In listing 13.5, in selection operations, we use the ByRow wrapper around operation functions. For example, in ByRow(x -> strip.(split(x, ";"))), it is a wrapper around an anonymous function.

The purpose of ByRow is simple: it turns a regular function into a vectorized one so that you can easily apply it to each element of a collection. In the case of Data-Frames.jl, these elements are rows of data frame objects, hence the name. Here is a minimal example how ByRow works:

```
julia> sqrt(4)          sqrt works on scalars.
2.0
                                            sqrt does not
julia> sqrt([4, 9, 16])                     work on vectors.
ERROR: MethodError: no method matching sqrt(::Vector{Int64})

julia> ByRow(sqrt)([4, 9, 16])      ByRow(sqrt) is a vectorized version
3-element Vector{Float64}:          of sqrt that works on vectors.
 2.0
 3.0
 4.0
```

```
julia> f = ByRow(sqrt)
(::ByRow{typeof(sqrt)}) (generic function with 2 methods)
```
←┐ **Creates a new callable
   object f that is vectorized**

```
julia> f([4, 9, 16])
3-element Vector{Float64}:
 2.0
 3.0
 4.0
```
←┐ **You can call f without writing a dot (.)
   after it to have a vectorized operation.**

`ByRow(sqrt)([4, 9, 16])` has the same effect as broadcasting `sqrt.([4, 9, 16])`. You might ask, then, why it is needed. Broadcasting requires a function call to be specified immediately, while `ByRow(sqrt)` creates a new callable object. Therefore, you can think of `ByRow` as a lazy signal that you want the function to be broadcasted later after you pass an argument to it. You can see this when we define the `f` callable object in our example.

13.2.3 Flattening data frames

Listing 13.5 also introduced the `flatten` function. Its purpose is to expand a column storing vectors into multiple rows of a data frame. Here's a minimal example:

```
julia> df = DataFrame(id=1:2, v=[[11, 12], [13, 14, 15]])
2×2 DataFrame
 Row │ id     v
     │ Int64  Array…
─────┼──────────────────
   1 │     1  [11, 12]
   2 │     2  [13, 14, 15]

julia> flatten(df, :v)
5×2 DataFrame
 Row │ id     v
     │ Int64  Int64
─────┼──────────────
   1 │     1     11
   2 │     1     12
   3 │     2     13
   4 │     2     14
   5 │     2     15
```

In this code, we expand vectors stored in the `v` column into multiple rows of a data frame. The values stored in the `id` column get appropriately repeated.

13.2.4 Using convenience syntax to get the number of rows of a data frame

You might have been surprised by the `nrow => :count` operation specification syntax in the `combine` call in listing 13.5, as it does not match any rules of the operation specification syntax you have learned so far. This case is an exception. This is because asking for the number of rows in a data frame, or in each group of a data frame, is a common operation. Additionally, the result of this operation does not require passing a source column (it would be the same for every source column).

Therefore, to support this case with a simpler syntax, two special forms are allowed: just passing `nrow` or passing `nrow => target_column_name`. In the first case, the default `:nrow` column name is used; in the second, the user passes the name of the column where we want to store the data. Here is an example showing both variants of this syntax:

```
julia> @chain DataFrame(id=[1, 1, 2, 2, 2]) begin
           groupby(:id)
           combine(nrow, nrow => :rows)
       end
2×3 DataFrame
 Row │ id     nrow   rows
     │ Int64  Int64  Int64
─────┼─────────────────────
   1 │     1      2      2
   2 │     2      3      3
```

In this example, the source data frame has five rows. In two of the rows, we have the value 1, and in three rows, we have the value 2 in the `:id` column. When passing `nrow`, we get the column named `:nrow` holding these numbers. Passing `nrow => :rows` produces the same values, but under the `:rows` column name.

13.2.5 Sorting data frames

Listing 13.5 uses the `sort` function to sort rows of a data frame. Since data frames can contain many columns, we pass a list of columns on which sorting should be performed (when passing multiple columns, sorting is performed lexicographically). Here are some examples of sorting a data frame:

```
julia> df = DataFrame(a=[2, 1, 2, 1, 2], b=5:-1:1)
5×2 DataFrame
 Row │ a      b
     │ Int64  Int64
─────┼──────────────
   1 │     2      5
   2 │     1      4
   3 │     2      3
   4 │     1      2
   5 │     2      1
```

```
julia> sort(df, :b)          ◁─────┐  Data frame is sorted in
5×2 DataFrame                      │  ascending order by column :b
 Row │ a      b
     │ Int64  Int64
─────┼──────────────
   1 │     2      1
   2 │     1      2
   3 │     2      3
   4 │     1      4
   5 │     2      5
```

```
julia> sort(df, [:a, :b])
5×2 DataFrame
 Row │ a      b
     │ Int64  Int64
─────┼──────────────
   1 │     1      2
   2 │     1      4
   3 │     2      1
   4 │     2      3
   5 │     2      5
```

◁── **Data frame is sorted in ascending order by columns :a and :b lexicographically**

13.2.6 *Using advanced functionalities of DataFramesMeta.jl*

Listing 13.5 works but is a bit verbose because we need to use `ByRow` and anonymous functions. For simple transformations, in my opinion, using `ByRow` is quite convenient and readable. Here's an example:

```
julia> df = DataFrame(x=[4, 9, 16])
3×1 DataFrame
 Row │ x
     │ Int64
─────┼───────
   1 │     4
   2 │     9
   3 │    16
```

```
julia> transform(df, :x => ByRow(sqrt))
3×2 DataFrame
 Row │ x      x_sqrt
     │ Int64  Float64
─────┼────────────────
   1 │     4      2.0
   2 │     9      3.0
   3 │    16      4.0
```

However, in listing 13.5, we work with very long expressions. In these cases, it is often easier to use the DataFramesMeta.jl domain-specific language to perform transformations. Let's rewrite the code from listing 13.5 using DataFramesMeta.jl to replace the `select` function calls:

```
@chain owensboro begin
    @rselect(:v=strip.(split(:violation, ";")))
    flatten(:v)
    @rselect(:v=contains(:v, "SPEEDING") ? "SPEEDING" : :v)
    groupby(:v)
    combine(nrow => :count)
    sort(:count, rev=true)
end
```

◁── ◁── **The @rselect macro is defined in the DataFramesMeta.jl package.**

The code is much easier to read now. Visually distinguishing the DataFramesMeta.jl macros is easy, as they are prefixed with @. As discussed in chapter 12, DataFramesMeta.jl macros use the domain-specific language following the assignment syntax instead of the operation specification syntax supported by DataFrames.jl.

In this example, we see the `@rselect` macro from the DataFramesMeta.jl package. It is an equivalent of the `select` function, but the `r` in front of it signals that all operations should be performed by row, or in other words, wrapped with `ByRow`. In addition, the `@select` macro works like the `select` function on entire columns of a data frame. Let's compare them by doing the same operation of computing a square root of a column in a data frame:

```julia
julia> df = DataFrame(x=[4, 9, 16])
3×1 DataFrame
 Row │ x
     │ Int64
─────┼───────
   1 │     4
   2 │     9
   3 │    16

julia> @select(df, :s = sqrt.(:x))
3×1 DataFrame
 Row │ s
     │ Float64
─────┼─────────
   1 │     2.0
   2 │     3.0
   3 │     4.0

julia> @rselect(df, :s = sqrt(:x))
3×1 DataFrame
 Row │ s
     │ Float64
─────┼─────────
   1 │     2.0
   2 │     3.0
   3 │     4.0

julia> select(df, :x => ByRow(sqrt) => :s)
3×1 DataFrame
 Row │ s
     │ Float64
─────┼─────────
   1 │     2.0
   2 │     3.0
   3 │     4.0
```

In this example, all code lines give an equivalent result. The difference between `@rselect` and `@select` is that in the latter, we need to add a dot (`.`) after the `sqrt` function.

Table 13.2 lists the relevant macros that DataFramesMeta.jl provides (you learned about `@combine` in chapter 12), mapped to DataFrames.jl functions.

Table 13.2 Mapping DataFramesMeta.jl macros to DataFrames.jl functions

DataFramesMeta.jl	DataFrames.jl
`@combine`	`combine`
`@select`	`select`
`@select!`	`select!`
`@transform`	`transform`
`@transform!`	`transform!`
`@rselect`	`select` with automatic `ByRow` of operations
`@rselect!`	`select!` with automatic `ByRow` of operations
`@rtransform`	`transform` with automatic `ByRow` of operations
`@rtransform!`	`transform!` with automatic `ByRow` of operations

This list seems long but is relatively simple to learn. The basic functions you need to know are `combine`, `select`, and `transform`. When constructing a macro call name, just remember that you can append `!` after the name to make the operation in place and place `r` in front of the name to make the operation automatically wrap all operations with `ByRow` (thus vectorizing them).

13.3 Preparing data for making predictions

In section 13.2, we extracted the most common violation types from the police stop data set. We are now ready to prepare data that we will use to predict the probability of arrest.

In this section, you will learn how to perform complex transformations of data frame objects, as well as how to join and reshape them. All these operations are often needed when you prepare data for modeling.

13.3.1 Performing initial transformation of the data

To prepare data so that it can later be used to fit a model predicting the probability of arrest, we want to create a data frame with the following structure:

- One Boolean column called `arrest` that indicates whether an arrest was made.
- One column named `day`, showing the day of the week on which the incident happened.
- A column `type` informing us of whom was stopped by police.
- Four Boolean columns, `v1`, `v2`, `v3`, and `v4`, indicating the four most common reasons for being stopped by the police. I use short column names in this case to save horizontal space in the output.

The following listing shows the syntax of the transformation creating the requested data frame.

Listing 13.6   Preparing data for making a prediction model

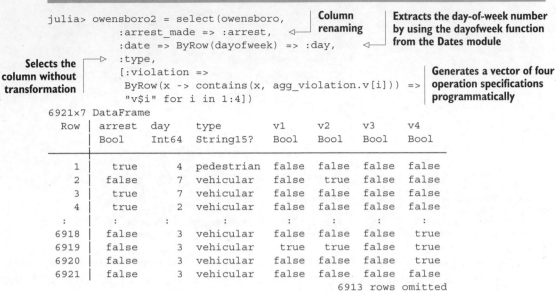

```
julia> owensboro2 = select(owensboro,                    Column        Extracts the day-of-week number
           :arrest_made => :arrest,          <──┘ renaming        by using the dayofweek function
           :date => ByRow(dayofweek) => :day,    <──┘             from the Dates module
           :type,
           [:violation =>                                         Generates a vector of four
             ByRow(x -> contains(x, agg_violation.v[i])) =>       operation specifications
             "v$i" for i in 1:4])                                 programmatically
6921×7 DataFrame
  Row │ arrest   day     type        v1      v2      v3      v4
      │ Bool     Int64   String15?   Bool    Bool    Bool    Bool
──────┼─────────────────────────────────────────────────────────
    1 │  true      4     pedestrian  false   false   false   false
    2 │ false      7     vehicular   false   true    false   false
    3 │  true      7     vehicular   false   false   false   false
    4 │  true      2     vehicular   false   false   false   false
    :  │   :        :         :        :       :       :       :
 6918 │ false      3     vehicular   false   false   false   true
 6919 │ false      3     vehicular   true    true    false   true
 6920 │ false      3     vehicular   false   false   false   true
 6921 │ false      3     vehicular   false   false   false   false
                                      6913 rows omitted
```

The most important part of this code is the last one, which shows us that operation specifications can also be passed in vectors. In this example, the vector of operations is as follows:

```
julia> [:violation =>
          ByRow(x -> contains(x, agg_violation.v[i])) =>
          "v$i" for i in 1:4]
4-element Vector{Pair{Symbol, Pair{ByRow{Base.Fix2{typeof(contains),
var"#66#68"{Int64}}}, String}}}:
 :violation => (ByRow{Base.Fix2{typeof(contains),
var"#66#68"{Int64}}}(Base.Fix2{typeof(contains),
var"#66#68"{Int64}}(contains, var"#66#68"{Int64}(1))) => "v1")
 ⋮
 :violation => (ByRow{Base.Fix2{typeof(contains),
var"#66#68"{Int64}}}(Base.Fix2{typeof(contains),
var"#66#68"{Int64}}(contains, var"#66#68"{Int64}(4))) => "v4")
```

We can see that it performs a lookup in the violation column for the four most common violations that we identified in the agg_violation data frame. Next, the select function properly handles this object as a vector holding four operation specification requests.

Let's see one more example of transformations generated programmatically. Assume that we want to extract minimum and maximum elements from the date and arrest_made columns in the owensboro data frame. We can express this operation as follows:

```
julia> combine(owensboro, [:date :arrest_made] .=> [minimum, maximum])
1×4 DataFrame
```

Row	date_minimum Date	date_maximum Date	arrest_made_minimum Bool	arrest_made_maximum Bool
1	2015-09-01	2017-09-01	false	true

This works because we broadcast one row matrix with a column vector to specify the transformation (this kind of application of broadcasting is discussed in chapter 5):

```julia
julia> julia> [:date :arrest_made] .=> [minimum, maximum]
2×2 Matrix{Pair{Symbol}}:
 :date=>minimum   :arrest_made=>minimum
 :date=>maximum   :arrest_made=>maximum
```

Additionally, as you can see in the output of the combine function, the autogenerated column names nicely describe the results of the performed operations.

EXERCISE 13.1 Rewrite the code from listing 13.6 using the @rselect macro from DataFramesMeta.jl.

Renaming a data frame's columns

The operation specification syntax allows you to rename columns of a data frame by using the form :old_column_name => :new_column_name.

However, column renaming is needed quite often. Therefore, DataFrames.jl provides two functions that are dedicated to this task: rename and rename!. As usual, the difference between these two functions is that rename creates a new data frame, while rename! changes the passed data frame in place.

The basic syntax is the same as for operations specification—that is, writing rename(df, :old_column_name => :new_column_name) renames the column :old_column_name to :new_column_name without changing any other column names in the data frame df. These two functions support several other styles of column renaming; refer to the package documentation (http://mng.bz/m2jW) to learn more about them.

As a rule, use rename when you want to only rename columns in a data frame. Use select when, apart from renaming columns, you also want to perform other manipulations on columns of the passed data frame.

13.3.2 Working with categorical data

This section covers working with categorical data by using the CategoricalArrays.jl package.

Now, in our owensboro2 data frame, we have the column day, which stores the day number, where Monday is 1, Tuesday is 2, . . . , and Sunday is 7. It would be nice to use day names instead of numbers in our analysis. Additionally, we would like day names to be correctly ordered—that is, Monday should be seen as the first day, through Sunday, which should be seen as the last day. This means that we cannot store day names as strings, as Julia would then use alphabetical order when sorting our data (alphabetically, Friday is the first day name and Wednesday is the last).

The functionality allowing us to specify a custom order for a predefined set of values is provided in other ecosystems by factors or categorical columns. It is also available in Julia and is provided by the CategoricalArrays.jl package.

Categorical values

Categorical variables can be unordered (nominal variables) or ordered categories (ordinal variables).

An example of a *nominal variable* is a color of a car that is one of several from a closed list, like blue, black, or green.

An example of an *ordinal variable* is, for example, traditional academic grading in the United States: A+, A, A–, B+, B, B–, C+, C, C–, D+, D, D–, and F, with A+ being the highest and F being the lowest.

The CategoricalArrays.jl package provides support for working with categorical values in Julia. The four most important functions that this package defines and that you need to learn are as follows:

- `categorical`—Creates arrays of categorical values
- `levels`—Checks levels of values stored in a categorical array
- `levels!`—Sets levels and their order in a categorical array
- `isordered`—Checks whether a categorical array is ordered (stores ordinal values) or unordered (stores nominal values)

We will use these functions when creating a reference data frame that stores a mapping between the day number and day name, as shown in the following listing.

Listing 13.7   Creating a reference data frame of day-of-week names

```
julia> weekdays = DataFrame(day=1:7,
                            dayname=categorical(dayname.(1:7);
                                                ordered=true))
7×2 DataFrame
 Row │ day    dayname
     │ Int64  Cat…
─────┼──────────────────
   1 │     1  Monday
   2 │     2  Tuesday
   3 │     3  Wednesday
   4 │     4  Thursday
   5 │     5  Friday
   6 │     6  Saturday
   7 │     7  Sunday
```

```
julia> isordered(weekdays.dayname)
true

julia> levels(weekdays.dayname)
7-element Vector{String}:
 "Friday"
 "Monday"
 "Saturday"
 "Sunday"
 "Thursday"
 "Tuesday"
 "Wednesday"

julia> levels!(weekdays.dayname, weekdays.dayname)
7-element CategoricalArray{String,1,UInt32}:
 "Monday"
 "Tuesday"
 "Wednesday"
 "Thursday"
 "Friday"
 "Saturday"
 "Sunday"
```

We first create a `weekdays` data frame storing a mapping between day number and day name. We create a column of day names by using the `dayname` function, which returns the text name of a given day number. Next, using the `categorical` function, we turn this column into a categorical one and make it ordered by passing the `ordered=true` keyword argument. Next, we check that the column is ordered and inspect its levels. As you can see, levels are ordered alphabetically by default. To fix this, we use the `levels!` function to set the order of days to be the same as the order of day numbers. This function takes a categorical array as a first argument and a vector containing new level ordering as a second argument.

You might ask what the benefit is of using a categorical array for day names. One benefit is that in this way, we clearly signal to the user that the column contains a closed set of allowed values. However, another important benefit exists. Later, if we use functions that are sensitive to the order of values (for example, `sort`), they will respect the order that we have set for the categorical vector.

13.3.3 *Joining data frames*

In this section, you will learn the functions from DataFrames.jl that allow you to join several data frames together.

We have a mapping of day numbers to categorical day names, but how do we put them in our `owensboro2` data frame? This can be done by joining the `owensboro2` data frame with the `weekdays` data frame. In this case, we need to perform a left join that we want to execute in place—that is, we want to add the column to the `owensboro2` data frame. The function that accomplishes this is `leftjoin!`, where we pass the `on` keyword argument specifying the column name on which the join should be performed (this is a column storing keys on which the join should be performed). In the result of the operation, the `owensboro2` data frame has all the columns that we have put into it in listing 13.6 (that is, arrest, day, type, v1, v2, v3, and v4) and additionally has the dayname column added from the joined weekdays data frame:

```
julia> leftjoin!(owensboro2, weekdays; on=:day)
6921×8 DataFrame
  Row │ arrest  day    type       v1     v2     v3     v4     dayname
      │ Bool    Int64  String15?  Bool   Bool   Bool   Bool   Cat…?
──────┼──────────────────────────────────────────────────────────────
    1 │  true      4   pedestrian false  false  false  false  Thursday
    2 │ false      7   vehicular  false  true   false  false  Sunday
    3 │  true      7   vehicular  false  false  false  false  Sunday
    4 │  true      2   vehicular  false  false  false  false  Tuesday
    ⋮ │   ⋮       ⋮        ⋮         ⋮      ⋮      ⋮      ⋮        ⋮
 6918 │ false      3   vehicular  false  false  false  true   Wednesday
 6919 │ false      3   vehicular  true   true   false  true   Wednesday
 6920 │ false      3   vehicular  false  false  false  true   Wednesday
 6921 │ false      3   vehicular  false  false  false  false  Wednesday
                                                        6913 rows omitted
```

In addition to leftjoin!, the most-often-used join functions provided by Data-Frames.jl create a new data frame from passed source data frames. These functions are the following:

- innerjoin—Includes rows with keys that match in all passed data frames
- leftjoin—Includes all rows from the left data frame and matching rows from the right data frame
- rightjoin—Includes all rows from the right data frame and matching rows from the left data frame
- outerjoin—Includes rows with keys that appear in any of the passed data frames

You can find more information about available join functions along with available options in the DataFrames.jl manual (http://mng.bz/wyz2) and in the documentation of the relevant functions.

EXERCISE 13.2   Write a select operation creating the owensboro2 data frame that immediately has the dayname column (without having to perform a join).

13.3.4 *Reshaping data frames*

In this section, you will learn to reshape a data frame by using the stack and unstack functions. Before moving forward, let's check in the next listing to see whether owensoboro2 has a correct mapping of day numbers to day names.

Listing 13.8   Mapping day numbers to day names in long format
---

```
julia> @chain owensboro2 begin
           groupby([:day, :dayname]; sort=true)
           combine(nrow)
       end
7×3 DataFrame
```

```
Row │ day    dayname      nrow
    │ Int64  Cat…?        Int64
────┼──────────────────────────
  1 │   1    Monday         913
  2 │   2    Tuesday       1040
  3 │   3    Wednesday     1197
  4 │   4    Thursday      1104
  5 │   5    Friday        1160
  6 │   6    Saturday       850
  7 │   7    Sunday         657
```

This looks to be the case. Additionally, we can see that the smallest number of police stops happen on Sundays. Another way to check the mapping is to build a frequency table:

```
julia> freqtable(owensboro2, :dayname, :day)
7×7 Named Matrix{Int64}
dayname ╲ day │    1     2     3     4     5     6     7
──────────────┼─────────────────────────────────────────
"Monday"      │  913     0     0     0     0     0     0
"Tuesday"     │    0  1040     0     0     0     0     0
"Wednesday"   │    0     0  1197     0     0     0     0
"Thursday"    │    0     0     0  1104     0     0     0
"Friday"      │    0     0     0     0  1160     0     0
"Saturday"    │    0     0     0     0     0   850     0
"Sunday"      │    0     0     0     0     0     0   657
```

We can see that we only have values stored on a main diagonal. The frequency table we produce is a matrix. Since in this chapter we are working with data frames, you might ask if we can obtain a similar result using a data frame. Indeed, it is possible, using the unstack function, as the following listing shows.

Listing 13.9 Mapping day numbers to day names in wide format

```
julia> @chain owensboro2 begin
           groupby([:day, :dayname]; sort=true)
           combine(nrow)
           unstack(:dayname, :day, :nrow; fill=0)
       end
7×8 DataFrame
Row │ dayname    1      2      3      4      5      6      7
    │ Cat…?      Int64  Int64  Int64  Int64  Int64  Int64  Int64
────┼──────────────────────────────────────────────────────────
  1 │ Monday       913      0      0      0      0      0      0
  2 │ Tuesday        0   1040      0      0      0      0      0
  3 │ Wednesday      0      0   1197      0      0      0      0
  4 │ Thursday       0      0      0   1104      0      0      0
  5 │ Friday         0      0      0      0   1160      0      0
  6 │ Saturday       0      0      0      0      0    850      0
  7 │ Sunday         0      0      0      0      0      0    657
```

As you can see, we get the same result, but this time as a data frame. The unstack function takes three positional arguments: the first is the data that should be used to specify row keys (dayname, in this case), the second is the column that should be used to specify column keys (day, in this case), and the third is the column that should be used to specify values for the row key-column key combinations (in this case, nrow). We additionally pass the fill=0 argument to signal that entries with missing combinations of keys should take this value (by default, it would be missing).

Reshaping data frames

Data analysis uses two approaches to representing data: wide and long (www.statol ogy.org/long-vs-wide-data/).

For data stored in wide format, also called *unstacked*, it is assumed that each entity is represented as one row of data and that each attribute is a column of data. Listing 13.9 presents an example of such a mapping, where day names are treated as entities (each row represents one day name) and day numbers as attributes (represented by columns with names from 1 to 7).

For data in long format, also called *stacked*, a single row represents a mapping from an entity-attribute combination to a value assigned to it. Listing 13.8 presents an example of such a mapping, where entity names are stored in the dayname column, attribute names are stored in the day column, and values related to them are stored in the nrow column.

In DataFrames.jl, you can reshape data frames from wide to long format by using the stack function, and from long to wide format by using the unstack function.

A related operation is transposition of a data frame, which is supported with the permutedims function.

You can find examples of how these functions can be used in the package manual (http://mng.bz/QnR1). For your reference, the following figure shows the relationship between the stack and unstack functions.

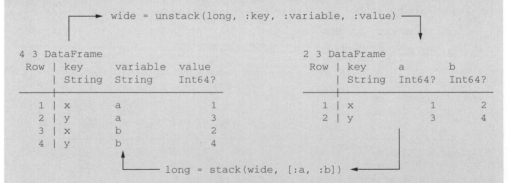

The stack function takes data in wide format and transforms it into long format. The [:a, :b] column selector indicates which columns should be transformed into variable-value pairs. The unstack function performs the reverse operation. We pass information to it: which columns should identify rows in an unstacked data frame (key, in our example), which column contains column names (variable, in our example), and which column contains the values to put in row-column combinations (value, in our example).

13.3.5 *Dropping rows of a data frame that hold missing values*

The last step in data preparation for modeling is related to `missing` values. In listing 13.1, we can see that the `type` column has 42 missing elements. Assume we want to remove them from the `owensboro2` data frame before the analysis. This can be done in place by using the `dropmissing!` function:

```
julia> dropmissing!(owensboro2)
6879×8 DataFrame
 Row │ arrest  day    type        v1     v2     v3     v4     dayname
     │ Bool    Int64  String15    Bool   Bool   Bool   Bool   Cat…
─────┼─────────────────────────────────────────────────────────────
   1 │ true        4  pedestrian  false  false  false  false  Thursday
   2 │ false       7  vehicular   false  true   false  false  Sunday
   3 │ true        7  vehicular   false  false  false  false  Sunday
   4 │ true        2  vehicular   false  false  false  false  Tuesday
   ⋮ │   ⋮      ⋮        ⋮          ⋮      ⋮      ⋮      ⋮        ⋮
6876 │ false       3  vehicular   false  false  false  true   Wednesday
6877 │ false       3  vehicular   true   true   false  true   Wednesday
6878 │ false       3  vehicular   false  false  false  true   Wednesday
6879 │ false       3  vehicular   false  false  false  false  Wednesday
                                                    6871 rows omitted
```

> **All element types do not have ? at their end, which signals that no columns contain missing data.**

The operation changes the data frame in place. If we wanted to create a new data frame with dropped missing values, we could use the `dropmissing` function. Note that now the data frame has 6,879 rows, which is 42 fewer than the original 6,921 row count, as expected.

Additionally, we can easily visually confirm that no columns hold missing data. If you look at listing 13.6, you can see that the element type of column `type` was `String15?`, and now it is `String15`. The question mark appended to the type signals that a column allows for missing values. Since it is now gone, this means that after the `dropmissing!` operation, our data frame has no missing values.

> **EXERCISE 13.3**   To practice the operations you have learned in this section, prepare the following two analyses. First, calculate the probability of arrest per `dayname` column. Second, compute the probability of arrest again, but this time, per the `dayname` and `type` columns, and present the results in wide form, where `dayname` levels are rows and `type` values form columns.

Before we move forward, let's drop the `day` column from `owensboro2`, as we will not need it in further analyses:

```
julia> select!(owensboro2, Not(:day))
6879×7 DataFrame
 Row │ arrest  type        v1     v2     v3     v4     dayname
     │ Bool    String15    Bool   Bool   Bool   Bool   Cat…
─────┼───────────────────────────────────────────────────────
   1 │ true    pedestrian  false  false  false  false  Thursday
   2 │ false   vehicular   false  true   false  false  Sunday
   ⋮ │   ⋮        ⋮          ⋮      ⋮      ⋮      ⋮        ⋮
```

```
6878 │  false  vehicular   false  false  false   true  Wednesday
6879 │  false  vehicular   false  false  false  false  Wednesday
                                           6875 rows omitted
```

13.4 *Building a predictive model of arrest probability*

In this section, we will build a predictive model of arrest probability. In comparison to methods presented in earlier chapters, we will use a more-advanced procedure. We will split the data randomly into training and test data sets to verify that our model is not overfitted (www.ibm.com/cloud/learn/overfitting). Learning how to do this with DataFrames.jl is useful, as ensuring that your model is not overfitted is a standard procedure in most data science workflows.

13.4.1 *Splitting the data into train and test data sets*

We start by adding the indicator variable `train`, signaling whether a row of the `owensboro2` data frame should go to a training or test data set. Assume we want to perform a 70/30 split between these sets.

Listing 13.10 Randomly generating the indicator column for our data

```
                                    Sets the seed of a random number generator
                                    for reproducibility of our experiment
julia> Random.seed!(1234);    ◁──┘

julia> owensboro2.train = rand(Bernoulli(0.7), nrow(owensboro2));    ◁──┐

julia> mean(owensboro2.train)               Draws random numbers from a
0.702427678441634                           Bernoulli distribution with a
                                        probability of success equal to 0.7
```

We can see that in around 70% of cases, the `train` column has the value `true`, indicating that the row should go to the training data set. With the `false` value, the row goes to the test data set. When generating the `train` column, we sample the `true` and `false` values from the Bernoulli distribution (http://mng.bz/Xaql) with 0.7 probability of success. The `Bernoulli` type is defined in the Distributions.jl package. This package provides a wide range of distributions you might want to use in your code—both univariate (like `Beta` or `Binomial`) and multivariate (like `Multinomial` or `Dirichlet`). See the package documentation for details (https://juliastats.org/Distributions.jl/stable/).

The design of this package is highly composable. For example, if you want to draw a random sample from a distribution, you pass it as a first argument to the standard `rand` function. In listing 13.10, we have written `rand(Bernoulli(0.7), nrow(owensboro2))` to sample from the Bernoulli distribution the same number of times as the number of rows in our `owensboro2` data frame.

In the next listing, we create `train` and `test` data frames that contain rows of the `owensboro2` data frame that have `true` and `false` values, respectively.

Listing 13.11   Creating `train` and `test` data frames

```
julia> train = subset(owensboro2, :train)
4832×8 DataFrame
  Row │ arrest   type         v1      v2      v3      v4      dayname    train
      │ Bool     String15     Bool    Bool    Bool    Bool    Cat…       Bool
──────┼──────────────────────────────────────────────────────────────────────
    1 │   true   pedestrian   false   false   false   false   Thursday    true
    2 │  false   vehicular    false    true   false   false   Sunday      true
    ⋮ │    ⋮         ⋮          ⋮       ⋮       ⋮       ⋮         ⋮          ⋮
 4831 │  false   vehicular     true    true   false    true   Wednesday   true
 4832 │  false   vehicular    false   false   false    true   Wednesday   true
                                                          4828 rows omitted

julia> test = subset(owensboro2, :train => ByRow(!))
2047×8 DataFrame
  Row │ arrest   type         v1      v2      v3      v4      dayname    train
      │ Bool     String15     Bool    Bool    Bool    Bool    Cat…       Bool
──────┼──────────────────────────────────────────────────────────────────────
    1 │   true   vehicular    false   false   false   false   Tuesday    false
    2 │   true   vehicular    false   false   false   false   Sunday     false
    ⋮ │    ⋮         ⋮          ⋮       ⋮       ⋮       ⋮         ⋮          ⋮
 2046 │  false   vehicular    false   false    true   false   Friday     false
 2047 │  false   vehicular    false   false   false   false   Wednesday  false
                                                          2043 rows omitted
```

Note that the `train` column in the `train` data frame contains only `true` values, and in the `test` data frame, it contains only `false` values. To perform row subsetting, this time we use the `subset` function that creates a new data frame based on passed conditions. As usual, its `subset!` equivalent operates in place. The `subset` function accepts operation specification syntax, just like `combine` or `select`. The only difference is that it requires forms that do not specify a target column name since we are not creating any columns, but subsetting rows. Also, naturally, the result of the operation must be Boolean, as we use it as a condition to subset rows.

As for other functions that accept operation specification syntax, DataFramesMeta.jl provides the `@subset`, `@subset!`, `@rsubset`, and `@rsubset!` convenience macros. Recall that the `r` prefix means that the passed operation should be performed by row, and the `!` suffix means that we want to update the data frame in place instead of creating a new data frame. Let's use the `@rsubset` macro to create the `test` data frame again as an exercise:

```
julia> @rsubset(owensboro2, !(:train))
2047×8 DataFrame
  Row │ arrest   type         v1      v2      v3      v4      dayname    train
      │ Bool     String15     Bool    Bool    Bool    Bool    Cat…       Bool
──────┼──────────────────────────────────────────────────────────────────────
    1 │   true   vehicular    false   false   false   false   Tuesday    false
    2 │   true   vehicular    false   false   false   false   Sunday     false
    ⋮ │    ⋮         ⋮          ⋮       ⋮       ⋮       ⋮         ⋮          ⋮
 2046 │  false   vehicular    false   false    true   false   Friday     false
 2047 │  false   vehicular    false   false   false   false   Wednesday  false
                                                          2043 rows omitted
```

EXERCISE 13.4   Create `train` and `test` data frames by using (a) data frame indexing syntax and (b) the `groupby` function.

13.4.2 *Fitting a logistic regression model*

We are now ready to build our model. We will use the GLM.jl package that you learned about in earlier chapters. We will build the model by using the `train` data set and then compare its predictive power between the `train` and `test` data sets:

```
julia> model = glm(@formula(arrest~dayname+type+v1+v2+v3+v4),
                 train, Binomial(), LogitLink())
StatsModels.TableRegressionModel{GeneralizedLinearModel{
GLM.GlmResp{Vector{Float64}, Binomial{Float64}, LogitLink},
GLM.DensePredChol{Float64, LinearAlgebra.Cholesky{Float64,
Matrix{Float64}}}}, Matrix{Float64}}

arrest ~ 1 + dayname + type + v1 + v2 + v3 + v4

Coefficients:
```

	Coef.	Std. Error	z	Pr(>|z|)	Lower 95%	Upper 95%
(Intercept)	0.28762	0.215229	1.34	0.1814	-0.134216	0.70946
dayname: Tuesday	0.13223	0.216134	0.61	0.5407	-0.291381	0.55585
dayname: Wednesday	0.07929	0.21675	0.37	0.7145	-0.34553	0.50411
dayname: Thursday	-0.03443	0.218522	-0.16	0.8748	-0.462734	0.39385
dayname: Friday	0.19434	0.202768	0.96	0.3378	-0.203075	0.59176
dayname: Saturday	0.59492	0.204298	2.91	0.0036	0.194504	0.99533
dayname: Sunday	1.02347	0.205539	4.98	<1e-06	0.620622	1.42632
type: vehicular	-1.34187	0.16969	-7.91	<1e-14	-1.67445	-1.00928
v1	-2.40105	0.147432	-16.29	<1e-58	-2.69001	-2.11208
v2	-2.46956	0.18695	-13.21	<1e-39	-2.83598	-2.10315
v3	-0.55070	0.149679	-3.68	0.0002	-0.844072	-0.25734
v4	-2.96624	0.289665	-10.24	<1e-23	-3.53397	-2.3985

From the model, we learn that the probability of arrest goes up the most on Sundays. If the type of stop is vehicular, the probability of arrest goes down. Also, for violation types `v1`, `v2`, `v3`, and `v4`, the probability of arrest goes down. This should be expected, as the violations are failure to wear seat belts, no registration plates, failure to produce proof of insurance, and speeding. None seems to be severe enough to typically lead to an arrest.

I would like to draw your attention to one property of the output that we have obtained. For the `dayname` variable, `Monday` is selected as the reference level (and thus is not present in the summary), and the remaining levels are properly ordered. This is possible because the `dayname` column is categorical, so the `glm` function respects the order of levels in this variable.

Let's now assess the predictive quality of our model. We start with storing its predictions in `train` and `test` data frames, respectively, using the `predict` function:

```
julia> train.predict = predict(model)
4832-element Vector{Float64}:
 0.5629604404770923
 0.07583480306410262
 ⋮
 0.00014894383671078636
 0.019055034096545412
```

<-- **By default, the predict function returns predictions for the data set that was used to build the model.**

```
julia> test.predict = predict(model, test)
2047-element Vector{Union{Missing, Float64}}:
 0.2845489586270871
 0.4923077257785381
 ⋮
 0.19613838972815223
 0.27389501945271594
```

<-- **If you pass a data set as a second argument to the predict function, you get predictions for new data.**

13.4.3 *Evaluating the quality of a model's predictions*

Let's compare histograms of model predictions in groups defined by the value of the `arrest` column. We expect that the histograms will not overlap much, as this would indicate that the model is able to separate arrests from non-arrests relatively well:

```
julia> test_groups = groupby(test, :arrest);

julia> histogram(test_groups[(false,)].predict;
                 bins=10, normalize=:probability,
                 fillstyle= :/, label="false")

julia> histogram!(test_groups[(true,)].predict;
                  bins=10, normalize=:probability,
                  fillalpha=0.5, label="true")
```

We group the `test` data frame by the `arrest` column. Then, to produce histograms, we extract from this grouped data frame the first group that represents a `false` value of arrest, and next, a `true` value of arrest. If you would like to refresh your understanding of `GroupedDataFrame` indexing, you can find all the needed explanations in chapter 11.

For the first group, we use the `histogram` function. For the second, we use the `histogram!` function, which adds a second histogram to the same plot. Both histograms are plotted with 10 bins, and the presented values are probabilities of these bins. With the `fillalpha=0.5` keyword argument, we make the second histogram transparent. The `fillstyle=:/` keyword argument adds lines to the first histogram so that it can be easily distinguished when printed in black and white. Figure 13.5 shows the result of our operation.

Figure 13.5 confirms that if `arrest` is `false`, predictions are low, while if it is `true`, predictions are high.

Now consider the following experiment. Assume you set a certain threshold—let's pick 0.15 as an example—and decide to classify all observations with predictions less than or equal to 0.15 as `false`, and greater than 0.15 as `true`. If we perform such a

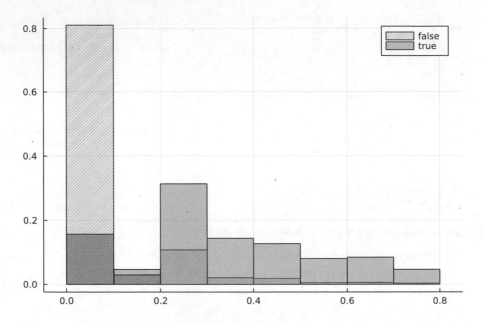

Figure 13.5　Histograms of predictions on a test data set for values in the `arrest` column equal to `true` and `false`. We can see that the model separates the observations relatively well.

classification, we sometimes make a correct decision (predict observed `true` as `true` or observed `false` as `false`) and sometimes make a mistake (predict observed `true` as `false` or observed `false` as `true`). In the following code, we make a table summarizing these results:

```julia
julia> @chain test begin
           @rselect(:predicted=:predict > 0.15, :observed=:arrest)
           proptable(:predicted, :observed; margins=2)
       end
2×2 Named Matrix{Float64}
predicted \ observed |    false      true
─────────────────────┼───────────────────
false                | 0.811154  0.169492
true                 | 0.188846  0.830508
```

This table is typically called a *confusion matrix* (http://mng.bz/yaZ7). We create it by using the `proptable` function from the FreqTables.jl package, and since we pass the `margins=2` keyword argument, the values in the columns add up to 1.

For example, the value `0.188846` in the second row and first column of our confusion matrix tells us that for the selected threshold, there is around an 18.88% probability that we will incorrectly classify an observed `false` as `true`. Let's call this a *probability of false alarm (pfa)*. Similarly, the value `0.169492` that we have in the first row and second column of our confusion matrix tells us that for the selected threshold, there is around a 16.95% probability that we will incorrectly classify observed true as false. Let's call this a *probability of miss* (*pmiss*). Figure 13.6 illustrates these relationships.

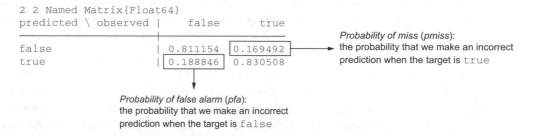

Figure 13.6 Elements in the columns of this confusion matrix add up to 1. The model makes two kinds of errors, whose probabilities are pmiss and pfa.

The lower the pfa and pmiss, the better the quality of our model. However, we have calculated them for a fixed-value classification threshold, 0.15 in the example, which was picked arbitrarily. A natural approach to resolve this problem is to plot how the relationship of pfa and pmiss changes for all possible values of cutoff thresholds. This functionality is provided by the ROCAnalysis.jl package.

We will now create a plot showing the relationship between pfa on the x-axis and pmiss on the y-axis. Additionally, we will calculate the probability that a randomly picked observation that has a true label has a lower prediction than the randomly picked observation that has a false label. We want this probability to be close to 0% for a good classifier. Note that for the random model (not making any useful prediction), this probability is equal to 50%. Let's call this value the *area under the pfa-pmiss curve* (*AUC*). Under our definition, the lower the AUC, the better the model.

Using the ROCAnalysis.jl package, we'll draw the pfa-pmiss curves for the test and train data set predictions of our model and calculate the AUC metric in the next listing.

Listing 13.12 Drawing pfa-pmiss curves for evaluating the model

```
julia> test_roc =  roc(test; score=:predict, target=:arrest)
ROC curve with 62 points, of which 14 on the convex hull

julia> plot(test_roc.pfa, test_roc.pmiss;
            color="black", lw=3,
            label="test (AUC=$(round(100*auc(test_roc), digits=2))%)",
            xlabel="pfa", ylabel="pmiss")

julia> train_roc =  roc(train, score=:predict, target=:arrest)
ROC curve with 73 points, of which 16 on the convex hull

julia> plot!(train_roc.pfa, train_roc.pmiss;
            color="gold", lw=3,
            label="train (AUC=$(round(100*auc(train_roc), digits=2))%)")
```

We first use the `roc` function from the ROCAnalysis.jl package. It takes a data frame as an argument, along with the `score` and `target` keyword arguments in which we pass the names of columns storing predictions and `true` labels of data, respectively. The produced object has two properties that we use: `pfa` and `pmiss`, which store information about the pfa and pmiss metric values for different values of the cutoff threshold, and thus can be used to produce the plots. Finally, using the `auc` function, we calculate the area under the pfa-pmiss curve. The operations are done for both the `test` and `train` data frames to check whether the obtained results are similar.

Figure 13.7 shows the result produced by listing 13.12. We can see that the pfa-pmiss curves for the `test` and `train` models are almost identical, so we can conclude that it is not overfitted. The AUC is below 15%, which shows that the model has a relatively good predictive power.

I have intentionally kept the model simple in order to not overly complicate the discussion presented in this chapter. If we wanted to use this model in practice, I would recommend adding more features and allowing for their interactions. Additionally, in the Julia ecosystem, in addition to generalized linear models, many other predictive models are available. You can find an example list in the MLJ.jl package documentation (http://mng.bz/M09E).

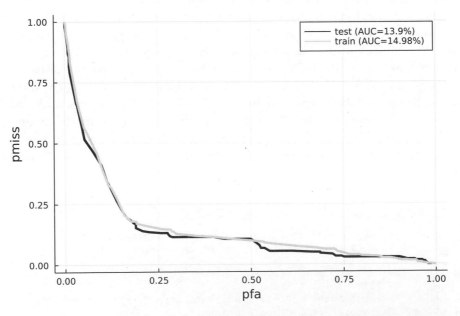

Figure 13.7 The pfa-pmiss curves for model predictions on the `test` and `train` data sets are almost identical, which shows that we do not have a problem with overfitting the model.

The ROCAnalysis.jl package takes a convention to analyze the area under the pfa-pmiss curve. In some other sources (for example, http://mng.bz/aPmx), the pmiss metric is replaced by a 1-pmiss measure. Then, on the y-axis of the curve, we plot the probability that we make a correct decision when the target is `true`. In such a situation, the area under the curve is maximized (not minimized, as in our case) and can be computed as 1 minus the return value of the `auc` function.

Doing machine learning with Julia

In this chapter, we have manually created and evaluated a simple predictive model. If you would like to create more-complex machine learning workflows, I recommend learning the MLJ framework (https://github.com/alan-turing-institute/MLJ.jl).

Machine Learning in Julia (MLJ) is a toolbox providing a common interface and meta-algorithms for selecting, tuning, evaluating, composing, and comparing over 160 machine learning models.

Additionally, appendix C lists various packages that you might find useful if you want to go beyond simple data analysis and start doing advanced data science projects in Julia.

13.5 Reviewing functionalities provided by DataFrames.jl

In this chapter, you have seen a lot of functionalities provided by DataFrames.jl. In conclusion, here's an overview of functions discussed throughout part 2 so that you can have a brief reference:

- *Constructing data frames*—`DataFrame` and `copy`
- *Providing summary information*—`describe`, `summary`, `ncol`, `nrow`
- *Working with column names*—`names`, `rename`, `rename!`
- *Adding rows to data frames*—`append!`, `push!`, `vcat`
- *Iterating*—`eachrow`, `eachcol`
- *Indexing*—`getindex`, `setindex!`
- *Adding columns*—`insertcols!`
- *Transforming columns*—`combine`, `select`, `select!`, `transform`, `transform!`, `flatten`
- *Grouping*—`groupby`
- *Subsetting rows*—`subset`, `subset!`, `dropmissing`, `dropmissing!`
- *Reshaping*—`stack`, `unstack`, `permutedims`
- *Sorting*—`sort`, `sort!`
- *Joining*—`innerjoin`, `leftjoin`, `leftjoin!`, `rightjoin`, `outerjoin`

This list is quite long. I have listed only functions presented in part 2. For a complete list of available functions, check the DataFrames.jl documentation (http://mng.bz/gR7Z). Also, for the functions we have discussed, I have omitted some of the functionalities they provide, and instead focus on only the most used ones. In the documentation, you will find a complete description of every function provided by DataFrames.jl, along with usage examples.

The operation specification syntax supported by `combine`, `select`, `select!`, `transform`, `transform!`, `subset`, and `subset!` also has more functionalities than are covered in this part of the book. I have selected only the most used patterns. You can find a complete explanation of all available features in the package documentation (http://mng.bz/epow). Additionally, in my blog post "DataFrames.jl Minilanguage Explained" (http://mng.bz/p6pE), I have prepared a review of operation specification syntax.

Many users of DataFrames.jl enjoy using the DataFramesMeta.jl domain-specific language, especially in combination with the `@chain` macro. This package also has many more functionalities than I am able to cover in this book; you can find more information in its documentation (http://mng.bz/O6Z2). In my blog post "Welcome to DataFramesMeta.jl" (http://mng.bz/YK7e), I have additionally created a short guide to the most used macros provided by this package.

In summary, you can consider DataFrames.jl a mature package. It has been developed for 10 years, and the vast number of functionalities it provides reflects the various requirements of its users over this period.

Additionally, the package is past the 1.0 release, which means that it gives a guarantee of not introducing breaking changes until its 2.0 release (which is not expected anytime soon). This promise is, in my experience, most relevant for users considering it for production use.

Another important design aspect related to production use of DataFrames.jl is that it was designed to either produce a correct result or raise an exception. You might have noticed that nowhere in this book have you seen any warning message printed. This is intentional. Warnings are often silently ignored when you run your code in production. In DataFrames.jl, in many functions, we instead provide keyword arguments that allow you to turn an error into accepted behavior. Let's look at one example.

In R, when you create a data frame with duplicate column names, it is silently accepted, and column renaming is done (this is R code):

```
> data.frame(a=1,a=2)
  a a.1
1 1   2
```

In DataFrames.jl, by default, we do not allow duplicate column names, as most of the time this code is incorrect and should be fixed:

```
julia> DataFrame(:a=>1, :a=>2)
ERROR: ArgumentError: Duplicate variable names: :a. Pass makeunique=true
to make them unique using a suffix automatically.
```

However, we allow you to opt in to accepting duplicate column names by passing the `makeunique=true` keyword argument if this is what you want:

```
julia> DataFrame(:a=>1, :a=>2; makeunique=true)
1×2 DataFrame
 Row │ a      a_1
     │ Int64  Int64
─────┼──────────────
   1 │     1      2
```

Summary

- You can create data processing pipelines by using the @chain macro. Functions and macros provided by DataFrames.jl and DataFramesMeta.jl integrate well with this macro, as typically they take an input data frame or grouped data frame as a first positional argument and return a data frame.
- DataFrames.jl defines five functions that allow you to perform operations on columns of data frames or grouped data frames: combine, select, select!, transform, and transform!. Functions with the ! suffix mutate the object passed to them in place, while functions without it allocate a new return value.
- The combine function is used to combine (aggregate) rows from a source object. The select and transform functions keep the same number and order of rows as are in the source object. The difference between them is that select keeps only columns that you specify, while transform additionally keeps all columns from the source object.
- If you have a function that works on scalars, wrapping it with the ByRow object turns them into vectorized (accepting) collections of data and applies the original function elementwise.
- Functions performing operations on columns use a common operation specification syntax. It uses the general pattern source_column => operation_function => target_column_name, but selected elements of this pattern can be dropped, as shown in listing 13.3. The three most common variants are as follows: (1) passing source_column stores it in the result without any modification, (2) passing source_column => operation_function automatically generates the target column name, and (3) passing source_column => target_column_name is a syntax used for column renaming.
- DataFramesMeta.jl provides macros for all column transformation functions provided in DataFrames.jl. An important rule is that macros can be prefixed with r in front of the macro name. This prefix signals that the operation specified in the macro should be automatically vectorized (performed rowwise). For example, the @select and @rselect macros are equivalents of the select function. The difference is that operations in @select operate on whole columns, while operations in @rselect operate on single elements.
- CategoricalArrays.jl provides support for categorical arrays. This data is useful if you want to treat your data as nominal or ordinal in a statistical sense.
- DataFrames.jl provides functions that allow you to perform all the standard join operations of several tables. These functions are used when you want to combine data from several source data frames.
- You use the stack and unstack functions to reshape data frames between long and wide formats. Such operations are often needed when you analyze data.
- The subset and subset! functions allow you to subset rows of a data frame. They use operation specification syntax that is the same as is used in combine

or `select`. DataFramesMeta.jl provides macros that are equivalents of these two functions. The benefit of using these functions, over, for example, data frame indexing, is that they are designed to be easily used in `@chain` operations.

- The ROCAnalysis.jl package provides a set of functionalities that allow you to evaluate the predictive power of classifiers. This functionality is needed essentially every time you build a model with a binary target variable.

Creating web services for sharing data analysis results

This chapter covers

- Implementing a Monte Carlo simulation
- Using multiple threads in computations
- Creating and running a web service in Julia

In chapter 1, we discussed a Timeline case study. Recall that the Timeline company provides a web application that helps financial advisers with retirement financial planning. This application needs to perform a lot of on-demand computations while having a fast response time. In this chapter, we will create a web service that serves a similar purpose in a simplified setting.

Imagine we are working at a company that offers its customers a service of evaluating financial assets. You are asked to create a web service that will perform pricing of an Asian option. *Asian options* are financial instruments whose price depends on an average price of an underlying asset (for example, a stock) over a certain period; in section 14.1, I give details of how this option is defined.

Since the Asian option is a complex financial instrument, there is no simple formula for its value. Therefore, you need to perform a Monte Carlo simulation to approximate this value. When doing a Monte Carlo simulation, we randomly sample the evolution of the underlying asset's price multiple times. Next, for each price path, we compute the payoff of the Asian option and use the average payoff to approximate the option's value.

The challenge is that Monte Carlo simulations are compute intensive. Therefore, in this chapter, you will learn how to use multiple cores of your CPU, taking advantage of Julia's support for multithreading, to produce the desired result as quickly as possible.

From the engineering side, the requirements are that your web service accepts JSON payloads in POST requests and also returns the response in JSON format. In this case, the POST request sends data to the server specifying the parameters of the Asian option that we want to valuate. These parameters are passed in JSON format to the server; information passed this way is often called a *JSON payload*. You will learn how to create such web services by using the Genie.jl package.

To test the created web service, we will write a client program that will analyze how the valuation of the Asian option changes with its parameters.

This chapter is divided into the following sections:

- Section 14.1 explains the theory of pricing Asian options by using a Monte Carlo simulation.
- In section 14.2, we implement the simulation while taking advantage of the multithreading support that Julia offers.
- In section 14.3, using the Genie.jl package, we create a web service that can respond to requests for valuation of the Asian option.
- In section 14.4, we test the created web service by writing a client that sends requests to it and fetches the returned response.

14.1   *Pricing financial options by using a Monte Carlo simulation*

In this section, you will learn the theory behind pricing Asian options by using a Monte Carlo simulation. Such pricing models are commonly used in the financial industry, so it is useful to know the details of how they work. Our example is adapted from *Foundations and Methods of Stochastic Simulation* by Barry L. Nelson (Springer, 2013).

14.1.1   *Calculating the payoff of an Asian option definition*

We start by giving a definition of an Asian option we consider. The payoff of such an option depends on an underlying financial instrument. Assume that this underlying instrument is a stock. We observe the price of this stock over a certain period of time. The Asian option gives an investor a payoff if the average price of the stock is greater than a value called the *strike price*. In such a case, the payoff of the Asian option is equal to the mean price of the stock minus the strike price. Now I'll formally define the way the payoff is computed.

Assume that a stock is traded on the market. We use $X(t)$ to denote its price at time t. For simplicity, assume that we are currently at time $t = 0$, so we know that the price of the stock is $X(0)$. We are interested in the average price of this stock in the period from $t = 0$ to $t = T$. During this period, the stock changes its price m times. Therefore, we will see its price at times $0, T/m, 2T/m, \ldots, (m-2)T/m, (m-1)T/m,$ and T. We use Y to denote the average price of the stock over these $m + 1$ points in time.

The Asian option we consider has the following rule of its valuation. At time T, we compute the average price of the stock Y. If this value is greater than the value K (called the *strike price*), we get a $Y - K$ payoff; otherwise, we get no payoff. More formally, our payoff is $\max(Y - K, 0)$. If you have experience with machine learning, you will recognize that this function is often called a *rectified linear unit* (*ReLU*).

Before we move forward, let's consider an example of such pricing. Assume that we have $T = 1.0$, $m = 4$, and $K = 1.05$. We are in time T, and we have seen the prices X that were 1.0, 1.1, 1.3, 1.2, 1.2. Therefore, Y is equal to 1.16, so the payoff is $\max(Y - K, 0) = 0.11$. We can visualize this scenario with the following code:

```julia
julia> using Plots

julia> using Statistics

julia> X = [1.0, 1.1, 1.3, 1.2, 1.2]
5-element Vector{Float64}:
 1.0
 1.1
 1.3
 1.2
 1.2

julia> T = 1.0
1.0

julia> m = 4
4

julia> Y = mean(X)
1.1600000000000001

julia> K = 1.05
1.05

julia> plot(range(0.0, T; length=m+1), X;
            xlabel="T", legend=false, color="black")

julia> hline!([Y], color="gray", lw=3, ls=:dash)

julia> hline!([K], color="gray", lw=3, ls=:dot)

julia> annotate!([(T, Y + 0.01, "Y"),
                  (T, K + 0.01, "K"),
                  (T, X[end] + 0.01, "X")])
```

In this example, we use three new functions. The `range` function creates a vector of equally spaced values, from the first to the second positional argument it is passed, and the `length` keyword argument specifies the number of points we want. The `hline!` function adds a horizontal line to the plot, and the `annotate!` function adds text annotations to it. The `annotate!` function takes a vector in which each element is a tuple specifying the *x* location, *y* location, and the text to be displayed.

Figure 14.1 shows the result produced by our code.

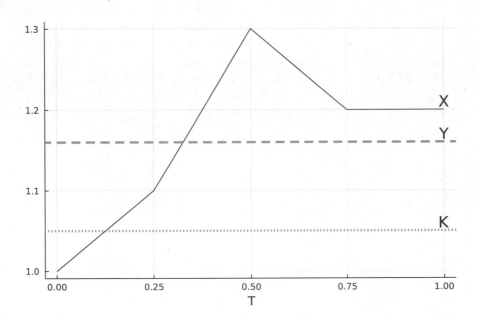

Figure 14.1   Since *Y* is above *K*, the Asian option gives a positive payoff for stock price *X*.

14.1.2 Computing the value of an Asian option

Our task is to compute the value of the Asian option at time 0. At this time, we do not know *Y*. What, then, is a fair value of our Asian option?

Imagine that we could buy such an option many times and observe the evolution of the stock prices underlying our option. The value of our option is defined to be the average payoff we could expect in such an experiment. Formally, using the language of probability theory, we say that we want to compute the expected value of our payoff via $E(\max(Y - K, 0))$. However, we need to consider one additional factor. Since the payoff is collected at time *T*, and we are at time 0, we need to discount it. Assume that *r* is a risk-free interest rate, and we use continuous compounding (this is a typical assumption made in financial calculations; see, for example, http://mng.bz/AV87). Therefore, we need to multiply the expected value of the payoff by discount factor $\exp(-rT)$. In summary, the value of the option at time 0 is $\exp(-rT) \cdot E(\max(Y - K, 0))$.

The challenge of computing the requested value is that at time 0, the value of *Y* is unknown. We will assume that the price of the stock in the period between 0 and *T* follows *geometric Brownian motion* (GBM, http://mng.bz/ZpRa). This stochastic process is often used to model prices of financial assets.

14.1.3 Understanding GBM

Typically, the GBM process is introduced as a solution of a stochastic differential equation, but for our purposes, it is enough that you have an intuitive understanding. The idea is as follows. If we have a stochastic process $X(t)$ representing a stock price, we want the logarithm of the ratio of this price between two times t_1 and t_2 (where $t_1 < t_2$) to follow a normal distribution. This ratio can be expressed using the formula $\log(X(t_2)/X(t_1))$ and is called the *log return* (http://mng.bz/RvmO). Since we assume that the log return follows a normal distribution, we should specify the mean and variance of this distribution.

Let's start with the variance of the distribution of the stock price's log return. In the GBM model, we assume that the variance is equal to $s^2(t_2 - t_1)$, where s is a parameter. As you can see, the variance is proportional to the difference between t_2 and t_1. To understand why this is a natural assumption, consider three time periods, $t_1 < t_2 < t_3$. The assumption in the GBM model is that the log returns between periods t_1 and t_2, and t_2 and t_3, respectively, are independent. Observe that $\log(X(t_2)/X(t_1)) + \log(X(t_3)/X(t_2)) = \log(X(t_3)/X(t_1))$. Therefore, if we want the GBM model to be consistent, the sum of variances of the two terms on the left-hand side of this equation must be equal to the variance of the term on the right-hand side. Indeed, this is the case, as $s^2(t_2 - t_1) + s^2(t_3 - t_2) = s^2(t_3 - t_1)$.

We are now ready to turn to the expected value of the distribution of the stock price's log return. Here the assumption I make in the book is that the log return on the expected stock price should be equal to the log return of the risk-free asset. Recall that we have used r to denote the risk-free interest rate with continuous compounding. This means that $r(t_2 - t_1)$ should be equal to $\log(E(X(t_2))/E(X(t_1)))$. It can be shown that if we want this property to hold, the mean of the distribution of the stock price's log return should be equal to $(r - s^2/2)(t_2 - t_1)$.

In summary, in our GBM model, we assume that the log return of the stock price $\log(X(t_2)/X(t_1))$ follows a normal distribution with mean $(r - s^2/2)(t_2 - t_1)$ and standard deviation $s^2(t_3 - t_1)$. Let's translate this assumption to the parameterization we use in the implementation. Recall that we assume that the stock price is measured at times $0, T/m, 2T/m, \ldots, (m-2)T/m, (m-1)T/m$, and T. Under these assumptions, the value of the ratio $X((I+1)T/m)/X(iT/m)$ is the random variable $\exp((r - s^2/2)T/m + s^2(T/m) \cdot Z(i))$, where $Z(0), Z(1), \ldots, Z(m-2), Z(m-1)$ are independent and identically distributed random variables having normal distribution with mean 0 and standard deviation 1. In this formula, r is the risk-free interest rate, and s is a measure of the stock price's variability.

Before we move forward, let's look at a minimal example of generating a single sample of the GBM process. In the computations, we use $X(0) = 1.0$, $T = 2.0$, $s = 0.2$, $r = 0.1$, and $m = 4$.

In the code, we collect the results of a simulation of a single sample of the GBM process in a data frame having two columns: simulated stock price X and time t. Next, we iteratively sample the log return of our stock price between two consecutive periods. Using it, we compute the updated stock price and store it as a new row of the gbm data frame using the push! function:

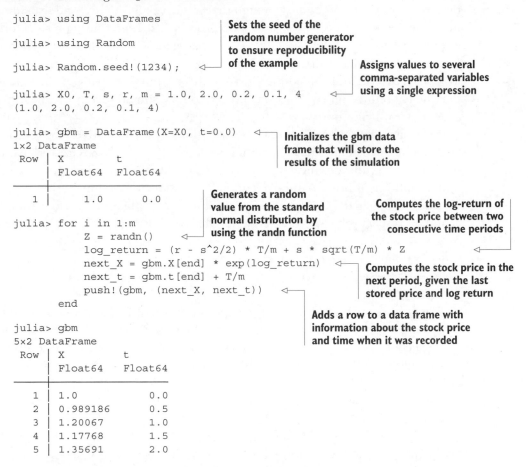

```julia
julia> using DataFrames

julia> using Random

julia> Random.seed!(1234);

julia> X0, T, s, r, m = 1.0, 2.0, 0.2, 0.1, 4
(1.0, 2.0, 0.2, 0.1, 4)

julia> gbm = DataFrame(X=X0, t=0.0)
1×2 DataFrame
 Row │ X        t
     │ Float64  Float64
─────┼──────────────────
   1 │     1.0      0.0

julia> for i in 1:m
           Z = randn()
           log_return = (r - s^2/2) * T/m + s * sqrt(T/m) * Z
           next_X = gbm.X[end] * exp(log_return)
           next_t = gbm.t[end] + T/m
           push!(gbm, (next_X, next_t))
       end

julia> gbm
5×2 DataFrame
 Row │ X         t
     │ Float64   Float64
─────┼───────────────────
   1 │ 1.0           0.0
   2 │ 0.989186      0.5
   3 │ 1.20067       1.0
   4 │ 1.17768       1.5
   5 │ 1.35691       2.0
```

Sets the seed of the random number generator to ensure reproducibility of the example

Assigns values to several comma-separated variables using a single expression

Initializes the gbm data frame that will store the results of the simulation

Generates a random value from the standard normal distribution by using the randn function

Computes the log-return of the stock price between two consecutive time periods

Computes the stock price in the next period, given the last stored price and log return

Adds a row to a data frame with information about the stock price and time when it was recorded

In the example, the stock price stored in column X of the gbm data frame changes randomly from period to period because in the calculation of the log_return variable, we have a random component represented by the Z variable.

14.1.4 *Using a numerical approach to computing the Asian option value*

The formulas describing the GBM process look complex. This suggests that there is no simple method allowing us to compute the value of the Asian option; recall that this value is defined as $\exp(-rT) \cdot E(\max(Y - K, 0))$. Indeed, in this case there is no closed-form formula for this expression. How should we compute its value? We will use a Monte Carlo simulation to approximate it. The algorithm of a Monte Carlo simulation is as follows.

In a single step of our Monte Carlo simulation, we need to compute the payoff of our Asian option for a single realization of the GBM process. Therefore, we need to perform the following operations:

1 Sample independent random values $Z(0)$, $Z(1)$, . . . , $Z(m-2)$, $Z(m-1)$ from the standard normal distribution.
2 Compute stock prices $X(0)$, $X(T/m)$, . . . , $X((m-1)/T)$, $X(T)$ by using the generated random values.
3 Compute Y as an average of the computed stock prices.
4 Compute $V = \exp(-rT) \cdot \max(Y-K, 0)$.

In our Monte Carlo simulation, we repeat this single step of the process independently many times. Use n to denote the number of times we perform this single step. We thus will collect n values $V(1)$, $V(2)$, . . . , $V(n-1)$, $V(n)$. The mean of these values approximates the value of our Asian option $\exp(-rT) \cdot E(\max(Y-K, 0))$. However, since the process I have described is randomized, this value is not exact. In such situations, we usually want to quantify this uncertainty somehow. We will therefore compute the 95% confidence interval of our Asian option price.

The 95% confidence interval is a range in which, if we ran the simulation and computed it multiple times, 95% of the intervals would contain the true (unknown) value of our Asian option price (www.simplypsychology.org/confidence-interval.html). If we have a set of n independent observations whose mean is m and whose standard deviation is sd, then the formula for approximation of the 95% confidence interval that we will use in this chapter is $[m - 1.96sd/\sqrt{n}, m + 1.96sd/\sqrt{n}]$.

Before we move on to implementing the Asian option valuation algorithm, I'll summarize the parameters that we need to know to calculate the value of the Asian option we are considering:

- Time horizon T
- Starting price of the stock $X(0)$
- Strike price K
- Risk-free interest rate r
- Stock's price volatility s
- Number of changes of the price of the stock m

We assume that the user asking for the valuation of the Asian option knows these parameters.

An additional technical parameter is n, which is the number of repetitions of the simulation. This parameter will affect the precision with which we will calculate the Asian option price.

We are ready to write code that will compute the approximate value of the Asian option, along with the 95% confidence interval of this price. Additionally, in our implementation, we want to determine the probability that the payoff of the option will be zero.

14.2 *Implementing the option pricing simulator*

In this section, you will learn how to implement the simulator that prices the Asian option, following the description from the last part of section 14.1. First, we will create a function that computes the payoff of our option for a single sample of stock prices. Next, we will create a function that computes the approximate price of the option by using the Monte Carlo simulation.

In the process, we will use multithreading so we can quickly get the results of the computation. Learning how to write multithreaded code is useful, as it can efficiently use your CPU cores and, consequently, deliver computation results faster.

14.2.1 *Starting Julia with multiple-thread support*

In this section, you will learn how to start Julia with multiple-thread support. This is useful when you want to use the full power of your CPU in the computations.

For our computations, we want to use multiple threads, so start Julia with support for four threads. This is done by passing the -t4 switch. If you work in the terminal, you should be in the directory where we store the repository of code associated with this book. Type the following:

```
julia --project -t4
```

If you use Visual Studio Code (see appendix A), you can set the number of threads that the Julia session should use in the settings of the Julia extension.

I assume that the processor on your computer has at least four physical cores. The code will work if your processor does not meet this requirement, but you might not see the performance improvements that I present.

Once you start your Julia session using four threads, we first check to see if we set things up properly. The Threads.nthreads function returns the number of threads available to the Julia process:

```
julia> Threads.nthreads()
4
```

As expected, we get 4, which means that code supporting multithreading will be able to use four cores of your CPU.

> **Starting Julia**
>
> You can choose from multiple options when you start the Julia process. You can get a list of those options by typing `julia --help` in the terminal or by checking the "Command-Line Options" section of the Julia Manual (http://mng.bz/2r7m).
>
> Here is a selected list of available switches:
>
> - -tN, *where N is a number*—Sets the number of threads to be used by Julia to N. In Visual Studio Code, you can set the value of N in the settings of the Julia extension.

- --project—Sets the current working directory as the home project (see appendix A for an explanation). If you use the terminal, you should use this option when starting Julia for all code presented in this book. In Visual Studio Code, this option is used by default if you start a Julia session and opened a directory earlier with the repository storing your code along with Project.toml and Manifest.toml files.
- -pN, *where N is a number*—Sets the number of additional worker processes that Julia should launch on this computer. (This option is used with distributed computing. We do not discuss this topic in this book; see the "Multiprocessing and Distributed Computing" section of the Julia Manual at http://mng.bz/19Jn for details.)
- --machine-file <file>—Starts additional worker processes on hosts listed in <file> . (This option is used with distributed computing. We do not discuss this topic in this book; see the "Multiprocessing and Distributed Computing" section of the Julia Manual at http://mng.bz/19Jn for details.)
- --depwarn={yes|no|error}—Decides whether Julia should print deprecation warnings (usually emitted when you use functionalities of some packages that are deprecated and might be removed or changed in the future). By default, deprecation warnings are not printed; if this option is set to error, all deprecations are turned into errors.
- -ON, *where N is a number from 0 to 3*—Sets the optimization level for the compiler. The default is 2 (the higher the optimization level, the more optimizations the compiler performs).

14.2.2 Computing the option payoff for a single sample of stock prices

In this section, we will implement the function that computes the payoff of the Asian option we consider in this chapter for a single sample of stock prices. We also will check whether we can use multiple threads to speed up the execution of the code computing this payoff.

Our code directly follows the specification presented in section 14.1. In the X variable, we keep the current price of the stock, and in the sumX variable, we keep the sum of all observed prices. We update the X and sumX variables *m* times. The X variable is iteratively multiplied by the sample of the $\exp((r - s^2/2)\,T/m + s^2(T/m)\,Z(i))$ expression. Recall that $Z(i)$ is normally distributed with a mean of 0 and a standard deviation of 1. We can sample this value in Julia by using the randn function. Listing 14.1 presents a complete implementation of the payoff_asian_sample function that calculates the payoff of the option for one sample of stock price trajectory.

Note in listing 14.1 that I have added the ::Float64 type annotation after the payoff_asian_sample(T, X0, K, r, s, m) signature. In this way, I ensure that the return value of this function is converted to a Float64 value. In other words, this function always returns a number that has the Float64 type.

This annotation is optional but occasionally useful. First, it explicitly signals the intention of the function's developer, so it is useful as documentation. Second, if we were to mistakenly try to return a value from this function that cannot be converted to

Float64, we would get an error, which would allow us to catch potential bugs faster. Finally, since we know that this function returns Float64, writing the code that uses this function can be made a bit simpler in some cases. For example, when we want to preallocate a collection that will store the values produced, then we can safely declare its element type as Float64.

Listing 14.1   Computing the payoff of the Asian option for one sample of price trajectory

The X variable keeps track of the current stock price.

The sumX variable accumulates the sum of all observed stock prices.

The d variable has a value equal to the time delta between measurements of the stock price.

```
function payoff_asian_sample(T, X0, K, r, s, m)::Float64
    X = X0
    sumX = X
    d = T / m
    for i in 1:m
        X *= exp((r - s^2 / 2) * d + s * sqrt(d) * randn())
        sumX += X
    end
    Y = sumX / (m + 1)
    return exp(-r * T) * max(Y - K, 0)
end
```

Changes the stock price by using the log return calculated following the GBM formula

The Y variable stores the average stock price over the considered period.

Execution of the payoff_asian_sample function involves random number generation, so running it several times will produce different results. For example, let's check it for the parameters T=1.0, X0=50.0, K=55.0, r=0.05, s=0.3, and m=200:

```
julia> payoff_asian_sample(1.0, 50.0, 55.0, 0.05, 0.3, 200)
0.0

julia> payoff_asian_sample(1.0, 50.0, 55.0, 0.05, 0.3, 200)
1.3277342904015152

julia> payoff_asian_sample(1.0, 50.0, 55.0, 0.05, 0.3, 200)
4.645749241587061
```

If you run this example, expect to get different results, since we have not set the seed of the random number generator.

As discussed in section 14.1, we want to run payoff_asian_sample many times to approximate the value of the Asian option. For the purposes of this example, we benchmark the amount of time it takes to run this function 10,000 times and collect the results in a freshly allocated vector:

```
julia> using BenchmarkTools

julia> @btime map(i -> payoff_asian_sample(1.0, 50.0, 55.0, 0.05, 0.3, 200),
                  1:10_000);
  21.783 ms (2 allocations: 78.17 KiB)
```

Can we run this simulation faster? We can, and one of the ways to do so is to use multi-threading. We will use the map function from the ThreadsX.jl package. This is a multithreaded version of the `map` function that will spawn multiple *tasks* (informally, portions of code that can be independently executed) that will be run in parallel to use all threads available in the Julia session:

```
julia> using ThreadsX

julia> @btime ThreadsX.map(i -> payoff_asian_sample(1.0, 50.0, 55.0, 0.05,
                           0.3, 200), 1:10_000);
  5.821 ms (413 allocations: 845.89 KiB)
```

Our code runs almost four times faster, so the use of multithreading is justified in this case.

Experienced programmers will notice that we need to consider one issue when we start to use a parallelized version of the `map` function. The `payoff_asian_sample` function uses the random number generator when it calls the `randn` function. Therefore, the question is whether it is safe to run this function in parallel since potentially it could lead to a race condition (http://mng.bz/PoRv), because when we generate pseudo random numbers, we update the internal state of their generator. The answer is that the code is correct since each task in Julia uses a separate instance of the random number generator, so tasks do not interfere with each other.

> **The ThreadsX.jl package**
>
> The ThreadsX.jl package provides parallelized versions of functions available in Base Julia. Here's a list of selected functions that are implemented: `any`, `all`, `map`, `prod`, `reduce`, `collect`, `sort`, `minimum`, `maximum`, `sum`, and `unique`. You can find more details in the package documentation (https://github.com/tkf/ThreadsX.jl).
>
> Remember that when using the functions that can take functions as arguments, we must make sure that using them will not lead to race condition bugs.
>
> As a more advanced topic, it is worth adding that the functions defined in the ThreadsX.jl package were designed to support reproducibility of the produced results even across sessions using different numbers of threads. To ensure such reproducibility, use the `basesize` keyword argument that specifies the number of input elements to be processed in each task.

14.2.3   Computing the option value

In this section, we will implement the function that approximates the Asian option value. Additionally, it will return an assessment of the uncertainty of the result by computing the 95% confidence interval of the value and will compute the probability that the option gives zero payoff.

IMPLEMENTING THE FUNCTION PERFORMING THE ASIAN OPTION VALUATION

Recall from section 14.1 that to approximate the value of the Asian option, we are going to use a Monte Carlo simulation. Therefore, we will need to run the `payoff_asian_sample` function defined in listing 14.1 multiple times. But how many times should we do this? In this section, we will use the following approach. Instead of specifying the number of repetitions *n* given in the formulas in section 14.1, we will allow the user to specify the time the simulation is allowed to run, and we will compute as many repetitions as possible within this time budget.

The reason we prefer to set a limit on computation time is that later we will use this function in a web service, and we want to be able to control the web service's response time to make sure its potential users do not have to wait very long for the results. Recall from chapter 1 that in the Timeline case study, long waiting times for a web application response were one of the reasons the company decided to switch to Julia.

To allow for controlling the maximum computation time, we will run the `payoff_asian_sample` function in batches of 10,000 by using the `ThreadsX.map` function, just as we did in section 14.2.2, until we reach the computation time passed by the user. We will repeatedly append the results of the `ThreadsX.map` function to a single collection of results. After finishing the computations using formulas given in section 14.1, we will compute the approximation of the option value, the 95% confidence interval of the price, and the probability that the option gives zero payoff. These steps are implemented in the `asian_value` function in the following listing.

Listing 14.2   Function that approximates the value of the Asian option

```
using Statistics

function asian_value(T, X0, K, r, s, m, max_time)
    result = Float64[]              ◁──── The result variable stores the simulated payoffs that are computed in 10,000-element batches.
    start_time = time()             ◁──── Records the time when we start the simulation
    while time() - start_time < max_time
        append!(result, ThreadsX.map(i -> payoff_asian_sample(T, X0, K,
                                                              r, s, m),
                            1:10_000))   ◁──── Until the max_time computation time is not exceeded, adds a 10,000-element batch of simulated payoffs
    end
    n = length(result)
    mv = mean(result)
    sdv = std(result)
    lo95 = mv - 1.96 * sdv / sqrt(n)
    hi95 = mv + 1.96 * sdv / sqrt(n)
    zero = mean(==(0), result)      ◁──── The ==(0) syntax is a shorthand for the x -> x == 0 anonymous function.
    return (; n, mv, lo95, hi95, zero)   ◁──── The (; n, mv, lo95, hi95, zero) syntax is shorthand for (n=n, mv=mv, lo95=lo95, hi95=hi95, zero=zero).
end
```

The `max_time` argument passed to the `asian_value` function should be given in seconds. In the function, we use the `time` function to get the current time measured in seconds. This measurement has microsecond resolution. In particular, the `time() - start_time` expression measures, in seconds, the time since the `while` loop present in the function body started.

In the `while` loop, we compute simulated payoffs of the Asian option in batches of 10,000 elements. We know from section 14.2 that computing each batch takes around

5 ms using four threads. We append the 10,000-element batches to the `result` vector by using the `append!` function.

After the loop finishes, we compute the following statistics by using formulas from section 14.1: the mean payoff, its 95% confidence interval, and the probability that the payoff is 0.

In the `mean(==(0), result)` expression, we use the same pattern that you learned in chapter 4 for the `sum` function. The `mean` function accepts a function as its first argument and a collection as its second argument. Then it efficiently computes the mean of values stored in the collection after transforming them by the passed function. Here is a simple example of this pattern at work:

```julia
julia> mean(x -> x ^ 2, 1:5)
11.0
```

The result of the operation is `11.0` since we compute the mean of squares of integers from 1 to 5—that is, `(1^2 + 2^2 + 3^2 + 4^2 + 5^2) / 5`.

USING PARTIAL FUNCTION APPLICATION SYNTAX

Another expression to note is `==(0)`. You know that, normally, the `==` operator requires two arguments and checks their equality. The `==(0)` is a *partial function application* operation (http://mng.bz/JVda). It fixes the right side of the `==` operation to be equal to 0.

The result of `==(0)` is a function that expects one argument and compares it to 0 by using the `==` operator. Therefore, you can think of `==(0)` as equivalent to defining an anonymous function `x -> x == 0` that fixes the right side of the operation to be 0. Here's an example of using the function returned by `==(0)`:

```julia
julia> eq0 = ==(0)
(::Base.Fix2{typeof(==), Int64}) (generic function with 1 method)

julia> eq0(1)
false

julia> eq0(0)
true
```

> ### Operations that support partial function application
>
> Partial function application is quite convenient because it makes the code more readable as compared to using anonymous functions.
>
> Additionally, repeatedly defining anonymous functions creates a new function each time, which requires their compilation each time (this is a more advanced topic). On the other hand, partial function application creates a definition only once, so it also is preferred from a compilation latency perspective.
>
> Therefore, in addition to `==`, common operations like `>`, `>=`, `<`, `<=`, and `isequal` also support the partial function application pattern.

EXERCISE 14.1   Using the @time macro, compare the time to compute the mean of values in the range -10^6:10^6 transformed by the <(0) and x -> x < 0 functions. Also check the timing when you predefine the lt0(x) = x < 0 function. Run each operation three times.

USING A CONVENIENT SYNTAX FOR CREATING A NAMEDTUPLE

The last new element that you learned in listing 14.2 is a notation that simplifies the creation of named tuples from variables. If you put in parentheses a semicolon (;) followed by a comma-separated list of variables, Julia creates a NamedTuple whose field names are the names of variables you used and whose values are the values of these variables. Here is an example:

```
julia> val1 = 10
10

julia> val2 = "x"
"x"

julia> (; val1, val2)
(val1 = 10, val2 = "x")
```

The result is equivalent to writing (val1=val1, val2=val2), but is shorter and more convenient to type and read. This pattern is commonly used when you want to return a NamedTuple from a function and want to store some variables that you have computed inside this function. This is what we did in the asian_value function.

TESTING THE ASIAN OPTION VALUATION FUNCTION

Before we move forward, let's test our asian_value function, giving it 0.25 seconds of computation time and keeping the values for all other parameters the same as those in our tests in section 14.2.2:

```
julia> @time asian_value(1.0, 50.0, 55.0, 0.05, 0.3, 200, 0.25)
  0.253619 seconds (19.76 k allocations: 30.483 MiB, 3.05% gc time,
                    18.78% compilation time)
(n = 300000, mv = 2.02427932454885, lo95 = 2.008366009684488,
 hi95 = 2.040192639413212, zero = 0.6931733333333333)

julia> @time asian_value(1.0, 50.0, 55.0, 0.05, 0.3, 200, 0.25)
  0.255105 seconds (17.30 k allocations: 39.226 MiB)
(n = 410000, mv = 2.026794692695957, lo95 = 2.01310815351485,
 hi95 = 2.0404812318770635, zero = 0.6940609756097561)

julia> @time asian_value(1.0, 50.0, 55.0, 0.05, 0.3, 200, 0.25)
  0.252337 seconds (16.89 k allocations: 38.398 MiB)
(n = 370000, mv = 2.0317793342921395, lo95 = 2.0173863909563443,
 hi95 = 2.0461722776279347, zero = 0.6943594594594594)
```

Each time, the function execution time is just a bit over 0.25 seconds. The first time, it is able to run 300,000 steps of the simulation, while the second and third times, respectively, it runs 410,000 and 370,000. This difference occurs because during the first run, Julia additionally needs to perform compilation of the code.

From a computational perspective, note that the obtained results are similar for all three runs of the simulation. With the 0.25-second time budget, the width of the 95% confidence interval is around 0.03. For the purposes of this chapter, let's assume that this is acceptable from the end user's perspective.

Multithreading in Julia

In this section, you have learned about the ThreadsX.jl package, which provides a high-level API enabling you to conveniently perform typical operations by using multiple threads.

Base Julia also has the `Threads` module, which provides a low-level API enabling you to write multithreaded code. The key element of this API is the `Threads.@spawn` macro (http://mng.bz/wyja), which creates a task and schedules it to run on an available thread. The `Threads` module also allows you to use locks (http://mng.bz/qoj6), which can help you avoid race condition problems and have support for atomic operations (http://mng.bz/5mo8) that are thread safe.

Many Julia packages take advantage of multithreading. For example, selected expensive operations in DataFrames.jl can take advantage of multiple threads. You can check the package documentation for the list (http://mng.bz/69np).

You can find more details about the functionality of the `Threads` module in the "Multithreading" section of the Julia Manual (http://mng.bz/o5ry).

14.3   Creating a web service serving the Asian option valuation

In this section, we will build a web service that will allow us to serve the Asian option valuation over the Hypertext Transfer Protocol (HTTP). For those who would like a refresher, see "An Overview of HTTP" on the MDN Web Docs site (http://mng.bz/ne1V).

Web services are currently one of the most popular methods of allowing applications to exchange messages. Their use became especially widespread when cloud computing became popular, since they allow for communication between software programs over the network, independent of the programming language used to create them or the platform on which they are run.

14.3.1   A general approach to building a web service

We want the web service to work as follows. Assume you have a client application and a web service running on a server. We want the client application to be allowed to send a request to the server, asking for the price of the Asian option. In response, the server returns information about the calculated price. The communication happens over the internet, using the HTTP protocol. Figure 14.2 shows a high-level view of this process.

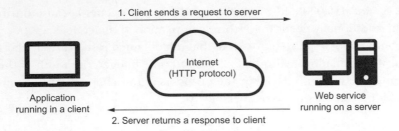

1. Client sends a request to server

Internet
(HTTP protocol)

Application
running in a client

Web service
running on a server

2. Server returns a response to client

Figure 14.2   Communication between a client application and a web service running on a server is done via HTTP.

How can the client send a request to the server? In this section, I show you how to use the POST method of HTTP to perform this action in Julia. To send such a request, we need to pass the following:

- The address we want to send the request to. In this chapter, we will use http:// 127.0.0.1:8000, which is the default in Genie.jl and refers to the current device (called the *local host*) and port 8000.
- The request header (request metadata).
- The request body (request data).

We want our web service to accept requests with data in JSON format. (We discussed JSON format in chapter 7.) The format of the request should allow the client to pass the parameters of the Asian option we are interested in. For simplicity, out of all parameters we discussed in section 14.1, we will allow the user to pass the value of the strike price *K*. An additional technical parameter that we will send is the time we allow the server to process the request before returning a response. To send such a query to the web service, we need to set in the request header the `Content-Type` metadata to `application/json`. The request body should be data in JSON format, specifying the value of *K* and the expected response time.

In response, the web service should return the values produced by the `asian_value` function defined in section 14.2—that is, the number of Monte Carlo samples used, the approximation of the Asian option price, the 95% confidence interval of this price, and the probability that the value of the option will be zero. All these values should also be sent using JSON format. We have already worked with this response type in chapter 7.

To create a web service, we will use the Genie.jl package. This full-stack web framework has all the components needed for developing web applications. In this section, I will use a limited and simplified set of functionalities of Genie.jl. If you would like to learn more about this package, check its documentation (http://mng.bz/qomJ).

> ### Web development in Julia
>
> In this chapter, we want to only build a web service. However, in general, Julia provides the full set of tools needed to build production web applications. The three key components of the Genie Framework are as follows:
>
> - *Genie.jl*—A web framework with features such as a flexible request router, web socket support, templating, and authentication
> - *SearchLight.jl*—Provides an object-relational mapping (ORM; www.altexsoft .com/blog/object-relational-mapping/) layer, allowing you to connect to PostgreSQL, MySQL, and SQLite databases
> - *Stipple.jl*—A reactive UI library for building interactive data applications
>
> If you would like to learn more about the Genie Framework, visit https://genieframe work.com.

14.3.2   *Creating a web service using Genie.jl*

To set up a simple web service, follow these steps:

1   Load the Genie.jl package.
2   Set `Genie.config.run_as_server` to `true` so that later the Genie.jl server will be started synchronously; the Julia process will handle the server operations only after the server is started. The visible effect will be that the `Genie .Server.up` function used to start the server will not return.
3   Define a mapping between a URL and the Julia function that should be invoked to send the response back to the client when it receives the request. This is achieved by using the `Genie.Router.route` function.
4   Start the server by calling `Genie.Server.up()`.

A crucial element of this procedure is understanding how to define the function that will handle the POST requests. In this section, we want our web service to accept JSON POST payloads; we want to allow clients of our web service to send JSON-formatted data in the request body. We also want the produced response to be in JSON format.

To process an `application/json` POST request, use the `Genie.Requests .jsonpayload` function. Then you can index the returned object to get its fields. If parsing JSON fails, `Genie.Requests.jsonpayload` returns `nothing`.

To produce a response that has the `application/json` content type, use the `Genie.Renderer.Json.json` function. We will pass `NamedTuple` value to it, as it conveniently gets converted to JSON in the body of the message, and an appropriate message header is added. Here is an example:

```
julia> using Genie

julia> Genie.Renderer.Json.json((firstname="Bogumił", lastname="Kamiński"))
HTTP.Messages.Response:
"""
HTTP/1.1 200 OK
```

```
Content-Type: application/json; charset=utf-8
```

```
{"firstname":"Bogumił","lastname":"Kamiński"}"""
```

We now know everything we need to create a web service. I have put its code in a separate ch14_server.jl file in the GitHub repository. The web service code is given in listing 14.3. The only new part is the handling of the web service. The payoff_asian_sample and asian_value functions are the same as we defined them in section 14.2.

In the code, we set a route for root ("/") accepting the POST payload. We use default settings of Genie.jl so we will be able to send POST requests to the address http://127.0.0.1:8000. For this route, we first store in the message variable the received JSON payload. We then have a try-catch-end block that tries to get data from the message and pass it to the asian_value function. Note that for simplicity, I have assumed that our web service accepts only the K and max_time parameters of the asian_value function.

We use the float function to make sure that both K and max_time, when passed to asian_value, are floating-point numbers. If the process of getting the JSON request and running the simulation is successful, we return a message with OK status and the value returned by the asian_value function. If anything breaks (for example, parameter K is not passed or is not numeric), an exception will be raised, and in the catch part of the block, we will return an ERROR status and an empty string as a value.

Listing 14.3   Creating the Asian option pricing web service

```
using Genie
using Statistics
using ThreadsX

function payoff_asian_sample(T, X0, K, r, s, m)::Float64
    X = X0
    sumX = X
    d = T / m
    for i in 1:m
        X *= exp((r - s^2 / 2) * d + s * sqrt(d) * randn())
        sumX += X
    end
    Y = sumX / (m + 1)
    return exp(-r * T) * max(Y - K, 0)
end

function asian_value(T, X0, K, r, s, m, max_time)
    result = Float64[]
    start_time = time()
    while time() - start_time < max_time
        append!(result,
                ThreadsX.map(i -> payoff_asian_sample(T, X0, K, r, s, m),
                        1:10_000))
    end
    n = length(result)
    mv = mean(result)
```

```
    sdv = std(result)
    lo95 = mv - 1.96 * sdv / sqrt(n)
    hi95 = mv + 1.96 * sdv / sqrt(n)
    zero = mean(==(0), result)
    return (; n, mv, lo95, hi95, zero)
end


Genie.config.run_as_server = true        ◁── Configures Genie.jl to
                                              start the web service
                                              synchronously

Genie.Router.route("/", method=POST) do                 ◁──
  message = Genie.Requests.jsonpayload()      ◁──
  return try
      K = float(message["K"])
      max_time = float(message["max_time"])
      value = asian_value(1.0, 50.0, K, 0.05, 0.3, 200, max_time)
      Genie.Renderer.Json.json((status="OK", value=value))
  catch
      Genie.Renderer.Json.json((status="ERROR", value=""))
  end
end

Genie.Server.up()   ◁──┤ Starts the web service
```

Uses the do-end block to define an anonymous function that will be invoked if the user passes the POST request to the root of the address where the web service will be made available

Parses the JSON payload sent in the POST request

Tries getting the parameters and computing the valuation of the Asian option; returns OK as a status and the value on success; otherwise, returns ERROR as a status

14.3.3 *Running the web service*

We are now ready to start our web service. Open a new terminal window, switch to the folder where you have cloned the GitHub repository, and run the `julia --project -t4 ch14_server.jl` command. You should see the following output:

```
$ julia --project -t4 ch14_server.jl
? Info:
? Web Server starting at http://127.0.0.1:8000 - press Ctrl/Cmd+C to stop
  the server.
```

Now we have a running server, so we can connect to it. Note that we have started it with four threads using the `-t4` switch. Do not close this terminal window.

Before we move forward, let me add one comment. In listing 14.3, when we get an incorrect request, we still send a response with the `200 OK` status to the client by using the `Genie.Renderer.Json.json((status="ERROR", value=""))` expression. An alternative way to handle this situation would be to return the `400 Bad Request` response. If you would prefer to respond with this status code, you should put the `Genie.Responses.setstatus(400)` expression in the `catch` part of listing 14.3 instead. If you would like to learn more about HTTP status codes, you can check the "HTTP Status Code Registry" page (http://mng.bz/4965).

14.4 *Using the Asian option pricing web service*

In this section, you will learn how to send requests to a web service and parse the received response. Learning how to do this is useful, as your programs will often need to use third-party web services. For this, we will use the HTTP.jl and JSON3.jl packages that you learned about in chapter 7.

As an example, we will check to see how the value of our Asian option changes as we change the strike price *K* in the range from 30 to 80, keeping all other parameters at values we fixed in section 14.3. This section is organized as follows:

1 We start with discussing how to send a single POST request to our web service.
2 We collect the results of multiple POST requests in a data frame.
3 The collected results have a complex structure, in which one column stores multiple values. We unnest each column into multiple columns to facilitate working with the data.
4 We visualize the results of our computations to verify that increasing the strike price *K* decreases the value of our Asian option and increases the probability that it gives zero payoff.

14.4.1 *Sending a single request to the web service*

Start a new Julia session (remember not to terminate the session where we are running our web service).

We start with sending a POST request to our web service. Recall that it is available at http://127.0.0.1:8000. Let's get the response for `K=55.0` and `max_time=0.25`, as these are values we already used in section 14.2. At a high level, figure 14.2 visualizes the process of communication between our client and web service:

```
julia> using HTTP

julia> using JSON3

julia> req = HTTP.post("http://127.0.0.1:8000",
                       ["Content-Type" => "application/json"],
                       JSON3.write((K=55.0, max_time=0.25)))
HTTP.Messages.Response:
"""
HTTP/1.1 200 OK
Content-Type: application/json; charset=utf-8
Server: Genie/Julia/1.7.2
Transfer-Encoding: chunked

{"status":"OK","value":{"n":190000,"mv":2.05363436780124,
"lo95":2.033372995802685,"hi95":2.0738957397997946,
"zero":0.6927631578947369}}"""

julia> JSON3.read(req.body)
JSON3.Object{Vector{UInt8}, Vector{UInt64}} with 2 entries:
  :status => "OK"
  :value  => {…
```

We already used the `JSON3.read` function in chapter 7 and know that it parses JSON data into a JSON object from which we can get data. The `JSON3.write` function, which we also use in the code, performs a reverse operation. It takes a Julia object and converts it to a JSON-formatted string. Let's see what `JSON3.write((K=55.0, max_time=0.25))` produces to make sure it is indeed properly formatted JSON data:

```
julia> JSON3.write((K=55.0, max_time=0.25))
"{\"K\":55.0,\"max_time\":0.25}"
```

We have not used HTTP.post yet either, since in chapter 7 we used the HTTP.get function. The difference between them is as follows. You use the HTTP.post function when you want to send a POST request, and you use HTTP.get when you want to send a GET request. Our web service expects the POST request, as we need to pass JSON data to it, called a *JSON payload* (the GET request does not support sending data in a request payload). You can find an overview of various HTTP request methods at the W3Schools website (www.w3schools.com/tags/ref_httpmethods.asp).

In the HTTP.post method, we pass the following arguments:

- The URL we want to query (http://127.0.0.1:8000 in our case).
- The header metadata. Since our content is application/json, we pass the "Content-Type" => "application/json" pair; it is wrapped in a vector, as potentially we might want to pass more metadata in the header.
- The body of the request, which is in JSON format.

Now switch for a moment to the terminal where you have our web service running. You will note that a message is printed there showing that the POST request was handled successfully:

```
:
[ Info: POST / 200
```

Now check to see what happens if we send an incorrect request to our web service:

```
julia> HTTP.post("http://127.0.0.1:8000",
                 ["Content-Type" => "application/json"],
                 JSON3.write((K="", max_time=0.25)))
HTTP.Messages.Response:
"""
HTTP/1.1 200 OK
Content-Type: application/json; charset=utf-8
Server: Genie/Julia/1.7.2
Transfer-Encoding: chunked

{"status":"ERROR","value":""}"""
```

This time, since we sent an empty string instead of a number as the K parameter, we get an ERROR in the status and an empty string as the value. Therefore, error handling in our web service seems to work correctly.

EXERCISE 14.2 Create a web service that accepts a JSON payload with a single element n that is an integer. It should return, in JSON format, a vector of n random numbers generated using the rand function. If the passed request is incorrect, a 400 Bad Request response should be produced. Run this web server on your local computer and test whether it works as expected.

14.4.2 *Collecting responses to multiple requests from a web service in a data frame*

Now we can collect the valuations of our Asian option for K varying from 30 to 80. In the code presented next, we first create a data frame in which each row stores the values of K that we want to check. Additionally, in this data frame, we store the max_time that we want to use (in the example, it is fixed to be equal to 0.25).

Next, for each row of our data frame, we run the HTTP.post function discussed in this section. To achieve this, we use the map function, passing the K and max_ time columns of the data frame as collections that we want to iterate. We store the results fetched from the web service in the data column. Since the process of getting the results is time-consuming, we print the value of K that we process by using the @show K macro call. In this way, we can easily watch the progress of the computations. Additionally, we print the time the web service took to produce the response to confirm that it is indeed around 0.25 seconds:

```julia
julia> using DataFrames

julia> df = DataFrame(K=30:2:80, max_time=0.25)
26×2 DataFrame
 Row │ K      max_time
     │ Int64  Float64
─────┼────────────────
   1 │    30      0.25
   2 │    32      0.25
   3 │    34      0.25
   ⋮ │    ⋮         ⋮
  24 │    76      0.25
  25 │    78      0.25
  26 │    80      0.25
        20 rows omitted
```

Initially populates the data frame with the values of the strike price K for which we want to compute the value of the Asian option and the maximum allowed computation time for each run

Sends a POST request to our web service for each pair of strike price K and computation time, using the map function, and stores the result in the data column of the data frame

```julia
julia> df.data = map(df.K, df.max_time) do K, max_time
           @show K
           @time req = HTTP.post("http://127.0.0.1:8000",
                                 ["Content-Type" => "application/json"],
                                 JSON3.write((;K, max_time)))
           return JSON3.read(req.body)
       end;
K = 30
  0.273856 seconds (194 allocations: 148.000 KiB)
K = 32
  0.282072 seconds (194 allocations: 12.500 KiB)
K = 34
  0.274884 seconds (194 allocations: 11.953 KiB)

...

K = 76
  0.271959 seconds (193 allocations: 11.609 KiB)
```

```
K = 78
  0.261515 seconds (194 allocations: 11.906 KiB)
K = 80
  0.269932 seconds (193 allocations: 11.625 KiB)
```

Now our `df` data frame has three columns: `K`, `max_time`, and `data`. The last column stores the JSON3 objects that are constructed from data returned by the web service:

```
julia> df
26×3 DataFrame
 Row │ K       max_time   data
     │ Int64   Float64    Object…

   1 │    30       0.25   {\n    "status": "OK",\n    "valu…
   2 │    32       0.25   {\n    "status": "OK",\n    "valu…
   3 │    34       0.25   {\n    "status": "OK",\n    "valu…
   ⋮ │    ⋮        ⋮                         ⋮
  24 │    76       0.25   {\n    "status": "OK",\n    "valu…
  25 │    78       0.25   {\n    "status": "OK",\n    "valu…
  26 │    80       0.25   {\n    "status": "OK",\n    "valu…
                                               20 rows omitted
```

First, check that in all cases we receive the `OK` status of the request, which will show that the web service processed them without a problem. To achieve this, we use the `all` function. We pass two positional arguments to this function. The first argument is a predicate function—in this case, an anonymous function checking whether the status is `OK`. The second is a collection of elements for which we want to check that the predicate is always `true`. Here is the code that performs the check:

```
julia> all(x -> x.status == "OK", df.data)
true
```

For all queries, we receive a response with the `OK` status.

14.4.3   Unnesting a column of a data frame

The information stored in the `data` column in the `df` data frame is slightly inconvenient to work with since it is nested. Each element of the `df.data` vector has an internal structure. Each entry of a vector stored in the `data` column has a `value` element. Recall from section 14.3 that each `value` element internally stores five sub-elements: `n`, `mv`, `lo95`, `hi95`, and `zero`. We want to create five new columns in our data frame using data extracted from these five sub-elements. This process is typically called *unnesting*.

Figure 14.3 illustrates an example of unnesting. The source data frame has a single column x. Each element of this column is a `NamedTuple` with fields a and b. When we unnest such a column, we create new columns in the target data frame, called a and b, that store the values from the respective fields of named tuples that form column x.

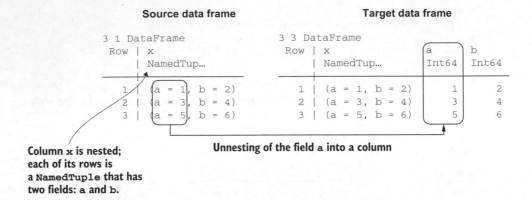

Figure 14.3   The x column in the source data frame is unnested into a and b columns in the target data frame. Unnesting often makes it easier to work with the stored data.

We can perform the unnesting by using the `select` function we already worked with in chapter 13. However, to perform this operation, we need to learn a new element of the operation specification syntax.

In chapters 12 and 13, you learned that the general structure of this syntax is `source_column => operation_function => target_column_name`. For example, when we write `:a => sum => :sum_a`, we want to get column a from a source data frame, apply the `sum` function to it, and store it in the `sum_a` column in the target data frame.

As we have already discussed, the `value` element of the stored JSON objects has five sub-elements: `n`, `mv`, `lo95`, `hi95`, and `zero`. Therefore, if we wanted to extract the n element, for example, we could write the following transformation specification (we discussed `ByRow` in chapter 13; recall that it transforms a function that accepts scalars to a function that is vectorized):

```
:data => ByRow(x -> x.value.n) => :n
```

However, we want to extract all five sub-elements of the `value` element. We could write five such transformation specification operations, but there is an easier way. In operation specification syntax, the `target_column_name` typically is the name of a column. However, we can instead pass a special `AsTable` expression as the target column name. If we do this, DataFrames.jl will try to extract the elements stored in the return value of the operation function into multiple columns. The names of the columns will be automatically generated using the names of the elements that are unnested. This process is easiest to explain by example. Assume, following figure 14.3, that we have a data frame whose column x stores named tuples that have properties a and b:

```
julia> small_df = DataFrame(x=[(a=1, b=2), (a=3, b=4), (a=5, b=6)])
3×1 DataFrame
```

```
Row | x
    | NamedTup...
    |
  1 | (a = 1, b = 2)
  2 | (a = 3, b = 4)
  3 | (a = 5, b = 6)
```

We now want to unnest the properties :a and :b as new columns. We can write this:

```
julia> transform(small_df, :x => identity => AsTable)
3×3 DataFrame
Row | x                 a       b
    | NamedTup...        Int64   Int64
    |
  1 | (a = 1, b = 2)         1       2
  2 | (a = 3, b = 4)         3       4
  3 | (a = 5, b = 6)         5       6
```

Or, as explained in chapter 13, you can omit the operation function if it is not required and write this:

```
julia> transform(small_df, :x => AsTable)
3×3 DataFrame
Row | x                 a       b
    | NamedTup...        Int64   Int64
    |
  1 | (a = 1, b = 2)         1       2
  2 | (a = 3, b = 4)         3       4
  3 | (a = 5, b = 6)         5       6
```

We now know that we can use AsTable as the target column name to unnest the data stored in the value element from the JSON objects contained in the data column of the df data frame. We also want to keep the K column to have information on which row represents which value of the strike price. Here is the code that performs the required operation:

```
julia> df2 = select(df, :K, :data => ByRow(x -> x.value) => AsTable)
26×6 DataFrame
Row | K       n        mv          lo95        hi95        zero
    | Int64   Int64    Float64     Float64     Float64     Float64
    |
  1 |    30   420000   20.2203     20.1943     20.2462     0.000795238
  2 |    32   370000   18.3586     18.3309     18.3863     0.0030973
  3 |    34   410000   16.4279     16.4017     16.4541     0.00917805
  : |    :        :         :           :           :           :
 24 |    76   400000    0.0566558   0.054339    0.0589726  0.988712
 25 |    78   400000    0.0378442   0.035959    0.0397294  0.9924
 26 |    80   390000    0.0256958   0.0241446   0.027247   0.994672
                                                       20 rows omitted
```

14.4.4 Plotting the results of Asian option pricing

To visualize the obtained results, we will create two plots. In the first, we want to show the value of our Asian option as a function of the strike price. In the second, the probability of zero payoff of this option as a function of the strike price is visualized. We expect that as the strike price grows, the value of the option drops, and the probability of zero payoff grows. We generate the plot with the following code:

```julia
julia> using Plots

julia> plot(plot(df2.K, df2.mv; legend=false,
                 xlabel="K", ylabel="expected value"),
            plot(df2.K, df2.zero; legend=false,
                 xlabel="K", ylabel="probability of zero"))
```

Figure 14.4 shows the result.

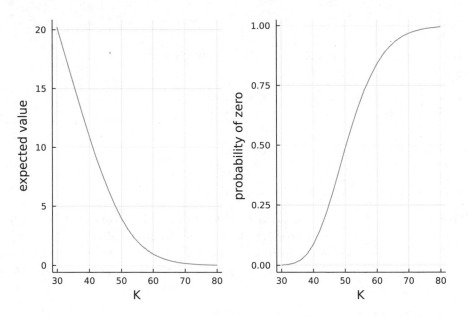

Figure 14.4   Plotting the approximated value of the Asian option and the probability of zero payoff of the option as a function of K**. The higher the probability of zero payoff of our option, the lower its value.**

Before we finish our work, remember to terminate the web service. Go to the terminal window where your web service is running, and press Ctrl-C (on Windows and Linux) or Cmd-C (on a Mac). Now the terminal should show your system prompt, indicating that the web service is terminated.

Summary

- Asian options are complex financial instruments. They often do not have a closed-form formula that would allow you to compute their value. In such situations, you can use a Monte Carlo simulation to approximate this value. In a

Monte Carlo simulation, we randomly sample the evolution of the stock price underlying the Asian option multiple times, and for each sample, we compute the option's payoff. The mean of these payoffs allows us to compute the approximate value of the Asian option.

- Pricing financial assets by using a Monte Carlo simulation is compute intensive. Julia is a good choice for this task since it is a fast language.

- Julia natively supports multithreading. To allow your Julia process to use multiple threads, pass the `-tN` option when you start it, where `N` is the desired number of threads. Built-in support for multithreading is one of the features that distinguishes Julia from R or Python. This functionality allows your programs to run faster, as they can take advantage of the multiple CPU cores on which Julia is run.

- The `Threads` module provides a low-level API for writing multithreaded code in Julia. It offers all standard components (like spawning tasks, atomics, and locks) that are needed to write advanced code using multithreading.

- The ThreadsX.jl package provides a high-level API allowing you to easily run standard functions (for example, `map` using multiple threads).

- The functionalities of the `Threads` module and the ThreadsX.jl package taken together enable simple operations to be easily parallelized in Julia, even by non-experts. In addition, writing complex multithreaded code is possible, and experts can squeeze out maximum performance from the available CPU.

- When you write code that has a limited time budget for computations and you still want it to use multithreading, a useful pattern is to process data in batches. The batch size should be big enough that you get the benefit of multithreading, but also small enough that performing computations for a single batch requires a small amount of the available time budget. This technique is often useful when you write applications that serve data interactively and need to ensure that your users can decide how long they can wait for the results.

- Several operators in Julia (like ==, >, and <) allow for partial function application. Therefore, writing `==(0)` has the same effect as defining an anonymous function `x -> x == 0`. Using the partial function application pattern leads to more-readable code that also requires less compilation than using anonymous functions.

- The Genie.jl package is a full-stack web framework that allows you to create complex web applications. In data science workflows using Genie.jl, you can easily create web services, which allow you to use HTTP to serve the results of your analysis.

- When designing web services, you can use the HTTP POST request method to allow client applications to send data to the server in the body of the request. The server is informed about the format of your data through the value of the `Content-Type` header of the request.

- Using Genie.jl, you can design your web service so that it accepts POST requests containing a JSON payload specifying the parameters of the user's request and also returns the response in JSON format. Using this web service design, you can easily integrate Julia code with code written in other programming languages, as HTTP and the JSON format abstract out the implementation details of your web service.

- You can easily unnest a column in a data frame that contains complex structures (for example, named tuples or JSON objects) by using `AsTable` as the target column name in the operation specification syntax. This functionality is useful when working with data organized hierarchically, which is often the case, for example, when data is stored in JSON format.

appendix A
First steps with Julia

This appendix covers

- Installing and setting up Julia
- Getting help in Julia
- Where to look for help about Julia
- Managing packages in Julia
- Overview about standard ways to work with Julia

A.1 Installing and setting up Julia

In this section, I explain how to get, install, and configure your Julia environment. First, visit the "Download Julia" web page (https://julialang.org/downloads/), and download the version of Julia appropriate for the operating system you use.

This book was written and tested with Julia 1.7. When you read this book, a newer version of Julia will likely be available in the "Downloads" section. This should not be a problem. The code we use should work under any newer 1.*x* version of Julia. Slight differences, however, might exist in, for example, the way Julia displays the output. If you would like to use the Julia version that matches the one that I used when writing this book, you should be able to find Julia 1.7 on the "Older Unmaintained Releases" page (https://julialang.org/downloads/oldreleases/).

After downloading the appropriate Julia version for your operating system, go to the "Platform Specific Instructions for Official Binaries" page (https://julialang.org/downloads/platform/), and follow the setup instructions for your operating system. In particular, make sure to add Julia to your PATH environment variable so the Julia executable can be easily run on your system (the instructions are operating-system specific and given on the website). After this process, you should be able to start Julia by opening a terminal and typing the julia command.

The following is a minimal Julia session run from a terminal. Before running the example, I opened a terminal on my computer. The $ sign is an operating system prompt on my machine.

You first start Julia by typing the julia command. Then the Julia banner and julia> prompt are shown, indicating that you can now execute Julia commands. To terminate Julia, type the exit() command and go back to the operating system, which is indicated by the $ prompt:

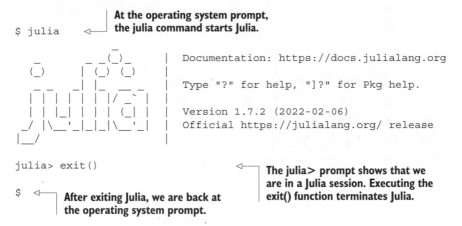

In this book, I consistently use this style of presenting output. All commands that you should send to Julia are given after the julia> prompt. The rest of the text shown is what is automatically printed on the terminal.

A.2   *Getting help in and about Julia*

In this section, I explain how to get help in Julia and how to find standard resources from which you can learn about Julia.

Julia has a built-in help mode. When you are in this mode, Julia will attempt to print documentation about the text you type.

Here's an example of how to get help regarding the && operator. Start following the example at the Julia prompt. First, press the question-mark key to type ?. The prompt will change from julia> to help?>, indicating that you are in help mode. Now type &&, and press Enter to get information about this operator:

```
julia> ?
                                    Upon typing ?, the prompt
help?> &&                           changes (in place) to help?>.
search: &&

  x && y

  Short-circuiting boolean AND.

  See also &, the ternary operator ? :, and the manual section on control
      flow.

  Examples
  ==========

  julia> x = 3;

  julia> x > 1 && x < 10 && x isa Int
  true

  julia> x < 0 && error("expected positive x")
  false
```

Typically, in Julia documentation, you will get an explanation about what a given command does, along with information about other related commands and examples of how it can be used.

Apart from the built-in help, Julia has extensive documentation available on the web. The most important resource is the Julia Documentation (https://docs.julialang.org/en/v1/), which has three parts. The first part is a complete manual of the language, the second covers documentation of all functions available in a standard Julia installation, and the third discusses Julia internals.

Most of the packages have documentation sites. For example, the DataFrames.jl package has documentation at https://dataframes.juliadata.org/stable/. Both Julia Documentation and documentation created for packages have a similar design. This is because the Documenter.jl package is used as a default method for building documentation from docstrings and Markdown files.

On the Julia website, you can find additional links to teaching materials in the "Learn" section (https://julialang.org/learning/). They include YouTube videos, interactive tutorials, and a list of books that can help you learn various aspects of working with Julia.

Julia's online communities are important resources for any Julia user. If you have any questions about Julia, I recommend you start with the Discourse forum (https://discourse.julialang.org). For more casual conversations, you can use Slack (https://julialang.org/slack/) or Zulip (https://julialang.zulipchat.com/register/). The Julia language and most of its packages are hosted on GitHub. Therefore, if you would like to report a bug or submit a feature request, open an issue in an appropriate GitHub repository. For example, for the DataFrames.jl package, you can do this by following https://github.com/JuliaData/DataFrames.jl/issues.

Finally, Julia has a presence on Stack Overflow under the [julia] tag (https://stackoverflow.com/tags/julia).

A.3 *Managing packages in Julia*

An integrated part of Julia is its package manager. It allows you to install and manage the packages that you might want to use in your projects. In this section, I present the most important information about managing packages in Julia. An in-depth discussion of this topic is available in the Pkg.jl documentation (https://pkgdocs.julialang.org/v1/).

A.3.1 *Project environments*

The key concept when discussing packages in Julia is *environments*: independent sets of packages that can be local to an individual project or shared and selected by name. The exact set of packages and versions in an environment is captured in the Project.toml and Manifest.toml files. For example, in the GitHub repository accompanying this book (https://github.com/bkamins/JuliaForDataAnalysis), you can find these two files in the root folder. You do not need to manually edit these files or understand their structure in detail, but it is useful to have a general understanding of their content.

The Project.toml file specifies which packages can be loaded directly in a given project. Here is part of this file taken from the book's code:

```
[deps]
Arrow = "69666777-d1a9-59fb-9406-91d4454c9d45"
BenchmarkTools = "6e4b80f9-dd63-53aa-95a3-0cdb28fa8baf"
CSV = "336ed68f-0bac-5ca0-87d4-7b16caf5d00b"
```

The Manifest.toml file contains more information. It includes all packages required by the project—that is, the ones listed in the Project.toml file (called *direct dependencies*) and all other packages that are required to properly set up the project environment (packages required by the packages listed in Project.toml, called *indirect dependencies*). For each package, exact information about the version used in your project is given. Here is part of this file taken from the book's code:

```
# This file is machine-generated - editing it directly is not advised

julia_version = "1.7.2"
manifest_format = "2.0"

[[deps.AbstractFFTs]]
deps = ["ChainRulesCore", "LinearAlgebra"]
git-tree-sha1 = "69f7020bd72f069c219b5e8c236c1fa90d2cb409"
uuid = "621f4979-c628-5d54-868e-fcf4e3e8185c"
version = "1.2.1"

[[deps.Adapt]]
deps = ["LinearAlgebra"]
git-tree-sha1 = "af92965fb30777147966f58acb05da51c5616b5f"
uuid = "79e6a3ab-5dfb-504d-930d-738a2a938a0e"
version = "3.3.3"
```

In summary, if a certain folder contains Project.toml and Manifest.toml files, they define a project environment.

A.3.2   *Activating project environments*

After you start your Julia session, you can start package manager mode by pressing the square bracket key (]) on your keyboard. When you do this, the prompt will change from `julia>` to `pkg>`, indicating that you are in package manager mode. By default, this prompt will look like this:

```
(@v1.7) pkg>
```

Note that before the `pkg>` prompt, you have the `(@v1.7)` prefix. It shows you that Julia is using the default (global) project environment. The default environment is provided by Julia for user convenience, but it is recommended to not rely on it in your projects and instead use project-specific Project.toml and Manifest.toml files. I will explain how to activate this environment by using the GitHub repository accompanying this book (https://github.com/bkamins/JuliaForDataAnalysis).

Before proceeding, download this repository to a folder on your computer. In the examples that follow, I assume you have this repository stored in the D:\JuliaForData-Analysis folder (this is an example path on Windows; under Linux or macOS, the path will look different).

To activate the project-specific environment, you need to do the following (this is the simplest scenario):

1. Change the working directory of Julia to the D:\JuliaForDataAnalysis folder, using the `cd` function.
2. Check if Project.toml and Manifest.toml are present in the working directory, using the `isfile` function. (This is not strictly required, but I include this step so you can be sure that you have these files in the working directory.)
3. Switch to package manager mode by pressing the] key.
4. Activate the project environment by using the `activate .` command.
5. Optionally, instantiate the environment by using the `instantiate` command. (This step makes sure Julia downloads all required packages from the web and is required if you are using a project environment for the first time.)
6. Leave package manager mode by pressing the backspace key.

Here is the code for these steps:

```
julia> cd("D:/JuliaForDataAnalysis")        ◁───   In Windows, you can use a
                                                    slash (/) instead of a backslash
julia> isfile("Project.toml")                       (\) as a separator in paths.
true

julia> isfile("Manifest.toml")
true
                                             ┌─  Press the ] key to switch to
(@v1.7) pkg> activate .         ◁────────────┘   package manager mode.
  Activating project at `D:\JuliaForDataAnalysis`
```

```
(JuliaForDataAnalysis) pkg> instantiate

julia>
```
◁─┐ **Press the Backspace key to
     switch back to Julia mode.**

Note that in Windows, you can use a slash (/) instead of a standard backslash (\) as a separator in paths.

In the `activate` command, we pass a dot (.), which indicates the current working directory of Julia. We can avoid changing the working directory via the `cd` function and instead pass the path to the environment in the `activate` command like this:

```
(@v1.7) pkg> activate D:/JuliaForDataAnalysis
  Activating project at `D:\JuliaForDataAnalysis`

(JuliaForDataAnalysis) pkg>
```

I prefer to switch the working directory of Julia to the place where the Project.toml and Manifest.toml files are stored because usually they are stored in the same directory as other project files (like Julia code or source data).

Observe that after changing the project environment, its name is shown as a prefix to the `pkg>` prompt. In our case, this prefix is (JuliaForDataAnalysis).

After you have activated the environment, all operations that you will perform (for example, using packages or adding or removing packages) will be done in the context of the activated environment.

In the following typical scenarios, activation of the project environment is simplified:

- If you are at the operating system prompt in a terminal in a folder containing the Project.toml and Manifest.toml files, then when you start Julia using a `julia --project` call, the project environment defined by these files will automatically be activated.
- If you are using Visual Studio Code (discussed in section A.4) and have opened a folder containing Project.toml and Manifest.toml files, and you then start Julia server, Visual Studio Code will automatically activate the project environment defined by these files.
- If you are using a Jupyter interactive environment (discussed in section A.4), then, similarly to the previous scenarios, if the folder containing the Jupyter notebook also has the Project.toml and Manifest.toml files, the environment defined by them is automatically activated.

Running code examples from this book

The GitHub repository accompanying this book (https://github.com/bkamins/Julia ForDataAnalysis) contains Project.toml and Manifest.toml files that specify the project environment used in all code examples I present. Therefore, I recommend that when you test any code examples from this book, you run them when this project environment is activated. This will ensure that you do not have to manually install any packages and that the versions of the packages you use match the versions of the packages I used when creating the book.

A.3.3 Potential issues with installing packages

Some Julia packages require external dependencies before they can be used. This issue is encountered mainly if you are working in Linux. If this is the case, the documentation of respective Julia packages typically provides all required installation instructions.

For example, if we consider packages used in this book, you might need some configuration if you want to use Plots.jl for plotting. By default, this package uses the GR Framework (https://gr-framework.org) to display created graphs. In Linux, to use this framework, you need to have several dependencies installed, as explained at https://gr-framework.org/julia.html. For example, if you use Ubuntu, use the following command to ensure that all dependencies are available:

```
apt install libxt6 libxrender1 libxext6 libgl1-mesa-glx libqt5widgets5
```

Another potential issue with using packages that rely on external binary dependencies is that you might need to manually invoke their build script. This is sometimes needed when, for example, the binaries of the dependencies that the package relies on change. In such a case, invoke the `build` command in package manager mode (the prompt should be `pkg>`). This will invoke build scripts of all packages that have them.

A.3.4 Managing packages

After you have activated and instantiated your project environment, you can start writing Julia programs that use the packages the given environment provides. However, you will occasionally want to manage available packages. The most common package management operations are listing available packages, adding packages, removing packages, and updating packages. I'll show you how to perform these operations. In the following examples, I will work in an empty folder, D:\Example, to make sure that we do not accidentally modify project environments you already have.

First, create the D:\Example folder (or any empty folder), and start your terminal in this folder. Next, start Julia by using the `julia` command, and use the `pwd` function to make sure that you are in an appropriate folder:

```
$ julia
               _
   _       _ _(_)_     |  Documentation: https://docs.julialang.org
  (_)     | (_) (_)    |
   _ _   _| |_  __ _   |  Type "?" for help, "]?" for Pkg help.
  | | | | | | |/ _` |  |
  | | |_| | | | (_| |  |  Version 1.7.2 (2022-02-06)
 _/ |\__'_|_|_|\__'_|  |  Official https://julialang.org/ release
|__/                   |

julia> pwd()
"D:\\Example"
```

Now switch to package manager mode by pressing the] key, and activate the environment in the current working directory:

```
(@v1.7) pkg> activate .
  Activating new project at `D:\Example`

(Example) pkg>
```

This is a new and empty environment. We can check it by running the status command:

```
(Example) pkg> status
      Status `D:\Example\Project.toml` (empty project)
```

We now add the BenchmarkTools.jl package to this environment by using the add BenchmarkTools command:

```
(Example) pkg> add BenchmarkTools
    Updating registry at `D:\.julia\registries\General`
    Updating git-repo `https://github.com/JuliaRegistries/General.git`
  Resolving package versions...
    Updating `D:\Example\Project.toml`
  [6e4b80f9] + BenchmarkTools v1.3.1
    Updating `D:\Example\Manifest.toml`
  [6e4b80f9] + BenchmarkTools v1.3.1
  [682c06a0] + JSON v0.21.3
  [69de0a69] + Parsers v2.2.3
  [56f22d72] + Artifacts
  [ade2ca70] + Dates
  [8f399da3] + Libdl
  [37e2e46d] + LinearAlgebra
  [56ddb016] + Logging
  [a63ad114] + Mmap
  [de0858da] + Printf
  [9abbd945] + Profile
  [9a3f8284] + Random
  [ea8e919c] + SHA
  [9e88b42a] + Serialization
  [2f01184e] + SparseArrays
  [10745b16] + Statistics
  [cf7118a7] + UUIDs
  [4ec0a83e] + Unicode
  [e66e0078] + CompilerSupportLibraries_jll
  [4536629a] + OpenBLAS_jll
  [8e850b90] + libblastrampoline_jll
```

In the process, we get information indicating that the BenchmarkTools entry is added to the Project.toml file and a list of packages is added to the Manifest.toml file. The plus (+) character indicates that a package was added. Recall that Manifest.toml contains both direct dependencies of our project and other packages that are required to properly set up the project environment.

Let's check the status of our project environment again:

```
(Example) pkg> status
      Status `D:\Example\Project.toml`
  [6e4b80f9] BenchmarkTools v1.3.1
```

We see that now we have the BenchmarkTools.jl package installed in version 1.3.1.

After some time, a new release of BenchmarkTools.jl might be made available. You can update the versions of the installed packages to their latest releases by using the update command. In our case, since we have just installed the BenchmarkTools.jl package, the command will not make any changes:

```
(Example) pkg> update
    Updating registry at `D: \.julia\registries\General`
    Updating git-repo `https://github.com/JuliaRegistries/General.git`
  No Changes to `D:\Example\Project.toml`
  No Changes to `D:\Example\Manifest.toml`
```

Finally, if you want to remove a package from your project environment, use the remove command:

```
(Example) pkg> remove BenchmarkTools
    Updating `D:\Example\Project.toml`
  [6e4b80f9] - BenchmarkTools v1.3.1
    Updating `D:\Example\Manifest.toml`
  [6e4b80f9] - BenchmarkTools v1.3.1
  [682c06a0] - JSON v0.21.3
  [69de0a69] - Parsers v2.2.3
  [56f22d72] - Artifacts
  [ade2ca70] - Dates
  [8f399da3] - Libdl
  [37e2e46d] - LinearAlgebra
  [56ddb016] - Logging
  [a63ad114] - Mmap
  [de0858da] - Printf
  [9abbd945] - Profile
  [9a3f8284] - Random
  [ea8e919c] - SHA
  [9e88b42a] - Serialization
  [2f01184e] - SparseArrays
  [10745b16] - Statistics
  [cf7118a7] - UUIDs
  [4ec0a83e] - Unicode
  [e66e0078] - CompilerSupportLibraries_jll
  [4536629a] - OpenBLAS_jll
  [8e850b90] - libblastrampoline_jll

(Example) pkg> status
    Status `D:\Example\Project.toml` (empty project)
```

The package manager not only removes the BenchmarkTools package from Project.toml but also removes all unneeded packages from Manifest.toml. The minus (-) character indicates the removal of a package.

A.3.5 *Setting up integration with Python*

The PyCall.jl package offers integration of Julia with Python. We discuss the use of this package in chapter 5. Here, I discuss the process of its installation on Windows and Mac systems.

In the Example project environment we have just created, add the PyCall.jl package (I cropped the list of packages added to Manifest.toml because it is long):

```
(Example) pkg> add PyCall
  Resolving package versions...
   Updating `D:\Example\Project.toml`
 [438e738f] + PyCall v1.93.1
   Updating `D:\Example\Manifest.toml`
 [8f4d0f93] + Conda v1.7.0
 [682c06a0] + JSON v0.21.3
 [1914dd2f] + MacroTools v0.5.9


...


 [83775a58] + Zlib_jll
 [8e850b90] + libblastrampoline_jll
 [8e850ede] + nghttp2_jll
```

Normally, the entire configuration process should happen automatically, and you should be able to start using Python at this point. Let's check the path to the Python executable that is used by the PyCall.jl package by default:

```
julia> using PyCall

julia> PyCall.python
"C:\\Users\\user\\.julia\\conda\\3\\python.exe"
```

As you can see, the Python installation is inside the Julia installation in the conda directory. This is because by default, on Windows and Mac systems, when you install the PyCall.jl package, a minimal Python distribution (via Miniconda) that is private to Julia (not in your PATH) is installed. Alternatively, you can specify another Python installation that should be used, as explained in the documentation (http://mng.bz/lRVM).

The situation is different under GNU/Linux systems, in which PyCall.jl will default to using the python3 program (if any—otherwise, python) in your PATH.

A.3.6 *Setting up integration with R*

The RCall.jl package provides integration of Julia with the R language. We discuss this package in chapter 10. I'll show you how to install it.

As a first step, I recommend you download and install R on your machine. You must do this before starting your Julia session, as otherwise you will get an error when trying to install the RCall.jl package.

Windows users can find installation instructions at https://cran.r-project.org/bin/windows/base/, and macOS users at https://cran.r-project.org/bin/macosx/.

If you are using Linux, the installation will depend on the distribution you use. If you are using Ubuntu, you can find instructions that you can follow at http://mng.bz/BZAg.

After you complete this installation, when the RCall.jl package is added, the operating system should be able to automatically detect it.

While in the Example project environment, we add the RCall.jl package (I cropped the list of packages added to Manifest.toml because it is long):

```
(Example) pkg> add RCall
   Resolving package versions...
   Installed DualNumbers _____ v0.6.7
   Installed NaNMath _____ v1.0.0
   Installed InverseFunctions _ v0.1.3
   Installed Compat _____ v3.42.0
   Installed LogExpFunctions __ v0.3.7
    Updating `D:\Example\Project.toml`
  [6f49c342] + RCall v0.13.13
    Updating `D:\Example\Manifest.toml`
  [49dc2e85] + Calculus v0.5.1
  [324d7699] + CategoricalArrays v0.10.3
  [d360d2e6] + ChainRulesCore v1.13.0

...

  [cf7118a7] + UUIDs
  [05823500] ⊢ OpenLibm_jll
  [3f19e933] + p7zip_jll
```

Normally, the RCall.jl package should be able to detect your R installation automatically. You can check that it is working by using the package and checking the location of the R executable:

```
julia> using RCall

julia> RCall.Rhome
"C:\\Program Files\\R\\R-4.1.2"
```

If you have problems with automatic detection of R installation on your machine, refer to the documentation (http://mng.bz/dedX) for more detailed instructions since they depend on the operating system you use.

A.4   Reviewing standard ways to work with Julia

In this section, I discuss the four most common ways users work with Julia:

- Using the terminal and the Julia executable
- Using Visual Studio Code
- Using Jupyter Notebook
- Using Pluto notebooks

A.4.1   Using a terminal

The terminal is the most basic way to work with Julia. You have two options for running Julia.

The first option is to start an interactive session by running the `julia` executable. Then, as discussed in section A.1, you will see the `julia>` prompt and will be able to execute Julia commands interactively.

The second option is to run Julia scripts. If your Julia code is stored in a file (for example, named code.jl), then by running `julia code.jl`, you will ask Julia to run the code stored in code.jl and then terminate.

Additionally, the Julia executable can take multiple command-line options and switches. You can find a complete list in the "Command-Line Options" section of the Julia Manual (http://mng.bz/rnjZ).

A.4.2   *Using Visual Studio Code*

A popular option for working with Julia is to use Visual Studio Code. You can download this integrated development environment at https://code.visualstudio.com/.

Next, you need to install the Julia extension. You can find instructions at http://mng.bz/VyRO. The extension provides such features as built-in dynamic autocompletion, inline results, plot pane, integrated REPL, variable view, code navigation, a debugger, and many more. Check the extension's documentation to learn how to use and configure all the options.

A.4.3   *Using Jupyter Notebook*

Julia code can be run in Jupyter notebooks (https://jupyter.org). This combination allows you to interact with the Julia language by using a graphical notebook, which combines code, formatted text, math, and multimedia in a single document.

To use Julia in Jupyter Notebook, first install the IJulia.jl package. Next, the simplest way to run an IJulia notebook in your browser is to run the following code:

```
using IJulia
notebook()
```

For more advanced installation options, such as specifying a specific Jupyter installation to use, see the IJulia.jl package documentation (https://julialang.github.io/IJulia.jl/stable/).

A.4.4   *Using Pluto notebooks*

Pluto notebooks allow you to combine code and text, just like Jupyter notebooks. The difference is that Pluto notebooks are reactive: if you change a variable, Pluto automatically reruns the cells that refer to it. Cells can be placed in arbitrary order in the notebook, as it automatically identifies dependencies between them. Additionally, Pluto notebooks understand which packages are being used in a notebook. You do not need to install packages yourself, as Pluto notebooks automatically manage the project environment for you.

You can learn more details about the features of Pluto notebooks and how to use them on the package website (https://github.com/fonsp/Pluto.jl).

appendix B
Solutions to exercises

EXERCISE 3.1

Create an x variable that is a range of values from 1 to 10^6. Now, using the collect function, create a y vector holding the same values as the x range. Using the @btime macro, check the time of sorting x and y by using the sort function. Finally, using the @edit macro, check the implementation of the sort function that would be invoked when you sort the x range.

SOLUTION

```
julia> using BenchmarkTools

julia> x = 1:10^6;

julia> y = collect(x);

julia> @btime sort($x);
  1.100 ns (0 allocations: 0 bytes)

julia> @btime sort($y);
  7.107 ms (2 allocations: 7.63 MiB)

julia> @edit sort(x)
```

Observe that sorting the x range is much faster than sorting the y vector. If you have a properly configured Julia environment (see appendix A for instructions), calling @edit sort(x) should take you to the editor and show you the following method definition:

```
sort(r::AbstractUnitRange) = r
```

EXERCISE 4.1

Rewrite the expression [cor(aq[:, i], aq[:, i+1]) for i in 1:2:7] by using views (either the view function or the @view macro). Compare the performance of both approaches by using the `@benchmark` macro from the BenchmarkTools.jl package.

SOLUTION

```
julia> using Statistics

julia> using BenchmarkTools

julia> aq = [10.0    8.04   10.0  9.14   10.0   7.46    8.0   6.58
                8.0    6.95    8.0  8.14    8.0   6.77    8.0   5.76
               13.0    7.58   13.0  8.74   13.0  12.74    8.0   7.71
                9.0    8.81    9.0  8.77    9.0   7.11    8.0   8.84
               11.0    8.33   11.0  9.26   11.0   7.81    8.0   8.47
               14.0    9.96   14.0  8.1    14.0   8.84    8.0   7.04
                6.0    7.24    6.0  6.13    6.0   6.08    8.0   5.25
                4.0    4.26    4.0  3.1     4.0   5.39   19.0  12.50
               12.0   10.84   12.0  9.13   12.0   8.15    8.0   5.56
                7.0    4.82    7.0  7.26    7.0   6.42    8.0   7.91
                5.0    5.68    5.0  4.74    5.0   5.73    8.0   6.89];
```

We now run the first benchmark:

```
julia> @benchmark [cor($aq[:, i], $aq[:, i+1]) for i in 1:2:7]
```

It produces the following output:

```
BenchmarkTools.Trial: 10000 samples with 199 evaluations.
 Range (min … max):  468.844 ns …   4.577 µs  │ GC (min … max): 0.00% … 88.63%
 Time  (median):     515.578 ns               │ GC (median):    0.00%
 Time  (mean ± σ):   546.053 ns ± 166.823 ns  │ GC (mean ± σ):  1.81% ±  5.68%
```

```
 469 ns        Histogram: log(frequency) by time        1.19 µs <
```

```
Memory estimate: 1.22 KiB, allocs estimate: 9.
```

Now run the second benchmark:

```
julia> @benchmark [cor(view($aq, :, i), view($aq, :, i+1)) for i in 1:2:7]
```

This time the execution is faster, as you can see in the following output:

```
BenchmarkTools.Trial: 10000 samples with 390 evaluations.
 Range (min … max):  243.077 ns …   1.632 µs  │ GC (min … max): 0.00% … 84.26%
 Time  (median):     254.103 ns               │ GC (median):    0.00%
 Time  (mean ± σ):   267.219 ns ± 56.193 ns   │ GC (mean ± σ):  0.39% ±  2.35%
```

```
 243 ns        Histogram: log(frequency) by time        476 ns <
```

```
Memory estimate: 96 bytes, allocs estimate: 1.
```

The results of the benchmarks show that using views almost halved the execution time of the code.

If you wanted to use the @view macro, the code would be as follows:

```
[cor(@view(aq[:, i]), @view(aq[:, i+1])) for i in 1:2:7]
```

In the example code, note that we used the $ prefix in front of the aq variable to correctly pass it to the @benchmark macro (see chapter 2 for an explanation of this rule).

EXERCISE 4.2

Rewrite the code solving the Sicherman puzzle, wrapping the logic of the processing in functions. Create one function, dice_distribution, that produces a dictionary with a distribution of the sum of possible combinations of values on two dice passed as its arguments. Next, write another function, test_dice, in which you create the all_dice variable and the two_standard variable, and you finally run the main loop comparing the distribution of all dice from the all_dice vector against the two_standard distribution.

SOLUTION

```
function dice_distribution(dice1, dice2)
    distribution = Dict{Int, Int}()
    for i in dice1
        for j in dice2
            s = i + j
            if haskey(distribution, s)
                distribution[s] += 1
            else
                distribution[s] = 1
            end
        end
    end
    return distribution
end

function test_dice()
    all_dice = [[1, x2, x3, x4, x5, x6]
                for x2 in 2:11
                for x3 in x2:11
                for x4 in x3:11
                for x5 in x4:11
                for x6 in x5:11]

    two_standard = dice_distribution(1:6, 1:6)

    for d1 in all_dice, d2 in all_dice
        test = dice_distribution(d1, d2)
        if test == two_standard
            println(d1, " ", d2)
        end
    end
end
```

Now you can test the solution by running the following command:

```
julia> test_dice()
[1, 2, 2, 3, 3, 4] [1, 3, 4, 5, 6, 8]
[1, 2, 3, 4, 5, 6] [1, 2, 3, 4, 5, 6]
[1, 3, 4, 5, 6, 8] [1, 2, 2, 3, 3, 4]
```

EXERCISE 4.3

Reproduce figure 4.6 using the `data` named tuple defined in listing 4.2.

SOLUTION

```
plot(scatter(data.set1.x, data.set1.y; legend=false),
     scatter(data.set2.x, data.set2.y; legend=false),
     scatter(data.set3.x, data.set3.y; legend=false),
     scatter(data.set4.x, data.set4.y; legend=false))
```

This code reproduces figure 4.6.

EXERCISE 5.1

The `parse` function can be used to convert a string into a number. For instance, if you want to parse a string as an integer, write `parse(Int, "10")` to get the integer 10. Assume you are given a vector of strings `["1", "2", "3"]`. Your task is to create a vector of integers by parsing the strings contained in the given vector.

SOLUTION

```
julia> parse.(Int, ["1", "2", "3"])
3-element Vector{Int64}:
 1
 2
 3
```

EXERCISE 5.2

Repeat the analysis presented in section 5.3, but instead of adding and subtracting 1 when creating data for clusters 1 and 2, add and subtract 0.4, respectively. This will reduce the separation between the two clusters in five-dimensional space. Check if this will reduce their separation in the two-dimensional space generated by t-SNE.

SOLUTION

```
julia> Random.seed!(1234);

julia> data5bis = [randn(100, 5) .- 0.4; randn(100, 5) .+ 0.4];

julia> tsne = manifold.TSNE(n_components=2, init="random",
                            learning_rate="auto", random_state=1234);

julia> data2bis = tsne.fit_transform(data5bis);

julia> scatter(data2bis[:, 1], data2bis[:, 2];
               color=[fill("black", 100); fill("gold", 100)],
               legend=false)
```

Figure B.1 shows the result. We can see that the clusters are overlapping more than in figure 5.3.

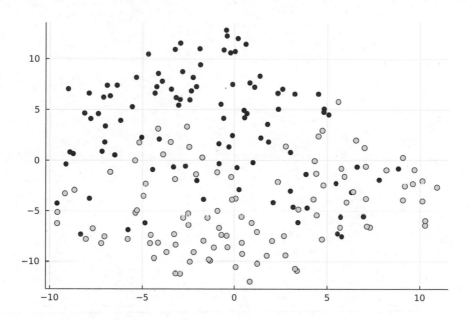

Figure B.1   In this result of the t-SNE embedding, the clusters, represented as points of different fill colors, are overlapping.

EXERCISE 6.1
Create a plot of the number of movies by year, using the `years` variable.

SOLUTION

```
julia> years_table = freqtable(years)
93-element Named Vector{Int64}
Dim1  |
──────┼──────
1913  |    1
1916  |    1
1917  |    1
:     |    :
2011  |  322
2012  |  409
2013  |   85

julia> plot(names(years_table, 1), years_table; legend=false,
            xlabel="year", ylabel="# of movies")
```

Your result should look like the plot in figure B.2, on which we see a sharp increase of movies per year, except for the last year, for which data was likely not collected for the whole period.

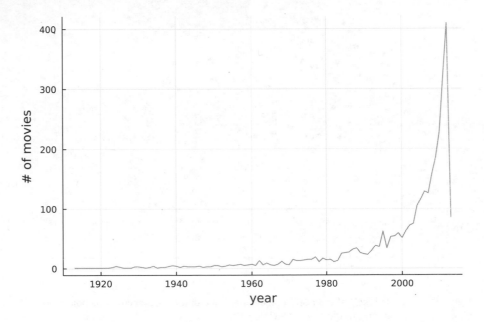

Figure B.2   In this plot of the number of movies per year, observed values increase sharply over the years.

EXERCISE 6.2

Using the s1 vector from listing 6.7, create the s3 vector consisting of symbols representing the same strings as those contained in the s1 vector. Next, benchmark how fast you can sort the s3 vector. Finally, benchmark how fast you can de-duplicate the s1, s2, and s3 vectors by using the unique function.

SOLUTION

```
julia> s3 = Symbol.(s1)
1000000-element Vector{Symbol}:
 :KYD
 :tLO
 :xnU
 :
 :Tt6
 Symbol("19y")
 :GQ7

julia> @btime sort($s3);
  193.934 ms (4 allocations: 11.44 MiB)
```

Sorting `Vector{Symbol}` bound to s3 is a bit faster than sorting `Vector{String}` bound to s1, but is slower than sorting `Vector{String3}` bound to s2.

Now we test de-duplication:

```julia
julia> @btime unique($s1);
  122.145 ms (49 allocations: 10.46 MiB)

julia> @btime unique($s2);
  29.882 ms (48 allocations: 6.16 MiB)

julia> @btime unique($s3);
  25.168 ms (49 allocations: 10.46 MiB)
```

De-duplicating `Vector{String}` is slowest, while for `Vector{Symbol}` and `Vector{String3}`, the performance is similar. Working with `Symbol` values is fast because comparing symbols for equality is efficient, as explained in section 6.1.

EXERCISE 7.1

Given a vector `v = ["1", "2", missing, "4"]`, parse it so that strings are converted to numbers and the `missing` value remains a `missing` value.

SOLUTION

I will show three ways to achieve the desired result. The first uses a comprehension, the second uses the `map` function, and the last employs the `passmissing` function and broadcasting:

```julia
julia> v = ["1", "2", missing, "4"]
4-element Vector{Union{Missing, String}}:
 "1"
 "2"
 missing
 "4"

julia> [ismissing(x) ? missing : parse(Int, x) for x in v]
4-element Vector{Union{Missing, Int64}}:
 1
 2
  missing
 4

julia> map(v) do x
           if ismissing(x)
               return missing
           else
               return parse(Int, x)
           end
       end
4-element Vector{Union{Missing, Int64}}:
 1
 2
  missing
 4
```

```
julia> using Missings

julia> passmissing(parse).(Int, v)
4-element Vector{Union{Missing, Int64}}:
 1
 2
  missing
 4
```

EXERCISE 7.2

Create a vector containing the first day of each month in the year 2021.

SOLUTION

I will show you two approaches for achieving the desired result. In the second one, we use a range, so I use the `collect` function to show you that the result is indeed as expected:

```
julia> using Dates

julia> Date.(2021, 1:12, 1)
12-element Vector{Date}:
 2021-01-01
 2021-02-01
 2021-03-01
 2021-04-01
 2021-05-01
 2021-06-01
 2021-07-01
 2021-08-01
 2021-09-01
 2021-10-01
 2021-11-01
 2021-12-01

julia> Date(2021, 1, 1):Month(1):Date(2021, 12, 1)
Date("2021-01-01"):Month(1):Date("2021-12-01")

julia> collect(Date(2021, 1, 1):Month(1):Date(2021, 12, 1))
12-element Vector{Date}:
 2021-01-01
 2021-02-01
 2021-03-01
 2021-04-01
 2021-05-01
 2021-06-01
 2021-07-01
 2021-08-01
 2021-09-01
 2021-10-01
 2021-11-01
 2021-12-01
```

Note that in the second case, Julia properly calculates the interval of one month, although different months have a different number of days. This is indeed the desired behavior.

EXERCISE 7.3

The NBP Web API allows you to get a sequence of rates for a period of dates. For example, the query `"https://api.nbp.pl/api/exchangerates/rates/a/usd/2020 -06-01/2020-06-30/?format=json"` returns a sequence of rates from June 2020 for dates when the rate is present. In other words, dates for which there is no rate are skipped. Your task is to parse the result of this query and confirm that the obtained result is consistent with the data we collected in the `dates` and `rates` vectors.

SOLUTION

```
julia> query2 = "https://api.nbp.pl/api/exchangerates/rates/a/usd/" *
                "2020-06-01/2020-06-30/?format=json";

julia> response2 = HTTP.get(query2);

julia> json2 = JSON3.read(response2.body)
JSON3.Object{Vector{UInt8}, Vector{UInt64}} with 4 entries:
  :table    => "A"
  :currency => "dolar amerykański"
  :code     => "USD"
  :rates    => JSON3.Object[{…

julia> rates2 = [x.mid for x in json2.rates]
21-element Vector{Float64}:
 3.968
 3.9303
 3.9121
 ⋮
 3.9697
 3.9656
 3.9806

julia> dates2 = [Date(x.effectiveDate) for x in json2.rates]
21-element Vector{Date}:
 2020-06-01
 2020-06-02
 2020-06-03
 ⋮
 2020-06-26
 2020-06-29
 2020-06-30

julia> has_rate = rates .!== missing
30-element BitVector:
 1
 1
 1
 ⋮
 0
 1
 1
```

```
julia> rates2 == rates[has_rate]
true

julia> dates2 == dates[has_rate]
true
```

In the solution, the `json2` object in the `:rates` field contains a sequence of rates. Therefore, we extract them to the `rates2` and `dates2` vectors by using comprehensions. Next, we want to compare the `rates2` and `dates2` vectors to the `rates` and `dates` vectors for entries where the `rates` vector does not contain a `missing` value. To do this, we create the `has_rate` Boolean mask vector by broadcasting the `!==` comparison of the `missing` value against the `rates` vector.

EXERCISE 8.1

Using the BenchmarkTools.jl package, measure the performance of getting a column from a data frame by using the `puzzles."Rating"` syntax.

SOLUTION

```
julia> using BenchmarkTools

julia> @btime $puzzles."Rating";
  36.831 ns (0 allocations: 0 bytes)
```

As expected, the performance is a bit worse than for `puzzles.Rating`.

EXERCISE 9.1

Calculate summary statistics of the `NbPlays` column under two conditions. In the first, select only puzzles that have popularity equal to 100, and in the second, select puzzles that have popularity equal to –100. To calculate the summary statistics of a vector, use the `summarystats` function from the StatsBase.jl package.

SOLUTION

```
julia> using StatsBase

julia> summarystats(puzzles[puzzles.Popularity .== 100, "NbPlays"])
Summary Stats:
Length:         148244
Missing Count:  0
Mean:           283.490280
Minimum:        0.000000
1st Quartile:   6.000000
Median:         124.000000
3rd Quartile:   396.000000
Maximum:        8899.000000

julia> summarystats(puzzles[puzzles.Popularity .== -100, "NbPlays"])
Summary Stats:
Length:         13613
Missing Count:  0
Mean:           4.337839
```

```
Minimum:        0.000000
1st Quartile:   3.000000
Median:         4.000000
3rd Quartile:   5.000000
Maximum:        35.000000
```

We can see that the puzzles that have popularity equal to −100 are indeed played infrequently. However, for puzzles that have 100 popularity, this relationship is not that strong. As you may recall from the output produced by the code in listing 8.2, the mean of the number of plays for the entire data set was around 891, and the median was 246. So the 100-popularity puzzles were played a bit less on average, but the relationship is not that strong. Some of these puzzles seem to just be very good ones.

EXERCISE 9.2
Make sure that the values stored in the `rating_mapping` dictionary add up to represent all row indices of our `good` data frame. To do this, check whether the sum of lengths of these vectors is equal to the number of rows in the `good` data frame.

SOLUTION
```
julia> sum(length, values(rating_mapping))
513357

julia> nrow(good)
513357
```

The use of the `sum` function with a transformation function passed as its first argument is explained in chapter 4.

EXERCISE 9.3
Check the consequences of changing the value of the `span` keyword argument in the `loess` function. By default, this argument has the value 0.75. Set it to 0.25, and add another prediction line to the plot presented in figure 9.4. Make the line yellow with its width equal to 5.

SOLUTION
```
julia> model2 = loess(ratings, mean_popularities; span=0.25);

julia> popularity_predict2 = predict(model2, ratings_predict);

julia> plot!(ratings_predict, popularity_predict2;
             width=5, color="yellow");
```

Figure B.3 shows the result. Note that by applying less smoothing, the curve has a slightly better fit to the data. In comparison to the predictions from figure 9.4, it has lower bias on the edge, a rating equal to around 1500 (the original prediction is slightly biased upward), and in the extremum, a rating equal to around 1750 (the original prediction is slightly biased downward).

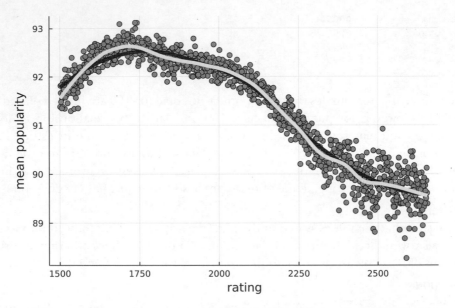

Figure B.3   This plot of the relationship between the number of web and machine learning neighbors and the fraction of machine learning developers is created without jittering.

EXERCISE 10.1

Compare the performance of creating a data frame holding a single random vector of one million elements with and without copying a source vector. You can generate this vector by using the rand(10^6) command.

SOLUTION

```
julia> using BenchmarkTools

julia> x = rand(10^6);

julia> @btime DataFrame(x=$x);
  1.010 ms (22 allocations: 7.63 MiB)

julia> @btime DataFrame(x=$x; copycols=false);
  827.941 ns (21 allocations: 1.50 KiB)
```

Using copycols=false leads to less memory allocation and faster code execution.

EXERCISE 10.2

Check the result of vcat on the two data frames, df1=DataFrame(a=1, b=2) and df2=DataFrame(b=2, a=1). Next, verify the result of the operation if we also pass the cols=:orderequal keyword argument.

SOLUTION

```
julia> df1 = DataFrame(a=1,b=2)
1×2 DataFrame
```

```
Row │ a       b
    │ Int64   Int64
────┼───────────────
  1 │   1       2

julia> df2 = DataFrame(b=3, a=4)
1×2 DataFrame
Row │ b       a
    │ Int64   Int64
────┼───────────────
  1 │   3       4

julia> vcat(df1, df2)
2×2 DataFrame
Row │ a       b
    │ Int64   Int64
────┼───────────────
  1 │   1       2
  2 │   4       3

julia> vcat(df1, df2, cols=:orderequal)
ERROR: ArgumentError: when `cols=:orderequal` all data frames need
to have the same column names and be in the same order
```

EXERCISE 10.3

Change the code from listing 10.7 so that we perform only two-steps-ahead verification if the random walk visits the same point again. Verify that under such a definition, the probability that we do not have duplicate visits to the same point is around 7.5%.

SOLUTION

```
julia> function walk_unique_2ahead()
           walk = DataFrame(x=0, y=0)
           for _ in 1:10
               current = walk[end, :]
               push!(walk, sim_step(current))
           end
           return all(walk[i, :] != walk[i+2, :] for i in 1:9)
       end
walk_unique_2ahead (generic function with 1 method)

julia> Random.seed!(2);

julia> proptable([walk_unique_2ahead() for _ in 1:10^5])
2-element Named Vector{Float64}
Dim1  │
──────┼────────
false │ 0.92472
true  │ 0.07528
```

The difference in this code as compared to listing 10.7 is that this time, the condition we check is `all(walk[i, :] != walk[i+2, :] for i in 1:9)`. As explained in section 10.2, we check whether we visit different points in instances 1 and 3, 2 and 4, ..., 9 and 11.

The result is around 7.5%, as expected.

EXERCISE 11.1

Measure the time required to create a data frame with one row and 10,000 columns consisting of only 1s. Use the matrix created by ones(1, 10_000) as a source and automatic column names. Next, measure the time required to create a NamedTuple of vectors from this data frame.

SOLUTION

```
julia> @time wide = DataFrame(ones(1, 10_000), :auto);
  0.092228 seconds (168.57 k allocations: 9.453 MiB,
                    94.13% compilation time)
julia> @time wide = DataFrame(ones(1, 10_000), :auto);
  0.006999 seconds (39.53 k allocations: 2.508 MiB)

julia> @time Tables.columntable(wide);
 18.517356 seconds (1.70 M allocations: 65.616 MiB, 0.08% gc time,
                    99.60% compilation time)
julia> @time Tables.columntable(wide);
  0.002036 seconds (25 allocations: 938.750 KiB)
```

Creating very wide data frame objects is fast, even on the first run. On the other hand, creating wide NamedTuple objects incurs a very high compilation cost. The second run of Tables.columntable(wide) is fast because Julia caches compilation results of the required functions for the used column names and types.

EXERCISE 11.2

Using the gdf_city grouped data frame, compute the mean temperature in each city by using the mean function from the Statistics module. Store the result as a dictionary in which keys are city names and values are corresponding mean temperatures. Compare your result with the output of the following call: combine(gdf_city, :rainfall => mean). (We will discuss the exact syntax of such expressions in chapters 12 and 13.)

SOLUTION

```
julia> using Statistics

julia> Dict(key.city => mean(df.rainfall) for (key, df) in pairs(gdf_city))
Dict{String7, Float64} with 2 entries:
  "Ełk"    => 2.275
  "Olecko" => 2.48333

julia> combine(gdf_city, :rainfall => mean)
2×2 DataFrame
 Row │ city     rainfall_mean
     │ String7  Float64
─────┼────────────────────────
   1 │ Olecko         2.48333
   2 │ Ełk            2.275
```

EXERCISE 12.1

Using the complete_graph(37700) call, create a complete graph on 37,700 nodes (the number of nodes we have in the gh graph). But beware: if you have less than 32 GB RAM on your machine, use a smaller graph size, as this exercise is memory intensive. Next, using the Base.summarysize function, check how much memory this graph takes. Finally, using the `@time` function, check how long the `deg_class` function would take to finish on this graph, using the `classes_df.ml_target` vector as the vector of developer types.

SOLUTION

```
julia> cg = complete_graph(37700)
{37700, 710626150} undirected simple Int64 graph

julia> Base.summarysize(cg)
11371828056

julia> @time deg_class(cg, classes_df.ml_target);
  7.114192 seconds (5 allocations: 589.250 KiB)
```

Consistent with our discussion in chapter 12, we see that a complete graph on 37,700 nodes has 710,626,150 edges. Creating the graph requires around 11 GB of RAM. Executing the `deg_class` function on this graph took around 7 seconds.

EXERCISE 12.2.

Check to see how the plot in figure 12.6 would look if you removed jittering from it.

SOLUTION

```
scatter(log1p.(agg_df.deg_ml),
        log1p.(agg_df.deg_web);
        zcolor=agg_df.web_mean,
        xlabel="degree ml", ylabel="degree web",
        markersize=2, markerstrokewidth=0, markeralpha=0.8,
        legend=:topleft, labels = "fraction web",
        xticks=gen_ticks(maximum(classes_df.deg_ml)),
        yticks=gen_ticks(maximum(classes_df.deg_web)))
```

This code produces the plot in figure B.4.

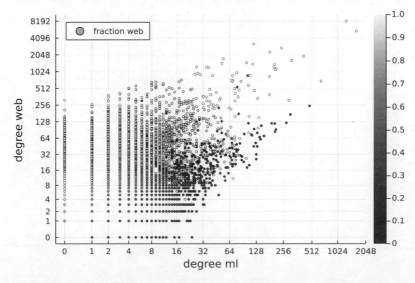

Figure B.4   Plot of relationship between number of web and machine learning neighbors and fraction of machine learning developers. The plot is created without jittering.

If you compare figures B.4 and 12.6, you will see that, indeed, the points plotted in Figure B.4 overlap a lot, which makes it possible that some dark points would be unnoticed because they would be covered by many light points.

EXERCISE 12.3

Fit a probit model instead of a logit model to predict the `ml_target` variable. Use the `ProbitLink()` argument to the `glm` function.

SOLUTION

```julia
julia> glm(@formula(ml_target~log1p(deg_ml)+log1p(deg_web)),
           classes_df, Binomial(), ProbitLink())
StatsModels.TableRegressionModel{GeneralizedLinearModel{
GLM.GlmResp{Vector{Float64}, Binomial{Float64}, ProbitLink},
GLM.DensePredChol{Float64, LinearAlgebra.Cholesky{Float64,
Matrix{Float64}}}}, Matrix{Float64}}

ml_target ~ 1 + :(log1p(deg_ml)) + :(log1p(deg_web))

Coefficients:
```

	Coef.	Std. Error	z	Pr(>|z|)	Lower 95%	Upper 95%
(Intercept)	0.142686	0.0161981	8.81	<1e-17	0.110939	0.174434
log1p(deg_ml)	1.02324	0.0119645	85.52	<1e-99	0.999791	1.04669
log1p(deg_web)	-0.91654	0.0108211	-84.70	<1e-99	-0.937749	-0.895331

EXERCISE 12.4

Create an empty data frame. Add a column a to it, storing values 1, 2, and 3 without copying. Next, create another column in the data frame, called b, that is the same vector as column a (without copying). Check that columns a and b store the same vector. Storing two identical columns in a data frame is unsafe, so in column b, store its copy. Now check that columns a and b store the same data but are different objects. Update in place the first two elements of column a by 10.

SOLUTION

```julia
julia> df = DataFrame()
0×0 DataFrame

julia> df.a = [1, 2, 3]
3-element Vector{Int64}:
 1
 2
 3

julia> df.b = df.a
3-element Vector{Int64}:
 1
 2
 3

julia> df.b === df.a
true
```

```
julia> df.b = df[:, "b"]
3-element Vector{Int64}:
 1
 2
 3

julia> df.b === df.a
false

julia> df.b == df.a
true

julia> df[1:2, "a"] .= 10
2-element view(::Vector{Int64}, 1:2) with eltype Int64:
 10
 10

julia> df
3×2 DataFrame
 Row │ a      b
     │ Int64  Int64
─────┼──────────────
   1 │    10      1
   2 │    10      2
   3 │     3      3
```

Of these operations, the trickiest one is df.b = df[:, "b"]. We assign to an existing column b its copied value df[:, "b"]. Alternatively, we could have written df.b = copy(df.b).

EXERCISE 13.1
Rewrite the code from listing 13.6, using the @rselect macro from Data-FramesMeta.jl.

SOLUTION
```
@rselect(owensboro,
    :arrest = :arrest_made,
    :day = dayofweek(:date),
    :type,
    :v1 = contains(:violation, agg_violation.v[1]),
    :v2 = contains(:violation, agg_violation.v[2]),
    :v3 = contains(:violation, agg_violation.v[3]),
    :v4 = contains(:violation, agg_violation.v[4]))
```

Note that with @rselect, we can specify simple transformations more easily, but the last four transformations, which we generated programmatically in listing 13.6, have to be explicitly written instead.

EXERCISE 13.2
Write a select operation creating the owensboro2 data frame that immediately has the dayname column (without having to perform a join).

SOLUTION

```
select(owensboro,
    :arrest_made => :arrest,
    :date => ByRow(dayofweek) => :day,
    :type,
    [:violation =>
     ByRow(x -> contains(x, agg_violation.v[i])) =>
     "v$i" for i in 1:4],
    :date => ByRow(dayname) => :dayname)
```

It is enough to apply the `dayname` function to the `:date` column to get the desired result. Note, though, that in this case, the obtained column is not categorical, so we would need to turn it into a categorical one later by using the `categorical` function.

EXERCISE 13.3

To practice the operations you learned in this section, prepare the following analyses. First, calculate the probability of arrest per `dayname` column. Second, compute the probability of arrest again, but this time, compute it per the `dayname` and `type` columns, and present the results in wide form, where `dayname` levels are rows and `type` values form columns.

SOLUTION

```
julia> @chain owensboro2 begin
           groupby(:dayname, sort=true)
           combine(:arrest => mean)
       end
7×2 DataFrame
 Row │ dayname     arrest_mean
     │ Cat…        Float64
─────┼─────────────────────────
   1 │ Monday        0.0825991
   2 │ Tuesday       0.0928433
   3 │ Wednesday     0.0780201
   4 │ Thursday      0.0834846
   5 │ Friday        0.112174
   6 │ Saturday      0.165485
   7 │ Sunday        0.258114
```

Observe that, in general, the highest probability of arrest is on weekends:

```
julia> @chain owensboro2 begin
           groupby([:dayname, :type], sort=true)
           combine(:arrest => mean)
           unstack(:dayname, :type, :arrest_mean)
       end
7×3 DataFrame
 Row │ dayname     pedestrian   vehicular
     │ Cat…        Float64?     Float64?
─────┼──────────────────────────────────────
   1 │ Monday        0.827586    0.0580205
   2 │ Tuesday       0.611111    0.0741483
   3 │ Wednesday     0.568182    0.0592334
   4 │ Thursday      0.568182    0.063327
```

```
5 │ Friday      0.596491   0.0869167
6 │ Saturday    0.638889   0.144444
7 │ Sunday      0.592593   0.243548
```

If `type` is `pedestrian`, the probability of arrest is much higher.

EXERCISE 13.4

Create train and test data frames by using (a) data frame indexing syntax and (b) the `groupby` function.

SOLUTION

```
julia> train2 = owensboro2[owensboro2.train, :]
4832×8 DataFrame
  Row │ arrest   type        v1      v2      v3      v4      dayname     train
      │ Bool     String15    Bool    Bool    Bool    Bool    Cat…        Bool
──────┼──────────────────────────────────────────────────────────────────────
    1 │  true    pedestrian  false   false   false   false   Thursday    truc
    2 │ false    vehicular   false   true    false   false   Sunday      true
    :     :         :          :       :       :       :        :         :
 4831 │ false    vehicular   true    true    false   true    Wednesday   true
 4832 │ false    vehicular   false   false   false   true    Wednesday   true
                                                         4828 rows omitted
```

```
julia> test2 = owensboro2[.!owensboro2.train, :]
2047×8 DataFrame
  Row │ arrest   type        v1      v2      v3      v4      dayname     train
      │ Bool     String15    Bool    Bool    Bool    Bool    Cat…        Bool
──────┼──────────────────────────────────────────────────────────────────────
    1 │  true    vehicular   false   false   false   false   Tuesday     false
    2 │  true    vehicular   false   false   false   false   Sunday      false
    :     :         :          :       :       :       :        :         :
 2046 │ false    vehicular   false   false   true    false   Friday      false
 2047 │ false    vehicular   false   false   false   false   Wednesday   false
                                                         2043 rows omitted
```

```
julia> test3, train3 = groupby(owensboro2, :train, sort=true)
GroupedDataFrame with 2 groups based on key: train
First Group (2047 rows): train = false
  Row │ arrest   type        v1      v2      v3      v4      dayname     train
      │ Bool     String15    Bool    Bool    Bool    Bool    Cat…        Bool
──────┼──────────────────────────────────────────────────────────────────────
    1 │  true    vehicular   false   false   false   false   Tuesday     false
    2 │  true    vehicular   false   false   false   false   Sunday      false
    3 │ false    vehicular   false   false   false   false   Tuesday     false
    :     :         :          :       :       :       :        :         :
 2046 │ false    vehicular   false   false   true    false   Friday      false
 2047 │ false    vehicular   false   false   false   false   Wednesday   false
                                                         2042 rows omitted
?
Last Group (4832 rows): train = true
  Row │ arrest   type        v1      v2      v3      v4      dayname     train
      │ Bool     String15    Bool    Bool    Bool    Bool    Cat…        Bool
──────┼──────────────────────────────────────────────────────────────────────
    1 │  true    pedestrian  false   false   false   false   Thursday    true
    2 │ false    vehicular   false   true    false   false   Sunday      true
```

3		true	vehicular	false	false	false	false	Sunday	true
:		:	:	:	:	:	:	:	:
4831		false	vehicular	true	true	false	true	Wednesday	true
4832		false	vehicular	false	false	false	true	Wednesday	true
								4827 rows omitted	

In the solution using the groupby function, it is important that we use sort=true. This ensures that groups are sorted by grouping column, so the false key is in the first group, and the true key is in the last group. Also, in this case, the train3 and test3 data frames have the SubDataFrame type, so they are views into the original owensboro2 data frame.

EXERCISE 14.1

Using the @time macro, compare the time to compute the mean of values in the range -10^6:10^6 transformed by the < (0) and x -> x < 0 functions. Also, check the timing when you predefine the lt0(x) = x < 0 function. Run each operation three times.

SOLUTION

```
julia> @time mean(x -> x < 0, -10^6:10^6)
  0.058563 seconds (124.09 k allocations: 6.868 MiB, 100.84% compilation
      time)
0.499999750000125

julia> @time mean(x -> x < 0, -10^6:10^6)
  0.058623 seconds (123.13 k allocations: 6.808 MiB, 99.25% compilation time)
0.499999750000125

julia> @time mean(x -> x < 0, -10^6:10^6)
  0.059394 seconds (123.13 k allocations: 6.808 MiB, 99.22% compilation time)
0.499999750000125

julia> @time mean(<(0), -10^6:10^6)
  0.000515 seconds
0.499999750000125

julia> @time mean(<(0), -10^6:10^6)
  0.000608 seconds
0.499999750000125

julia> @time mean(<(0), -10^6:10^6)
  0.000523 seconds
0.499999750000125
```

As you can see in the results of the @time macro, the code using < (0) is faster because it does not have to be compiled each time, as opposed to the code using x -> x < 0.

This difference would not be important in scripts, in which everything is typically compiled only once. But it is most relevant when you work interactively with Julia, as in such cases, you are often manually repeating the same operation in global scope several times.

Another way to solve this issue is to define a named function:.

```
julia> lt0(x) = x < 0
lt0 (generic function with 1 method)

julia> @time mean(lt0, -10^6:10^6)
  0.000433 seconds (4 allocations: 112 bytes)
0.499999750000125

julia> @time mean(lt0, -10^6:10^6)
  0.000420 seconds (4 allocations: 112 bytes)
0.499999750000125

julia> @time mean(lt0, -10^6:10^6)
  0.000400 seconds (4 allocations: 112 bytes)
0.499999750000125
```

However, in interactive sessions, users often prefer to define anonymous functions inline rather than predefining them as named functions.

EXERCISE 14.2

Create a web service that accepts a JSON payload with a single element n that is an integer. It should return in JSON format a vector of n random numbers generated using the rand function. If the passed request is incorrect, a 400 Bad Request response should be produced. Run this web server on your local computer and test whether it works as expected.

SOLUTION

In the solution, we now have the server and the client parts. First, start a Julia session that will be a server, and run the following code in it:

```
using Genie
Genie.config.run_as_server = true
Genie.Router.route("/", method=POST) do
    message = Genie.Requests.jsonpayload()
    return try
        n = message["n"]
        Genie.Renderer.Json.json(rand(n))
    catch
        Genie.Responses.setstatus(400)
    end
end
Genie.Server.up()
```

Now, start another Julia session, and test the web service we have created:

```
julia> using HTTP

julia> using JSON3

julia> req = HTTP.post("http://127.0.0.1:8000",
                       ["Content-Type" => "application/json"],
                       JSON3.write((n=3,)))
```

```
HTTP.Messages.Response:
"""
HTTP/1.1 200 OK
Content-Type: application/json; charset=utf-8
Server: Genie/Julia/1.7.2
Transfer-Encoding: chunked

[0.5328896673008208,0.832033459458785,0.4955600307532585]"""

julia> JSON3.read(req.body)
3-element JSON3.Array{Float64, Vector{UInt8}, Vector{UInt64}}:
 0.5328896673008208
 0.832033459458785
 0.4955600307532585

julia> HTTP.post("http://127.0.0.1:8000",
                      ["Content-Type" => "application/json"],
                      JSON3.write((x=3,)))
ERROR: HTTP.ExceptionRequest.StatusError(400, "POST", "/",
     HTTP.Messages.Response:
"""
HTTP/1.1 400 Bad Request
Content-Type: application/json; charset=utf-8
Server: Genie/Julia/1.7.2
Transfer-Encoding: chunked

""")
```

In the first call, we pass a correct request, and we obtain a three-element array of random numbers (your numbers might be different). In the second example, the request is malformed, as instead of n, we pass x. In this case, the server returns the 400 Bad Request response.

appendix C
Julia packages
for data science

After reading this book, you have a solid foundation for performing data analysis with Julia. However, knowledge of Base Julia and the selected packages that we used will likely not be enough for real-life applications. Therefore, this appendix reviews the Julia package ecosystem that you will find useful in your data science work.

In data science projects, apart from simple data ingestion and analysis tasks that we focused on in this book, you typically encounter challenges related to scaling of your computations, working with various data sources and formats, or building advanced machine learning models. All these topics are essential for data scientists, who not only want to perform simple data analysis, but also need to create complex analytical models that are scalable and can be deployed in production environments where they typically also need to be integrated with other software components.

This appendix is an overview of useful functionalities that the Julia ecosystem offers that allow you to build complex data science solutions. To avoid providing an overly long list, I had to omit many great packages. In particular, I focus this appendix only on data-science-related packages, skipping many that have a different focus (like Genie.jl, which we used in chapter 14 for creating a web service). Fortunately, you can conveniently explore the entire Julia package ecosystem on Julia-Hub at https://juliahub.com/ui/Packages.

The list I provide may feel overwhelming. However, I am convinced that after reading this book, you will have acquired adequate fundamentals to be able to confidently learn and use these packages in your projects. To add structure to this material, I have organized it into four sections covering the following topics:

- Plotting
- Scaling computational tasks

- Working with databases and various data storage formats
- Using data science methods

C.1   Plotting ecosystems in Julia

Julia provides several plotting ecosystems. In data science, plotting is one of the fundamental requirements, while at the same time, you might want to use completely different tools in different contexts. For example, different aspects of plotting are important when you want to create an interactive dashboard as compared to when you want to prepare a static plot that should have publication quality.

In this section, I present four selected plotting packages and highlight their features. I recommend you try each of them to see which one best fits your needs:

- *Gadfly.jl*—A package whose API is heavily influenced by Leland Wilkinson's book *The Grammar of Graphics* (Springer, 2005) and Hadley Wickham's ggplot2 package for R. The grammar-of-graphics approach to specifying plots is currently one of the most popular methods in data science.
- *Makie.jl*—A plotting ecosystem that enables creating high-performance, GPU-powered, interactive visualizations, as well as publication-quality vector graphics with one unified interface.
- *Plots.jl*—A package that we use in this book; it provides a unified interface into several available plotting backends, like GR, PyPlot, PGFPlotsX, and Plotly. It is bundled with StatsPlots.jl, which contains many recipes for statistical plotting.
- *UnicodePlots.jl*—A plotting library that produces plots directly in a terminal.

C.2   Scaling computing with Julia

With Julia, you can easily run multithreaded code and leverage distributed computing, as well as execute your programs on GPUs or Spark. If you do not have much experience with this topic, *Parallel and High Performance Computing* by Robert Robey and Yuliana Zamora (Manning, 2021) can serve as a good introduction to the related concepts and approaches.

Here is a selection of the relevant packages in the Julia ecosystem:

- *AMDGPU.jl*—Tools for writing programs for AMD GPUs.
- *CUDA.jl*—A programming interface for working with NVIDIA CUDA GPUs.
- *Dagger.jl*—A scheduler allowing you to run computations represented as directed acyclic graphs efficiently on many Julia worker processes and threads, as well as GPUs.
- *Distributed*—A Julia standard module providing an implementation of distributed memory computing.
- *MPI.jl*—An interface to the message passing interface (MPI).
- *Spark.jl*—A package that allows the execution of Julia programs on the Apache Spark platform.
- *Threads*—A Julia standard module providing basic functionalities, allowing you to write multithreaded code.

- *ThreadsX.jl*—A package we use in chapter 14. It provides an API that's compatible with Base Julia functions to easily parallelize Julia programs.

C.3   Working with databases and data storage formats

Another important aspect of scaling computing programs is connectors to databases and various data storage types. Here are some of the available packages:

- *Arrow.jl*—An implementation of the Apache Arrow standard we use in chapter 8.
- *AVRO.jl*—A pure Julia implementation of the Apache Avro data standard.
- *AWSS3.jl*—An interface for Amazon Simple Storage Service (S3). AWS.jl is a related package that provides an interface for Amazon Web Services (AWS).
- *CSV.jl*—A package for working with CSV files and fixed field width files.
- *DuckDB.jl*—An interface to the DuckDB SQL OLAP database management system.
- *HDF5.jl*—An interface for reading and writing data stored in the HDF5 file format.
- *JSON3.jl*—A package for working with JSON files.
- *LibPQ.jl*—A wrapper for the PostgreSQL libpq C library.
- *Mongoc.jl*—A MongoDB driver.
- *MySQL.jl*—An interface to MySQL server.
- *ODBC.jl*—An interface to the ODBC API.
- *Parquet2.jl*—A pure Julia implementation of the Parquet tabular data binary format.
- *SQLite.jl*—An interface to the SQLite library we use in chapter 8.
- *RData.jl*—A package for reading R data files.
- *ReadStatTables.jl*—A package for reading data files from Stata, SAS, and SPSS.
- *TOML*—A standard module for parsing TOML files.

C.4   Using data science methods

The Julia ecosystem provides a rich collection of packages allowing you to perform advanced data science projects. Their functionalities cover machine learning, probabilistic programming, optimization, statistics, and numerical computing:

- *Agents.jl*—A library for creating agent-based models in Julia.
- *DifferentialEquations.jl*—A suite for numerically solving differential equations. It is a key package of Julia's SciML ecosystem (https://sciml.ai).
- *Flux.jl*—A library for machine learning geared toward high-performance production pipelines.
- *Gen.jl, Soss.jl/Tilde.jl, Turing.jl*—Three alternative frameworks for probabilistic programming (each has unique features, so I recommend you check which one best fits your needs).
- *JuliaStats*—An ecosystem of packages for statistics listed at https://github.com/JuliaStats. They provide probability distributions, various univariate and multivariate statistical models, hypothesis testing, and related functionalities.

- *JuMP.jl*—A domain-specific modeling language for mathematical optimization. It supports a range of problem classes, including linear programs, integer programs, conic programs, semidefinite programs, and constrained nonlinear programs.
- *Knet.jl*—A mature deep learning framework.
- *MLJ.jl*—A toolbox written in Julia providing a common interface and meta-algorithms for selecting, tuning, evaluating, composing, and comparing over 160 machine learning models.
- *OnlineStats.jl*—A library providing high-performance single-pass algorithms for statistics.
- *Optim.jl*—A package for univariate and multivariate nonlinear optimization in Julia.
- *ReinforcementLearning.jl*—A package for reinforcement learning in Julia.
- *Roots.jl*—A library providing routines for finding roots of continuous scalar functions of a single real variable.

The potential list here is so long that I needed to restrict myself to only the most popular ones covering the most important data science tools and techniques. In particular, I omit listing various packages providing implementations of concrete machine learning models, as they are all available via a common interface provided by the MLJ.jl ecosystem (which you can learn about at http://mng.bz/xMjY).

Summary

- Julia has a rich ecosystem of packages allowing you to implement complex data science projects.
- Julia has several mature plotting ecosystems. Each has a different API and focus area. I recommend you try different options and pick one that works best for you.
- If you do high-performance computations, Julia has comprehensive support for multithreading, distributed, and GPU computing. Therefore, you have the flexibility of choosing the best way to scale your computations.
- Julia has support for reading and writing data in multiple formats and connecting to popular database systems. You can easily perform your data analysis projects by integrating with existing data stores.
- The ecosystem of data science tools and algorithms available in Julia is extensive. Their number is so large that in some domains, umbrella organizations were created to group them. From the data science perspective, important projects include JuliaStats, JuMP.jl, MLJ.jl, and SciML.

index

Symbols

::AbstractString type annotation 50
::Float64 type annotation 373
::Function type annotation 50
:auto option 236
@assert macro 65–66
@benchmark macro 67–68, 83, 406–407
@btime macro 68–69, 199, 405
@chain macro 328–332, 362
@code_warntype macro 271–272, 308–309
@debug macro 188
@edit macro 69, 405
@error macro 188
@formula macro 96, 320
@info macro 188
@macroexpand macro 65, 67
@rselect macro 344–345, 347, 421
@rselect! macro 345
@rsubset macro 355
@rsubset! macro 355
@rtransform macro 345
@rtransform! macro 345
@select macro 344–345
@select! macro 345
@show macro 304, 386
@subset macro 355
@subset! macro 355
@time macro 7, 12, 65–66, 151, 308–309, 378, 419, 424
@transform macro 345
@transform! macro 345
@view macro 80–81, 83, 129, 223, 405, 407
@warn macro 188

Numerics

1-based indexing 74

A

abs function 105
abstract syntax tree 65
AbstractDataFrame supertype 225
AbstractString type 129, 141, 151
AbstractVector type 114
activate command 398
add BenchmarkTools command 400
add_edge! function 303
Agents.jl package 429
all function 375, 387
AMDGPU.jl package 428
annotate! function 368
anonymous function 40–41
Anscombe's quartet data
    analyzing data stored in named tuples 95–96
    analyzing using broadcasting 109, 112
    plotting data in arrays 86–88
any function 375
Any type 51–52, 55, 108–109, 116, 141
Apache Arrow 204–205
append! function 136, 254–256, 274, 377
area under the pfa-pmiss curve (AUC) 359
arguments
    functions passed as arguments to other
        functions 40
    keyword 37–38
    positional 37–38
    rules for passing to functions 39

arrays 70–88
  calculating correlations between variables 82–83
  copying vs. making views 81–82
  indexing into 78–81
  linear regressions 83–86
  matrices 72–76
    computing basic statistics of data stored in 76–78
    creating 72–73
    tuples 73–76
Arrow.jl package 429
Arrow.List type 205
Arrow.Table object 204–205
Arrow.write function 204
ASCII strings 134–135
Asian option 365
AsTable expression 388
AUC (area under the pfa-pmiss curve) 359
AVRO.jl package 429
AWSS3.jl package 429
axes function 79, 301

B

bar function 56
Base module 64, 79
Base.summarysize function 145, 147, 149, 309, 419
BenchmarkTools package 145
Bernoulli type 354
Between expression 217
bitstring function 22
Bool type 53
break keyword 33
broadcast fusion 111
broadcasting 101–112
  analyzing Anscombe's quartet data 111–112
  creating columns 322
  expanding length-1 dimensions in 103–106
  protecting collections from being broadcasted over 106–109
  syntax and meaning of 101–103
  updating columns by replacing 322
  updating columns in place 322–323
  updating contents of data frames 299–303
build command 399
ByRow wrapper, vectorizing functions by using 340–341
byte indexing 133–134
bzip2 files and algorithm 188–189

C

capturing group 130
Cartesian product 104
catch keyword 162
categorical data 347–349
categorical function 348–349, 422
Categorical type 150
cd function 50–51, 397–398
cell 10
Char character type 135
Char type 135
character indexing 133–134
coalesce function 165, 167
code indentation 27
codec 189
codeunits function 132–133
collect function 58, 69, 83, 171, 240, 251, 375, 405, 412
collections 70–122
Cols selector 218
columnindex function 201, 212
columns
  creating
    using broadcasting 322
    via copying 322
    without copying 321
  extracting 196–203
    data frame indexing 200–202
    indexing 210–225
    storage model 196–197
    treating data frame columns as properties 197–200
    visualizing data stored in columns 202–203
  text processing 337–345
    advanced functionalities of DataFramesMeta.jl 343–345
    finding most frequent types 337–340
    flattening data frames 341
    sorting data frames 342
    using convenience syntax to get number of rows 341–342
    vectorizing functions by using ByRow wrapper 340–341
  type-unstable iterators of 277–279
  unnesting 387–389
  updating
    by replacing 322
    by using broadcasting to replace 322
    in place 322
    in place by using broadcasting 322–323

combine function 289, 312–314, 325, 333, 335–336, 345, 347, 362

complete_graph function 309, 418

compose function 38, 40

composite structures 96

composite types 97

compound expressions 33–34

compression 146

computing node features 303–311
  computing features of nodes by using Graphs.jl package 305–306
  counting node neighbors 307–311
  creating SimpleGraph objects 303–304

concrete types 51

conditional evaluation 26–32
  code indentation 27
  combining logical conditions 29
  conditional expressions
    introduction to 26–27
    returning values 31–32
  floating-point numbers
    comparing 27–28
    inexact representation of numbers by floating-point values 28–29
  short-circuit conditional evaluation 29–30
  ternary operator 31

conditional expressions
  introduction to 26–27
  returning values 31–32

confusion matrix 358

constant term 83

Content-Type metadata 380

continue keyword 33

control-flow constructs 26–36
  compound expressions 33–34
  conditional evaluation 26–32
    code indentation 27
    combining logical conditions 29
    conditional expressions 26–27, 31–32
    floating-point numbers 27–29
    short-circuit conditional evaluation 29–30
    ternary operator 31
  loops 32–33
  winsorized mean 35–36

convenience syntax
  creating named tuples 378
  getting number of rows of data frame 341–342

convert function 267

copy operation 205

copycols keyword argument 241

cor function 82, 247

count function 213

covariance function 116

CRISP-DM (cross-industry standard process for data mining) 15

CSV files
  inspecting 190
  reading into data frames 190–192
  saving data frames to 195

CSV.jl package 429

CSV.read function 191, 193, 196, 281, 298

CSV.write function 195–196

CUDA.jl package 428

D

Dagger.jl package 428

data collections 70

data frame mutation 291

data frames 185–364
  converting 266–280
    to iterator of named tuple 277
    to matrices 268–269
    to named tuple of vectors 269–275
    to type-unstable iterators of rows and columns of data frame 277–279
    to vector of named tuple 277
    to vector of vectors 279–280
  creating
    from matrices 235–237
    from vectors 237–244
    incrementally 248–263
    using Tables.jl interface 244–246
  extracting columns 196–203
    indexing 200–202, 210–225
    storage model 196–197
    treating data frame columns as properties 197–200
    visualizing data stored in columns 202–203
  functionalities provided by DataFrames.jl 361–362
  grouping 280–289
    comparing performance of indexing methods 285–286
    getting group keys of grouped data frame 282–283
    grouping data frame 281–282
    indexing grouped data frame with multiple values 286–287
    indexing grouped data frame with single value 283–285
    iterating grouped data frame 288–289
    preparing source data frame 280–281
  inspecting CSV files 190

data frames *(continued)*
  loading data 190–195
    inspecting contents of data frames 192–195
    reading CSV files into data frames 190–192
    saving data frames to CSV files 195
  mutation operations 321–324
    insertcols! function 323–324
    low-level API operations 321–323
  plotting correlation matrix of data stored in data frame 246–248
  police stop data set 328–337
    short forms of operation specification syntax 336–337
  reading and writing 203–207
    Apache Arrow 204–205
    SQLite 205–207
  split-apply-combine approach 311–320
    computing summary statistics 311–315
  text processing columns
    advanced functionalities of DataFramesMeta.jl 343–345
    flattening data frames 341
    sorting data frames 342
    using convenience syntax to get number of rows of data frame 341–342
    vectorizing functions by using ByRow wrapper 340–341
data science packages 427–430
  data science methods 429–430
  databases and data storage formats 429
  plotting ecosystems 428
  scaling computing 428–429
data scientists 1
data.table package 4
databases and data storage formats 429
DataFrame constructor 204, 225, 235–236, 238, 240–244, 246, 323, 325
DataFrame type 10, 186–187, 190, 196–198, 223, 225, 234, 243–244, 270, 273–275, 310
DataFrameColumns collection 279
DataFrameRow object 215
DataFrameRows 278
DataFrames.jl package 5
  functionalities provided by 361–362
  performing object consistency checks in 310–311
DataFramesMeta.jl package
  advanced functionalities of 343–345
  domain-specific language 314–315
Date constructor 170
DateFormat object 170
Dates module 169

dayname function 349, 422
DBInterface.execute function 206
DecisionTree.jl package 5
deepcopy function 99
degree 293
degree function 305
dependency hell 10
dependent variable 72
describe function 193–194, 298–299, 332
deserialize function 263, 267
Dict type 93, 97
dictionaries
  creating 88–91
  creating data frames from vectors 240–241
  mapping key-value pairs 88–93
DifferentialEquations.jl package 429
direct dependencies 396
Distributed package 428
do blocks 41–42
do-end notation 77
download function 125
downloading data files from web 187–188
Downloads module 125
dropmissing function 353
dropmissing! function 353
DRY (don't repeat yourself) principle 92
DuckDB.jl package 429
dump function 307

E

eachcol function 110, 247, 279
eachindex function 102–103, 133
edges function 307
else keyword 27
elseif keyword 27
eltype function 113
empty! function 98–99
end keyword 27, 37, 60
enumerate expression 226
environments 396
Example project environment 401–402
exception 160
execution speed 6
exercises and solutions 405–426
exit() command 394
export keyword 60
extrema function 260–261

F

factor 328
features 72

fieldnames function 198
fill function 120
findall function 297, 299
first function 128, 132
fitting LOESS regression 229–231
fitting logistic regression model 319–320
fixed-width string types 143–145
    available fixed-width strings 143–144
    performance of fixed-width strings 144–145
flatten function 341
float function 229, 382
Float64 type 22, 24, 55, 97, 113, 373
floating-point numbers
    comparing 27–28
    consequences of inexact representation of
        numbers by floating-point values 28–29
Flux.jl package 5, 429
Foundations and Methods of Stochastic Simulation
    (Nelson) 366
freqtable function 136–137
Friedl, Jeffrey E. F. 130
function keyword 37
Function type 50–51
function-barrier technique 273, 308–309
functions 36–43
    anonymous functions 40–41
    covariance function 116
    defining
        short syntax for 39–40
        using function keyword 37
    do blocks 41–42
    missing value propagation 164–165, 168–169
    naming convention 42–43
    passed as arguments to other functions 40
    positional and keyword arguments 37–38
    rules for defining methods of 55
    rules for passing arguments to 39
    winsorized mean 43

G

Gadfly.jl package 428
GBM (geometric Brownian motion) 369–370
gbm data frame 370
GC (garbage collection) 75
Gen.jl package 429
Genie.jl package, creating web service
    using 381–382
Genie.Renderer.Json.json function 381
Genie.Requests.jsonpayload function 381
Genie.Router.route function 381
Genie.Server.up function 381

get_rate function 172–173
getfield function 198
getproperty function 197, 240
GitHub developers data set 292–303
    fetching from web 294–295
    graphs 293–294
    implementing function that extracts data from
        ZIP files 296–298
glm function 320, 356, 420
global keyword 33
global scope 44
Grammar of Graphics, The (Wilkinson) 428
Graph object 303
graphs
    introduction to 293–294
    iterating edges of 307
Graphs.jl package, computing node features
    using 305–306
groupby function 223, 266, 281–282, 312, 356,
    423–424
GroupedDataFrame indexing 287, 357
GroupedDataFrame object 266, 280, 283, 286,
    288–289, 312–313
GroupedDataFrame objects 266, 280, 283, 313
GroupKey indexing 286
GroupKey objects 283, 289

H

Hadamard product 101
haskey function 89
hasproperty function 201
HDF5.jl package 429
heatmap function 247
help resources 394–396
histogram function 357
histogram! function 357
hline! function 368
HTTP (Hypertext Transfer Protocol) 379
HTTP.get function 157, 160, 385
HTTP.post function 385–386
HTTP.post method 385

I

identity function 116, 279
if expressions 30
if-elseif-else-end expressions 31
immutable type 97
import statement 61
Impute.interp function 177
in function 106–107

in operator 138
include function 59–60
independent variable 72
indexing
    arrays 78–81
    data frames 200–202, 210–225
        allowed column selectors 215–220
        allowed row-subsetting values 220–223
        comparing methods 285–286
        grouped data frames with multiple
            values 286–287
        grouped data frames with single value
            283–285
        making views of data frame objects 223–225
    extracting subsets of strings 132–135
        ASCII strings 134–135
        Char type 135
        character vs. byte indexing 133–134
        UTF-8 encoding of strings 132
indicator vector 212
indirect dependencies 396
InlineString function 143
inlinestrings function 143, 145
innerjoin function 350
insertcols! function 323–324
instantiate command 397
Int type 97, 113
Int64 type 22, 52
Integer type 52–53
integrating with Python 117–120
    calling Python from Julia 118–120
    preparing data for dimensionality reduction
        using t-SNE algorithm 117–118
    visualizing results of t-SNE algorithm 120
interactive mode 15
IOBuffer function 281
isa operator 23
isabstracttype function 51
isapprox function 29
isascii function 134
isequal function 165–166, 262
isfile function 127, 397
isless function 165
ismissing function 163, 176
isodd function 108
isordered function 348
Iterator of NamedTuple output value 276

J

JSON for Beginners (iCode Academy) 156
JSON payload 366, 385

JSON3.jl package 429
JSON3.read function 158
JSON3.write function 384
Julia 1–16, 393–404
    collections 70–122
        arrays 70–88
        broadcasting 101–112
        integrating with Python 117–120
        mapping key-value pairs with
            dictionaries 88–93
        named tuples 93–99
        parametric types 112–116
    control-flow constructs 26–36
        compound expressions 33–34
        conditional evaluation 26–32
        loops 32–33
        winsorized mean 35–36
    defining variables 23–26
    drawbacks of 11–13
    help resources 394–396
    installing and setting up 393–394
    integration with R 243–244
    introduction to 2–6
    key features of 6–10
        built-in package manager 9–10
        compiled language 6–8
        easy composition 8–9
        execution speed 6–8
        integration of existing code 10
        interactive workflow support 8
        reusability 8–9
    package management 396–403
        activating project environments 397–398
        managing packages 399–401
        potential issues with installing packages 399
        project environments 396–397
        setting up integration with Python 401–402
        setting up integration with R 402–403
    representing values 20–23
    scaling projects 49–69
        macros 65–69
        modules 59–60
        multiple dispatch 55–58
        packages 61–64
        type system 50–55
    usage scenarios 10–11
    using for data analysis 13–15
    variable scoping rules 44–48
    working with 403–404
        using Jupyter Notebook 404
        using Pluto notebooks 404
        using terminal 403–404
        using Visual Studio Code 404

julia –project call 398
julia command 394, 399
Julia compiles code 5
julia executable 403
JULIA_EDITOR environment variable 69
julia> prompt 394, 403
JuliaStats.jl package 429
JuMP.jl package 430
Jupyter Notebook, working with Julia
    through 404

K

k-times winsorized mean 20
KDD (knowledge discovery in databases) 15
key-value pairs, mapping with dictionaries 88–93
    creating dictionaries 88–91
    Sicherman puzzle
        introduction to 88
        solving 91–93
keys function 91, 283
keyword arguments 37–38
    copycols keyword argument 241
    creating data frames from vectors 238
    handling nonstandard arguments 242–243
Knet.jl package 430

L

leftjoin function 350
leftjoin! function 349
levels function 348
levels! function 348–349
LibPQ.jl package 429
library code 5
linear regression 83–86
LinearAlgebra module 84
literals 21
lm function 96
load function 263
local host 380
local scope 45
LOESS (locally estimated scatterplot smoothing)
    regression 229–231
loess function 231, 415
Loess.jl package 229
log return 369
Logging module 188
logical conditions, combining 29
loops 32–33
loss function 5

M

Machine Learning in Julia (MLJ) 361
macros 65–69
Main module 60, 79
Makie.jl package 428
map function 40, 77–78, 95, 100–101, 103, 111,
    245, 249, 375, 386
mapping key-value pairs with dictionaries 88–93
    creating dictionaries 88–91
    Sicherman puzzle 88, 91–93
Mastering Regular Expressions (Friedl) 130
match function 130
matrices 72–76
    computing basic statistics of data stored in
        76–78
    converting data frames to 268–269
    creating 72–73
    creating data frames from 235–237
    plotting correlation matrix of data stored in
        data frame 246–248
    tuples 73–76
matrix 104
Matrix constructor 268
Matrix type 97
maximum function 375
mean function 62–63, 76–77, 86, 110, 168, 173,
    289, 313, 377, 418
median function 212
metaprogramming 143
methods 41
methods function 50, 230
minimum function 375
Mining Complex Networks (Pralat and
    Theberge) 294
Missing type 54, 163
missing values 163–169
    comparison operators guaranteeing Boolean
        result 165–166
    defined 163–164
    enabling missing propagation in
        functions 168–169
    propagating in functions 164–165
    replacing in collections 167
    skipping in computations 167–168
    working with 164–169
ml_target variable 319–320, 420
MLJ (Machine Learning in Julia) 361
MLJ.jl package 430
modules, defined 59–60
Mongoc.jl package 429
Monte Carlo simulation 366–371

calculating option payoff 366–368
computing option value 368–369
GBM 369–370
numerical approach to computing option
value 370–371
Mount, John 146
MPI.jl package 428
multiple dispatch 50–51, 55–58
method ambiguity problem 56
rules for defining methods of functions 55
winsorized mean 57–58
mutable keyword 97
mutable type 97
mutation operations 321–324
creating columns
using broadcasting 322
via copying 322
without copying 321
insertcols! function 323–324
updating columns
by replacing 322
in place 322
in place by using broadcasting 322–323
using broadcasting to replace 322
MySQL.jl package 429

N

name property 296
named tuples 93–99
analyzing Anscombe's quartet data stored
in 95–96
composite types 97
converting data frames to iterators of named
tuple 277
converting data frames to named tuple of
vectors 269–275
converting data frames to vectors of named
tuple 277
defining and accessing contents 94
mutability of values 97–99
using convenient syntax for creating 378
NamedTuple indexing 286
NamedTuple objects 11, 93, 97, 245–246, 270,
275
names function 137, 139, 194–195, 217–218, 220
NaN (not a number) 28
NBP (National Bank of Poland) Web API
155–162
analyzing data fetched from 173–179
computing summary statistics 174
finding which days of week have most missing values 174–175

plotting PLN/USD exchange rate 175–179
fetching data by using Julia 157–159
fetching data via web browser 155–157
getting time-series data from 169–173
fetching data for range of dates 172–173
working with dates 170–172
handling NBP Web API query fails 159–162
ncol function 194
ne function 310
neighbors, of a node 293
Nelson, Barry L. 366
nested arrays 85
nested data 11
node 293
node classification 294
node features 303–311
computing using Graphs.jl package 305–306
creating SimpleGraph objects 303–304
nominal variable 348
not a number (NaN) 28
Not expression 217
Not selectors 221
nrow function 194–195
nv function 310

O

object term 20
observations 71
ODBC.jl package 429
OLS (ordinary least squares) 83
ones function 82, 84
OneTo type 79
OnlineStats.jl package 430
only function 159, 162
open function 146, 189, 295
operation specification syntax
computing summary statistics of developer
features 312–314
short forms of 336–337
Optim.jl package 430
option pricing simulator 372–379
computing option payoff for single
sample 373–375
computing option value 375–379
implementing function performing option
valuation 375–377
testing option valuation function 378–379
using convenient syntax for creating named
tuple 378
using partial function application
syntax 377

starting Julia with multiple-thread support 372–373
option pricing web service 379–390
  collecting responses to multiple requests from web service in data frame 386–387
  creating web service using Genie.jl 381–382
  general approach to building of web service 379–380
  plotting results of option pricing 389–390
  running web service 383
  sending single request to web service 384–385
  unnesting column of data frame 387–389
OrderedDict dictionary 93
OrderedSet set 93
ordinal variable 348
ordinary least squares (OLS) 83
outerjoin function 350

P

package management 396–403
  managing packages 399–401
  potential issues with installing packages 399
  project environments
    activating 397–398
    introduction to 396–397
  setting up integration with Python 401–402
  setting up integration with R 402–403
packages
  using 61–63
Pair object 99
Pair type 114
pairs function 288
pairs, creating data frames from vectors 238–240
pairwise function 247
Parallel and High Performance Computing (Robey and Zamora) 428
parameters 22
parametric types 112–116
  defining covariance function 116
  introduction to 112–114
  rules for subtyping of 114–115
parentindices function 225
Parquet2.jl package 429
parse function 109, 131, 408
parseline function 131, 135–136
partialsort! function 68
pass-by-sharing feature 39
passmissing function 169
PATH environment variable 394
PCRE (Perl-Compatible Regular Expressions) library 130

permutedims function 352
pfa (probability of false alarm) 358, 360
pkg> prompt 397–398
plot function 12, 87–88, 175, 203, 268–269
Plots.jl package 428
plotting ecosystems 428
Pluto notebooks, working with Julia through 404
pmiss (probability of miss) 359–360
PooledArrays.jl, compressing vectors of strings with 146–150
  internal design of PooledArray 148–150
  reading data into vector and compressing 147–148
PooledVector type 147
positional arguments 37–38
Practical Data Science with R (Zumel and Mount) 146
Prałat, Pawel 294
predict function 229–230, 356
predictive models 354–361
  evaluating quality of predictions 357–361
  fitting logistic regression model 356
  splitting data into train and test data sets 354–355
predictive models of probability 354–361
  evaluating quality of predictions 357–361
  fitting logistic regression model 356
  splitting data into train and test data sets 354–355
preparing data for making predictions 345–353
  categorical data 347–349
  dropping rows of data frame that hold missing values 353
  joining data frames 349–350
  performing initial transformation of data 345–347
  reshaping data frames 350–352
print function 127, 129, 147
println function 147, 189
probability of false alarm (pfa) 358, 360
probability of miss (pmiss) 359–360
prod function 375
project environments
  activating 397–398
  introduction to 396–397
promote keyword 255
proptable function 138, 174, 358
pseudo broadcasting 242
push! function 225–226, 256, 274, 370
pwd function 399

Python, integrating Julia with 117–120
  calling Python from Julia 118–120
  preparing data for dimensionality reduction
    using t-SNE algorithm 117–118
  setting up integration 401–402
  visualizing results of t-SNE algorithm 120
python3 program 402
PyTorch package 4

Q

quantile function 61, 213

R

R language 243, 402
R² function 85–86
r2 function 96
rand function 68, 258, 354, 385, 425
randn function 118, 373, 375
Random package 145
Random.seed!(1234) command 118, 145
randstring function 145
range function 261, 367
raw string literals 126
RData.jl package 429
read function 195, 297
readlines function 127, 147
ReadStatTables.jl package 429
Real-World Cryptography (Wong) 295
reduce function 251, 375
Ref type 108
regular expressions 130–131, 217
  working with 130–131
  writing parser of a single line of files 131
ReinforcementLearning.jl package 430
ReLU (rectified linear unit) 367
remove command 401
rename function 347
rename! function 347
REPL (read-eval-print loop) 8
rethrow function 162
return keyword 37, 173
rightjoin function 350
Robey, Robert 428
Roots.jl package 430
rows
  adding to existing data frames 256–257
  dropping rows that hold missing values 353
  type-unstable iterators of 277–279
  using convenience syntax to get number
    of 341–342

S

save function 263
scaling computing 428–429
scaling projects 49–69
  macros 65–69
  modules 59–60
  multiple dispatch 55–58
    method ambiguity problem 56
    rules for defining methods of functions 55
    winsorized mean 57–58
  packages 61–64
  type system 50–55
    multiple dispatch 50–51
    subtypes 52–53
    supertypes 52
    type hierarchy 51
    type restrictions 54–55
    Union keyword 53–54
scatter function 120
scatter! function 178
SearchLight.jl 381
select function 327, 333, 335–336, 344–346, 362,
    388
select! function 327–328, 333, 336, 362
SEMMA (Sample, explore, modify, model, and
    assess) 15
Serialization module 263
serialize function 263
Set type 92–93
SHA module 295
sha256 function 295
short-circuit conditional evaluation 29–30
show function 194
Sicherman puzzle
  introduction to 88
  solving 91–93
Signed subtype 53
SimpleGraph function 303
SimpleGraph type 303
single-column selectors 215
size function 73, 79
skipmissing function 168, 174
sort function 42, 58, 69, 229, 342, 375, 405
sort! function 42, 58, 137
Soss.jl package 429
source data ingestion 14
span keyword 415
Spark.jl package 428
splatting 88
split function 128–130, 136

split-apply-combine approach 311–320
  computing summary statistics 311–315
    approach using indexing 311–312
    DataFramesMeta.jl domain-specific
      language 314–315
    operation specification syntax 312–314
SQL select query 205
SQLite, reading and writing data frames
  205–207
SQLite.columns function 206
SQLite.DB function 206
SQLite.jl package 429
SQLite.load! function 206
SQLite.tables function 206
sqrt function 330, 344
stack function 328, 350, 352
stacked data 352
Statistics module 61–64, 76, 82, 86, 174,
  212–213, 247, 289, 418
StatsBase.jl package 63–64
status command 400
std function 61, 76–77, 174
step function 258
step parameter 82
Stipple.jl 381
strike price 366–367
String constructor 158
string function 106, 150, 239
String type 97, 129, 143–145, 151, 193
String3 type 145
String7 type 193
strings 123–153
  compressing vectors of strings with
    PooledArrays.jl 146–150
    internal design of PooledArray 148–150
    reading data into vector and
      compressing 147–148
  fixed-width string types 143–145
    available fixed-width strings 143–144
    performance of fixed-width strings 144–145
  getting and inspecting data 124–128
    common techniques of string
      construction 125–127
    downloading files from web 125
    reading file contents 127–128
  indexing 132–135
    ASCII strings 134–135
    Char type 135
    character vs. byte indexing 133–134
    UTF-8 encoding of strings 132
  regular expressions 130–131
    working with 130–131

writing parser of a single line of files 131
  splitting 128–129
  storage for collections of 151
  symbols 140–143
    creating 140–141
    using 141–143
struct composite type 97, 197, 275
StructArray type 275
SubDataFrame objects 225
SubDataFrame type 225, 424
subset function 327, 355, 362
subset! function 327, 362
SubString{String} object 128
subtypes
  finding all subtypes of a type 52–53
  rules for subtyping of parametric types
    114–115
sum function 41–42, 50–51, 58, 104, 167–168,
  213, 330, 375, 377, 388, 415
  104
summary function 298, 332
summarystats function 215, 414
supertype function 51–52
supertypes 52
Symbol type 140–141
symbols 140–143
  creating 140–141
  using 141–143

T

t-SNE (T-distributed stochastic neighbor embedding)
  preparing data for dimensionality
    reduction 117–118
  visualizing results of 120
-t4 switch 383
Table type 275
TableRegressionModel type 97
tables, appending to data frames 253–256
Tables.jl interface, creating data frames
  using 244–246
Tables.namedtupleiterator function 279
tabular data 10, 244
targets 72
TDSP (Team Data Science Process) 15
terminal, working with Julia through 403–404
ternary operator 31
Théberge, Francois 294
Threads module 379
Threads package 428
Threads.@spawn macro 379

Threads.nthreads function 372
ThreadsX.jl package 429
ThreadsX.map function 376
three-valued-logic 164
throw function 58
Tilde.jl package 429
time function 66, 376
time to first plot problem 11
time-series data 154–181
  analyzing 173–179
    computing summary statistics 174
    finding which days of week have most miss-
      ing values 174–175
    plotting PLN/USD exchange rate 175–179
  fetching 169–173
    fetching data for range of dates 172–173
    using Julia 157–159
    via web browser 155–157
    working with dates 170–172
  handling query fails 159–162
  missing values 163–169
    comparison operators guaranteeing Bool-
      ean result 165–166
    defined 163–164
    enabling missing propagation in
      functions 168–169
    propagating in functions 164–165
    replacing in collections 167
    skipping in computations 167–168
    working with missing values 164–169
TOML package 429
transcode function 188–189
transform function 327, 333, 335–336, 345, 362
transform! function 327, 333, 362
Tuple indexing 286
tuples
  introduction to 73–76
  named 93–99
    composite types 97
    converting data frames to iterators of named
      tuple 277
    converting data frames to named tuple of
      vectors 269–275
    converting data frames to vectors of named
      tuple 277
    defining and accessing contents 94
    mutability of values 97–99
    using convenient syntax for creating 378
Turing.jl package 429
two-dimensional random walks
  analysis of simulation output 261–262
  defined 257–259

serialization of Julia objects 262–263
simple simulator of 259–261
two-language problem 5
type piracy 266, 270
type piracy in Julia 274–275
type stability in Julia 270–274
type stability of code 266
type system 50–55
  Char type 135
  composite types 97
  fixed-width string types 143–145
  multiple dispatch 50–51
  parametric types 112–116
  subtypes
    defining covariance function 116
    finding all subtypes of a type 52–53
    rules for subtyping of parametric types
      114–115
  supertypes 52
  type hierarchy 51
  type piracy in Julia 274–275
  type restrictions 54–55
  type stability in Julia 270–274
  Union keyword 53–54
typejoin function 54
typeof function 21, 23

U

UInt32 type 149
UInt8 type 113
uncompressed vector 147, 149
UnicodePlots.jl package 428
Union keyword 53–54
unique function 98, 146, 227, 262, 274, 375, 410
unique! function 98, 262, 274
unnesting 387
Unsigned subtype 53
unstack function 328, 350–352
unstacked format 352
update command 401
using keyword 61–62
using statement 61–62
UTF-8 encoding of strings 132

V

value element 387–389
values
  defined 20
  missing 163–169
  mutability of 97–99

representing 20–23
returned by conditional expressions 31–32
values function 91
variables
    defining 23–26
    scoping rules 44–48
vcat function 118, 250–251, 274
Vector type 51, 58, 74, 97, 115, 205, 280
Vector{String} type 128
vectorized operations 101
vectors 22
    converting data frames to named tuple of
        vectors 269–275
        type piracy in Julia 274–275
        type stability in Julia 270–274
    converting data frames to vector of
        vectors 279–280
    converting data frames to vectors of named
        tuple 277
    creating data frames from 237–244
        constructor using dictionary 240–241
        constructor using keyword arguments 238
        constructor using pairs 238–240
        copycols keyword argument 241
        handling nonstandard arguments
            242–243
        integration of Julia with R 243–244

view function 80, 83, 129, 405
Visual Studio Code, working with Julia
    through 404

W

weekdays data frame 349–350
where keyword 54
while keyword 32
while loop 32–33, 45, 376
Wilkinson, Leland 428
winsor function 63, 69
winsorized mean 20
    computing in Julia REPL 35–36
    multiple dispatch 57–58
    StatsBase.jl package 63–64
Wong, David 295
write function 189

Z

Zamora, Yuliana 428
zeros function 307
ZIP files, implementing function that extracts
    data from 296–298
ZipFile.Reader object 296
Zumel, Nina 146

MANNING

A new online reading experience

liveBook, our online reading platform, adds a new dimension to your Manning books, with features that make reading, learning, and sharing easier than ever. A liveBook version of your book is included FREE with every Manning book.

This next generation book platform is more than an online reader. It's packed with unique features to upgrade and enhance your learning experience.

- Add your own notes and bookmarks
- One-click code copy
- Learn from other readers in the discussion forum
- Audio recordings and interactive exercises
- Read all your purchased Manning content in any browser, anytime, anywhere

As an added bonus, you can search every Manning book and video in liveBook—even ones you don't yet own. Open any liveBook, and you'll be able to browse the content and read anything you like.*

Find out more at www.manning.com/livebook-program.

Open reading is limited to 10 minutes per book daily